BAKHTIN AND CULTURAL THEORY

edited by Ken Hirschkop and David Shepherd

BAKHTIN AND CULTURAL THEORY

revised and expanded second edition

MANCHESTER UNIVERSITY PRESS

MANCHESTER AND NEW YORK

distributed exclusively in the USA by Palgrave

Published by Manchester University Press
Oxford Road, Manchester M13 9NR, UK
and Room 400, 175 Fifth Avenue, New York, NY 10010, USA
www.manchesteruniversitypress.co.uk

Distributed exclusively in the USA by
Palgrave, 175 Fifth Avenue, New York NY 10010, USA

Distributed exclusively in Canada by
UBC Press, University of British Columbia, 2029 West Mall,
Vancouver, BC, Canada V6T 1Z2

British Library Cataloguing-in-Publication Data
A catalogue record for this book is available from the British Library

Library of Congress Cataloging-in-Publication Data
A catalog record for this book is available from the Library of Congress

ISBN 0 7190 4990 3 paperback

ISBN 13: 9780719049903

First published 1989

This edition first published 2001

First digital, on-demand edition produced by Lightning Source 2006

CONTENTS

CONTENTS

NOTES ON THE CONTRIBUTORS

Carol Adlam is Lecturer in Russian at the University of Exeter. She is co-editor of *Face to Face: Bakhtin in Russia and the West* (Sheffield Academic Press, 1997), and is completing a doctoral thesis on contemporary Russian women writers. Formerly a Research Assistant at the Sheffield Bakhtin Centre, she is now Co-Director of the AHRB Project 'Russian Visual Arts, 1863–1913: Documents from the British Library Collection'.

Tony Crowley is Professor of Modern English Literature at the University of Manchester. His publications include: *The Politics of Discourse: The Standard Language Question in British Cultural Debates* (Macmillan, 1989); *Proper English? Readings in Language, History and Cultural Identity* (Routledge, 1991); *Language in History: Theories and Texts* (Routledge, 1996), *The Politics of Language in Ireland 1366–1922* (Routledge, 1999), and *The Language and Cultural Theory Reader,* which he co-edited with Lucy Burke and Alan Girvin (Routledge, 2000).

Terry Eagleton is Professor of Cultural Theory and John Rylands Research Fellow at the University of Manchester. His latest book is *The Idea of Culture* (Blackwell, 2000).

Nancy Glazener is Associate Professor of English at the University of Pittsburgh. Her book *Reading for Realism: The History of a Literary Institution, 1850–1910* was published in 1997 by Duke University Press in the New Americanists series. She is currently working on a project bringing together feminist work in ethics and some contemporary works of fiction.

Ken Hirschkop is Senior Lecturer in English at the University of Manchester. He is the author of several articles on language and cultural theory and of *Mikhail Bakhtin: An Aesthetic for Democracy* (Oxford University Press, 1999). He is currently working on the social and political significance of the 'linguistic turn'.

Ann Jefferson is a Fellow in French at New College, Oxford and is the author of *The Nouveau Roman and the Poetics of Fiction* (1980), *Reading Realism in Stendhal* (1988), *Nathalie Sarraute Fiction and Theory: Questions of Difference* (2000) and the co-editor of *Modern Literary Theory: A Comparative Introduction* (1982 and 1986).

Nikolai Pan'kov is Director of the Bakhtin Centre at the Russian State University for the Humanities in Moscow and has been chief editor of the Bakhtin journal *Dialog Karnaval Khronotop* since its inception in 1992. He has published several important articles on Bakhtin and is one of the contributing editors to the Moscow *Collected Works*. He is currently at work on a new biography of Bakhtin.

Graham Pechey is Visiting Research Fellow in English at the University of Hertfordshire. In addition to his work on Bakhtin, he has written a number of articles in the fields of Romantic writing, literary and cultural theory, and the post-colonial. He is currently completing a book provisionally entitled *Word Made Flesh: Essays in the Understanding of Bakhtin*.

Brian Poole is currently teaching at the Institut für Allgemeine und Vergleichende Literaturwissenschaft, Freie Universität Berlin and is a member of the editorial group for the Russian edition of Bakhtin's *Collected Works*. He has published many articles on Bakhtin and his translation of Viktor Duvakin's interviews with Bakhtin is forthcoming from University of Texas Press.

David Shepherd is Professor of Russian and Director of the Bakhtin Centre at the University of Sheffield. His publications include *Beyond Metafiction: Self-Consciousness in Soviet Literature* (1992), and (as editor) *Bakhtin: Carnival and Other Subjects* (1993) and *The Contexts of Bakhtin: Philosophy, Authorship, Aesthetics* (1998). He is the editor of *Dialogism: An International Journal of Bakhtin Studies* and Director of a Bakhtin Centre project that will lead to an electronic scholarly edition of the works of Bakhtin and the Bakhtin Circle.

Clair Wills is Reader in Modern Poetry at Queen Mary, University of London. She is the author of *Improprieties* (Oxford University Press, 1993) and *Reading Paul Muldoon* (Bloodaxe Books, 1998).

ACKNOWLEDGEMENTS

David Shepherd's 'Bakhtin and the reader' contains some material first used in an article in *Poetics Today*; permission to re-publish is hereby gratefully acknowledged. Graham Pechey's 'Not the novel: Bakhtin, poetry, truth, God' first appeared in *Pretexts* IV: 2, 1993 (the journal's website is *http://www.tandf.co.uk/journals*); for permission to publish it in the present volume the editors wish to thank Taylor & Francis Ltd, PO Box 25, Abingdon, Oxfordshire OX14 3UE.

The editors would also like to thank Anita Roy for suggesting a new edition of this book and Matthew Frost for having the inexhaustible patience to wait for it.

TRANSLITERATION OF RUSSIAN

Russian words are transliterated according to British Standard 2979 (1958), with the exception of some names which appear in their most familiar form (e.g. Gorky rather than Gor'kii).

Ken Hirschkop

Bakhtin in the sober light of day (an introduction to the second edition)

Shortly after *Bakhtin and Cultural Theory* was first published, the Soviet state which did so much to shape Bakhtin's fate fell to pieces. The manner of its fall might have made Bakhtin smile. There was no civil war, and no spontaneous popular uprising. At a critical moment a coup by the old guard, the Rabelaisian 'agelasts' of their day, presented the Russian people with the familiar threat of official power. This time, however, gloomy seriousness and fear failed. There was no counterattack, but enough Russian people (both ordinary citizens and, crucially, members of the armed forces) made clear they were not afraid, or not afraid enough, and this being the case the coup collapsed. Could one have asked for a more elegant demonstration of the impotence of official fear in the modern historical world, the world of the novel? In fact, one could have, and the proof of it was in what followed.

For the peoples of the former Soviet Union had no opportunity to bask in their fearlessness: they found out there were all sorts of new things to be scared of once they had thrown off their Communist shackles – unemployment, gang warfare, homelessness, rampant inflation, the collapse of a welfare system. Once the official lid was off, the field should have been free for history to surge forward in its many voices. Instead it stuttered, seemed to go backwards for a moment, and finally took off in a direction no one, except a few well-placed bureaucrats, had expected. The thinking had been that Communism was a nightmare from which the Soviet people would finally wake up. When dawn breaks, however, the demons that haunted you resume an everyday, but no less terrifying, form.

Bakhtin scholars were no less susceptible to these illusions than their compatriots. If anything, the substance of what Bakhtin had to say seemed to encourage the belief that a kind of desirable 'normality', a world in which dialogue and 'becoming' thrived, was simply there for the taking. Had Bakhtin not implied that 'official culture' – the culture of the State, of power, of politics – was the sole impediment to the unfettered flow of dialogue? Had he not urged us to protect, above all, the 'fragile and easily destroyed' sphere of dialogue from all outside interference, from every historical attempt, however well meaning, to institutionalise our talk politically or socially?[1] If monological thinking and speaking were the consequence of an alien force squeezing the dialogism out of language, then it stood to reason that once the pressure was off the task of intellectuals would be to keep it off.

With Communism dead and Lenin almost buried, Russian Bakhtin scholars could be forgiven for thinking that the pressure was off Bakhtin, too, and that, freed from the partisan political squabbling of the Soviet era, he would emerge in his true colours, as a philosophical spokesperson for humanity at large. Even in 1976 Sergei Averintsev had insisted that to 'drag Bakhtin into the dualism of arguments between circles' was to obscure the larger view which he strove for: 'The essence of Bakhtin's position', he claimed, 'always consisted not of "against" but of "for", not of contention or of rejection but of affirmation, of defence of the rights of the whole against the unjustified pretensions of the part.'[2] At last untethered from the murky and corrupt world of political manoeuvre and social struggle, Bakhtin would be allowed to ascend to the perspective destined for him. Gazing across the entirety of human history, scanning its literary and cultural achievements from antiquity to modernity, Bakhtin had articulated a 'social ontology', a 'first philosophy', a 'philosophical anthropology' remote from the grosser realities of political and social life.[3]

Scholarship always dreams of a straight and steady passage, forgetting that history is not only the storm that blows it off course but also the wind that fills its sails. The upsurge in Bakhtin scholarship that also followed in the wake of *glasnost'* and the sudden opening up of archives led, as it turned out, to more, not less, controversy. Scholars looking through newly available public and private documents, or scrutinising manuscript versions of by now canonical texts, discovered that much of what we thought we knew about Bakhtin – concerning his background, his education, his life, his actual written output – was false or distorted. Distorted, in fact, by no other person than Bakhtin himself. A couple of examples should suffice.

The earliest accounts of Bakhtin's life were necessarily sketchy, but they included the information that Bakhtin had been a student at the Novorossisk University in Odessa for a year, transferring afterwards to the then University of Petrograd, where he completed a degree in classics and philology in 1917.[4] Certain teachers at the latter university (Losskii, Vvedenskii and Zelinskii were the usual suspects) were apparently particularly important to Bakhtin, and their relative influence soon became a topic within Bakhtin commentary. In one of the most interesting and substantial works to emerge after the break-up of the Soviet Union, the transcript of six interviews conducted in 1973 by the scholar V. D. Duvakin, Bakhtin confirmed this sketch of his university education. Mind you, the confirmation was a little strange. Having been unable to recall the details of his higher education, Bakhtin at last came up with the right dates, and then concluded: 'I do not remember the dates exactly ... There are reminiscences of my brother, they are ... in this ... English ... memorial volume'.[5] Why would Bakhtin refer to his brother's reminiscences? For the simple reason that the education he has recalled is that of his brother: archival research in the 1990s revealed that Bakhtin had never been registered at either Novorossisk or Petrograd University.[6] And the Duvakin interview was not the first time he recalled it so: on a number of official forms Bakhtin presented the same false account, and on one occasion an even more ingenious one, in which he credited himself with having studied at several German universities before the First World War. (Here, too, the education was not so much invented as borrowed: his friend Matvei Kagan had attended the universities Bakhtin claimed for himself.)[7]

Very well, then, Bakhtin had no first degree (although he later acquired the equivalent of a doctorate without it: but that's another story). Doesn't this make his depth of knowledge even more impressive? It would, except that work on Bakhtin's manuscripts and typescripts, which are now being edited in Moscow for a definitive *Collected Works*, has revealed previously unacknowledged sources for a good deal of Bakhtin's work. In a series of remarkable studies, Brian Poole has shown that footnotes to sources for 'Discourse in the novel' were excised when it was edited for publication, that the unacknowledged source for much of Bakhtin's commentary on ancient literature is Georg Misch's *Geschichte der Autobiographie*, and that Bakhtin's book on Rabelais not only borrows from Ernst Cassirer's study of the Renaissance, *The Individual and the Cosmos in Renaissance Philosophy*, but plagiarises, *word for word*, entire pages of it.[8] In the one volume of the *Collected Works* which has already been published, the editors (to their credit) admit that Bakhtin relied extensively on German secondary sources for much of his material on classical literature.

The obvious response to these revelations comes from Bakhtin himself, who admitted in conversation with Sergei Bocharov that 'everything that was created during this half-century on this barren soil, under this unfree sky; all of it is to some degree defective'.[9] Perhaps the further controversies represent just the unfinished business of the past, the inevitable consequence of untangling a personal biography from perverse and extraordinary circumstances? While there is indisputably an element of truth in this, once you begin to separate off the genuine man from the compromising moments around him, it can be hard to know where to stop. Is Bakhtin so wholly out of his time that every reference to it should be expunged? This appears to be the strategy adopted in some of the editing of Bakhtin's *Collected Works*. In the volume just mentioned, which covers Bakhtin's writings from the early 1940s to the early 1960s, the editors have felt justified in deleting from a text such as 'The problem of speech genres' 'direct references and citations (together with their surrounding context) from J. V. Stalin's work *Marxism and Questions of Linguistics* and certain other references of a similar nature, explained, of course, by the official character of the text as a work plan for the Mordovia Teacher Training Institute'.[10] Without access to the manuscript or typescript one can't judge just how extraneous to the substance of the text these references are, but the strategy is a risky one, despite the editors' confidence in its appropriateness. Bocharov himself had claimed earlier that a clear distinction could be made in Bakhtin's work between the inner kernel of Bakhtin's thought and the terminological shell in which it was sometimes encased. Thus the concepts of *narodnost'* (closeness to the people) and realism, which played so large a part in Bakhtin's analysis of Rabelais, were, Bocharov argued, only surface concessions to the political demands of his time.[11] In a similar vein, N. I. Nikolaev, discussing Bakhtin's 1929 book *Problems of Dostoevsky's Art*, has suggested that it is a 'sociologised' version, rewritten to be in tune with the times, of an earlier wholly philosophical and theological book on Dostoevsky.[12]

The ultimate limit of this mode of interpretation, however, comes in comments made by L. A. Gogotishvili respecting Bakhtin's preparatory notes for 'The problem of speech genres'. Claiming that the presence of linguistic terminology in this text was yet one more 'concession' or ruse, she argues that a text such as this should be interpreted like Voloshinov's *Marxism and the Philosophy of Language*, which she regards as written by Bakhtin in a consciously alien Marxist idiom. 'The problem of speech genres', written roughly twenty-five years later, when Bakhtin had steady employment and had no need to circumlocute, should nevertheless be considered 'deutero-canonical' – as only half Bakhtin's:

> However, on their [the preparatory materials'] basis one can at a minimum come to the conclusion that the text of 'The problem of speech genres', usually perceived as the direct discourse of Bakhtin is, conventionally speaking, as 'deutero-canonical' as the text of *Marxism and the Philosophy of Language*. They are constructed on identical principles and from analogous authorial positions, from which it follows in particular that the language of positive or normative linguistics, and likewise the logical presuppositions of structuralism, were as distant from M. M. Bakhtin as the language of Marxism. All these languages are to an equal degree conventional and *equally alien* to him. (*SS*5, pp. 558–9)

One of the things revealed in this editorial paragraph is that the debate over the so-called 'disputed texts' (texts authored by Voloshinov and Medvedev which were claimed for Bakhtin in the 1970s) was about more than the correct attribution of copyright. It was also a debate about Bakhtin's relationship to the historical events of his time, and whether it would be possible to separate him from their contaminating influence once and for all. When the metaphor of kernel and shell is applied universally and rigorously to Bakhtin's texts, it suggests one can, and should, literally strip history away from them.

The irony in this is that the critics backing this interpretation are also the ones doing the most to make the historical study of Bakhtin's work as precise and careful as possible. Volume 5 of the Russian *Collected Works*, published in 1996, is the crowning glory of recent efforts to base the study of Bakhtin on evidence rather than speculation. One of its most striking features is the sheer amount of space, roughly 300 pages, given over to notes and commentary on the primary texts. Editorial annotation in earlier editions of Bakhtin was for the most part limited to occasional notes and a short intro-duction (although the essays on the novel translated in *The Dialogic Imagination* didn't even have notes). The sheer bulk of the new apparatus is a sign that this time things are going to be different. The manuscripts and typescripts which have been transcribed for the edition, almost all of them in notebook form, are described in minute physical detail, the rationale for the dating of each text is discussed openly and often at length, and commentary to a work like 'The problem of speech genres' provides almost a blow-by-blow account of the intellectual arguments framing its composition. Much of the commentary is devoted to an unceasing and adventurous search for theological subtexts in the material; but even this cannot take away from the positivistic sobriety of the whole enterprise.

Of course, reverence for a great man and positivistic scholarship have been happy bedfellows for a long time. The accumulation of ordinary facts typically does not subtract anything from the exceptional status of the great thinker; if anything it adds to it. As Roland Barthes has observed:

> To endow a writer publicly with a good fleshly body, to reveal that he likes dry white wine and underdone steak, is to make even more miraculous for me, and of a more divine essence, the products of his art. Far from the details of his daily life bringing nearer to me the nature of his inspiration and making it clearer, it is the whole mythical singularity of his condition which the writer emphasises by such confidences.[13]

If, in Bakhtin's case, the weight of facts seems rather more threatening to the cause of hagiography, it is because the latter depended so much on keeping Bakhtin apart from other thinkers and others' 'thoughts' rather than banal human preferences and needs. The world from which Bakhtin supposedly took a distance was not the everyday one of eating, sleeping and going to the movies, but the intellectual world of publication and public argument. The danger for his devotees is not that he will turn out to be a human with needs – if anything, his vulnerability and weakness is often explicitly tied to his insight – but that he will turn out be one more intellectual. The more he gets the usual positivistic treatment, though, the more he assumes his place in that not necessarily august company.

In their different ways, the four new contributions in this revised edition of *Bakhtin and Cultural Theory* encourage this new sobriety. Carol Adlam has replaced the earlier bibliographical essay with a sharp and concise overview of changes in Bakhtin scholarship since the first edition. By far the most important of these is, of course, the expansion of Russian Bakhtin scholarship and its increasing contacts with Western work. Before the 1990s, Western scholarship on Bakhtin had, by its own account, passed the point of industrial take-off, its Russian cousin remaining something of a cottage industry (whose craftsmanship, it goes without saying, was generally far superior to that of its 'market-led' counterpart). Now that the native industry has found its feet, however, it has wasted no time in declaring the distinctiveness of its products, occasionally resorting to intellectual protectionism on the part of its native son. In her wide-ranging discussion of Russian and Western criticism, Adlam shows how the two styles both conflict and overlap, each moving in the direction of the kinds of historicising and contextualising work I have already mentioned.

Since 1992 Nikolai Pan'kov has edited a journal wholly devoted to Bakhtin, *Dialog Karnaval Khronotop*, and his remarkable even-handedness and good judgement have made it a constant source of valuable information and provocative opinion. Pan'kov's authorial contributions to the journal have consisted of extremely intelligent introductions to archival studies and several important transcriptions of material drawn from institutional archives. For *Bakhtin and Cultural Theory* we have chosen one of the most important of his introductory articles, a lengthy discussion of the preparations for and conduct of the defence of Bakhtin's dissertation on Rabelais, which was later published as *Rabelais and His World*. Pan'kov's article is a gem: it not only reveals the drama behind one of Bakhtin's few explicit confrontations with Russian colleagues – some sympathetic, some not – but also shrewdly demonstrates that the objections raised at the dissertation defence were the same ones which scholars, Russian and Western alike, would make when the book was published in the 1960s. In this way Pan'kov demonstrates that the defence, while certainly dramatic in its own terms, was not simply a matter of genius confronting Party-minded mediocrity, but involved serious and substantial intellectual debate.[14]

Graham Pechey's contribution to the first edition was an article which probed the logic of Bakhtin's concepts and in particular their tendency to cross intellectual boundaries and shift direction without much notice. His contribution to the new edition is a characteristically brilliant analysis of Bakhtin's theory of genres. Using Blake and current South African writing as his testing-ground, Pechey demonstrates that Bakhtin's well-known and often derided tendency to overdramatise the difference between genres in fact reveals the inner logic of the idea of novelistic, dialogical writing. Here, without even having to refer to Bakhtin's 'early

7

works', Pechey argues that the necessity of thinking the absolute is revealed in Bakhtin's tendentious account of the history of genres. All those who have felt uneasy about Bakhtin's apparent dismissal of poetry, drama and prophecy will be simultaneously reassured and provoked by Pechey's argumentative tour-de-force.

Nothing has done more to bring Bakhtin down to earth than the revelation of his sources, however, particularly when these sources provided not just vague themes or inspiration, but concrete arguments and particular concepts, many of which became central to his project. 'Discourse in the novel', which at least referred to contemporaries like Gustav Shpet and V. V. Vinogradov, always appeared as a dialogic bolt from the blue. We now know, thanks to the efforts of the editors of the *Collected Works* and to Brian Poole, that deleted from the published version were references to scholars who had already broached the problem of dialogue and to the philosopher Ernst Cassirer (the fact that the deleted references all involved German-Jewish scholars has not gone unnoticed).

As mentioned above, Poole has already shown how Bakhtin in his work in the 1930s continually relied on the works of the neo-Kantian Cassirer for concepts, arguments and insights. In this volume he makes an equally striking and radical argument in relation to Bakhtin's writing in the 1920s. Drawing on sources from Bakhtin's archive, Poole demonstrates that the relation of 'author' to 'hero', so central both to the essay of the same name and the later book on Dostoevsky, was modelled on Max Scheler's idea of 'sympathy'. By examining Bakhtin's extensive notes on Scheler, Poole reveals a considerable specific and unacknowledged debt. The ramifications of this discovery do not end there, however. For the connection between Scheler's *Essence of Sympathy* and Bakhtin's early philosophy leads Poole to the conclusion that the philosophical works which everyone has claimed Bakhtin abandoned by the time he arrived in Leningrad in 1924 could not have been written before that time, and that they represent not an early philosophy thrown aside so that Bakhtin could write the 'disputed texts', but work which Bakhtin must have done *while* Voloshinov was composing his own, quite different, text, influenced in the main by Cassirer and not Scheler. By opening up the apparently settled question of the dating of Bakhtin's works, Poole in fact throws into question the model of Bakhtin's career that lies behind Bakhtin's image as a philosopher gone astray.

The articles which we have retained from the earlier edition of *Bakhtin and Cultural Theory* acquire a new resonance in the intellectual context which they played a part in creating, for they were distinguished, then as now, by their insistence on placing Bakhtin in a larger intellectual world and probing his weaknesses. The articles by Clair Wills and Nancy Glazener explored the very different meanings that carnival, carnivalesque, and the novel would have for feminists and for women writers more generally. Rather than take Bakhtin's worship of the public festive culture at face value, Wills showed that concepts of publicity and privacy were shaped by the facts of gender difference, such that women writers might find gestures towards privacy, in form and content, more politically compelling than the simple act of going public. Glazener's piece emphasised the need to think of the novel's subversive potential in more historically nuanced terms, requiring different formal strategies according to the changing habits of patriarchy.

David Shepherd's discussion of Bakhtin and theories of reading was one of the first to put Bakhtin where he belongs: in the middle of an ongoing intellectual debate, where at best he might assume the role of *primus*, or even *secondus inter pares*. His subtle consideration of what Bakhtin might contribute to the analysis of readers and reading exemplifies an approach to Bakhtin which is alert and appreciative without being idolatrous. Tony Crowley's discussion of Bakhtin and the history of language shows how Bakhtin's polemical concepts cast new light on existing histories of the European languages. At the same time, Crowley shows that Bakhtin's account of language's history is itself often not as historical as it should be, assigning to monoglossia and heteroglossia singular and unchangeable political functions.

The final two essays of the collection focus on the status of the body and embodiment in Bakhtin, a strikingly proleptic theme in 1989, but here treated with a care and shrewdness usually missing from analyses on this topic. Ann Jefferson discusses Bakhtin's early work 'Author and hero in aesthetic activity', but in a spirit wholly different from what has become standard in commentary on this text. By using Sartre and Barthes as comparators, and drawing together 'Author and hero' with the book on Rabelais, Jefferson is able to pinpoint the strengths and weaknesses of Bakhtin's interesting connection of bodiliness and literariness. Finally, Terry Eagleton provides a polemical reminder of the ambiguities that any appeal to the body entails. For however much we would like to believe what we read about Bakhtin, he has not left us with a theory instantly adaptable to the social or political needs of the Left (or the Right, for that matter).

9

These careful analyses, and the philological work of people like Poole and Pan'kov, draw our attention to the ambiguities encircling any attempt to reconstruct Bakhtin's career after the fact. For the end of historical Communism has led many Russian intellectuals to believe that by capturing the facts of Bakhtin's life and restoring his texts they will pull him out of the historical rubble in which he remains partly buried. When the texts themselves, however, have an unfinished and distorted character, when political history has decreed that most of them shall never be more than notebooks and sketches, it's not clear what reconstruction ought to amount to. Is the historical rubble something which can be brushed off the surface of works that will stand on their own? Or are these texts so closely bound to their own painful history that they cannot be separated from it without losing the very thing that lends them their truth?

The reconstruction of Bakhtin's work now taking place in Russia seems guided by the first perspective; I think the second is closer to the mark. No one doubts that Bakhtin's work was warped and garbled by Stalinism. He could not write what he wanted to write and he could not publish what he would have liked to publish. Even a tragic history, however, cannot be cleanly separated from those who did their best to resist it. What I would like to demonstrate in the remainder of this introduction is that Bakhtin did not have a coherent argument to make *apart* from the history he lived through, which is to say that history did not just get in the way, but gave him both something to think about and the means to do so. And this is so even though Bakhtin himself sometimes denies it.

Commentators who wish to divide Bakhtin's work into kernel and shell define the two aspects in disciplinary terms: the shell is 'sociological', the kernel philosophical. In part this is an entirely reasonable reaction to Soviet Marxism's use of sociology as a code word for a certain kind of class rhetoric, but it is not only that. What makes sociology shell-like is its empirical reference, its dependence on changing social roles and institutions, all of which, to a certain kind of intellectual, makes it a look a bit unsteady as a moral compass. By contrast philosophy's truths are *a priori* and unchanging, whether they derive from the theory of knowledge, theological argument or phenomenological investigation. They can provide a solid guide to moral conduct when the world around you is filled with the rhetoric and reality of 'struggle'.

Confronting a world racked by a European war and a seemingly endless series of national revolutions, Bakhtin had opted for this higher philosophical road. In 1921 he wrote to his friend Matvei Kagan: 'I have begun a work which I now intend to finish – "The subject of ethics and the subject of right". I hope in the near future to put this work in its final and finished form; it will serve as an introduction to my ethical philosophy.'[15] The ambition of the project is clear from the promise made at the end of the introduction, which has been published with the title 'Toward a philosophy of the act':

> The first part of our investigation will be devoted to an examination of precisely the fundamental moments of the actual world, not as it is thought, but as it is experienced. The following part will be devoted to aesthetic activity as an act, not from within its product, but from the point of view of the author as a responsible participant and [missing] the ethics of the artistic work. The third part is on the ethics of politics and the final one, of religion.[16]

The promise was not kept: only the chapter on 'aesthetics', 'Author and hero in aesthetic activity', is extant (although a lecture on the philosophy of religion for which we have notes may be a précis of the chapter on that topic). According to N. I. Nikolaev, who has put the reconstructors' hypothesis in the most detail, Bakhtin did not finish the work because he realised it was a hopeless task in present conditions: too distant from Bolshevik ideas, it would never, the story goes, be publishable. When the journal *Russkii sovremennik*, which was to publish an excerpt from the aesthetics chapter, was shut down by the government in 1924, Bakhtin in effect gave up. He decided the only way to put his ideas into the public realm would be to disguise them in acceptable sociological, Marxisant language of the day. Thus, the disputed texts were composed, the Dostoevsky book was recast in the acceptable sociological form, and Bakhtin set off on a long career of dissimulation and indirect speech.[17] Every apparent conceptual innovation – the theory of the novel, the idea of carnival, the notion of double-voiced discourse – therefore should be understood as a philosophical idea masked by a scientific one, leading right up to the 'deutero-canonical' 'Problem of speech genres' and its feigned interest in linguistics. From this perspective, quibbling with the historical accuracy or precision of any of these texts is missing the point. For Bakhtin's philosophical case depends on a revolution in one's way of thinking, and such a far-reaching transformation can't be called to account for every historical nicety. Historical circumstances left the project in pieces, but with will and intelligence the shattered vase can be put together again.

Suppose, though, that Brian Poole is right, and that Bakhtin didn't compose his so-called early work until, say, 1926 (that is, *after* the journal *Russkii sovremennik* had closed)? What if his change in direction can't be explained by external circumstances? Maybe Bakhtin didn't finish his 'ethical philosophy' because he *couldn't* finish it, historical circumstances having defeated it not from the outside, but *from the inside.*

For even if Bakhtin thought the solution was philosophy, he was aware from the start that the problem was a particular historical trauma. The First World War, the Revolution and civil war in Russia, more generally the apparent end of a relatively confident nineteenth-century liberal culture, which had placed its faith in the consensus-making power of modern law: these are the reference points, alluded to throughout 'Toward a philosophy of the act', for what Bakhtin called the 'crisis of the *contemporary* act' (TPA, p. 123/54; emphasis mine). Their cause is the loss of what Bakhtin called 'obligation' or 'oughtness' (*dolzhenstvovanie*). The norms are there, but they no longer bind or motivate, and as a consequence, 'responsibility' is neither practised nor acknowledged:

> All the forces of responsible accomplishment pass into an autonomous sphere of culture, while the act which has been separated from them descends to the level of elementary biological and economic motivation, it loses all its ideal moments: this precisely is the condition of civilisation.[18] (TPA, p. 123/55)

How had this come to pass? In 'Toward a philosophy of the act' Bakhtin blames the hegemony of lawlike scientific knowledge, which now penetrates even into ethical life in the form of a legalistic conception of morality. The foolish belief that rational argument can produce the 'conscience' which alone can lead to moral action has led the contemporary world to reduce all morality to law. But laws are like 'a document without a signature, not obligating anyone to anything' (TPA, p. 115/44), for while they instruct the person intent on being moral how to behave, they themselves cannot persuade anyone that they should act morally:

> I can agree with this or that position as a psychologist, a sociologist, a jurist *ex cathedra*, but to assert that by this alone it becomes a norm for my act means to leap over the fundamental problem. Even for the very fact of my actual assent to the validity of a given position *ex cathedra* – as *my act* – the validity of the position in itself

and my psychological faculty of understanding is not enough, there must be something which comes from me, namely the morally obligating orientation of my consciousness in relation to a position which is in itself theoretically valid ... (TPA, p. 99/23–4)

No amount of science or critical philosophy could produce the 'morally obligating orientation' which alone made for truly responsible subjects, for it was science itself that had created the problem. In a 'theoreticist' culture which believes only in science, culture ends up chasing its own tail in the search for ethical life.

As a critic of modern culture, Bakhtin was hardly original, and he knew it. Writers were lining up in the first decades of the twentieth century to denounce Europe for its scientism, its degeneracy, its being in thrall to objective culture, but they naturally could not agree on the solution. The adherents of 'philosophy of life' – Spengler, Simmel, Bergson, Nietzsche a few years earlier – sought to dispense with the ethical altogether, relying on a concept of 'life' which Bakhtin thought no more than a generalisation of the idea of the individual biological instinct. The squadrons of self-critical philosophy – Hermann Cohen, Husserl, Rickert, Max Scheler – formalised ethics to the point where it was just another science. Christian and Jewish writers thought obligation would be restored via a renewal of religious faith, sociologists argued that modernity demanded new forms of 'legitimacy' or social 'solidarity', political thinkers looked for the charisma of a strong leader (Schmitt) or the inspiration of a great myth (Sorel), and not a few looked to social revolution itself as the catalyst for a revived culture. Bakhtin was confronting a historical problem which was no secret, either to the peoples of Europe (who had their own ideas about how to sort it out) or to its intelligentsia. It was patently obvious that 'oughtness' or a sense of obligation was in short supply, particularly after a European war which, for no apparent good reason, had left millions dead. Political arrangements were antique, economic arrangements anarchic and dysfunctional, and religion no longer persuasive as a legitimating force. What Bakhtin called 'oughtness' Weber called 'legitimacy' – and with the end of the great empires and the crisis of liberal states it was sorely lacking in Europe.

Could a magisterial 'ethical philosophy' restore it? On the evidence, even Bakhtin didn't believe that it could. For rather than complete the project, Bakhtin abandoned it. Or rather, he rewrote it, not once, but several times – as 'Author and hero', *Problems of Dostoevsky's Art*, 'Discourse in the novel', *Rabelais*, and so on. If we cast our eye over Bakhtin's career, we observe not smooth development or the careful cultivation of various fields, but an endless, almost compulsive, dwelling on a few key problems. The usual interpretation of this obsessiveness is that Bakhtin had a moment of glorious philosophical insight which, for political reasons, he then transposed into a variety of disciplinary idioms. But the actual succession of the texts implies something else: that Bakhtin kept going because he couldn't solve the problem or exorcise the trauma which started him off.

What could produce the 'oughtness' characteristic of a 'morally obligating position'? According to 'Toward a philosophy of the act', it depends on the ethical subject realising that 'Man-in-general does not exist: *I* exist and a particular concrete *other* exists' (TPA, p. 117/47). Although we usually speak of subjective acts (expression, actions, emotions, thoughts, etc.) as such, Bakhtin claimed that this is just a theoretical abstraction: in actuality, one experiences *one's own* thoughts, feelings, linguistic expressions and bodily gestures in a manner absolutely distinct from the way one experiences these same acts in *others*. As Bakhtin puts it in 'Author and hero': 'any inner experience and mental whole can be concretely experienced – can be inwardly perceived – either in the category of the *I-for-myself* or in the category of the *other-for-me*, that is, either as my experience or as the experience of this definite singular other person'.[19] And although this phenomenological insight could be described, in theoretical language, as true 'in general', what was essential was for the subject, so to speak, to believe it. For once such a division in subjective experience was *acknowledged* – it couldn't, you see, be 'proved' – it would instill a new ethical orientation in the subject acknowledging it.

Its thoughts, after the ethical lightning struck, would apparently go something like this: 'In all of Being, I experience only my unique self as an *I*. All other *I*s (theoretical ones) do not exist as an *I* for me ...' (TPA, pp. 112–13/41). Experiencing itself as unique, grasping (perceiving? understanding?) what Bakhtin infamously called its 'non-alibi in being', the subject interprets moral requirements in the form of a 'conscience' which addresses it and it alone, rather than a law. This stems from the fact that the *I* lives (as it did for Husserl) in its acts: it presses forward, it regards everything in the light of the future, shapes every object as an element of the 'horizon' (another Husserlian term) of its active subjectivity. In short, this is an I which cannot remain neutral in relation to practical (moral or ethical) demands: it experiences them as the voice of conscience, which it can defy, but to which it cannot remain indifferent.

'Toward a philosophy of the act' describes the architectonic split as that which holds the key to the 'oughtness' missing from modern Europe. But as it tails off into the beginning of a chapter on aesthetics, it shifts focus. Art, although 'closest of all the distinct cultural worlds (taken in isolation) to the singular, unique world of the act' (TPA, p. 128/61), is nevertheless more interesting for what it does for the *other* than for what it does for the *I*. For the focus of art is the person as a 'lovingly affirmed concrete actuality' (TPA, p. 129/61), that is, the person not as something in general, but as an '*other*' for a particular *I*. According to Bakhtin's aesthetic theory, the interplay of author and hero (in the sense of protagonist) in the artwork echoes and intensifies the fundamental relationship between *I* and *other*. But to understand this we have to wait until Bakhtin redrafts his aesthetics chapter in the form we know as 'Author and hero in aesthetic activity'.

'Author and hero', in fact a much longer fragment than 'Toward a philosophy of the act', differs from it in several important respects. It lays out, in much more substantial detail, the difference between subjective experience in the register of the *I* and subjective experience in the register of the *other*. But now the *I*, which seemed so impressive and morally compelling in 'Toward a philosophy of the act', cuts a more worried and anxious figure. Its constant pressing forward is now a problem, for it leads to an 'infinite discontentedness', based on the fact that every object or moment must be transcended, or perhaps merely left behind, by the subject's endless striving after an ideal which can never be actualised in a particular object or situation. Instead of precious oughtness, Bakhtin now speaks of merely ethical – *etichnye* – values. Suddenly acting doesn't look like the solution, but like the problem. The solution is art.

For in art the 'forward-directed life' of the *I* is seen from outside, that is, from the perspective of an author for whom this life is the life of an *other*. And the author can do something for this *other* which the *other* can't do for itself: it can love it, which means, for Bakhtin, affirming it as a whole, beyond any particular good or bad, admirable or despicable qualities, it might have. The 'outsidedness' which we maintain in relation to others is 'the bud in which [artistic] form slumbers, and whence form unfolds like a blossom' (AH, p. 27/24). The act of grasping and shaping a life in an aesthetic work is therefore for Bakhtin the paradigmatic act of love.

In short, the separation of *I* from *other*, presented as simple phenomenological fact, verifiable through introspection, contains within itself the seed of Christian ethics. The architectonic of *I* and *other* dictates 'absolute sacrifice for myself, and loving mercy towards the other' (AH, p. 56/56) and it means every *I* will not only save others though its love but will know in turn that it depends on them for its own salvation. This is, of course, very convenient. But also very problematic. For it means Bakhtin is trying to solve a historical crisis with unhistorical means. The architectonic of *I* and *other* which holds the key to Europe's redemption is, according to him, not itself the product of historical evolution (let alone historical conflict!), but the absolute and invariable structure of experience. That experience in the register of the *I* (or *I-for-myself* as he sometime calls it) – characterised by an inability to ground its life in values beyond itself, a constant orientation to the future, a desperate search for a lasting kind of happiness – sounds very familiar, very European, very modern, seems not to bother Bakhtin. That the perception by *others* which saves the *I* is structured by an 'aesthetic love' which, one presumes, demanded both the development of modern art and the emergence of modern love seems also not to ruffle Bakhtin's philosophical confidence. The 'contemporary crisis of the act' may have been brought on by modernity, but it will be solved by eternity, in the form of a sudden acknowledgement of what has always been the case.

But using the interplay of author and hero in art as your model for the saving of an *I* by an *other* has risks, the most important of which is the possibility that art will let the historical cat out of the bag. Its structures, its forms of authorship, the nature and style of its heroes or characters have all been historically variable, the most recent forms building on artistic achievements which came before them. So while the first half of 'Author and hero' shows us how to derive the forms of 'author' and 'hero' from the structures built into our experience, the second shows us how they evolve through a long and complicated cultural history. The forms of author and hero do not just jump out at us from behind the wings where they've been hiding: they come from ancient tragedy, from the forms of confession, from biography, romanticism, classicism.

But not, at this point in time, from Dostoevsky. 'Author and hero' finishes with an evocation of what Bakhtin calls a 'crisis of authorship' stretching 'from Dostoevsky to Bely' (AH, p. 186/203): its essence is the inability of authors (and by implication, everybody else) to get 'outside' the narrowly ethical perspective of the *I*. But a little later (how much later we don't know, but probably two or three years) Bakhtin changes his mind about Dostoevsky, and sets off on the road which leads to a lifetime of writing about literary and cultural history. The first half of *Problems of Dostoevsky's Art* retains the focus on the relationship between 'author' and 'hero', but the substance of the relationship has changed dramatically. Dostoevsky doesn't smother his heroes with a love which sees them from all sides: he discovers how to artistically represent them in all their *I*-centred open-endedness. In 'Toward a philosophy of the act' Bakhtin sought to remind subjects of their responsibility; in 'Author and hero' he focused on the need to save them. Now he thinks Dostoevsky has shown us that you must save them precisely by making them into ideals of responsibility. And the only way to do this is through a peculiarly dialogical art, which it was Dostoevsky's genius to invent.

And the rest, to coin a phrase, is history *and* eternity. From this point on Bakhtin devotes himself to describing, in ever more precise detail, the historical development of the dialogical relationship which will at last make Europeans responsible, at the same time trying to ground this relationship in something more permanent than history's ebb and flow. So while Dostoevsky's dialogical approach to his heroes is presented as a historical innovation (on a par with the discovery of relativity), its form depends on an act of wilful abstraction:

> An exceptionally sharp sense of the other person as *other* and of one's own *I* as a bare *I* presupposes that all those determinations which envelop the *I* and the *other* in socially concrete flesh – kin, social, class and all other determinations – have lost their authority and form-shaping force. It is as if the person senses himself immediately in the world as a whole, without any kind of mediating factors, beyond any kind of social collective to which he or she might have belonged.[20]

The get-out clause which follows this passage – Bakhtin claims that this merely represents the disorientation of a classless intelligentsia – is a rather gauche attempt at displacement.

There was, of course, one other major shift signalled in *Problems of Dostoevsky's Art*: the idea that a dialogical relationship between a hero and a framing author is embodied in prose style. In this Bakhtin was following in the footsteps of Voloshinov, who had made the 'transmission of another's speech' the focus of the final section of *Marxism and the Philosophy of Language*.[21] Voloshinov's insight was that the forms of indirect and so-called quasi-direct style developed in European prose were markers for changed possibilities in the relation of authors and heroes. Being Voloshinov, he offered a typology that was strictly chronological, leading from the 'linear style' of medieval writing, in which the object language was sharply demarcated from the narrative voice, to the 'relativistic individualism' of the moderns, in which the line of prose was able to reflect simultaneously the perspective of both the hero and the author. For Bakhtin, as for so many others, there was no author more modern than Dostoevsky: he announced him as the founder of the dialogical style Voloshinov had dubbed relativistic individualism. But once Bakhtin agreed that dialogism is embodied first and foremost in language, he effectively tied himself to the limits imposed by language's peculiar but verifiable historical development.

The full consequences of this would only become apparent in the 1930s, when literary and cultural history became Bakhtin's full-time occupation. However much he idealised the 'novel' or played games with its commonly accepted history, he could not fail to address it as a historical achievement. And, indeed, this is how it appears throughout the several texts devoted to the novel, both those that address it as distinctive stylistically, 'Discourse in the novel' and 'From the prehistory of novelistic discourse', and those essays that define it as a special form of narrative – the fragments of the *Bildungsroman* project (including 'Forms of time and of the chronotope in the novel'), 'Epic and novel', 'Towards a stylistics of the novel', 'Towards a theory of the novel', and 'On Flaubert'.[22] In all these works, the novel refers to a narratively and stylistically distinctive genre embodying the defining attributes of 'modernity'. And the distinguishing feature of modernity is its 'orientation to the future':

> This reorientation was first accomplished during the Renaissance. In that era the present, contemporaneity, for the first time began to experience itself as not only the unfinished continuation of the past, but also a kind of new and heroic beginning. To grasp something on the level of contemporaneity now meant not only to bring it down to earth, but also to raise it to a new heroic sphere. In the Renaissance the present first experienced itself clearly and consciously as something incomparably closer and more akin to the future than to the past.[23]

Without ever owning up to what he is doing, Bakhtin here admits that the experience he had attributed to the *I-for-myself* in the 1920s was in fact dependent on the dawning of a historical consciousness in the Renaissance.[24]

But if you redefine a type of consciousness in historical terms, you inevitably have to redefine the conditions which make it possible as well. The 'orientation to the future' was no longer something subjects simply inherited by virtue of being subjects: it depended on a sense of the world as historical, on ethics being guided by self-criticism rather than tradition, and on the conviction that one's personal actions were somehow connected, bound up, with that historical future. Clearly some novels were better at endowing their heroes with this sense of 'historical becoming' than others. 'Dialogical' novels could accomplish their task stylistically, by representing language as a kind of social 'heteroglossia', in which 'the formal markers of languages, manners and styles' were interpreted as 'symbols of social points of view'.[25] Novels of becoming would accomplish their task by virtue of a distinctive narrative practice:

> In novels such as *Gargantua and Pantagruel*, *Simplicissimus*, and *Wilhelm Meister* the becoming of a person has a different character. It is no longer his private affair. He becomes *together with the world*, he reflects the historical becoming of the world itself within himself. He is no longer within an epoch, but on the border of two epochs, at the point of transition from one to the next. The transition is achieved in him and through him. He is forced to become a new, unprecedented type of human being. The issue here is precisely the becoming of a new person; the organising force of the future is therefore extraordinarily great and it is, of course, not a private–biographical future, but a historical future. It is the *foundations* of the world that change, and the person must change with them.[26]

Foundations? The ante for becoming a responsible person has been upped considerably, so much so that it seems responsibility depends not only on a certain aesthetic practice but on particular political conditions as well. If the transition to a new kind of world is to be accomplished through the hero, than the world will have to be organised such that its inhabitants can determine not only the course of their own lives (rare enough anyhow) but even the foundations, the basic structures, which determine what kinds of lives are possible to begin with.

Bakhtin could not go this far: as far as he was concerned, politics was a sphere 'not illuminated by truth': there was something *per se* inauthentic about it. So he acknowledged the worldly conditions of responsibility in his own way, by admitting that what stood in the way of responsible human beings was not 'theoreticism', but other human beings. As everyone knows, the essays on the novel are unusually militant, and their militancy affects the core of their case and not just their tone. For in texts like 'Discourse in the novel', 'Epic and novel' and the book on Rabelais the social world is bisected into a novelistic side and a poetic or epic side, into a culture of laughter and a culture of seriousness, a dialogical culture of the people and a monological 'official' culture. Bakhtin cannot bring himself to say that the distribution of power in the world is what creates *I-for-myselves* who see only their own lives and not the world as historical. But he recognises that something stands in the way of the historical becoming he craves, and that this something is itself a kind of cultural practice.

Bakhtin's brilliant insight is to see that responsibility in a world like modern Europe will not flow from even the most delicately framed legal procedures. It will depend in the final analysis on a sense of connection to historical change embodied in particular kinds of narrative, which he calls novels. An 'orientation to the future' maintained by an isolated *I* breeds only anxiety, but an 'orientation to an historical future', one that involves the 'foundations of the world', comes about through specific cultural forms, themselves the fruit of a long and complex history.

But though Bakhtin welcomes History at the front door, he quietly shuffles it out the back. The same essays which map out the modern task of the novel suggest that success is somehow preordained. 'Discourse in the novel' not only describes what it takes to turn language into an 'image of a language' with historical force: it argues that when the novel does this it is doing no more than exploiting an innate dialogism available in language as such. When Bakhtin claims that 'a living utterance ... cannot avoid becoming a participant in social dialogue' (DN, p. 90/276) he effectively builds the connection with history he craves into language itself. Similarly, the literary and cultural history which distinguishes these works is not all that it seems. For while novelistic writing develops, its root source is a millennial popular culture which keeps its own counsel throughout history, occasionally providing the inspiration for a modern artist – Goethe, Rabelais, Dostoevsky – who is willing to make a break for it. Here eternity takes the form not of something transcending our culture, but of a culture mysteriously sustaining itself throughout history: 'the social life of discourse ... in the open spaces of public squares and streets' (DN, p. 73/259), which is always in the background, ready to break out, yet always (here the note of realism sounds) ultimately driven back or suppressed.

Cultural history is treated with the same ambiguous feelings in Bakhtin's book on Rabelais, where the distinctiveness of the latter's Renaissance achievement is balanced by an emphasis on its deep roots in popular festive tradition. And if the ambiguity isn't obvious enough in the published text, it's put in the sharpest possible terms in the recently published 'On questions of self-consciousness and self-valorisation', dated between 1943 and 1946 by its editors:

> The system of folkloric symbols laid down over the millennia, which gave form to the ultimate whole. In them one finds the great experience of humanity. In the symbols of official culture one finds only the petty experience of a specific part of humankind (at a given moment, interested in its stabilisation). Characteristic of these petty models, created on the basis of petty and private experience, is a specific pragmatism, a utilitarianism. They serve as a scheme for the practically interested action of a person, in them, actually, practice determines thought ... They are interested, least of all, in the truth of the all-embracing whole (this truth of the whole is non-practical and disinterested; it is indifferent to the temporal fates of the partial).[27]

The 'great experience' of humanity embodied in the symbolic forms of popular culture is not really a form of experience at all. It is the transcendence of experience, the means by which humanity achieves a wholly disinterested view of the 'ultimate whole'. The abstraction of Bakhtin's cultural history of carnival, which has annoyed social historians for decades, is not accidental. For the very anonymity of popular culture is what, in Bakhtin's view, allows it to function as an equivalent for the transcendent, ahistorical view of the philosopher.

These shrewd moves cannot be simply brushed aside: they make possible those whiggish interpretations of Bakhtin's theory which see modern novels, no matter what God-forsaken world they live in, doing no more than fulfilling language's immanent ethical destiny. To the extent that dialogism, novelistic writing, the chronotope, and the rest are conceived of as natural properties of language or narrative, all one has to do is set them loose, free them from any kind of external constraint. It's this ambiguity that lends credence to 'liberal' readings of Bakhtin, despite the fact that it's precisely the liberal conception of the individual that the whole theory is ranged against. If all that prevents a responsible, dialogical form of culture emerging is some kind of constraint on the natural operation of language, then it's clear the wisest policy will be to leave language and culture alone, to restrict social interventions to a minimum.

But what if the good and the bad, the dialogical and the monological, the chronotopic and the abstract, are equally natural to language and culture? What if the dialogues which make for responsible people don't emerge naturally from language, like Athena from the head of Zeus? Bakhtin tried to derive the culture he saw as necessary from a philosophy of language and culture, but he couldn't do it. His failure marks the presence of an unsolved problem, which can only be resolved by forcing apart what Bakhtin felt compelled to weld together.

The thesis that Bakhtin's work consists of a sociological outside and a philosophical or theological inside is one such forcing apart. It reduces the ambiguities by insisting that the philosophical meaning of each term (dialogism, responsibility, chronotope) is the real one and the historical derivation of it mere window dressing for the Soviet censor. But the pattern of Bakhtin's writing suggests that while he never quite shook off this temptation, he was also shrewd enough not to succumb to it. The more he looked, the more clearly the history of 'dialogue' came into focus. And if Bakhtin could not resist the temptation to 'examine everything from the standpoint of redemption', as Adorno put it, he also figured that redemption would come through human culture and not from outside of it.

In a brilliant and as yet untranslated essay on Bakhtin entitled 'The event of being', Sergei Bocharov described the aesthetics of the fragment 'Author and hero' as a 'dam' temporarily holding back the flow of metaphysical questions and conclusions.[28] Put thus, the dam sounds like an external constraint on Bakhtin's natural inclinations, which commentary and criticism might be able to posthumously loosen, if not remove. It's equally possible, however (and Bocharov admits this), that the dam is intrinsic to the intellectual construction. Everyone likes their rivers to flow free, and the image of history as an endless riverine 'becoming' is an almost irresistible temptation. In Bakhtin's work, however, the dams are as important as the flow they impede, for they alone produce the intellectual tension which makes the work compelling and relevant. Take them away and, after the first rush of water, you'll find just a slack, enervating current.

Elsewhere in his essay Bocharov comments that Bakhtin

preferred 'problems which "stick out" over conceptions'.[29] He's absolutely right. The conceptions for which Bakhtin is most renowned aren't really conceptions at all, but signs of problems unsolved. It's entirely legitimate to dream of their solution. In the sober light of day, however, one has to confront the problems themselves.

Notes

1 'Iz zapisei 1970–1971 godov', in *Estetika slovesnogo tvorchestva*, 2nd edn, ed. S. G. Bocharov, Moscow, 1986, p. 375. English translation: 'From notes made in 1970–71', in *Speech Genres and Other Late Essays*, ed. Caryl Emerson and Michael Holquist, trans. Vern W. McGee, Austin, Texas, 1986, p. 150.

2 Sergei Averintsev, 'Lichnost' i talant uchenogo', *Literaturnoe obozrenie*, 10, 1976, p. 59.

3 See, for example, Vitalii Makhlin, 'Face to face: Bakhtin's programme and the architectonics of being-as-event in the twentieth century', in Carol Adlam *et al.*, eds, *Face to Face: Bakhtin in Russia and the West*, Sheffield, 1997, pp. 46–7.

4 See V. Kozhinov and S. Konkin, 'Mikhail Mikhailovich Bakhtin: kratkii ocherk zhizni i deyatel'nosti', in S. Konkin, ed., *Problemy poetiki i istorii literatury*, Saransk, 1973, p. 5; Katerina Clark and Michael Holquist, *Mikhail Bakhtin*, Cambridge, Mass., and London, 1985, pp. 27–30.

5 *Besedy V. D. Duvakina s M. M. Bakhtinym* (*Conversations between V. D. Duvakin and M. M. Bakhtin*), interviews from 1973, ed. V. B. Kuznetsova, M. B. Radzishevskaya and V. F. Teider, Moscow, 1996, p. 35.

6 The documentary evidence is discussed in N. A. Pan'kov, 'Zagadki rannego perioda (Eshche neskol'ko shtrikhov k "Biografii M. M. Bakhtina")', *Dialog Karnaval Khronotop*, 1, 1993, pp. 74–89, and V. I. Laptun, 'K "Biografii M. M. Bakhtina"', *Dialog Karnaval Khronotop*, 1, 1993, pp. 67–73.

7 See A. G. Lisov and E. G. Trusova, 'Repliki po povodu avtobiografi-cheskogo mifotvorchestva M. M. Bakhtina', *Dialog Karnaval Khronotop*, 3, 1996, pp. 161–6.

8 Brian Poole, 'Bakhtin and Cassirer: the philosophical origins of Bakhtin's carnival messianism', *South Atlantic Quarterly*, XCVII: 3–4, 1998, pp. 537–78.

9 S. G. Bocharov, 'Ob odnom razgovore i vokrug ego', *Novoe literaturnoe obozrenie*, 2, 1993, p. 71; an abridged translation into English by Stephen Blackwell and Vadim Liapunov is 'Conversations with Bakhtin', *PMLA*, CIX: 5, 1994, p. 1012.

10 Editorial commentary (by L. A. Gogotishvili) to 'Problema rechevykh zhanrov', in *Sobranie sochinenii v semi tomakh, tom 5: Raboty 1940-kh – nachala 1960-kh godov* (*Collected Works in Seven Volumes, Vol. 5: Works from the 1940s to the Beginning of the 1960s*), ed. S. G. Bocharov and L. A. Gogotishvili, Moscow, 1996, p. 536. All further references to this volume

are given in the text and notes of this chapter in the form *SS5* followed by the page number.

11 S. G. Bocharov, 'Ob odnom razgovore i vokrug nego', pp. 78–9; 'Conversations with Bakhtin', p. 1017.

12 N. I. Nikolaev, '*Dostoevskii i antichnost'* L. V. Pumpyanskogo (1922) i M. M. Bakhtina (1963)', [Proceedings of] The Seventh International Bakhtin Conference, Book I, Moscow, 1995, pp. 1–10.

13 Roland Barthes, 'The writer on holiday', in *Mythologies*, trans. Annette Lavers, London, 1973, p. 31.

14 Pan'kov himself, however, was accused of still contributing to the mythology by V. M. Alpatov, whose critique of his introductory article was printed, together with a response from Pan'kov, in a later issue of *Dialog Karnaval Khronotop*. See Alpatov, 'Zametki na polyakh stenogrammmy zashchity dissertatsii M. M. Bakhtina', *Dialog Karnaval Khronotop*, 1, 1997, pp. 70–97; and N. A. Pan'kov, '"No my Istorii ne pishem ..."', *Dialog Karnaval Khronotop*, 1, 1997, pp. 98–139.

15 The final phrase – *nravstvennaya filosofiya* – is usually translated as 'moral philosophy'. I think the term 'ethical' is more appropriate as Bakhtin clearly means to emphasise the presence of the ethical relation of *I* and *other*, and wishes to contrast this to the tradition of Kantian *Moralität*.

16 'K filosofii postupka', in *Filosofiya i sotsiologiya nauki i tekhniki*, Moscow, 1986, p. 122. English translation: *Toward a Philosophy of the Act*, trans. Vadim Liapunov, Austin, Texas, 1994, p. 54. Hereafter references to the original and the translation will be provided in the form TPA, followed by the respective page numbers (e.g. TPA, p. 122/54).

17 See N. I. Nikolaev, 'The Nevel school of philosophy (Bakhtin, Kagan and Pumpianskii) between 1918 and 1925: materials from Pumpianskii's archives', in David Shepherd, ed., *The Contexts of Bakhtin: Philosophy, Authorship, Aesthetics*, Amsterdam, 1998, pp. 29–41.

18 I've borrowed certain elements of my translation here from Galin Tihanov's superb article 'Culture, form, life: the early Lukács and the early Bakhtin', which brilliantly reconstructs the historical context of Bakhtin's early philosophical work: in Craig Brandist and Galin Tihanov, eds, *Materializing Bakhtin: The Bakhtin Circle and Social Theory*, London, 2000, pp. 43–69.

19 'Autor i geroi v esteticheskoi deyatel'nosti', in *Estetika slovesnogo tvorchestva*, p. 26. English translation: 'Author and hero in aesthetic activity', in *Art and Answerability: Early Philosophical Essays*, ed. Michael Holquist and Vadim Liapunov, trans. Vadim Liapunov, Austin, Texas, 1990, p. 24. Hereafter references to this essay and its translation appear in text as, e.g., Att, p. 26/24.

20 M. M. Bakhtin, *Problemy tvorchestva Dostoevskogo*, Leningrad, 1929, p. 240. English translation: in an appendix to *Problems of Dostoevsky's Poetics*, trans. Caryl Emerson, Manchester, 1984, p. 280.

21 Nikolai Pan'kov's research into Voloshinov's academic papers at the Institute for the Comparative Study of Eastern and Western Languages and Literatures has turned up a detailed plan for a book to be entitled *Marxism and the Philosophy of Language* and an outline for an article entitled

BAKHTIN IN THE SOBER LIGHT OF DAY

'Problems in the transmission of another's speech', both dated 1928. The book plan corresponds (with some modifications) to the first two parts of the published *Marxism and the Philosophy of Language*; the article corresponds to its third part. On the basis of these archival discoveries it seems reasonable to conclude that Voloshinov was the principal author of the book in question, and that the decision to make the study of indirect forms of speech a part of it was taken relatively late. See 'Lichnoe delo V. N. Voloshinova' and N. A. Pan'kov, 'Mifologema Voloshinova (neskol'ko zamechanii kak by na polyakh arkhivnykh materialov', *Dialog Karnaval Khronotop*, 2, 1995, pp. 70–99 and 66–9 respectively.

22 The last three titles are probably unfamiliar to English-language readers, as they have only been published in Russian so far. They are, nevertheless, important and distinctive contributions to Bakhtin's writing on the novel. See 'K stilistike romana', 'K voprosam teorii romana' and 'O Flobere', in Bakhtin, *SS5*, pp. 138–40, 48–9 and 130–7 respectively.

23 'Epos i roman', in *Voprosy literatury i estetiki: issledovaniya raznykh let*, Moscow, 1975, p. 482–3. English translation: 'Epic and novel', in *The Dialogic Imagination: Four Essays by M. M. Bakhtin*, ed. Michael Holquist, trans. Caryl Emerson and Michael Holquist, Austin, Texas, 1981, p. 40.

24 On the creation of a distinct sense of history in the Renaissance, see Reinhart Koselleck, *Futures Past: On the Semantics of Historical Time*, trans. Keith Tribe, Cambridge, Mass., 1985.

25 'Slovo v romane', in *Voprosy estetiki i literatury*, p. 169. English translation: 'Discourse in the novel', in *The Dialogic Imagination*, p. 357. Hereafter references to this essay and its translation will appear in text as, e.g., DN, p. 169/357.

26 'Roman vospitaniya i ego znachenie v istorii realizma', in *Estetika slovesnogo tvorchestva*, p. 214. English translation: 'The *Bildungsroman* and its significance in the history of realism', in *Speech Genres and Other Late Essays*, pp. 23–4.

27 'K voprosam samosoznaniya i samootsenki', in *SS5*, p. 77.

28 Sergei Bocharov, 'Sobytie bytiya', *Novyi mir*, 11, 1995, p. 220.

29 Bocharov, 'Sobytie bytiya', p. 216.

Nikolai Pan'kov

'Everything else depends on how this business turns out ...': Mikhail Bakhtin's dissertation defence as real event, as high drama and as academic comedy[1]

> Mikhal Mikhalych used to speak of the phenomena of a certain 'false prophecy': 'the self-proclaimed seriousness of culture' (pronouncing these words slowly and carefully).   M. V. Yudina

It is common knowledge that when Mikhail Mikhailovich Bakhtin died in 1975 he had lived long enough to achieve international recognition while at the same time remaining a mere Candidate of Philological Sciences (the lower scholarly rank in the USSR).[2] True, in the mid-1960s there was an attempt to have conferred on him the rank of Professor (and shortly after even to propose him as a candidate for the Lenin Prize – the highest of honours!), and these moves might well have been successful (although in the case of the Lenin Prize this is perhaps unlikely). However, Bakhtin calmly and with dignity disavowed any claims to official regalia, asking that no one be troubled or disturbed on his account.

The principled nature of this refusal of honours is beyond doubt. First, Bakhtin always measured life from the perspective of 'great time', and, consequently, in his eyes a successful career or material goods possessed no significance in themselves. Moreover, Bakhtin considered himself not a literary scholar, but a philosopher, and a philosopher 'should be nobody, because if he becomes somebody, he begins to make his philosophy fit in with his professional position' (V. V. Kozhinov told me that this aphoristic, albeit somewhat joking, phrase was Bakhtin's response when asked about his reasons for refusing professorial honours and conditions.[3]) Second, Bakhtin knew perfectly well that among the people who determined the fate of such applications no small number were either openly or secretly hostile to him: those who had forced him into silence for several decades, those who had obstructed the re-issue of his book on Dostoevsky and the publication of his study of

Rabelais, and those who could not agree with his ideas and were afraid of their unfettered freedom, their alluring drive towards the unexplored spaces of thought. To depend upon a decision of the 'powerful of this world' and even – such miracles may happen! – to accept something from somebody's tainted hands, be it a prestigious testimonial or a laurel wreath, was something he clearly did not want. And, third and last, one should not overlook the fact that Bakhtin had already effectively been deprived of the rank of Professor (having not been awarded the degree of Doctor, which was essential for a professorship and without which only a few, in exceptional circumstances, have become professors). To have renewed efforts in this regard would have signified becoming reconciled with an earlier injustice, and this Bakhtin had manifestly not forgotten.

On 15 November 1946 the Academic Council of the USSR Academy of Sciences' Institute of World Literature convened for Bakhtin's defence of his Candidate's dissertation 'F. Rabelais in the history of realism'. This was far from the first and far from the last time the Council had met, and it met as it usually did on the days of traditional routine dissertation defences. Before long, however, it became clear that the proceedings were not following the usual pattern, for controversy immediately flared up in earnest: from the very outset things took a turn that was anything but predictable, and they culminated in a dramatic and colourful finale. What took place, and how, will be related in due course; but at this stage I need to reconstruct the prehistory of this tempestuous scholarly engagement.

Bakhtin probably began to contemplate the necessity of defending a dissertation under the pressure of the difficult circumstances in which he found himself living: after his exile in Kustanai he experienced continual difficulties in finding employment – and a higher degree, of course, could help him overcome these. Furthermore, the salary of a Candidate of Sciences was at that time significantly higher than the earnings of a 'degreeless' lecturer or researcher, and evidently Bakhtin, who lived perpetually on the edge of starvation, could not after all resist the prospect of relative well-being. True, it is perhaps not difficult to see in this a certain retreat from the maximalist ascetic stoicism spoken of above and to which, as I understand it, Bakhtin always gravitated consciously. However, Bakhtin, it seems, at no time imagined himself a heroic figure who had completely avoided visible, if forced, compromises with an unforgiving reality. And God grant that we all get through life with nothing more serious than 'transgressions' such as these.

It was not without hesitation that Bakhtin made this small accommodation with the Stalinist literary establishment. Most likely he simply heeded the persistent and stubborn urgings of M. V. Yudina, who may be seen as the true inspiration for this tactical manoeuvre by the recent political exile. At least Yudina herself acknowledged this fact, recalling in one of her letters to Irina Nikolaevna Medvedeva, the wife of B. V. Tomashevskii: 'when Mikh. Mikh. finally put into his pocket his Candidate's Diploma (which he had earlier considered "filthy lucre", but which later, in Saransk, came in very useful), he said to me "It was you who did this ..." I did not argue ... So it was, *by the grace of God* and many years of constant anxiety about him and his dissertation ...' (Yudina's emphasis).[4]

To judge from all the evidence, Bakhtin himself was initially interested not in the 'scholastic' genre of the dissertation, but in that of the book. He would rather have spoken to a much wider audience than those attending a dissertation defence, and even much later he tried not to refer to his work on Rabelais as a dissertation.[5]

At one point during his long hours of tape-recorded discussions with V. D. Duvakin Bakhtin said: 'I began Rabelais when I was still in Kustanai.'[6] But the idea for the work probably crystallised even earlier, in Leningrad in the late 1920s, because, as V. N. Turbin has recalled, in response to a direct question about when Rabelais might have appeared had there been no external impediments, Bakhtin answered without even stopping to think about it: 'In 1933, I think.'[7] And during the defence he said several times that work on the book had taken 'over ten years' (which means we can assume the original impetus dates back to the pre-Kustanai period).[8]

In 1940 the book was basically finished. But much remains unclear. Bakhtin remarked in his opening speech at the defence: 'Six years have passed since I completed my book. I finished it and submitted it to this Institute back in 1940, in the spring of 1940.'[9] And the autobiographical note written in 1944 in Saransk states: 'This dissertation (a book of 40 printer's sheets) was finished in 1940 and presented to the Institute of World Literature of the USSR Academy of Sciences in Moscow and the Institute of Western European Literature of the Academy of Sciences in Leningrad.'[10] But I have not been able to find any trace of Bakhtin's having submitted his manuscript to the Institute of World Literature in 1940.

At his defence Bakhtin repeatedly insisted that the text of the work had not changed since 1940 – 'It was written and handed in,

I did not see it again and could not make corrections' (Transcript, p. 99). For me this too is still an enigma. On the one hand it raises suspicion: where was the manuscript stored so securely that even its own author could not see it? (Was all this perhaps a tactical ruse with the aim of avoiding the obligatory, almost ritual at the time, citation of the aphorisms of A. A. Zhdanov?[11] It is telling that Bakhtin should refer with particular insistence to 1940 precisely in response to reproaches that he had not reflected the latest Party decisions.) But on the other hand it was not at all characteristic of Bakhtin to 'tremble over his manuscripts', and therefore it cannot be ruled out that all the copies of his book were constantly 'wandering' from one reader or 'interpreter' to the next. For example, in May 1946 he wrote to Yudina:

> I know nothing about you ... And I know nothing about my own business either (in particular, whether my Rabelais manuscript is still in one piece).
>
> I've telegraphed Iv. Iv. [Kanaev] to tell him I will be in Moscow after 20 May, and asked him to bring his copy of Rabelais. If he comes and can't wait for me, have him leave the manuscript with you.[12]

Whatever happened, Bakhtin did not of course stop thinking about the work after 1940: he sought to strengthen his argument in every possible way right up to the defence. It is no accident that we 'hear' in his concluding remarks: 'I was searching and I continue to search, I became convinced and continue to become convinced that this is the way it was ...' (Transcript, p. 92). It is no accident that he ordered books upon books through Yudina in 1945–46. It is no accident that during the discussion of his dissertation he referred to an article by A. A. Fortunatov about Virgilius Maro Grammaticus which he had read literally a few days before.[13]

If it is not completely clear whether Bakhtin attempted to set official procedures in motion for the defence of his dissertation in 1940, we can, as L. S. Melikhova says, know for certain that as early as late 1940 or early 1941 he launched his first attempt to have *Rabelais* published as a book.[14] Evidence for this is contained in the correspondence between Bakhtin and A. A. Smirnov (regrettably, I have not had the opportunity to consult this correspondence). Bakhtin was not discouraged by his failure, and his efforts were evidently renewed in late 1943 and early 1944. In January 1944 Smirnov forwarded the Rabelais manuscript from Yaroslavl with his report and asked D. E. Mikhal'chi to pass it on either to B. V. Tomashevskii (the other reader) or directly to P. I. Chagin at Litizdat.[15] But things were moving slowly, something was not quite right. In a letter of 22 October Bakhtin asked Yudina despairingly:

> You say nothing about how the Rabelais business is going: has the manuscript been passed on to Chagin, has it reached the stage of being sent to readers (in particular, has it gone to Boris Viktorovich [Tomashevskii]), has Nusinov phoned, what is the outcome of all this? I haven't received any communication from Chagin either. Everything else depends on how this business turns out.[16]

I have not yet located the report on the manuscript written by Smirnov in January 1944. Yudina's archive in the Manuscript Section of the Russian State Library contains reports by Smirnov and Tomashevskii dated December 1944.[17] Both readers offer a very positive evaluation of the book. At the beginning of 1945 everyone had the sense that just one last effort was needed. Then, in two letters, of 3 and 8 January, Bakhtin, using almost the same words on both occasions, urged Yudina to do everything she possibly could:

> The present moment is most important. Unfortunately I am ill myself, and there is no way that I can come to Moscow. Nevertheless, we must act quickly to ensure that things work out favourably. Please do everything you can. It's very important that Nusinov should 'put pressure on'. Perhaps we can get someone else with connections to Litizdat interested in the book. It would be a good idea to get advice from Bor. Vikt. Tomashevskii and Nik. Mikh. Lyubimov. You are closer to things and can see more clearly what can and needs to be done.[18]

Alas, in February 1945 Litizdat turned the book down. Smirnov explained the decision in a letter to Bakhtin:

> I think that there are two reasons: it is possible that they were in the end nervous about the specific nature of a certain part of the material, although they don't want to admit this. But the second reason is even more important: they have accepted for publication ... this book on Rabelais by E. Evnina from the Institute of World Literature, and they dare not risk publishing two books on Rabelais in the same year.[19]

But still Bakhtin did not let up. In May he worried in a letter to Yudina about 'what the position is with my Rabelais book (I find it hard to get any idea from your brief communications), what new prospects there might be now that the war is over'.[20] At the end of November in the same year (1945) he wrote to her again: 'It would be good to clarify what the prospects for Rabelais at Litizdat are now. I've heard that there's somebody new in charge there, one Sergei Mitrofanovich Petrov, who used to work in the Saransk Institute, he was my successor in the department. If this is true, then we could go to him directly (I don't think he knows me personally, but he will have heard of me in any case).'[21] These hopes were evidently not justified, but at more or less the same time – and, most likely, not without Petrov's good offices – a new and very promising turn of events almost became a genuine possibility. At the very end of December 1945 I. N. Medvedeva tried to cheer Yudina up: 'We've received news that Goslitizdat has sent Bakhtin's book to Aragon (the writer), and he's taken it to Paris, where it is to be published. This was done on the basis of Bor. Vikt.'s report, which impressed Aragon. We must assume that this will mean not only fame, but also money ...'[22]

Unfortunately, for some reason Rabelais was not published in France at that time either. And there was by now no alternative to a dissertation defence. The arrangements took rather a long time. But things were made easier by the fact that they were not starting from scratch. During the battle to have the work published as a book a certain number of contacts in academic circles had been made or renewed. I have already mentioned Smirnov (the first official examiner) and Tomashevskii. The name of I. M. Nusinov, who would become another official examiner, has also been mentioned once or twice. Yudina was the first to draw attention to Nusinov. She had written to Bakhtin back in the late 1930s:

> Mikhail Mikhailovich, I have unexpectedly discovered some direct routes to a certain Professor Nusinov – I have come across this name in journals, and in connection with Western literature at that; I've been told that he is a good man and 'non-standard'. Let me know at once whether we need him, in which case we will have to decide as soon as possible who will go to see him.[23]

It is a vitally important point that what they were looking for were good and 'non-standard' people, that is, people who did not have ulterior motives, and who were able to turn a blind eye to departures from Marxist dogma. L. I. Timofeev proved to be such an individual: 'there is no need to go to see L. I. Timofeev: I have already been in touch with him by letter, he is very kind and will do everything he can', Bakhtin wrote in September 1943 in an attempt to temper Yudina's enthusiasm.[24] E. V. Tarle, too, demonstrated similar qualities. Bakhtin had known him (he lived in Yudina's neighbourhood) in Leningrad. In the summer of 1946 he decided to ask Tarle for assistance. At the end of June I. I. Kanaev wrote to Yudina: 'After the first of July I will be living out of town, therefore send M. M.'s dissertation directly to Tarle. Then I can call on him to get the dissertation and his report. You should write to tell him this, and let me know when I should go to see him.'[25]

Tarle, who had himself lived through a fall from favour in the 1930s, was very understanding of Bakhtin's position, something of which Bakhtin informed Yudina with satisfaction in August, intending even 'to ask him to be an examiner'.[26] He went on: 'I do not know whether he will find this convenient. There is still no answer from him.'[27] Tarle probably declined the offer, but his report on the dissertation was read out at the defence. And instead of Tarle (and, perhaps, at his suggestion, as they had been corresponding since 1913),[28] A. K. Dzhivelegov agreed to act as the third examiner; Dzhivelegov, incidentally, was the supervisor of E. M. Evnina, whose book had 'got in the way of' Bakhtin's plans.[29]

On 28 June 1946 Bakhtin applied to the Institute of World Literature for leave to submit his Candidate's dissertation on the theme 'F. Rabelais in the history of realism': 'The established requirements for the degree of Candidate have been fulfilled by me. I append herewith the manuscript of the dissertation and all necessary documentation.'[30] This included an autobiographical statement, personnel record, and various certificates and references. But the key document is a certificate, dated 24 June 1946, that Bakhtin had passed the Candidate's examinations. The place where the examinations were taken was the Moscow State Pedagogical Institute. All the examinations – in ancient literature, literature of the Middle Ages and Renaissance, literature of the eighteenth, nineteenth and twentieth centuries, German and French language, the history of philosophy, dialectical and historical materialism – were passed with the highest grade of 'Excellent'.[31] This certificate was to play a vitally important role, for it would allow Bakhtin to perform another miracle: he would overcome the fatal bureaucratism of the VAK (*Vysshaya attestatsionnaya komissiiya*, Higher Attestation Commission). The fact was that Bakhtin did not have a first-degree certificate, and so could not submit it along with his other documents. On 10 May 1947, the defence now over, the Academic

Secretary of the Institute of World Literature B. V. Gornung would reply with obviously feigned innocence to an enquiry from the VAK Inspector, Belova:

1   Comrade Bakhtin was granted leave to defend his Candidate's dissertation on the basis of a certificate showing that in 1946 he had satisfied the Candidate's requirements at the Moscow State Pedagogical Institute. The certificate has been submitted to VAK (no. 13 on the inventory of documents accepted by VAK Inspector comrade Mokhova on 11 April 1947).

2   A copy of his 1918 first-degree certificate from Petrograd University has been requested from Bakhtin by telegraph, but the Institute did not require its submission by comrade Bakhtin at the time of the defence, since the document regarding the satisfaction of the requirements for the degree of Candidate was available.

3   Published notice of the defence of the dissertation will be delivered to you in the next few days.[32]

Subsequently VAK for some reason did not insist on presentation of the degree certificate, and a difficult moment for the candidate was successfully overcome.

The nearer the day of the defence drew, the greater the atmosphere of chaos and uncertainty became. On 3 September 1946 Smirnov confided in Mikhal'chi: 'The Bakhtin dispute, it appears, will not be all that soon after all – in October, perhaps even in November, since not all the examiners in Moscow have yet been able to read the dissertation. But perhaps it will take place in October.'[33] Incidentally, the reason given by Smirnov for the delay looks rather strange: all the evidence suggests that both Dzhivelegov and Nusinov must have read the work long before, particularly if it had not changed since 1940. Smirnov himself would write a more extensive version of his report for the defence than the one written in December 1944.

At its meeting on 24 September the Western Literature Section heard A. A. Smirnov's report on the dissertation and took the decision to set in motion arrangements for its defence. At the same time it was proposed that three official examiners be appointed (as for a doctoral dissertation, although the dissertation is nevertheless referred to as a Candidate's).[34]

By 13 October the date of the defence was apparently known, but there was still no certainty. Bakhtin complained to Yudina: 'I have waited for official communications from the Institute, but have not received any. I don't know anything about whether all *three* examiners have submitted their reports and in what spirit, and whether the defence (or an approximate timescale for it) has already been announced.'[35] And two weeks later nothing had changed: 'I know nothing about my dissertation defence, except that it has been set for 15 November. That would mean that I would have to leave no later than 8 or 9 November. But how can I leave, given that I don't know anything either about you or about the position with the dissertation?'[36]

On that day, 28 October, things evidently still hung by a thread, and could still have gone wrong. Not until 2 November was everything finally resolved, as we learn from a letter from Smirnov to Mikhal'chi: 'I have just received a telegram from B. V. Gornung telling me that the Bakhtin defence (Rabelais) has been set for 15 November and that my presence is required! So I will have to go. The only thing I don't know is at what time they hold their dissertation defences.'[37] In the following paragraph of the same letter Smirnov mentions that after the defence 'there will be a symposium at the apartment of the pianist M. V. Yudina, a great friend of Bakhtin'. They must have rejoiced very sincerely, wildly – carnivalesquely! A few days later I. I. Kanaev would send Yudina a postcard from Leningrad: 'I remember with pleasure the time spent on Begovaya Street, and I will await further news from you about Rabelais ... '[38]

And so, on 15 November 1946 the Institute of World Literature's Academic Council met for Bakhtin's defence of his Candidate's dissertation 'F. Rabelais in the history of realism'. The Council members present were V. F. Shishmarev, V. Ya. Kirpotin, L. I. Ponomarev, S. I. Sobolevskii, L. I. Timofeev, N. K. Piksanov, N. L. Brodskii, I. N. Rozanov, N. K. Gudzii, B. V. Mikhailovskii, I. M. Nusinov, A. K. Dzhivelegov and M. A. Tsyavlovskii.[39] There was also an audience (some 25–30 people, according to the recollection of Kirpotin, the only person actually involved in the defence that I have managed to track down),[40] some of whom took part in the discussion. And the odd thing is that while these spectators were drawn by their anticipation that the defence would have a somewhat unusual, scandalous character (as Kirpotin put it, they knew that the politically disgraced author of the dissertation intended to 'take a swipe at Marxism'), the members of the Academic Council apparently did not even suspect this, and were caught unawares.

Jean Vilar famously staged in his theatre a play based on the transcript of the court case against Robert Oppenheimer, the renowned American physicist condemned for refusing, after Hiroshima, to carry out atomic research or contribute to the creation of the hydrogen bomb. History, the age, the twentieth century – however one puts it – was revealed in a drama of near-Shakespearian intensity, without even a single word needing to be changed: the transcript contained a ready-made play. I am convinced that the minutes of Bakhtin's dissertation defence at the Institute of World Literature would also make a brilliant stage production, and then a different facet of more or less the same epoch in world history, a facet rather less familiar to Jean Vilar, would come alive before our eyes, and would probably shock some with its play of great passions and petty calculations, with its interweaving of tragedy, paradox and farce. True, the quality and state of preservation of these particular minutes are far from ideal, and so it would be helpful to be able to place them in the experienced and tactful hands of a willing dramatist in order that he might penetrate with genuine interest to the heart of the intrigue, offer coherent elucidation of the many 'obscure' passages, and impart to the text not, of course, completeness (that would be totally at odds with the spirit of Bakhtin), but a minimum of balance, plasticity and a capacity to be heard and apprehended from the outside. This would require considerable and, I fear, far from easy labour, as will be amply evident to a reader with a knowledge of Russian, for the minutes of the defence have been published in a completely unpolished form, with virtually all errors, inaccuracies and defects preserved.

Yet the defence will be interesting first and foremost as a major event in Bakhtin's personal destiny and in twentieth-century Russian academic life. Let us try, as though following in Jean Vilar's footsteps, to present the documentary record of the defence as a stage production – as high drama, but partly also as scholarly comedy and even farcical spectacle. Most important, of course, is the drama, and a drama is above all else characters. For want of space and adequate information I do not presume to offer detailed portraits of the players in this particular intrigue. I will limit myself merely to making a few 'remarks for the actors', as they say, to highlighting some individual features of the intellectual and external profiles of the *dramatis personae*.

Mikhail Mikhailovich Bakhtin

The central hero of our dramatic conflict, so certain facets of his personality have already been mentioned. Here, as before, we will not impose upon him an image of monolithic bravado, lest we lapse into the 'pretender's serious posturing' that was so inimical to him. The rich and varied hues of human existence are present in full measure in Bakhtin's case, and our protagonist is not only surrounded by an aura of courage and valour, but brings a smile to our lips with his naïve helplessness when faced with either cynical trimming to political circumstance, or timid doctrinairism.

On the one hand the defence was effectively deciding Bakhtin's fate. More than fifteen years of enormous labour, failure and concessions, and the only fruit of his compromises was this right to a desperate storming of the academic Bastille. Victory or breakthrough would mean escape from his position outside the law, and the prospect of at least having some work published, and of being able to continue his research. But the circumstances were thoroughly hostile: immediately after Bakhtin had submitted the necessary documentation to the Institute there came Zhdanov's notorious speech and the Central Committee's infamous resolution concerning the journals *Zvezda* and *Leningrad*.[41] The chances were virtually nil, but Bakhtin did not seek to avoid the battle, and fought like a lion. B. I. Purishev, who attended the defence, recounted that at climactic moments Bakhtin had shouted 'Obscurantists! Obscurantists!' at those opposing him, and angrily banged his crutches on the floor (I am grateful to Yu. M. Kagan for this information). True, this story is apocryphal, and is not substantiated by the minutes; nor does Kirpotin, the only witness and participant that I was able to speak to, recall anything of the sort. And in my view it is easier to imagine the cry of 'Obscurantists!' coming from the lips of Purishev himself (he knew and admired the *Epistolae obscurorum virorum*) than from those of Bakhtin. Nevertheless this small story conveys wonderfully well the tempestuous atmosphere of a discussion high in tension.[42]

But on the other hand there is an indefinable air of comedy: not cheerful, light comedy, but comedy of ideas, ornately rhetorical, complete with *raisonneur* and satirically coloured *staffage* – like Molière's *Misanthrope* or Griboedov's *Wit's End* (*Gore ot uma*). Four months earlier the same Academic Council had unanimously resolved to confer the degree of Doctor of Philological Sciences 'without dissertation defence' upon A. M. Egolin, an employee of the Central Committee's Department of Culture, an 'absolutely faceless' individual whose contribution to scholarship was non-existent.[43] And now here they were literally parading reckless adherence to principle, albeit accompanied by generosity of spirit: while rejecting root and branch the dissertation's principal theoretical contention, they were inclined actually to praise the author himself. Moreover, through some misunderstanding none of them (besides the official examiners), naturally, had actually read the work. It was a slippery case, and they were on their guard: if Bakhtin should get through, fine (after all, in general they were supportive of him), if not, then they would have shown due watchfulness. But to have read the work would have meant having to adopt a firm position from the outset: that would have been tricky, a bit of a risk!

In accordance with established ritual, the defence opened with introductory remarks by the author of the dissertation. I have already discussed some of the details that Bakhtin mentioned in these remarks, but more needs to be added. First, Bakhtin referred all those present to the substantial (twenty-page) abstract of the dissertation as an important source of additional information (*Tr. note*: The Russian text of the abstract was published as an appendix to the minutes of the defence, to which the present article was an introduction.)[44] Second, Bakhtin was of course aware that 'F. Rabelais in the history of realism' totally failed to meet the requirements of the dissertation genre in the USSR at that time, something to which he immediately alerted the members of the Academic Council and the others present: 'if anyone expects a complete picture, a biography and Rabelais's precise place in his immediate historical context, in the French Renaissance in the sixteenth century in France, then my study will disappoint them ... this is an issue that I have left to one side, although I have succeeded in reflecting the role of this tradition in my study' (Transcript, p. 58). Bakhtin's prediction was borne out: there was no discernible shortage of disappointed customers during the defence. It was this that kept at permanent boiling point a discussion that got under way even as the official examiners read out their responses.

Aleksandr Aleksandrovich Smirnov

Aged 63. While a student at St Petersburg University was a friend of the poet Aleksandr Blok.[45] A fierce supporter of avant-gardism in the 1910s who had close ties with many members of the artistic groups of the time.[46] Later he would become more interested in the classics. He was a highly professional researcher with a wide variety of interests, and a talented organiser. (In RGALI I leafed through a file on Smirnov's editing of a *Collected Works* of Molière for the 'Academia' publishing house: a vast labour.[47] And this was not the only collected works that Smirnov edited.) There is no doubt that Smirnov was sincerely convinced of the value of Bakhtin's work. Otherwise he would not either have been led by his personal sympathies, or argued for the award of the degree of Doctor. In his letters to Mikhal'chi he repeatedly praised N. G. Elina for her 'fine' work. But in December 1945 he refused to recommend her as a doctoral candidate at the Institute for World Literature, saying that it was 'a little early', and that he 'was afraid that the Institute might find him importunate'[48] (and later: 'Elina accepted my response kindly and nobly: she obviously understood my position totally'). Smirnov was by no means spineless, and was capable of, in his own words, 'rather sharply' criticising even quite major authorities.

Although he was the first to suggest that application should be made to turn the Candidate's defence into a Doctoral one, Smirnov made a number of serious critical points in his response. Without at this stage dwelling in any detail on these, I will note one point that I will need to return to later on. Smirnov agreed with Bakhtin that Rabelais's grotesque imagery, taken as a whole, had certainly not died out, but was a living aesthetic phenomenon. However, he argued that 'by no means all of the forms of grotesque imagery that occur in [Rabelais] remain alive to the same degree' (Transcript, p. 63), that many of them had been reinterpreted in a new fashion, were used as purely decorative elements, and so on.

Isaak Markovich (Moiseevich) Nusinov

Aged 57. Active in the revolutionary movement from an early age, and a member of the Bund, a Jewish Social Democratic movement. Spent many years in emigration, returning only after the February 1917 Revolution. Like Bakhtin, a victim early in life of serious illness (in his case, tuberculosis of the spinal column). Joined the Communist Party in 1919. In 1925 successfully defended his dissertation on 'The problem of the historical novel'. Taught in the Communist Academy, the Institute of Red Professors and Moscow State Universities (nos 1 and 2, i.e. the present Moscow State University and Moscow Pedagogical State University – formerly

Moscow State Pedagogical Institute).[49] At the start of his career he was frequently prone to extremes of vulgar sociologism, and in the 1940s was criticised for departures from orthodox Marxism and for abstract humanist tendencies. Ultimately, several years after Bakhtin's defence, he was repressed and died during the infamous campaign against cosmopolitanism.

Nusinov supported Smirnov's proposal that VAK be requested not to consider Bakhtin's dissertation for the degree of Candidate only. He saw 'the great positive value of Bakhtin's research' as its demonstration of how Rabelais's images 'grew out of the respective elements of the everyday life of the popular masses in the Middle Ages, out of medieval festivities, out of the whole of medieval popular anti-ecclesiastical play' (Transcript, p. 66). But Nusinov felt that the strengths of the work were also responsible for its numerous shortcomings. Above all, as a result of Bakhtin's fascination with the genesis of the novel, 'Rabelais [was] presented outside the atmosphere of the French Renaissance', was divorced from his 'immediate literary milieu', from the context of the ideas of scholarly humanism (the Abbaye de Thélème, the struggle with scholasticism, and so on).

Aleksei Karpovich Dzhivelegov

Born in 1875. Graduated from Moscow University in 1897. From 1915 taught in various institutes of higher education – Nizhegorod People's University, the Shanyavskii Moscow People's University, Moscow State University (no. 1) and others.[50] In the 1930s was awarded the degree of Doctor of Art History without dissertation defence and was offered a post in the Institute of World Literature, where until 1946 he was Head of the Western Literatures Section – moving, however, to the Institute of the History of the Arts shortly before Bakhtin's defence.[51]

We can best get a sense of Dzhivelegov's view of Bakhtin's dissertation by comparing the conclusion of his report with that of his reports on other dissertations. For instance, of G. N. Boyadzhiev's work he wrote: 'This book, as both parts and whole, undoubtedly merits the award to its author of the degree of Candidate of Art History.' Similarly: 'These criticisms in no sense detract from the merits of comrade Kuchborskaya's work, and I believe that it fully merits the award of the degree of Candidate of Philological Sciences.'[52] But at Bakhtin's defence Dzhivelegov exclaimed emotionally: 'when I look at the huge volume that lies

39

before me, full of such erudition, testifying to outstanding mastery of research methodology and, put simply, constituting a very talented work of scholarship, I think: can the degree of Candidate of Philological Sciences really be sufficient recognition of the merits of such a work?' (Transcript, p. 69). He went on to say: 'It would be ridiculous, of course, to award the degree of Candidate for a work like this, it is clear that it merits the degree of Doctor of Philological Sciences' (Transcript, p. 71). Dzhivelegov did comment, however, that there were aspects of Bakhtin's research 'that are not by any means beyond dispute': 'Thus ... the idea of the almost mystical significance for Rabelais of what Bakhtin calls the material lower-bodily stratum strikes me as excessively exaggerated' (Transcript, p. 68). While reluctant to argue 'on points of detail' with a scholar who had won him over with his obsession and erudition, Dzhivelegov nevertheless endorsed Smirnov's, and especially Nusinov's, point about the dissertation's failure to study adequately 'the unremitting struggle of social groups that was going on at the time that [Rabelais] lived, worked and wrote' (Transcript, p. 70).

Following Dzhivelegov's contribution Academician Evgenii Viktorovich Tarle's report – brief, somewhat restrained, but unambiguously positive – was read out. The information I have suggests that the renowned Soviet historian was not present at the defence, but he must nevertheless also be mentioned as an 'off-stage character' in our imagined drama.[53] Tarle praised Bakhtin for the 'subtlety' and 'originality' of his study, describing the chapters about Rabelais's literary influence on the seventeenth and eighteenth centuries as 'excellent' (Transcript, p. 71). What is perhaps especially noteworthy here is that Tarle found the connections and parallels that Bakhtin had established between Rabelais and Gogol to be undeniably interesting and important (Transcript, p. 71). Almost everyone else who contributed to the discussion either spoke of these parallels very cautiously, or criticised them. For instance, Nusinov, as though foreseeing his own persecution as a 'rootless cosmopolitan', did not miss the opportunity to distance himself explicitly from such risky assumptions: 'Gogol's laughter was nourished by Ukrainian reality itself, not by these literary influences brought in from the West' (Transcript, p. 67). After the defence, when VAK was deciding whether or not to award Bakhtin the degree of Doctor, the problem of the relationship between Gogol and Western popular culture acquired particularly keen significance, becoming one of the 'stumbling blocks' to the scholar's difficult progress towards his goal.[54]

After Smirnov, Nusinov, Dzhivelegov (and Tarle) it was the turn of the 'unofficial examiners' to give their views. The first was M. P. Teryaeva. It is unfortunate that from this point onwards I will not be able to describe all that took place in chronological sequence, observing properly the order in which the actors in this dramatic 'performance' appeared centre stage. My overriding aim is to reproduce the subsequent progress of the defence in a more conceptual and compressed form, and here what comes to the fore is not mere empirical detail, but the psychological core of the *dramatis personae*, the most important nuances of the ideas and problems discussed. The order of events is of course extremely interesting and will not escape attention altogether, but lack of space obliges me to sacrifice, at least in part, the 'context' of the event in favour of its 'subtext'.

Teryaeva's lengthy contribution was followed by interventions from: N. K. Piksanov, N. L. Brodskii, D. E. Mikhal'chi, (I. L.) Finkel'shtein, (E. Ya.) Dombrovskaya, Dzhivelegov, Smirnov, Nusinov and Brodskii (all for the second time), Kirpotin, B. V. Zalesskii, Smirnov (for the third time!), and B. V. Gornung. In total the discussion lasted more than seven hours.[55] Moreover, it is difficult to know which of its moments were the most tense, and thus most deserving of inclusion in our survey: odd though it may sound, the whole thing is one long climax. Reconciling ourselves to the inevitability of not offering a complete picture, and of having to omit descriptions of some of the key players, let us continue our account.

Mariya Prokof'evna Teryaeva

I have not been able to establish her age. Some biographical information may be gleaned from a letter she wrote in 1947 to the Union of Soviet Writers' Commission on Literary Theory and Criticism, addressed to the Union's Chairman Aleksandr Fadeev: 'I am a member of the Party and a graduate of Moscow State University where, back in 1923–30, I fought against the vulgar Menshevik sociology of Pereverzev.'[56] In the same paragraph she states that until July of the previous year (1946) she had worked at Moscow State Pedagogical Institute for Foreign Languages.

In the late 1920s Teryaeva sought to crush Pereverzev; in 1946 she struck at Bakhtin, and in the letter to Fadeev cited above she came down hard on 'the flawed theories and practice of Professor

Nusinov'. She details all the stages and the ups and downs of her 'battles': how she had spoken out in Ministries, at Party and Party Committee meetings, how she had bombarded the editors of numerous newspapers and journals with her letters and denunciatory articles, demanding that Nusinov's book *Pushkin and World Literature* be anathematised. Quoting T. L. Motyleva's comments at a meeting of the Academic Council of Moscow State Pedagogical Institute for Foreign Languages ('Nusinov's error is that he gets carried away with unhistorical comparisons of various images and phenomena'), she described these as an example of 'the terminology of a lady, not of Marxist, Party-minded criticism'.

Teryaeva's monologue and her sinister 'image' overall are essential for a full characterisation of the academic (and indeed the political) mores of the age, although they add next to nothing to the scholarly content of the discussion. In response to doubts expressed by Boris Zalesskii as to Teryaeva's competence, Kirpotin exclaimed: 'The comrade who spoke first is not someone who has wandered in off the street, she holds a Candidate's degree in Western literature.' I have not been able to find Teryaeva's personal file in any of the GARF collections pertaining to VAK or the Ministry of Enlightenment, so that I do not even know what the topic of her dissertation was, or when she defended it. But the archive of the journal *Literaturnyi kritik* in RGALI does contain two articles, 'Stendhal and bourgeois realism' and 'Stendhal as the founder of the nineteenth-century realist novel', written by her in the mid-1930s.[57] We may thus assume that Teryaeva had made a 'profound' and successful (i.e. one informed by the latest Party resolutions) study of Stendhal.

Nikolai Kir'yakovich Piksanov

Aged 68. Corresponding Member of the USSR Academy of Sciences since 1931. Graduate of Yur'ev (Derpt) University. Author of over 700 scholarly works.[58] In the context of the scholarly drama entitled 'Bakhtin's defence' whose plot I am seeking to trace, a section about Piksanov in E. G. Gershtein's memoirs is especially interesting:

> When I was a student at Moscow State University I took his seminar on Karamzin. This left me with a hostile feeling towards him, because he took a jaundiced view of my work. I thought he was a pedant. Perhaps I was wrong at the time, but later, when he lambasted Bakhtin at his dissertation defence, there could be no

doubt about the pedantic Piksanov's conservatism. By then it was 1947, i.e. immediately after the Central Committee's resolution on Zoshchenko and Akhmatova that placed the seal of obscurantism on our culture for long years thereafter. In his written response Tarle spoke of the international significance of Bakhtin's book on Rabelais, Dzhivelegov described Bakhtin's erudition as over-whelming and relentless, and a young graduate student, wringing his hands in his confusion, said that Bakhtin's works brought enlightenment, while Piksanov, referring extensively to Chernyshevskii, expressed his indignation that Bakhtin was driving a genius of the Renaissance back into the Middle Ages! Bakhtin became so worked up that, leaning on his crutches, he leapt nimbly about on his one leg and shouted at those opposing his views 'It's time the whole lot of you were replaced!' Dzhivelegov, in an attempt to defuse the atmosphere, declared 'One more dissertation like this and I'll have a stroke.' I had a kind of presentiment of all this on that day in Peterhof when I saw the pompous Piksanov strolling importantly along the paths of the Academy sanatorium.[59]

As soon as I read these lines I searched out the author's telephone number and rang her at once. It emerged that, unfortunately, Gershtein had not been present at Bakhtin's defence and knew of it only from the accounts of eyewitnesses (though she no longer remembered their identities). As we can see, the event was quite simply legendary in the second half of the 1940s. Gershtein's recol-lections give the date of the defence wrongly, but many other details are accurate, except that Bakhtin's cry of rebellion is not quite the same as in Purishev's account. This may be because Bakhtin has been quoted incompletely in both cases, and he might have shouted 'Obscurantists! It's time the whole lot of you were replaced!', or a result of the inevitable distortion of originally reli-able information as it is passed from one person to the next, or a function of the variability of motifs that is found in all myths.

Valerii Yakovlevich Kirpotin

Aged 48. Studied, and later taught, at the Institute of Red Professors. Secretary of the Commission responsible for the organ-isation of the first Congress of Soviet Writers in 1934 and of the Union of Soviet Writers. In 1946 was Deputy Director of the Institute of World Literature.[60]

I was able to arrange a meeting with Kirpotin in 1992. As he was by then a very old man, he was, alas, able to remember very little. But his account – the account of the only witness of the defence that I know to be still alive – has a certain value:

> I remember I was sitting in my office at the Institute when Bakhtin came in and asked to be allowed to defend his work. He said 'I need a higher degree so as to get ration coupons' (they wouldn't give him food coupons without this).
>
> At the time I was Deputy Director of the Institute. The Director was Shishmarev. You know, a major scholar. He was not much interested in the business of the Institute, it has to be said. He was interested in his own specialism, but not in broader scholarly issues. I had to handle everything.
>
> I hadn't known Bakhtin personally before then. I knew he'd been exiled from Leningrad, but I pretended not to. Those were very harsh times ... I thought highly of his book on Dostoevsky, although I didn't agree with it.
>
> I'd already read the dissertation, was familiar with it. Through Tarle.[61]
>
> I suggested he submit the book for the degree of Doctor. Bakhtin was a calm individual, not very ambitious – at least not outwardly. He said: 'If the dissertation doesn't get through, then I won't get any coupons ... '. He knew the psychology of the people he would be dealing with: run-of-the-mill, average Doctors of Science who'd got their degrees through years of labour were not particularly keen on allowing others into their circle.
>
> I rang the Ministry. They told me that the procedure was to have both defences on the same day. Bakhtin went off for a day to the Lenin Institute and brought back the certificate showing he had passed the Candidate's examinations.
>
> I prepared all the documents with a favourable outcome in mind: there were three official examiners. Bakhtin was happy with the defence. He said: 'I got what I came for.'
>
> We met a couple of times afterwards. I visited him when he lived in Peredelkino. He realised that I wished him well.
>
> My impression of him was that he was a modest, self-possessed person. His attitude to me was friendly and reserved.

Kirpotin told me almost nothing about the actual defence. He said that Tarle was not present, but that he could not remember who was. There were 25 or 30 people, or thereabouts: 'I remember that the defence was held in the Director's office. It was a small room, and wouldn't have held a lot of people. It was very tense. The first sensation was that a political exile was defending a dissertation. The second was that everyone knew that it was an anti-Marxist work, that it would be possible to take a swipe at Marxism.'

When I asked whether Bakhtin had shouted 'Obscurantists!' at those who opposed him Kirpotin replied that he could not remember anything of the sort, and repeated that Bakhtin always behaved in a very restrained manner.

The minutes of the defence steer us towards the firm conclusion that Kirpotin had not read the dissertation (Transcript, p. 87: 'I have not read the dissertation'). But in 1992 he thought that he had. Perhaps it was a trick of his memory, or possibly an involuntary desire to stress how conscious and significant his contribution to the whole business had been. His role was indeed a major one. There were, as he said, three official examiners from the outset, as for a Doctoral dissertation. This could not have happened without the knowledge of the Institute's management. Kirpotin chaired the defence with total objectivity. (At one point he exclaimed: 'Order, please. Everyone has the right to speak, everyone will have the opportunity to do so' (Transcript, p. 75) – which was exactly what happened.) When he spoke he did not deny Bakhtin's achievements or merits. Only on the matter of awarding the degree of Doctor was he evasive. Many believed that he was against this. (For example, the author of the official notice of the defence wrote: 'Substantive objections to the basic positions of the dissertation's author were voiced by N. K. Piksanov, Corresponding Member of the USSR Academy of Sciences, and Professors N. L. Brodskii and V. Ya. Kirpotin'.) But according to his own version Kirpotin was, on the contrary, the first to suggest that Bakhtin's work be submitted for the degree of Doctor rather than just that of Candidate. It is unlikely we will ever know who voted which way: the ballot of the members of the Academic Council was a secret one. All we can do is speculate.

In his concluding remarks Bakhtin acknowledged that it was natural that his 'basic conception appears both incorrect and strange': for a long time even he had found it utterly implausible (Transcript, p. 92). Therefore there is nothing surprising about the reaction of non-acceptance or rejection displayed by some of those involved in the defence. The only thing that may cause some surprise is that in articulating 'substantive objections' to Bakhtin, Piksanov, Brodskii and Kirpotin all effectively said the same as is said now by critics of Bakhtin's theory of popular culture. It is clearly not simply a matter of Bakhtin's being a progressive, bold innovator, while these three 'unofficial examiners' were adherents of conservative, curatorial views of Rabelais and the Middle Ages (although to a significant extent this is the case). The real nub of the disagreement lies somewhat deeper.

As far as the surface manifestation of the conflict is concerned, what is immediately obvious is the disagreement of all three with Bakhtin's assertion of the close connection between the progressive (according to the commonly accepted view) writer and humanist Rabelais and medieval popular culture. Piksanov expressed this with particular clarity:

> Mikhail Mikhailovich, you have entitled your dissertation 'The work of Rabelais in the history of realism'. In my view this is a wholly misleading title. With the same degree of exaggeration as you have indulged in in your choice of title, I will allow myself to propose to you an alternative: 'Rabelais pushed back, Rabelais pushed back into the Middle Ages and antiquity'. That is how your dissertation should be titled. (Transcript, p. 78)

Brodskii made the same point, playing on other categories from the dissertation. In Bakhtin's emphasis on the role of 'Gothic realism' (based precisely on the idea of the eternal unfinalisedness, 'unreadiness' of the human being and the world), he saw an understatement of the significance of 'the most progressive artistic method' – the traditional critical realism with which Marxist literary scholars were most comfortable:

> According to your conception there is one kind of realism, Gothic realism, and another, classical realism, and your preference is for the Gothic ... I am completely unable to agree with comrade Bakhtin that what is valuable in Gothic realism is its connection with folklore ... This connection is exactly what characterises the antipode of this Gothic method, i.e. classical realism.
>
> I am a supporter of classical realism. (Transcript, p. 81)

To conclude this account of the Marxist traditionalists' objections to Bakhtin, let me recall part of Kirpotin's contribution:

> [I]t has been argued here that as a humanist and an ideologue of the Renaissance, [Rabelais] is an ordinary figure who becomes remarkable only when he conveys the elemental life that takes place below the waist, and that this is what makes his book a great masterpiece. But this judgement leads to an underestimation of the ideology of the Renaissance and an exceedingly crude *idealisation* of the Middle Ages. (Transcript, p. 89; emphasis added)

Rejecting this rearrangement of established emphases, Kirpotin touches in passing on another very important facet of the problem: even if one were to agree in principle with Bakhtin's initial premiss, how should the Middle Ages then be interpreted (put another way, how accurately are the Middle Ages interpreted in Bakhtin's theory of popular–festive life)? At this point we are getting to the heart of the discussions of the Rabelais book that began in 1946 and were subsequently taken up again.

I cannot of course list all of the criticisms made by Piksanov, Brodskii and Kirpotin, nor indeed all the contradictory, at times mutually exclusive, views of later interpreters of Bakhtin. But I cannot fail to note that both during the defence and after it the most serious criticisms would seem to have been in response to Bakhtin's assertion that the character of popular culture is based on laughter. As Piksanov put it at the defence, 'all these Saturnalias and phallic cults, they distort terribly your own concept of the Middle Ages and of the kind of traditions that Rabelais inherited' (Transcript, p. 79). He went on to add: 'I am afraid that when we evaluate the popular or non-popular nature of a movement only from the perspective of laughter, then we will diminish any notion of popular character (*narodnost'*), whether it be medieval or Russian' (Transcript, pp. 79–80). This is still seen as one of the principal flaws in Bakhtin's theory.[62] And indeed popular culture would not have been so sharply opposed to official culture (a charge constantly laid at the door of the theorist of carnival) had the contrast between them not been so sharply drawn along the lines of 'laughter-based' and 'serious'.[63] Kirpotin raised this point at the defence:

> I find this division of the Middle Ages into the official life of the church and feudal elite on the one hand, and the life of the people on the other, a very artificial one, in the sense that we are dealing with an ideology that applies only to the façade, and that if we go behind this façade, kick it away, take a peek under the priest's soutane, then we will discover something completely different. In my view this division is too mechanistic. (Transcript, p. 88)

Moreover, had Bakhtin not insisted on a 'laughter-based' approach to popular culture, then the accusations of ignoring the historical context would have been much more moderate.[64] For example, Piksanov reproved Bakhtin: 'You talk about laughter. It has to be said that the way you talk about laughter, the way you have of universalising laughter, turning it into an essence, the very element of some state within a state, this is something that I have to oppose'

(Transcript, p. 80). Furthermore, arguing against Bakhtin's hypostatisation and idealisation of laughter, his unofficial opponents on several occasions stressed that laughter could be associated with violence and tragedy, that the medieval period was not a particularly cheerful age, and so on. (Brodskii: 'No, not a festival, but a tragedy by the greatest tragedian in Russia and the world. That is what I sense in Dostoevsky's *Bobok*. I cannot see any Gothic realism in this' (Transcript, p. 81). Kirpotin: 'What are you saying – that religious fanaticism did not affect men and women from the people, did these popular masses themselves not take part in the crusades?' (Transcript, p. 88). Piksanov: 'For example, Gogol's *Dead Souls* has an account of how the people tore a council chairman to pieces and he could only be identified from scraps of his clothing. Was this a popular uprising or not? Did this happen in the Middle Ages or not?' (Transcript, p. 80.)

Evgeniya Yakovlevna Dombrovskaya

This is someone about whom I know little. She is a rather mysterious creature, in many respects similar to Teryaeva. Firstly, Dombrovskaya also either craved notoriety, or kept selflessly (and dogmatically, complacently and narrowly) to the 'letter' of Marxist principles. Secondly, her personal file in VAK papers has also been either secreted away or for some reason destroyed: I could not find it! Unlike Teryaeva, in the minutes of Bakhtin's defence she is not described as a holder of the Candidate's degree.[65]

Dombrovskaya also acted in the same style as Teryaeva. Her 'specialism' was writing letters to various bodies. For example, in late 1947 she wrote to Konstantin Simonov, who at the time was editor of the literary journal *Novyi mir*. 'In a letter to the editorial staff of the journal Professor Nusinov attempts to refute and discredit the review in which I criticise his article about Romain Rolland. These efforts by Professor Nusinov to portray himself as a simple soul and as unjustly persecuted should not mislead the editorial board.'[66] Nusinov again! I am no great admirer of the man, but the campaign that was unleashed against him does produce a very unpleasant impression. We are obviously dealing here with a despicable rush to attack in a pack when the victim is no longer in a position to defend himself. Dombrovskaya repeats, like a zombie, rote-learned Marxist basics: 'Marxism recognises that class struggle, and class struggle alone, determines the direction in which culture and literature develop.' In seeking to establish the slightest depar-

ture from dogma by Nusinov, she naturally refers to the apostle of
Marxism: 'Comrade Zhdanov has characterised analysis of this kind
as metaphysics, "an idealistic conception of the supra-historical
nature of ideas".'[67] Some passages are quite simply brazen in their
denunciatory intonation: 'It is a matter not of correcting this
Professor who so persists in his errors, but rather of reaching certain
organisational conclusions, of protecting young people from this
politically illiterate and compromised Professor.' She goes on: 'I
consider it my duty to remind the editorial board of comrade
Nusinov's *political and scholarly past*' (her emphasis). And so on, in
the same spirit.

Dombrovskaya's oratory at Bakhtin's defence was less expressive and inspired than Teryaeva's. Nevertheless, she stated her
negative verdict firmly and definitively, not neglecting to play the
trump card of a couple of banal dogmas or to quote from some of
the 'fathers' of historical materialism:

> In my view Rabelais does not form part of medieval realism, is not
> an heir to it. The Renaissance is an entirely new quality. Although
> this is a commonly known truth, allow me to quote: 'What was the
> age of the Renaissance? The age of the Renaissance', says Engels,
> 'was an overcoming of the Middle Ages.' I shan't quote his famous
> words about the giants of the Renaissance, but will just cite one
> short passage: 'The ideologues of the French bourgeoisie criticised
> a great deal ...'. It was not just laughter, but criticism, it was by
> this stage the decay of the feudal world. (Transcript, p. 83)

In this passage Dombrovskaya is criticising both the placing of
Rabelais within the medieval tradition, and Bakhtin's accentuation
of the aspect of laughter in *Gargantua and Pantagruel*. (Here she
develops an idea which came up in an earlier paragraph:
'According to you laughter in Rabelais is only merry, carefree
laughter. You have nothing to say about the fact that Rabelais is
a satirist.') It is telling, however, that, as is shown by the minutes
of the defence, her clumsy attempts at polemic amused those
present.

Boris Vladimirovich Gornung

Aged 47. Graduated from Moscow University in 1921. From 1918
to 1922 worked in Narkompros, the People's Commissariat for
Enlightenment. From 1924 worked for the Russian Academy of the
Arts (as learned secretary of a commission on the study of time, and

then a commission on the study of form in the Philosophy Department). From 1925 to 1926 was General Secretary of the Academy's Committee for the Exhibition of Western Revolutionary Art. His own entry on a personnel form reads: 'Following graduation from university in 1921 I undertook, under the supervision of Professor G. G. Shpet, special training in those areas of philosophy essential to theoretical linguistics and poetics.'[68] His contacts with Shpet continued subsequently, as did his work on philosophical, linguistic and aesthetic issues.[69] He translated poetry by Gilbeau, Chennevier, Becher, Toller, and prose by Moran, Zola and others. In the 1940s he worked on a Candidate's dissertation to be defended in the Institute of World Literature and entitled 'An investigation in the area of ancient Greek literature and language', and acted as Secretary to the Institute's Academic Council.[70]

Gornung brought the discussion to a close, speaking immediately before Bakhtin's closing remarks. In the style of an artful sophist, he sought as far as possible to smooth over or at least camouflage the contradictions that had emerged. His principal technique was to find various Marxist postulates to underpin Bakhtin's theses. Thus he described 'the idea of two medieval periods' as one of the most valuable in the dissertation, one that was, moreover,

> valuable first and foremost from a Marxist point of view ... I shan't mention Marx's words, which will be familiar to all present here, about the unity of cultural development as it passes through various socio-economic formations ... The development of the life of the people, notwithstanding changes in social structures and the means of production, always has a unity, a unity from prehistoric times until the historical period ... And Bakhtin is perfectly correct when he takes back through the Middle Ages the Rabelaisian humanism and realism that can be traced back to certain sources in antiquity. (Transcript, p. 91)

After making a number of sarcastic digs at those who spoke out against Bakhtin ('one would need to have absolutely no idea of any aspect of ancient culture or the Middle Ages in order to see Bakhtin as arguing for some sort of endless, merry carnival'), Gornung did distance himself from some controversial points of the dissertation that 'merit severe criticism', at this point nominally associating himself with the views of those who had spoken out against Bakhtin, and whom he had just treated with such irony: 'I must state that I am in agreement with a number of the general positions outlined by Kirpotin in his intervention' (Transcript, p. 92).

At the end of this lengthy exchange of views, Bakhtin was once more given the floor. He spoke for rather a long time, replying to the comments of official and unofficial examiners alike. His closing remarks are an important document for our understanding of the early version of the theory of carnival as embodied in his dissertation. Close textological analysis of 'F. Rabelais in the history of realism' is something for the future; for the moment I will limit myself to some reflections on this matter, with reference principally to the dissertation defence.

Bakhtin agreed with the epithet 'obsessed' applied to him by Dzhivelegov, and called himself 'an innovator obsessed' (Transcript, p. 92). He thanked all who had spoken for not showing any 'inclination simply to brush the whole thing to one side', and for the great interest in his paradoxical theory, an interest that had been expressed in the form both of support and, in a different manner, of substantive objections. He accepted some of the criticisms made (for example, he did not seek to dispute the notion that the dissertation needed a further chapter which would show, in Dzhivelegov's words, 'with the requisite thoroughness ... the essentially Renaissance character of Rabelais's work and ideology'), but rejected others, in a number of cases acknowledging in doing so that he himself was to blame for a possible lack of clarity in expression that had given grounds for the criticism. I will pay particular attention to the points where Bakhtin robustly defended his approach to the study of Rabelais and of popular culture.

Responding to Piksanov's reproaches, Bakhtin stated in the most decisive possible manner: 'Nikolai Kir'yakovich was bound to be disconcerted by my theory, but his view that it means Rabelais is inevitably pushed backwards is one that I do not accept. Do we really, when we try to establish the roots of a tradition, do we really push it backwards?' (Transcript, p. 95). No less resolute was Bakhtin's refutation of Piksanov's accusation that he had hypostatised laughter: 'I do not turn laughter into an essence. Ancient laughter and Gothic laughter are historical categories, but this laughter in the public square enjoyed almost juridical rights of extraterritoriality. That is a historical fact' (Transcript, p. 97). Nor did the dissertation, in Bakhtin's view, at all idealise the Middle Ages, which, as had actually been shown, was characterised by acute contradictions: 'I do not at all mean to say that medieval laughter is merry, carefree and joyful laughter. It was one powerful weapon of struggle. The people fought with laughter, and they also fought with real weapons – fists and sticks. And the people on the public square which is a constantly recurring theme in my work is a people that rises up in rebellion' (Transcript, p. 97).

Not long after, however, Bakhtin would be forced to introduce into his texts changes of a kind apparently not anticipated by his concluding remarks. The most significant such change was of course his rejection of the term 'Gothic realism'. At the defence Bakhtin, holding unwaveringly to the position he had adopted, saw his introduction of this term into scholarly usage as one of his major contributions: 'I show Rabelais in the history of realism. Perhaps I am mistaken, but I believe that I have added a new page to the history of realism. The term "Gothic realism" did not previously exist in French or Russian literature. Nobody would be able to cite any examples of anybody, anywhere, at any time writing about Gothic realism. I have enriched the history of realism' (Transcript, p. 96). But M. P. Alekseev's report, and later the resolution of VAK's Expert Commission on Western Literature, would consider the term inappropriate, and in preparing a revised version of the dissertation for the Commission Bakhtin would replace it with the term 'grotesque realism'.[71] It was in this form that one of his key terms would find its way into the canonical published text of 1965. This change of epithet, incidentally, signified an essential corrective to Bakhtin's system of priorities.

In the 1940 version of the dissertation Bakhtin was rather inconsistent in defining the degree of significance of the various aspects of his theme. At first he wrote: 'This work is devoted ... not at all to folkloric or Gothic realism, but exclusively to the work of Rabelais.'[72] But this statement of position was followed by a whole series of qualifications suggesting that Rabelais's work 'is distinguished by exceptional revelatory force ... Many coarse and even repulsive pages in the manuscript book of the development of Gothic realism ... are given remarkable commentary in Rabelais's images.' Ultimately it became clear that Rabelais had nevertheless attracted Bakhtin's attention not in his own right, but as a figure who crowned the tradition of Gothic realism: 'It is this revelatory significance in the history of realism that is *at the forefront* for us. We focus on the *distinctiveness* of Rabelais's realism ... his *distinctiveness* from the point of view of subsequent centuries.' And, a little later, 'characterising the particular type of realism that is most vividly and completely represented by Rabelais's work' now features as the principal aim.[73]

At the defence Bakhtin, in both his introductory and his concluding remarks, expressed clearly and unambiguously his preference for popular culture: 'the hero of my monograph is not Rabelais, but these popular, festive–grotesque forms, the traditions revealed, illuminated for us in the work of Rabelais' (Transcript, p. 57); 'the whole of the Gothic is the history of realism. I would agree that this is not a book about Rabelais, but a book about the history of realism, a book about the history of pre-Renaissance realism' (Transcript, p. 96).

But, faced with the harsh criticism of VAK's reviewers and experts (R. M. Samarin, V. A. Dynnik and others), Bakhtin gradually moved away from this stress on Rabelais's pre-Renaissance Gothic roots.[74] In a letter to L. E. Pinskii of 21 February 1963 he stated remorsefully: 'I must acknowledge a certain one-sided character to my work: the common characteristics of the language of popular-laughter culture – common to a whole millennium – did to a certain extent dissolve the specific features of Rabelais's age and his creative individuality.'[75] By the time of the canonical text of 1965, however, we read: 'the immediate subject of our investigation is not popular laughter culture, but the work of François Rabelais'. True, later on it is again stated that Rabelais helps to reveal the essence of popular culture. However, Bakhtin continues: 'in using Rabelais to reveal the essence of popular-laughter culture, we are in no sense turning him merely into a means to an external end'.[76] Even the very semantics of the titles of the early and canonical versions also, of course, points to the re-evaluation of landmarks and reference points that had taken place. 'F. Rabelais in the history of realism' denotes the location of the phenomenon of Rabelais as it were 'within' the Gothic ('Gothic realism'); *The Work of François Rabelais and the Popular Culture of the Middle Ages and Renaissance* (*Tr. note*: the title of the book when it was published in Russian in 1965) merely brings together two related but ultimately distinct phenomena.

Even as he moved gradually in the direction of a more consistent historicism, seeking to separate himself clearly from the archaic thrust of 'the language of popular-laughter culture' and to focus on the work of Rabelais, Bakhtin nevertheless became oddly more vulnerable to criticism. The notorious accusations of seeing the world purely in terms of laughter would evidently have lost all meaning had Bakhtin on the contrary (or in parallel with his move towards historical detail) brought Rabelais closer to the syncretising world-picture of the archaic. This issue came up several times during the defence. For example, Gornung stood up for Bakhtin at one point by explaining to those present how claims that the conception of carnival was confined to the narrow sphere of laughter were without foundation: 'the author was not thinking about farce or merry entertainment when he wrote about this tradition in Rabelais that goes back to distant antiquity, not only to the ancient slave-owning world, but even further back, to magic and other cults' (Transcript, p. 91). Bakhtin himself also stressed carnival's link with ancient myth-making thinking that did not yet distinguish the comic and the tragic: 'This is the laughter of the public square, popular laughter that has nothing in common with the laughter of entertainment. It is laughter of a different kind, this is a laughter that mortifies, and death always appears here' (Transcript, p. 97). And later: 'This is very typical. Yet merriment and laughter were located in the same place. This was where they put death, the dying breath, and yet here was laughter as well ... As regards carnival. I did not have in mind carnival as something cheerful. Not at all. Death is present in every carnival image. In your terms, it is tragedy. But it is not tragedy that is the last word' (Transcript, p. 98).[77]

The shift of Bakhtin's original idea in the direction of greater historicism was of course logical and helpful in its way, and for this reason we should not see absolutely all the critical remarks made during the defence and during VAK's subsequent scrutiny of the dissertation as damaging and reactionary, or as having led to distortion of the core of the work. But all the evidence is that the dissertation did lose something in the reworking. Had the development of Bakhtin's ideas taken a different course, one without severe slopes or sharp turns, this might possibly have led to more profound philosophical and anthropological conclusions about the fundamental principles of ancient and medieval popular culture. However, as already indicated, this is a separate topic.

After Bakhtin's concluding remarks the members of the Academic Council conducted a secret ballot on the outcome of the defence. Thirteen people took part in the ballot: the number of votes for the award of the degree of Candidate of Philological Sciences was thirteen, with no votes against; the number of votes for the award of the degree of Doctor of Philological Sciences was seven, with six votes against.

There have been many celebrated defences in the history of Russian scholarship: V. S. Solov'ev's defence of his Master's and Doctoral dissertations, P. A. Florenskii's defence of his Master's dissertation, I. A. Il'in's defence of his Master's dissertation. Bakhtin's defence of 'F. Rabelais in the history of realism' is worthy of being set alongside these. Moreover, in some respects it even surpasses these other noteworthy events. Bakhtin's predecessors were opposed only by their opponents' scholarly arguments, while he had to overcome hostile circumstance, to confront a whole ideological system. Il'in's biographer, N. P. Poltoratskii, wrote: 'Il'in's work ('Hegel's philosophy as a doctrine of the concreteness of God and man, I: Doctrine of God', Moscow, 1918, 300pp.) was of such exceptional quality that the Faculty unanimously awarded him both degrees, Master and Doctor, at the same time.'[78] This was in 1918, when Moscow University's Law Faculty was not yet under Bolshevik control. By 1946 the principle of Party-mindedness and Communist ideological rectitude now loomed over Soviet scholarship: it was no longer a faculty (or an institute) that decided the fate of a dissertation, but a specially created bureaucratic office (VAK), which did not so much 'reject' weak or third-rate works as monitor the correct completion of extensive paperwork and authors' loyalty to the existing regime. In 1946, following Il'in's brilliant defence of his exceptional work, the Law Faculty would no doubt have voted somewhat differently. And the author, had the Soviet Higher Attestation Commission so wished, would have waited a long time for the award of his Doctoral degree (the wait would probably never have ended). This is why I am convinced that the dramatic subtext of Bakhtin's defence is far richer, more complex and more 'concentrated' than in the case of other (earlier) famous scholarly debates.

VAK spent six years reaching a decision on Bakhtin's dissertation. In 1952 it was decided to issue a Candidate's certificate to the excessively independent and zealous student of Rabelais. (Had Bakhtin kept a diary, he might have borrowed Pushkin's remark: 'The day before yesterday I was made a Kammerjunker, which is somewhat indecent at my age.'[79]) But Bakhtin's VAK epic is a separate topic, on which I have written elsewhere.[80]

Notes

   1 *Tr. note*: This article is an abridged translation of a revised version of '"Ot khoda etogo dela zavisit vse dal'neishee ..." (Zashchita dissertatsii M. M. Bakhtina kak real'noe sobytie, vysokaya drama i nauchnaya komediya)', *Dialog Karnaval Khronotop*, 2–3, 1993, pp. 29–54. The original article introduced a transcript of Bakhtin's dissertation defence (see note 9 below); the revision is translated in full in *Dialogism*, 1, 1998, pp. 11–29, and 2, 1999, pp. 7–40.

2 *Tr note.*: In the USSR, there were two degrees awarded on the basis of advanced research: the degree of Candidate and the degree of Doctor. The difference between them is similar to the difference in the German system between the doctorate, awarded on the basis of a long dissertation, and the *Habilitation*, awarded on the basis of a much longer text, intended for immediate scholarly publication.

3 V. V. Kozhinov, 'Kak pishut trudy, ili Proiskhozhdenie nesozdannogo avantyurnogo romana (Vadim Kozhinov rasskazyvaet o sud'be i lichnosti M. M. Bakhtina)', *Dialog Karnaval Khronotop*, 1, 1992, p. 120.

4 Otdel rukopisei Rossiiskoi gosudarstvennoi biblioteki (Manuscript Department of the Russian State Library, hereafter OR RGB), f. 645, karton 42, d. 22, l. 23. (*Tr. note*: Here and subsequently, materials held in Russian archives are referred to using the following standard indicators of location: f. (*fond*, collection); op. (*opis'*, inventory); karton (box); d. (*delo*, file); l. (*list*, sheet); ob. (*oborot*, verso).]

5 Letter from Bakhtin to Kozhinov, *Moskva*, 11–12, 1992, pp. 180f.

6 *Besedy V. D. Duvakina s M. M. Bakhtinym*, Moscow, 1996, p. 211.

7 V. N. Turbin, 'Karnaval: religiya, politika, teosofiya', *Bakhtinskii sbornik 1*, Moscow, 1990, p. 9.

8 Bakhtin left for Kustanai on 29 March 1930: see S. S. Konkin and L. S. Konkina, *Mikhail Bakhtin: Stranitsy tvorchestva*, Saransk, 1993, p. 198.

9 'Stenogramma zasedaniya Uchenogo soveta Instituta mirovoi literatury im. A. M. Gorkogo. Zashchita dissertatsii tov. Bakhtinym na temu "Rable v istorii realizma". 15 November 1946' ('Transcript of a meeting of the Academic Council of the Gorky Institute. Comrade Bakhtin's defence of his dissertation on the theme "Rabelais in the history of realism". 15 November 1946'), *Dialog Karnaval Khronotop*, 2–3, 1993, pp. 58ff, emphasis added. Further references to the Transcript of Bakhtin's defence are provided in the text.

10 See G. V. Karpunov, V. M. Boriskin and V. B. Estifeeva, *Mikhail Mikhailovich Bakhtin v Saranske: Ocherk zhizni i deyatel'nosti*, Saransk, 1989, p. 7. (*Tr. note*: a printer's sheet, or signature, is equivalent to 16 or 32 printed pages.)

11 *Tr. note*: Party spokesman on cultural matters.

12 OR RGB, f. 527, karton 10, d. 41, ll. 26, 26 ob.

13 See A. A. Fortunatov, 'K voprosu o sud'be latinskoi obrazovannosti v varvarskikh korolevstvakh (Po traktatam Virgiliya Marona Grammatika)', *Srednie veka*, 2, 1946, pp. 114–34.

14 L. S. Melikhova, 'Ot publikatora "Dopolnenii i izmenenii k *Rable*"', *Voprosy filosofii*, 1, 1992, p. 134.

15 OR RGB, f. 768, karton 43, d. 33, l. 21. (*Tr. note*: Litizdat (also Goslitizdat, Gosudarstvennoe literaturnoe izdatel'stvo): State Literary Publishing House.)

16 OR RGB, f. 527, karton 10, d. 41, l. 14.

17 OR RGB, f. 527, karton 24, d. 31. On 21 December Smirnov wrote to Mikhal'chi that he had received 'the Rabelais manuscript': see OR RGB, f. 768, karton 43, d. 33, l. 44.

18 See Gosudarstvennyi muzei muzykal'noi kul'tury im. Glinki (Glinka State

Museum of Musical Culture), f. 439. I am citing from copies generously made available to me by A. M. Kuznetsov.

19 See Melikhova, 'Ot publikatora', p. 134. See also 'Prilozhenie 3 k publikatsii stenogrammy zashchity (Iz vospominanii E. M. Evninoi)', *Dialog Karnaval Khronotop*, 2–3, 1993, pp. 114–17.

20 OR RGB, f. 527, karton 10, d. 41, l. 21.

21 OR RGB, f. 527, karton 10, d. 41, l. 10 ob.

22 OR RGB, f. 527, karton 19, d. 13, l. 21.

23 OR RGB, f. 527, karton 24, d. 32, l. 1; Yudina's emphasis.

24 OR RGB, f. 527, karton 10, d. 41, l. 5.

25 OR RGB, f. 527, karton 14, d. 13, l. 5.

26 See the letter requesting Tarle's rehabilitation, written in the hand of A. K. Dzhivelegov (Rossiiskii gosudarstvennyi arkhiv literatury i iskusstva (Russian State Archive for Literature and Art, hereafter RGALI), f. 2032, op. 1, d. 239, l. 13 ob.). Incidentally, the cases of Bakhtin and Tarle (*Tr. note*: their arrests in the late 1920s) were handled by the same team of investigators. At the end of 1974 Bakhtin told S. G. Bocharov: 'Later [the investigators] were liquidated, of course. I remember Tarle wrote to me in triumph: "Our lot have been liquidated, you know." But I could not share this feeling of triumph' (see S. G. Bocharov, 'Ob odnom razgovore i vokrug nego', *Novoe literaturnoe obozrenie*, 2, 1993, p. 84; abridged English version: Sergey Bocharov, 'Conversations with Bakhtin', *PMLA*, CIX: 5, 1994, p. 1021).

27 OR RGB, f. 527, karton 10, d. 41, l. 18.

28 See letters from E. V. Tarle to A. K. Dzhivelegov, RGALI, f. 2032, op. 1, d. 239.

29 In his concluding remarks Bakhtin mentioned that he had discussed his work with Dzhivelegov as early as 1940 (Transcript, p. 92).

30 Gosudarstvennyi arkhiv Rossiiskoi Federatsii (State Archive of the Russian Federation, hereafter GARF), f. 9506, op. 73, d. 70, l. 142.

31 GARF, f. 9506, op. 73, d. 71, l. 64.

32 GARF, f. 9506, op. 73, d. 71, l. 56. The published notice of the defence is in *Vestnik AN SSSR*, 5, 1947, p. 123.

33 OR RGB, f. 768, karton 43, d. 34, l. 28.

34 GARF, f. 9506, op. 73, d. 71, l. 88.

35 OR RGB, f. 527, karton 10, d. 41, l. 29, Bakhtin's emphasis.

36 OR RGB, f. 527, karton 10, d. 41, l. 8.

37 OR RGB, f. 768, karton 43, d. 34, ll. 29–30.

38 OR RGB, f. 527, karton 14, , d. 13, l. 6.

39 See GARF, f. 9506, op. 73, d. 70, l. 141.

40 Kirpotin's account is cited in abbreviated form below. For the full version, see 'Prilozhenie 2 k publikatsii stenogrammy zashchity (Beseda s V. Ya. Kirpotinym)', *Dialog Karnaval Khronotop*, 2–3, 1993, pp. 112–14.

41 *Tr. note*: Zhdanov's speech and the subsequent Central Committee resolution castigating these journals, and the writers Anna Akhmatova and Mikhail Zoshchenko, for ideological deviations marked the beginning of a new period of conservatism in official cultural policy following the comparative liberalisation of the war years.

42 *Tr. note*: the Epistolae obscurorum virorum (The Letters of Obscure People, 1515–17) was an anonymous satire in support of the Hebrew scholar Reuchlin, who had been accused of heresy because of his tolerant attitude towards Jews, in opposition to the Dominicans of Cologne. The work ostensibly supported the Dominican cause, but in reality was a humanistic attack on narrow-minded scholasticism.

43 See Arkhiv Rossiiskoi akademii nauk (Archive of the Russian Academy of Sciences, hereafter RAN), f. 397, op. 1, d. 149, l. 95, and N. Yanevich (E. Evnina), 'Institut mirovoi literatury v 1930–70 gg.', *Pamyat': Istoricheskii sbornik V*, Paris, 1992, pp. 101f.

44 See 'Prilozhenie 1 k publikatsii stenogrammy zashchity (Tezisy k dissertatsionnoi rabote M. M. Bakhtina "Rable v istorii realizma")', *Dialog Karnaval Khronotop*, 2–3, 1993, pp. 103–12.

45 See L. A. Iezuitova and N. V. Skvortsova, 'Novoe ob universitetskom okruzhenii A. Bloka (A. A. Blok i A. A. Smirnov)', *Vestnik Leningradskogo universiteta: Seriya 'Istoriya Yazyk Literatura'*, 3:14, 1981, pp. 49–58.

46 Cf. A. A. Smirnov, 'Moi zhiznennyi put': Nabroski k vospominaniyam', OR RGB, f. 572, karton 1, d. 14, l. 2.

47 See RGALI, f. 629, op. 1, d. 125.

48 OR RGB, f. 768, karton 43, d. 34, l. 20.

49 See 'Lichnoe delo Nusinova I. M., deistvitel'nogo chlena Gos. akademii iskusstvovedeniya', RGALI, f. 984, op. 2, d. 8; 'Avtorskoe delo Nusinova I. M. v Gosizdate', RGALI, f. 613, op. 7, d. 331; and Ya. M. Metallov, 'Literator-uchenyi', in I. M. Nusinov, *Izbrannye raboty*, Moscow, 1959, pp. 3–13.

50 See 'Lichnoe delo Dzhivelegova A. K. (Institut istorii, Rossiiskaya assotsiyatsiya nauchno-issledovatel'skikh institutov po obshchestvennym naukam [RANION])', GARF, f. A-4655, op. 2, d. 252.

51 GARF, f. A-2306, op. 70/2, d. 6252, l. 58.

52 RGALI, f. 2032, op. 1, d. 183, ll. 6 ob., 20.

53 On Tarle, see E. I. Chapkevich, *Evgenii Viktorovich Tarle*, Moscow, 1977, and B. S. Kaganovich, *Evgenii Viktorovich Tarle i peterburgskaya shkola istorikov*, St Petersburg, 1995.

54 See GARF, f. 9506, op. 73, d. 71, ll. 14, 35, 36, 53 and *passim*.

55 This was noted in the published account of the defence: see *Vestnik AN SSSR*, 5, 1947, p. 123.

56 RGALI, f. 631, op. 24, d. 55, l. 22.

57 RGALI, f. 614, op. 1, d. 308.

58 On Piksanov, see A. Revyakin, ed., *Nikolai Kir'yakovich Piksanov (Materialy k bibliografii uchenykh SSSR, Seriya literatury i yazyka, 8)*, Moscow, 1968; and K. Azadovskii and B. Egorov, 'O nizkopoklonstve i kosmopolitizme: 1948–1949', *Zvezda*, 6, 1989, pp. 175–6.

59 E. G. Gershtein, 'Lishnyaya lyubov': Stseny iz moskovskoi zhizni', *Novyi mir*, 11, 1993, pp. 160.

60 See 'Lichnoe delo prepodavatelya Instituta krasnoi professury Kirpotina V. Ya.', GARF, f. 5146, op. 2, d. 56, and V. Ya. Kirpotin, *Nachalo: Avtobiograficheskie stranitsy*, Moscow, 1986.

61 Some accounts suggest that Tarle took a sharply negative view of

Kirpotin's publications and his work in general: see, for example, E. L. Lann's notes 'Tarle v zhizni', RGALI, f. 2210, op. 1, d. 137, l. 11.

62 For example, one of the first reviews of the Rabelais book stated that 'popular culture was not only laughter-based, while carnival did not consist only of free laughter and merriment. Throughout the whole of the medieval period human consciousness was virtually always beset by fears, mass psychoses, and convulsive ecstatic explosions that embraced whole areas and whole strata of the population' (A.Ya. Gurevich, 'Smekh v narodnoi kul'ture srednevekov'ya', *Voprosy literatury*, 6, 1966, p. 209). In a recent article S. S. Averintsev has also reproached Bakhtin for advancing 'laughter itself as the criterion of the spiritual quality of laughter – not, of course, laughter as an empirical, concrete, palpable given, but a hypostatised and extremely idealised essence of laughter' (S. S. Averintsev, 'Bakhtin, smekh, khristianskaya kul'tura', in L. A. Gogotishvili and P. S. Gurevich, eds, *M. M. Bakhtin kak filosof*, Moscow, 1992, p. 12).

63 See, among others, A. Ya. Gurevich, *Problemy srednevekovoi narodnoi kul'tury*, Moscow, 1981, p. 274 and *passim*, and *Srednevekovyi mir: Kul'tura bezmolvstvuyushchego bol'shinstva*, Moscow, 1990, pp. 12–13; and R. M. Berrong, *Rabelais and Bakhtin: Popular Culture in* Gargantua and Pantagruel, Lincoln, Nebraska and London, 1986, pp. 9–16.

64 For example, '"Violence never lurks behind laughter" – how strange that Bakhtin should have made this categorical assertion! The whole of history literally cries out against him; there are so many examples of the opposite that it is beyond my capacity to select the most vivid' (Averintsev, 'Bakhtin, smekh, khristianskaya kul'tura', p. 13); again: 'Bakhtin's success both as a theorist and as an analyst of these particular works of literature is severely undermined by his failure to accord either the sixteenth-century French upper classes or Rabelais's novels any of the dynamism and change that he constantly proclaimed to be the very essence of "eternal" popular culture' (Berrong, *Rabelais and Bakhtin*, p. 15; see also esp. Chapter 3 of Part 2).

65 GARF, f. 9506, op. 73, d. 70, l. 138.

66 RGALI, f. 1702, op. 2, d. 260, l. 2.

67 RGALI, f. 1702, op. 2, d. 260, l. 3 ob.

68 'Lichnoe delo Gornunga B. V.', RGALI, f. 941, op. 10, d. 155, l. 4.

69 See Gornung's letter to Shpet from the mid-1920s: RGALI, f. 1495, op. 1, d. 32.

70 Arkhiv RAN, f. 397, op. 1, d. 149, l. 95.

71 See GARF, f. 9506, op. 73, d. 70, ll. 2–8; d. 71, ll. 12, 15; and d. 71, l. 29, which states: 'In accordance with the instructions of the Expert Commission the inappropriate term "Gothic realism" has been replaced with the term "grotesque realism" (a term which is also, of course, provisional). Also in accordance with the Commission's instructions, the title of the work has been slightly amended: instead of "Rabelais in the history of realism" the dissertation is now entitled "Rabelais and the problem of popular culture in the Middle Ages and Renaissance". This new title gives a rather more precise definition of the basic topic of the work, without, of course, altering the substance

of the argument, since popular culture is consistently and profoundly realistic.'

See in this connection N. A. Pan'kov, 'The creative history of Bakhtin's *Rabelais*', in Carol Adlam *et al.*, eds, *Face to Face: Bakhtin in Russia and the West*, Sheffield, 1997, pp. 196–202.

72 Otdel rukopisei, Institut mirovoi literatury (IMLI: Manuscript Division of the Institute of World Literature, hereafter OR IMLI), f. 427, op. 1, d. 19, l. 44.

73 OR IMLI, f. 427, op. 1, d. 19, l. 45 (first emphasis added, remaining two in original).

74 GARF, f. 9506, op. 73, d. 71, ll. 18–25, 42–54.

75 'Pis'ma M. M. Bakhtina k L. E. Pinskomu', *Dialog Karnaval Khronotop*, 2, 1994, p. 58.

76 Bakhtin, *Rabelais and His World*, trans. Hélène Iswolsky, Cambridge, Mass., 1968, p. 58. But, on the other hand, in his introductory remarks at the defence, Bakhtin stated: 'Rabelais *originally*, when I began my work, was not an end in himself' (p. 55; emphasis added), i.e. the logic is that Bakhtin can also be understood as meaning that as he worked, and without pressure from anyone else, Rabelais's work moved to centre stage.

77 Cf. 'Neither the tragic nor the comic is yet "in the words", just as they are not in rhythm, in ritual, in material culture, or in characters. However, two kinds of "word" unfailingly march side by side: tear-words and laughter-words ... I draw attention to the fact that any death may be an object of laughter rather than tears, provided that it is presented in the phase of conceptions and births. Any grotesque, any terrifying masks are intended, as metaphors of death, to provoke not tears but laughter' (O. M. Freidenberg, *Mif i literatura drevnosti*, Moscow, 1978, p. 106). Cf. also Freidenberg's treatment of a motif touched on by Bakhtin in connection with *The Covetous Knight*: 'Thus, three structurally identical versions of a myth ... In all three versions the children kill the fathers or the fathers the children, or the children kill for the fathers, or the children are killed because of the fathers. This "because of" is a later motivation by virtue of both its causality and its morality. The myth clearly transmits an image of mortification and devouring. The old is killed by the young, the young by the old; both are devoured ... An unreplaceable replacement, and unreplaceability constantly replaced: such is the mechanics of primitive thought' (*ibid.*, p. 51). It would appear that the themes 'Freidenberg and Bakhtin', 'Bakhtin and the archaic', 'Bakhtin and mythology' and the like still await detailed study, although some work has already been done: see, for example, V. V. Ivanov, 'Iz zametok o stroenii i funktsiyakh karnaval'nogo obraza', in S. S. Konkin *et al.*, eds, *Problemy poetiki i istorii literatury*, Saransk, 1973, pp. 37–53, and 'K semioticheskoi teorii karnavala kak inversii dvoichnykh predstavlenii', *Trudy po znakovym sistemam*, 8, 1977, pp. 45–64; E. M. Meletinskii, *Poetika mifa*, Moscow, 1976, pp. 134–47; and D. K. Danow, *The Spirit of Carnival: Magical Realism and the Grotesque*, Lexington, Kentucky, 1995, pp. 137–53.

78 N. P. Poltoratskii, *Ivan Aleksandrovich Il'in: Zhizn', trudy, mirovozzrenie. Sbornik statei*, Tenafly, NJ, 1989, p. 12.

79 A. S. Pushkin, diary entry of 1 January 1834, in *Pushkin on Literature*, ed. and trans. Tatiana Wolff, London, 1971, p. 343. (*Tr. note*: the rank of Kammerjunker at court was normally awarded to young men of 18 or so; Pushkin was 34 at the time.)

80 *Tr. note*: See the two articles on the 'VAK epic' published by Pan'kov in *Dialog Karnaval Khronotop* after the completion of this article: V. M. Alpatov, 'VAKovskoe delo M. M. Bakhtina' and N. A. Pan'kov, '"Rable est' Rable ...": Materialy VAKovskogo dela M. M. Bakhtina', *Dialog Karnaval Khronotop*, 2, 1999, pp. 36–49 and 50–137, respectively.

I would like to thank V. V. Babich, S. G. Bocharov, V. V. Kozhinov, Yu. M. Kagan, A. M. Kuznetsov and L. S. Melikhova, who have helped and continue to help me in my work.

Graham Pechey

Not the novel: Bakhtin, poetry, truth, God

'The novel' in the work of Mikhail Bakhtin is at once an empirical phenomenon and a transcendental category. It is not only a fact of literary history: it is also the rubric under which Bakhtin wishes us to think about the forms of sociality and subjectivity that belong to everyday life and to modernity. One of the ways in which he detaches the novel from its banal phenomenal familiarity and enforces its anti-generic non-self-identity is by contrast with the forms of writing which are – or at least have been – 'genres' in the proper sense: the older, canonical, classical or (as he puts it) 'straightforward' genres of poetry and drama. These forms have not of course been superseded by the novel upstart in their midst: they live on, transformed, bereft of their original innocence. Bakhtin veers between an insistence on their categorical difference from the novel and a case for their historical interaction, a power struggle among forms in which the novel always calls the shots. The test of Bakhtin's concepts lies, here as elsewhere, in confronting them with that to which (usually for very good conjunctural or strategic reasons) they accord only a secondary or instrumental theorisation. This means two (complementary) things: first, examining certain manifest exceptions to the monologism of the older genres; second, showing that the old forms are not just a convenience of Bakhtin's thinking but are inwardly constitutive of it, intimations of the absolute that live in the closest intimacy with its far more developed and overt celebration of relativity. In the scattered remarks he makes on these generic others of the novel we can trace the outlines of an idea whose importance to our experience of being human may be measured by the number of obituaries it has prompted and yet still refuses to go away: that of God. The upshot will be a Bakhtin who may be strange to some but who none the less has much to say to sociopolitical scenarios such as that of South Africa in the process of transformation, as I hope to show in my conclusion.[1]

I

We might begin by observing that for Bakhtin the novel stands to the other genres as the textuality of incarnation to the textuality of transcendence. There are strong hints in the Dostoevsky book of a homology between the authorial position in the polyphonic novel and the mediating figure of Christ, the 'highest and most authoritative orientation' perceived as 'another authentic human being and his voice'.[2] There are equally strong hints in 'Discourse in the novel' that the task of the poet is an impossible approximation to the figure of Adam. While the prose word foregrounds the difficult drama of arriving at its object, the word in poetry seeks a direct relation with an object conceived as 'virginally full and inexhaustible', behaving for all the world as if it had not had to struggle with other words in order to reach the latter.[3] Every word in poetry strives ideally towards the status of the first word ever uttered, uniquely and primally naming alien things while acknowledging no alien words. The epic thematises this putative condition of the poetic word by encoding the values of 'best' and 'highest' in the 'first', in a narrative of beginnings. Poetry, in short, names a postlapsarian impossibility: language living wholly inside itself; a language of the Name and the Same. The historicity and social specificity that are so sensitively and minutely registered by novelistic prose escapes poetry altogether, whose temporality is that of the epoch rather than the moment. True, in periods of change in 'literary poetic language' a certain hybridisation may take place – poetry might admit the Other into itself – but the outcome is an instant codification, rather like the Saussurean *langue* which opens itself momentarily to take in change from the world of *parole* and diachrony, reshuffling its internal relations only to close ranks again immediately afterwards.

Now of course in all this I am using the somewhat qualified case Bakhtin makes in 1934–35, where he confronts the novel's generic others more directly and extensively than before, and where he is describing not the actual status of all poetic discourse but only 'the extreme to which poetic genres aspire' (DN, p. 287). (Neither does he in any sense equate 'poetry' with 'writing in verse': Pushkin's 'novel in verse' *Eugene Onegin*, for example, is so thor-

oughly novelised as to render its verse form a matter of indifference, a mere technicality. In 1940 he was to analyse it as a novel.)
In 'Discourse in the novel' he finds a way of insisting on a categorical distinction between novel and poetry which none the less
avoids the trap of seeming to assign an essence to poetry which is
only contingently modifiable, as he was to do in the typology of
prose discourses in *Problems of Dostoevsky's Poetics*. There, poetry is
relegated to a brief afterword and is summarily characterised as
requiring 'the uniformity of all discourses, their reduction to a
common denominator' (*PDP*, p. 200). This typology is (perhaps
like all taxonomic projects) dominated by a functional rather than a
genetic perspective, very much in keeping both with the character
of the whole book and with its subject, whose novelistic imagination has, Bakhtin claims, a synchronic rather than a diachronic cast.
Even as it breaks with the old hierarchy of traditional poetics, it is
in this residual way haunted by the shadow of the classical division
of kinds which runs all the way from Plato and Diomedes to Hegel
and Lukács. In this ahistorical schema, epic, lyric and drama realise
and thereby exhaust three logical possibilities founded in the
'compositional' presence or absence (speech or silence) of author
and/or characters: in the lyric only the poet speaks; in drama only
the characters speak; in the epic both speak. Bakhtin here seeks to
overthrow the monopoly of the classical kinds by a sort of parody
of their triadic division, rejecting it as a valid division of the verbal
arts of European modernity and remapping a version of it onto the
field of prose. Thus his first 'type' is directly authorial discourse; his
second is the 'objectivised' speech of characters; and in the third
type Bakhtin unveils his (or rather the novel's) special discovery:
'double-voiced' discourse, in which author and other speak
together in the sense of *with each other at the same time*. Far from
being a mechanical sum of the first two types, the third embodies a
counter-logic in which, as Julia Kristeva would put it, their 0–1
interval is challenged by that of 0–2 in priority.[4] Where this
discourse of the other-in-dominance is itself the 'dominant' of a
text, dissolving the logic of plot, flouting and outliving all resolutions, we have novelistic polyphony.

In the attempt to account theoretically for the novel's dialogism, then, Bakhtin's earliest move is one of dialogising the very
triad by which the monological forms of writing are demarcated,
putting in the place where the epic 'should' be the discourse type
most closely identified with the novel. A radical semantic ambiguity crossing author with other reigns where epic homophony would

place the referential transparency of 'one's own' speech over the referential opacity of 'somebody else's', an omniscient metalanguage over an oblivious object language. The corollary of Bakhtin's theorisation of the novel in a parodic internalisation of the old classical threesome is a further implicit move whereby epic is first subsumed under the more general head of the poetic, then lumped together with drama, and both finally counterposed to the novel. If this new and recognisably modern triad of genres seems to be a simple correlative of the 1929 typology of prose discourses – with poetry and drama and novel, in that order, as generic reflexes of the three intranovelistic types – then it must be said that such simplicity is qualified even in that earlier text. The summary definition of poetry quoted above adds that the poetic word 'can either be discourse of the first type, or can belong to certain weakened varieties of the other types' (*PDP*, p. 200). By poetic speech of the second type Bakhtin would seem to mean the forms that in the English tradition are known as the epistle or the complaint – that is to say, recognised canonical forms in which a speaker other than the straightforwardly lyrical 'I' is represented as speaking, and which are among the forerunners of the nineteenth-century 'dramatic monologue'. With the third type Bakhtin is more specific, even proffering illustrations: the '"prosaic" lyric' of 'weakened' dialogism is exemplified in 'Heine, Barbier, some works of Nekrasov and others' (*PDP*, p. 200). In 1926 his friend Voloshinov (also citing Heine) had instanced a cognate type of 'lyric irony' which violates that 'unhesitating confidence in the sympathy of the listeners' which is 'the underlying condition for lyric intonation'.[5] The later Bakhtin would doubtless ascribe this inwardly anti-lyrical lyric to the work of 'novelisation' in the late eighteenth and early nineteenth centuries, and we might add that the lineage thus begun issues in the poetry of the various European modernisms.

Of William Blake's *Songs of Innocence and of Experience*, arguably the earliest English examples of this generic anomaly, I have more to say below. My present purpose is to situate the change in Bakhtin's understanding of the poetic that takes place between the Dostoevsky book and 'Discourse in the novel' within a more general shift in his theory of discourse from *forms* to *forces*, from 'types' within structures to 'lines' within histories. In short, his 'sociological poetics' is reinflected, with a stronger stress on the adjective than on the noun within that phrase. Whatever the problems involved in this shift – and Bakhtin's undertheorisation of the institutional dimension of these forms that he now frees from their static functional definition has been discussed elsewhere – its interest for us here is the greater exposure of the novel to its generic others that this shift brings in its train.[6] A whole chapter in this book-length essay is headed 'Discourse in poetry and discourse in the novel', and this issue refuses to be thus confined, spilling over as it does into the next, headed 'Heteroglossia in the novel'. As the novel is more fully exposed to its others, and as the genres are linked in relations of analogy and participation to particular social forces, so certain highly productive complexities and incoherences which had been repressed by the schematism of a taxonomic imperative come to light. The typology of 1929 had, as we have seen, somewhat rhetorically and decorously dialogised the logical schema of traditional poetics; the essay of 1934–35 is in a different theoretical style altogether. Carrying forward the typology's firm refusal of purely linguistic categories (its 'meta-linguistics'), 'Discourse in the novel' signals by its very repetitious prolixity a dialogism of theory less reined in by system, more in touch with its own unconscious.

The concept of the poetic is extended in two ways. First, looking at poetry's ideological effects, Bakhtin insists on its complicity in the project of linguistic and sociopolitical unification. Secondly, looking at its formal features, he both specifies in more detail the status of the poetic word (its would-be unconditionality) and critically refashions from the metalinguistic standpoint some of the established categories of poetic analysis (rhythm, image, symbol). It is from a difference in the tone of these two elaborations that we become aware of an ambiguity in Bakhtin's thinking about the poetic, an ambiguity which – far from threatening that think-ing with collapse, as it would any systematic or monological conceptual edifice – actually opens it up further, taking us into some highly engaged ethico-political and theologico-political reflections that were inapposite (perhaps quite inchoate as conscious themes) in the Russia of the mid-1930s, but whose moment may now have come.

Consider: when Bakhtin writes that 'the poet is a poet in so far as he accepts the idea of a unitary and singular language and a unitary, monologically sealed-off utterance' (DN, p. 296), he makes poetry out to be an accomplice in the cultural centralisation and linguistic standardisation that historically created the modern European polities. The poetic genres are the prime literary agents of that sociopolitical unity which is never given but always a matter of struggle from above, always *posited against* the actual heteroglot stratification of language. The intonation in these passages is militant and polemical, its intention demystifying. When, however, Bakhtin turns to the characteristics of the poetic word that fit it for this ideological instrumentality, a modulation takes place in his tone. These genres in which 'the natural dialogisation of the word is not put to artistic use' – which mimic the project they subserve in so far as they do not abolish dialogism (an impossibility) but rather 'suspend' it by 'convention' – attract to themselves a description that we would otherwise associate with his valorisation of carnival: 'utopian' (DN, pp. 284, 288). Popular they certainly are not; none the less they represent that ideal of a 'utopian philosophy of genres', a 'language of the gods' (DN, p. 331). poetic monologism may be bound up with a project that subordinates the individual to the state; novelistic dialogism may by the same token be understood as a metaphor for the subject in civil society constituted by multiple intersecting identities and positionalities; but any language that places itself in a ventriloquial relation to God can only be an instrument of the centralising state by a continuing political effort of insulation and a deliberate monopoly over its use. The 'hierarchical relations' which poetic and other monologisms seek to set up between stratified and (potentially) mutually dialogising languages can always be translated into 'contradictory relations'.[7] The history of heretical and antinomian sects within Christianity has shown that part of this process will be the transvaluation of the idea of God, its refunctioning away from hierarchy and submission and towards community and struggle. No notion is more powerful than this personification of the unconditional, yet none is more at the mercy of conditions.

Bakhtin does not of course *say* all this; I am not paraphrasing. Rather I am trying to show that Bakhtin in this moment of his thinking is more Nietzschean than we, or even perhaps he, might have supposed; that the 'linguistic and stylistic worlds' which he opposes as Edenic to Babelic, or as Ptolemaic to Galilean – these are his terms – are no more to be counterposed as (cognitively speaking) false to true or (ethically speaking) bad to good than those Apollonian and Dionysiac principles which they so insistently recall. Bakhtin follows Nietzsche in his conception of epic as a 'wholly Apollonian' genre, and he would not dissent with the latter's identification of its perennial Dionysiac other in the 'uneven and irregular imagery' of folk song:[8] we are not after all surprised at these echoes of *The Birth of Tragedy* in someone who had been a pupil of the Polish Nietzschean classical scholar Tadeusz Zelinskii.[9] What is more interestingly at stake here is the theoretical standing of the poetic word, which we might see as Bakhtin's equivalent of the Apollonian *principium individuationis*. For Nietzsche, that principle may well show its repressive side when 'Apollonian forces' constitute 'a perpetual military encampment' against the 'titanic and barbaric menace of Dionysos'; with the rise of tragedy it enters into a benign interaction with its opposite.[10] Making the appropriate adjustments, we might translate this into Bakhtinian terms by saying that both monologism and dialogism have a utopian dimension. Imagining a condition in which one person was everybody, the pseudo-Adamite language towards which poetry aspires asks of us a certain binocular vision, a perspective 'beyond good and evil' which is able to hold together at all times both its promise and its mystification.

It is worth following up this issue of 'individuation', for if dialogism is the substratum of all monologism – if from within a sense of the ubiquity of the dialogical we are enabled to 'see' or 'hear' monologism for what it is and does, if we are freed from the mystification of its naturalness – then it is also true that a dialogised heteroglossia as it were *needs* the moment of individuation whose hypostasis generates the monological genres. Bakhtin's revolutionary postulate of the primacy of dialogue (in his strong sense) must be sustained, but it must also be qualified by a consideration we could call its obverse: without individuation, that primal state of all discourse would not only not be known, it would be immobile and would mobilise nothing and nobody. Everybody speaking at once is unimaginable except as noise: not polyphony, but cacophony, aesthetically unpleasing and ethicopolitically null.

Perhaps it is now time to give this other side of Bakhtin's case a hearing, and to say that while all 'voices' in the novel are 'worldviews' and potential 'social languages', those languages and ideologies can only make themselves heard as *voices*. Poetry and drama, along with the 'rhetorical genres', survive as the bearers of this counter-truth to that of the novel. Dialogism is a reality of discourse precariously suspended between twin impossibilities: an experience of one as two which, if realised, would bring us back to one again by reducing two to a mechanical sum of two units. It is what would be lost (though not quite without trace) if the 'not as yet unfolded' dialogue 'embedded' in one utterance were actually to be 'unfolded' into 'individual argument and conversation between two persons' (DN, pp. 324–5) – as happens, for example, in dramatic dialogue. Drama in the typology of *Problems of Dostoevsky's Poetics* had been described somewhat formalistically as objectivised speech (speech of the second type) organised in relations that are themselves objectivised (*PDP*, p. 188). In the essay of 1934–35 drama is far more dialogically and hence productively redefined as the suicidal realisation of the inner dialogism of all discourse, as the manifestation of that towards which dialogism tends but which it can only reach at the cost of its own dissolution. The individuation which makes it possible to speak of two 'voices' within a single linguistic construction is taken a step further. Laid out sequentially as the lines of speaking subjects empirically present to each other, these voices are articulated as different semantic positions within what then becomes – with the displacement of all difference on to the signified – the same 'unitary' language. We might say that this externalising move which founds drama as we know it is fatal for dialogism, if it were not also the case that drama is the mirror in which novelistic and other dialogisms recognise their own composed and finished image. Without that dramatic model of individuation constantly before them, the voices of novelistic prose would be scarcely formed. The same goes for resolution: without the provisional closure of plot, dialogism as the irresolvable infinity of dialogue would be mere endlessness.

Bakhtin might, then, insist that the novelistic voices which retain their full power to mean in the face of this abstract dialectic of drama are always more than 'individual dissonances'; that, knowing themselves as 'only surface upheavals of the untamed elements in social heteroglossia' (DN, p. 326), they are at their most characteristic when they more or less explicitly open out all personal disagreement into that heteroglot matrix of sociolinguistic stratification and social contradiction from which they spring in the first place; and that any novel which approaches the condition of drama ends up as 'bad drama', with the narrative 'in the awkward and absurd position of stage directions in plays' (DN, p. 327). We can concede all this and yet still argue that the interacting voices of the novel cannot put on the ineluctably social and historical clothing of languages if they do not first of all experience as a moment of their constitution the individuating and finalizing imperative of the dramatic. The novel may weave at will in and out of that 'finite dialogue' of which the drama in its verbal aspect is wholly composed, but without this clarified micro-dialogue as its other the novel's inexhaustible macro-dialogue would not be 'itself'. The potential at least of inscription in manifested (if not necessarily attributed) 'voices' is perhaps the condition of dialogism's elementary audibility or legibility.

These reflections could be summed up by saying that the individuation of drama is not merely the result of an Apollonian reduction of the 'untamed' Dionysiac infinity of heteroglossia to persons, but is always already within heteroglossia as the precondition of our even beginning to enter and conceive the latter. What post-structuralist discourses speak of as a 'play of signifiers' is just that: a *play*, a drama of signification at the heart of all meaning. This metaphor of 'play', of a 'playing out' or staging, is never far off in Bakhtin's accounts of the varieties of meaning-making. We have seen the trope at work in what I have called the 'difficult drama' which takes place when the word strives to reach its object, that battle with other words in a 'tension-filled environment' (DN, p. 276) which the novel is unique in putting on display, thematising rather than suppressing. Now with the poetic genres it is not the case that there is no drama; it is simply that this drama of semiosis takes place in a different theatre. The product of this relocated 'play' is the symbol, the characteristic sign of poetic discourse and (for Bakhtin) just as 'central' to the theorisation of poetry as the 'double-voiced, internally dialogised word' is to the theory of prose (DN, p. 330). The little drama which gives us the poetic symbol or image is 'played out' not between one fully valued word and another but 'between the word and its object'; all of the symbol's play is 'in that space' (DN, p. 328). The distance between the symbol's 'double meaning' and the prose word's ambiguity can be measured by introducing dramatic dialogue as a middle term: where drama gives us two voices within a single language, symbolism can never be other than two meanings within a single voice. It shares with the novel's incarnate contradiction (dialogism) an intersection of meanings; at the same time it shares with drama the impulse towards unification. Another voice 'break[ing] into this play of the symbol' destroys the 'poetic plane' and 'translate[s]' it 'onto the plane of prose' (DN, p. 328). Figured diagrammatically, Bakhtin's conception of the dramatic and poetic words might be seen as occupying the middle of a scale which has at one end the novel's orchestration of many languages into a 'world' and at its other extreme the discourse of philosophy, a language of the 'term' and the 'concept' in which (one presumes: Bakhtin does not spell this out) a single meaning inhabits a single voice. Or: at the broad top of an imagined inverted pyramid is a form of mimesis which is dialogically open to the world which it also structurally replicates in its own infinite difference from itself; at the apex below is a sort of verbal position without magnitude, a form of conceptuality which has renounced all ambiguity in order to keep at bay the world it makes into the object of its monologue.

We have seen that for Bakhtin symbolism differs from dialogism in the space of its signifying event: the varieties of signification that he brings under the comprehensive rubric of the symbol correspond to different dramatic actions, different relationships between the figure's meanings. The relationship may be logical: of part to whole, for example, or of concrete to abstract.[11] Or it may be ontological: 'as a special kind of representational relationship, or as a relationship between essence and appearance' (DN, p. 328). Bakhtin might have said that symbolism is that form of verbal signification whose productivity could be exhausted by using the categories of either a structuralist or a metaphysical hermeneutic. The slightest touch of irony – of 'another's accent' intruding 'between the word and its object' – does not so much destroy the symbol as refunction it beyond the reach of both of these kinds of analysis (DN, p. 328). Irony or parody cutting across the poetic symbol behaves rather like an unruly fool erupting on to the space where the latter's decorous dance of meaning is being staged.

Bakhtin cites the similes of Lensky's lyrics in *Eugene Onegin* as an instance of this more or less blatant dialogisation of the poetic word. Similar English examples could no doubt be found with a sharp satirical edge in Byron, and in a slightly different vein in the novelised quasi-lyrical and narrative poetry of Browning and Clough. The less patent, more complex case of Blake's lyric irony will be elaborated later. A related case, one to which Bakhtin gives little space, is the 'novelistic image'. Its difference from the poetic image is worth briefly pursuing, if only because some dominant twentieth-century critical arguments have effected a certain poeticisation of the novel as a condition of its being treated as 'art', and Bakhtin can help us to resist such residual power as they still have. One thinks of F. R. Leavis's characteristically tautological dictum about 'major' fiction 'counting' in the same way as 'major' poetry 'counts'; or of the effort to present Dickens as a spontaneous 'symbolist'.[12] The motif of the prison in *Little Dorrit*, for example, has been seen as a symbol thanks to whose magic potency social criticism becomes high art, as the text's otherwise monstrously disparate sprawl of character zones and narrative lines is conjured into a unity offering aesthetic satisfactions beyond the mere story-telling ingenuity of the 'mystery' plot. Structuralist analysis might trace its productivity as an image in the abstract to its formal combination of metaphor and metonymy – the prison as part of a social whole which is itself prison-like – without ever taking us back to the discursive and historical roots of the life of that particular motif, which surely lie deep in metropolitan English heteroglossia. Dickens's image has none of the radiant translucence and single tone of the symbol: at once opaque and dissonant, it springs from a popular and radical consciousness of long standing and may be guessed as having its origins in or after 1789. Far from effacing the traces of its endless ironic as well as straightforward recycling through countless fictional and polemical contexts, Dickens's multifaceted 'prison' mobilises these diverse uses and draws its vitality from them. English Jacobinism is one such context: William Godwin's chauvinistic Englishman who exclaims 'Thank God, we have no Bastille!' finds an echo in the xenophobic politics of the plebeian occupants of Bleeding Heart Yard.[13] Also resonating here is the nickname 'Poor Law Bastilles' given to the workhouses after 1834; Mary Wollstonecraft's Maria who declares that marriage 'bastilled her for life'; and beyond and behind all of these that old tactic of radical polemic whereby the Whiggish critique of French institutions was turned against England itself (as if to underline this, the novel begins in a French prison).[14] The force of this 'novelistic image' is, then, anything but 'symbolic' – not unifying but displacing, moving the text beyond its own boundaries as an aesthetically finalised whole. Centrifugal rather than centripetal, it is less the all-resolving focus of the novel's 'great dialogue' than that dialogue's catalyst, the guarantee that it is unfinishable.

II

And so we come to Blake, the first of our generalisable exceptions.[15] If Blake is taken to be a 'Romantic' poet – and he was a latecomer to that company, itself only constituted by criticism after all of its members had already died – then his practice of writing hardly corresponds either to Bakhtin's view of Romantic discourse as a single-voiced authorial expressivity hostile to irony and parody, or to the more general view that in the poetic signification of Romanticism the symbol has triumphed over allegory. For Bakhtin, Romanticism breaks with the 'stylisation' of the single-voiced classicist word only to put in its place a yet purer monologism of utterance from which all hint of refraction through another's word has been eliminated. Combining a Chicago Aristotelian reading of literary history with a Russian Formalist conceptual vocabulary, we might extend this by saying that the lyric in all its forms, even the 'lowest', becomes the poetic norm of a new literary system, and that in the process both itself and the system are radically changed. As the latter sheds its hierarchy, so the lyric sheds its conventionality, offering itself as the quasi-spontaneous speech-act of a person empirically given and without any difference in kind from the reader. Now while Blake undoubtedly participates in this mutation whereby (to adopt yet another idiom) the 'bourgeois revolution' is at last fought to a finish on the field of poetics – the kinship between his *Songs* and the *Lyrical Ballads* of Wordsworth and Coleridge is evidence enough – his writing from first to last is very plainly both open to the dialogised heteroglossia of his time and alert to the revolutionary possibilities of the allegorised literary language then passing into obsolescence. His solution to the crisis of that language was not to forsake it altogether for an empiricism of 'feeling' but to re-invigorate it, thereby uncovering the ethics and the theology and the politics that lie buried in poetics. It is this act of compelling the poetic to yield up its ethical and theologico-political potential that he calls Imagination. Blake in this way forces upon Bakhtinian thinking an exception not only to its conceptualisation of poetry in general but to its characterisation of Romantic writing in particular, and seems to hold up before us a stark choice between *correcting* Bakhtin and *reclassifying* Blake. The Russian perhaps knew only the Romanticisms of his own country and Germany (and perhaps also France); the Englishman is a maverick, member of a class of one.

There is of course a third possibility, and that is to bring Bakhtin and Blake into dialogue with each other. My deconstruction of Bakhtin's opposition between the novelistic and the poetic will be interestingly elaborated if we follow through to some sort of answer these hitherto unposed questions: why was Blake not a novelist? If he was neither (quite) a Romantic nor (quite) a 'neo-classical' poet, what deflected him from taking the path to prose that a superficial reading of Bakhtin might see as the logical choice – at least of so sensitive and politically engaged a listener to the voices and languages of the revolutionary years? Or, to rephrase: what truth was it about poetic discourse and human potentiality that took on exceptional clarity under the signature of William

Blake? What I said earlier about the coexisting utopian and demystifying dimensions in Bakhtin's discussion of the poetic genres begins to clarify if we understand how Blake's writing is a powerful hybrid of allegory and parody, the sublime and the grotesque, a peculiar productivity and interaction of modes and effects that are traditionally opposed.

Demonstrating all this demands that we take a detour first of all into the fortunes of these modes as they came down to Blake and as they have since been (mis)represented. Allegory has suffered over the past 200 years from a critical discourse still under the dominance of symbol, whose terms cast it in an inferior signifying role, constructing it as the crude corporealisation of elements from an already given conceptuality, its arbitrary signifiers lacking that necessary relation to a signified with which the symbol instantaneously impresses us.[16] It suited the high-Romantic polemic against allegory to take the classicist conception of its conventional working at face value in order to sustain a notion of the symbol as no mere 'figure' but as a minor miracle of writing in which there is at once and inseparably meaning and materiality: always just enough of each but never too much of either. Nothing that Blake wrote can be understood in these terms: he works in a space before this move towards a punctual specularity of poetic signification is made, and what he retains from the allegorical tradition is its inherent narrativity, its intrinsically unstable dependence upon speaking and acting persons. If it is true that his polemical statements about allegory are (with one exception) denunciatory, his practice shows that what he there denounces is the 'fable' conceived as subordinated to the 'moral', allegory as narrativity in thrall to conceptuality. For the practice itself must be grasped not as leaping at one bound from the artificiality of the allegorical into the authenticity of the symbolic, but rather as exploiting a contradiction that was then opening up in poetics. 'Allegory' on the one hand was a tissue of 'improbabilities' licensed (within limits) by its 'moral', relegated to the half-life of mere exemplification. On the other hand it is the mode that enables the most unrestricted 'invention', the 'boldest' of 'fiction'. The allegory that Blake renews from within is the name that stood in his time for both the bondage and the freedom of the poetic signifier.

The means of this renewal is our other mode: parody. Whereas the Romantic symbol realises the monological potential in allegory, Blake's writing is a continuous opening-out of the dialogism that lies only just beneath the surface of an idea that has been made to speak. Parody is an unsublatable moment of that process whereby the always animated signifiers of allegory are freed to mean on their own. We might say that allegorical 'fiction' generates a truth strong enough to challenge the meaning which orthodoxy and authority intend it to deliver and whose very embodiment carries the risk of a subversion in the first place. Parody as the agent of a renovating subversion of allegory is everywhere in Blake: it is there in his claim that his narrative works make up an alternative Scripture, a 'Bible of Hell'; it is there also in his profoundly allusive and ironic lyrics. Typically he takes a dominant cultural text and literalises it at those highly vulnerable points where it makes a tactical use of allegory: the new narrative produced out of these materials is then offered as the text's occluded subtext, the state of affairs it does not wish us to see or hear. In 'A Poison Tree' and 'The Human Abstract' from the *Songs of Experience* Blake lays bare this device of his writing, above all in the relation between the first stanza and the rest of the poem. The first poem dialogises a voice of 'forbearance', elaborating out of its casual metaphors a little narrative of murderous consequences which that same voice is ironically forced to tell:

> In the morning glad I see
> My foe outstretch'd beneath the tree[17]

In the second poem (p. 75) the abstractions of 'Pity' and 'Mercy' clothed in the tones of ruling-class complacency are (in a first move) contextually re-accentuated as personifications:

> Pity would be no more
> If we did not make somebody Poor;
> And Mercy no more could be
> If all were as happy as we.

Another voice of vatic intonation then (p. 75) invents other actors in a full-blown allegory of social and psychic alienation which makes up the body of the text:

> And mutual fear brings peace,
> Till the selfish loves increase:
> Then Cruelty knits a snare,
> And spreads his baits with care.

These parodied allegories have their place in a set of lyrics produced in a parodic re-accentuation of the *Songs of Innocence*, themselves in turn already parodies of contemporary verse for children. Into the form which was even then becoming the paradigm of high-Romantic expressivity Blake introduces an unheard-of density of verbal refractions and displacements which extend beyond the parodic to take in the whole range of irony, ambiguity, and what Bakhtin calls 'hidden polemic' (*PDP*, p. 196). It seems we have no choice but to speak in Blake's case, and against the grain of Bakhtin's more categorical distinctions, of a specifically poetic dialogism – one which, while it could never match the range of its novelistic near relation, is none the less no mere rhetorical reduction or rarefaction of the latter, but deeply form-determining and with its own distinctive effects.

What then does this strong poetic dialogism offer that novelistic dialogism cannot? To answer this I need to be more specific about the type of allegorising poetic discourse that is dialogically revitalised in Blake. Let us call it, in a Bakhtinian coinage, the *apostrophic word*. By this I mean that so-called 'personification allegory' which in his time was exemplified in the 'great' or 'sublime' ode, the major lyric genre in which (normally) an abstraction like 'Peace' or 'Liberty' is launched into life by being apostrophised and made the hero(ine) of a short narrative of origins. For an idea to speak or act it has first to be spoken to by the poet; it was from this merely conventional odic gesture that Blake developed a whole ontology by the simple move of refusing to exempt anything from a universal addressivity. The programmatically 'third-person' discourse that tried to escape this condition he called Reason, the ultimate monologism. Blake's claim for the performative status of the apostrophic word is to be read not only in his occasional terse maxims on the topic but also in that transition in his writing which took him from the early lyrics, through the carnivalesque clarification of his great Menippean satire *The Marriage of Heaven and Hell*, to narrative poems where the notion that everything is alive only in so far as it is created and sustained by acts of apostrophe meets head on the criterion of 'probability'. Truth-claims that were suspended in the lyric held good for the epic kinds; hence to make lyric 'vision' the continuous texture of narrative, as Blake does in the prophetic books, is to flout the dominant rationality and flaunt the referentiality of the apostrophic word. Like Bakhtin, Blake poses discourses of integral personification against those rationalising discourses that reify everything they touch. The personification need not be explicit, in the sense of being spelt out, realised semantically: any speech of marked intonation (as Voloshinov observes in 'Discourse in life and discourse in poetry') turns its referent into an addressee, implicitly calls a hero into being, animates the world in a replay of our ontogenetic and phylogenetic childhood. Blake's fondness for such intonational heightening is to be seen in those intensely pointed and emphatically repeated questions, appeals and exclamations that fill whole lyrics and punctuate the 'epic' writing.

This dialogue between Bakhtinian theory and Blakean practice might perhaps be brought to a provisional focus by what must surely rank as the best-known Blakean text of this kind. In 'The Tyger' the central issue of any consequent spirituality is brought before us in poetic writing of the most relentlessly reiterative materiality: an utterance that undoes the pseudo-objectivity of the declarative sentence by being made of nothing but questions. To talk about God, Blake had to write a poem – a poem, moreover, that was poetic (read: apostrophic) to the nth degree; to transvalue the godhead that he rejected he had at the same time to refract his intentions parodically and polemically through the words of others. In this dense fabric of allusion to aesthetic and theological and political discourses, none is either finally detachable from its source in the current heteroglossia or finally reducible to the others' terms. Blake's revolutionary praise of (his) God is nothing if not oblique, having to fight its way through the outright abuse of anti-Jacobin reaction to reach its object: more than one conservative voice had by 1792–93 begun to recast the 'swinish' people as fearful 'tigers'. Blake's sublime is produced by reminding the arch-conservative Edmund Burke of that passage in his aesthetic treatise where he cites the tiger 'in the gloomy forest' as the quintessence of the sublime of 'power' which rises from 'terror, the common stock of everything that is sublime'.[18] The terrified split subject who speaks the poem is made to realise an image of unbridled Energy in an echo of the terms of William Collins's monstrous figure of 'Danger' in the 'Ode to Fear', whose 'Limbs of Giant Mold/ What mortal Eye can fix'd behold?'[19] His quest for an answer is both revealing and creatively misdirected: the artisanal maker that he imagines for the tiger tells us which earthly class-subject he most fears; while the 'distant deeps or skies' in which he imagines the making as happening show his fixation upon a conception of the divine Subject as both far removed in time and space and inwardly undivided. The poem's climax is yet another, and still more agonised, question: 'Did he who made the Lamb make thee?' In the absence of an answer the speaker repeats in intensified form the question that invoked the beast at the beginning. We then understand: the work of creation that he vividly though mistakenly thinks of as taking place in some indefinite past is the work of the heteroglot words that speak through him, coming together in his monologue. But we know also that though his idea of the nature and locus of God is at fault, though in some sense the tiger is of his own making – is a human possibility – his quest for a unified truth, a transcendence, is not. This need to imagine the unconditional author of everything is indeed no less human, inasmuch as it is the constitutive obverse of that knowledge of finitude which defines our humanity and which (as both Bakhtin and Blake understand) does not have to entail a disempowering obedience to any hierarchised authority actually in place in the world. Through and beyond the multiple ironies of its poetic dialogism, and taking its strength from them, 'The Tyger' remains a sublime lyric, a poem whose generic memory, extending back to ancient prayer and cultic ritual, ensures that it cannot do other than praise.

III

In Bakhtin's terms, then, Blake's extraordinary project is one of re-inventing within an irreversible European modernity the 'proclamatory genres', restoring to poetry its prophetic and performative dimension in an age when irony or speech 'with reservations' has so wholly entered the national vernaculars as to have become codified in their very syntactic forms.[20] Blake would have agreed with Bakhtin that the old authorial positions whose styles and settings were not a matter of choice have gone for good. However strongly the image of the author as prophet that he assumes in the narrative works alludes to one such superseded speaking subject, it is precisely *an* image, one among many he might have chosen. If he doesn't write novels, neither does he in any Bakhtinian sense write epics: in texts that refer so immediately to the present and the future there is no correlation whatever between a 'high' style and the absolute past; the genre of prophecy speaks to the present by bringing past and future into familiar contact with one another. In Blake an 'old' genre makes a bid for renewed authority in the modern world, openly reviving a 'proclamatory' mode of speech that other authorial images ironise almost to death (a negation which needless to say binds them no less firmly to what they negate). The hard thing, perhaps, for us to understand is that while this act of discursive renewal is always and necessarily a matter of 'stylisation' rather than of 'style', it is by no means less authentic for that reason. We might say that modern authorship strives in its Blakean move to be authoritative without being authoritarian, and that this persistence of the will to truth through a discourse that insistently frames and contextualises itself is a paradigm of poetry's accommodation to modernity.

The political character of this accommodation is never constant or assured: in late eighteenth-century England it was undoubtedly revolutionary in its implications, if not always in its effects. Percy Shelley's 'Ode to the West Wind' is perhaps the last brave attempt to mobilise a hybrid of prophecy and prayer for emancipatory ends, in the long aftermath of the French Revolution. Whatever the future fortunes and political effects of this kind of 'proclamatory' poetic writing in the modern world's European heartland, it has a long life ahead of it in other places, where modernisation is a recent experience or has taken a skewed path: South Africa, for example. A play of the 1980s like *Woza Albert!* suggests that in the township heteroglossia from which it manifestly draws its strength we might anywhere find working together (often coinciding in the same text or practice or individual) the radical parodist and the radical *imbongi* (praise singer), latterday prophet and holy fool alike speaking of the people's freedom as forms of pleasure and forms of worship unite to shadow forth a state beyond or before the cruel commodification of their bodies in the present. It is moreover no coincidence that this place where a prophetic poetic discourse has survived not only print culture and literacy but the coloniser's cultural exterminism should be a prime site of efforts to transform the God who came in the coloniser's missionary train, across a range which runs from the independent African churches in the early days of conversion to the black theology of more recent date; from the spontaneous and local spiritual revolt of the first elites, all the way to the consciously liberationist and global project espoused by black Christians who have sought roles in one or other of the (socialist, liberal or radical–democratic) emancipatory narratives of modernity. Whether oriented to the past or to the future, whether in identifying saints or prophets as ancestors or in identifying the regulative ideas of modern sociopolitical narratives with the Kingdom of God – in short, whether traditionalist or revolutionary – the effect of these phenomena is to show that the authoritative word can be wrested from 'authority' and reinflected from below as a discourse now of frontal challenge, now of everyday survival, sometimes (again) ambivalently poised between these postures.

We might usefully take some of these reflections into the polemical field latterly opened up in South Africa over the appropriate mode of post-apartheid cultural forms. The culture of slogans and of the 'spectacle', we are told in the most compelling of the arguments now making themselves heard, will (or should) now give way to a new culture of 'irony' and of the quotidian, models for which already exist in some of the writing produced under the old regime of apartheid.[21] Timely as this case is – and I have warmly underwritten it elsewhere – it needs to be hedged about with the kind of caveat that perhaps only the Bakhtinian perspective developed in this essay could make enterable.[22] Anyone brought to acknowledge that the 'proclamatory' genres do not necessarily oppress must also entertain the notion that the 'ironic' genres might not necessarily liberate, or at least not on their own. Strong and positive versions of this counter-argument have already surfaced in reference to metropolitan Europe: Russell Berman has, for example, recently argued that the 'charismatic modernism' of the avant-garde in our century is complicit with the very bureaucratic rationalisation that it is conventionally seen to oppose.[23] At the very least we might speculate that perhaps the idiom which links the double-voiced genres with civil society and the single-voiced genres with the state is a dangerous idiom – if only because it is self-fulfilling: monologism will seem the language of centralised authority just in so far as we confine that category's empirical instances to the State's monologues; in our loud denunciation of malign voices of authority such benign 'popular' correlatives of those voices as exist might be lost to hearing.

To pose the slogan against irony, as if irony were the sole alternative to the slogan's simplification, the only sure guarantee against its illegitimate trespass upon the field of knowledge, is to miss what is distinctive about the forms of modern authority. The slogan, it is true, does not admit of ambiguity or hesitation: as that micro-genre in which the collective praises its own qualities – wishes itself long life or proclaims its own *amandla* or *maatla* (strength, power) – and/or denounces the evils of its others, it cannot live in the company of sceptical tones, let alone admit semantically explicit qualifiers or modifiers of any kind; as the distant echo within modernity of ancient battle-cries, it bears within it the residual magic of all optatives or performatives. At the same time, it has an instrumental cast which puts it in that distinctively modern category of forms that belong to what Bakhtin calls the 'small time' of short-term ends and immediate resolutions. The slogan celebrates the certainties of the collective in an epoch that began in Europe with a revolutionary gesture of doubting everything, and whose hero is the one (literally 'one', typically 'the individual') who claims the right to demur.[24]

It has then to be said that the slogan carries no fixed valency, independent of context. The State-sponsored slogans of the May Day and October marches in the old Soviet Union had of course nothing whatever to do with democracy, or with the collective, and everything to do with a bureaucratic elite devoid of all popular legitimation. What then of the slogans of 'national liberation' movements? Any actual movement of that kind will be a hybrid: at its best, a living utopian image of civil-society-in-the-making, a focus for variously oriented social forces; at its worst, a bureau-cracy-in-waiting, becoming more like a mirror-image of the state the longer it has to wait in illegality and exile, while its hierarchies harden into military structures of command. The slogan in the latter context, emanating from that source and feeding its finished iden-tity, differs only in tone and content, but scarcely in effect, from the state decree; it is only on entering civil society that a slogan escapes the monopoly of any one movement and can carry the intentions of those who pragmatically put it to use on the ground. There, too, it finds itself in a spectrum of (oral) discourses that, as it were, qualify it from without, challenging its logic of if-not-for-then-against with a counter-logic which says that not to be unambiguously 'for' is not necessarily to be 'against'. The slogan chanter also laughs or prays, or is exposed to laughter and prayer, and in so far as this happens the slogan is placed in the context of a macro-dialogue without dates or bounds in space. The slogan that does not live at peace with the profane *carnivalisation* of the one form or the sacred *consum-mation* of the other may issue at length (and all too often does) in the blow that maims or kills.

Now of course much South African poetry lives in the atmos-phere inhabited by the slogan, an atmosphere in which primary and secondary oralities meet and cross-fertilise, and where the written word might paradoxically seem at once superseded and still to come.[25] A literature – that is to say, a tradition specifically of writing – whose organising principle is the slogan would indeed be giving up on any active role, would not be doing what it does best. Irony is one of its modes, the dominant mode of novelistic prose in particular; and a South Africa in transformation needs novels with their valuable orchestration of incommensurable stories and privacies, if the pretensions of the totalising narratives that have obsessed both oligarchy and opposition are to be cut down to size. But then a culture breaking out of the grip of such narratives also needs friendly forms of authority. Myths, hymns, anthems, prophecies, proverbs: all of these court the danger that they can become terroristic under modern conditions, bearers of exclusive and monopolistic narratives. Properly contextualised, these forms counter the *hubris* of the 'nation' with a sense (a knowledge only ever agonistically, rather than cognitively, acquired) of the boundlessness of semantic space–time, in which any given community forms only a local and finite coherence. With their focus on the eternities that surround our finitude, they remind us that no speech would begin if besides our interlocutor we did not posit what Bakhtin calls the 'third': an instance of absolute understanding and truly caring listening, a 'super-addressee' more or less personified. If they are not to be the mere means of groups bonding themselves and banding together against their others, these proclamatory forms of the authoritative word need interpreters, and an appropriate technology for their distribution in a 'developing' society.

Writers are those interpreters; print is their medium. The riches of an oral and vatic past are not the less authentic for being 'quoted', ventriloquised, as they cannot but be now. A literature that is the custodian of all times makes the conditions for their continued meaning within our late modernity.[26] The nation that thinks of itself as a village is the enemy of all other villages; condensing the wisdom of its villages in the second-order though no less authentic authority of writing and putting it in everybody's hands, the nation – through its writers – redeems itself. The 'battle-hymns' of the time of insurgency (as Nadine Gordimer called them) may not be a foundation for the future, but even at their first moment of declamation they had behind them and around them the tones of Ntsikana's hymn and Sontonga's famous anthem: lodged in comprehensive anthologies, sung at meetings, globally reproduced in recorded sound, these are songs not *of* but *for* the 'nation'.[27] They belong to nobody in this world; what we say in singing them contradicts and forbids any monopoly of their use. Their matter is not thought or even feeling but rather the invocation of that which in some sense thinks us before we think; and what we who sing them 'believe' matters not in the slightest. Calling on God to bless Africa and on the Holy Spirit to 'descend', we celebrate community by imagining what transcends and holds community itself. Blake would have valued (had he known them) these sublime lyrics in which Africa ceaselessly re-images her own bounding outline in eternity. And so too would Bakhtin: for whom the grotesque body was only half the story of our humanity, the novel no absolute model, and the absolute a human reality.

Notes

1 The bulk of this essay was written in late 1989; the concluding section on South Africa dates from September 1993. At the time of writing in 1989 there was no English translation of Bakhtin's earliest writings, where the 'theological' dimension of his thinking is quite explicit. Though I have, of course, since read these essays, and indeed written about them, I have chosen not to rewrite this essay in their light.

2 *Problems of Dostoevsky's Poetics*, trans. Caryl Emerson, Manchester, 1984, p. 97. Further references to this book are given in the text as *PDP* followed by the page number. For further reflections on Christ in Bakhtin–Dostoevsky see the chapter 'Human and interhuman: Mikhail Bakhtin', in Tzvetan Todorov, *Literature and its Theorists*, New York, 1987.

3 'Discourse in the novel', in M. M. Bakhtin, *The Dialogic Imagination*, ed. Michael Holquist, trans. Caryl Emerson and Michael Holquist, Austin, Texas, 1981, p. 278. Further references to this essay will be given in the text as DN followed by the page number.

4 Julia Kristeva, *Desire in Language: A Semiotic Approach to Literature and Art*, London, 1980, pp. 70–2.

5 Valentin Voloshinov, 'Discourse in life and discourse in poetry (concerning sociological poetics)', an appendix to Voloshinov, *Freudianism: A Marxist Critique*, trans. I. R. Titunik, New York, 1976, p. 113.

6 Ken Hirschkop, 'Bakhtin, discourse and democracy', *New Left Review*, 160, 1986, pp. 92–113.

7 Ken Hirschkop, 'Dialogism as a challenge to literary criticism', in Catriona Kelly *et al.*, eds, *Discontinuous Discourses in Modern Russian Literature*, London and New York, 1989, p. 27.

8 Friedrich Nietzsche, *The Birth of Tragedy*, trans. F. Golffing, New York, 1956, pp. 42–3.

9 James Curtis, 'Michael Bakhtin, Nietzsche, and Russian pre-revolutionary thought', in B. G. Rosenthal, ed., *Nietzsche in Russia*, Princeton, NJ, 1986, pp. 331–54.

10 Nietzsche, *Birth of Tragedy*, p. 35.

11 Though Bakhtin does not use these terms, we can recognise here the classic figures of metonymy and metaphor later to be correlated by Roman Jakobson with 'contiguity' and 'similarity' and elevated to the status of semiotic universals. See Jakobson, 'Two aspects of language and two types of aphasic disturbances', in Roman Jakobson and Morris Halle, *Fundamentals of Language*, 2nd edn, The Hague, 1971, pp. 69–96.

12 F. R. Leavis, *The Great Tradition*, London, 1948, p. 2.

13 William Godwin, *The Adventures of Caleb Williams; or, Things as They Are*,

ed. D. McCracken, Oxford, 1970, p. 181.

14 Mary Wollstonecraft, *Maria*, ed. Janet Todd, Harmondsworth, 1992, p. 115. For a discussion of this transvaluation by radical writers of key elements of the Whiggish national self-image (with special reference to Blake's *London*), see my 'The London motif in some eighteenth-century contexts: a semiotic study', *Literature and History*, 4, 1976, pp. 2–29.

15 Much of the rest of this section draws on a paper I presented to the University of Essex Sociology of Literature Conference in 1981: see my '1789 and after: mutations of "Romantic" discourse', in Francis Barker *et al.*, eds, *1789: Reading Writing Revolution*, Colchester, 1982, pp. 52–66.

16 The great and pioneering exception to this unanimity on allegory among post-Romantic commentators (long before Paul de Man) is of course Walter Benjamin: see his *The Origins of German Tragic Drama*, trans. John Osborne, London, 1977, pp. 159ff.

17 *Poetry and Prose of William Blake*, ed. Geoffrey Keynes, London, 1961, p. 77. Further references to this edition are given in the text.

18 The reference here is to *A Philosophical Inquiry into the Origin of Our Ideas of the Sublime and the Beautiful*, ed. J. T. Boulton, London, 1958: see Part II, Section 5, p. 64.

19 *The Poems of Gray and Collins*, ed. Austin Poole, London, 1961, p. 246.

20 'From notes made in 1970–71', in *Speech Genres and Other Late Essays*, ed. Caryl Emerson and Michael Holquist, trans. Vern W. McGee, Austin, Texas, 1986, pp. 132–3.

21 Njabulo Ndebele, *South African Literature and Culture: Rediscovery of the Ordinary*, Manchester, 1994.

22 Graham Pechey, 'Post-apartheid narratives', in F. Barker *et al.*, eds, *Colonial Discourse/Postcolonial Theory*, Manchester, 1994, pp. 151–71.

23 Russell Berman, 'The routinization of charismatic modernism and the problem of postmodernity', *Cultural Critique*, 5, 1987, pp. 49–68.

24 The best examination of the slogan as a micro-genre in the context of South Africa in the last days of the struggle against the apartheid regime is a novel which has a slogan for its title: *Longlive!*, by Menan du Plessis. See my review of this book, 'Voices of struggle', in *Southern African Review of Books*, III: 2, 1989–90, pp. 3–5.

25 Jeremy Cronin, '"Even under the rine of terror": insurgent South African poetry', *Research in African Literatures*, XIX: 1, 1988, pp. 12–23.

26 These remarks were strongly inspired by my reading – repeatedly, over many years – of Njabulo Ndebele's poem *The Revolution of the Aged*: see *The Penguin Book of Southern African Verse*, ed. Stephen Gray, Harmondsworth, 1989, pp. 296–8.

27 Non-South African readers will need to be told that the reference here is to the 'Great Hymn' by Ntsikana (one of the first black South African converts to Christianity in the early nineteenth century) and to the South African national anthem 'Nkosi Sikelel' iAfrika'. For the texts, see Gray, *ibid.*, pp. 47–8 and 149–50.

Clair Wills

Upsetting the public: carnival, hysteria and women's texts

Reading Bakhtin, it's hard not to envy Rabelais. However much one extols the virtues of *Ulysses*, or the more popular pleasures of Brighton beach or the Costa del Sol, they still lack that combination of critique and indecency typical of the carnival Rabelais could take as his source. So it appears a mostly compensatory gesture when critics enthuse about the 'carnival*esque*' they find in the latest (post-)modernist novel. Surely they can't really confuse reading a good book with the experience of carnival grounded in the collective activity of the people? What seems to be lacking in this textual carnival is any link with a genuine social force. This is an argument made by Peter Stallybrass and Allon White in *The Politics and Poetics of Transgression*, where they reject some of the easy appropriations of Bakhtin's too often populist and utopian theory of carnival, which argue for the 'transgressive' potential of carnivalesque literature.[1] The authors point out that literary carnival doesn't possess the same social force as actual carnival may once have done. Displaced from public sphere to the bourgeois home (let alone to the novel read by its fire), carnival ceases to be a site of actual struggle. Shifting the emphasis slightly, I want to ask whether some women's texts may not have a more productive relationship to carnival, leading to a closer connection between literary transgression and cultural transformation.[2] I will draw an analogy between Bakhtinian carnival, hysteria and women's texts in terms of their capacity to disrupt and remake official public norms, arguing firstly that carnival and hysteria are linked in terms of the content of their representations, as critics such as Stallybrass and White and Catherine Clément have maintained.[3] Moreover, just as the hysteric seems to 'store' the misplaced carnival content, representing the past in the present, so, I will argue, this cyclical return to the past mirrors the relation to the past which Bakhtin takes as the mark of carnival: in opposition to 'official' time, which presents a linear and hierarchical teleology of events, carnivalesque time is aware of 'timeliness' and crisis in the version of history which it presents. But while both carnival and hysteria are excluded from official public norms, the question should be how to dialogise the public realm by bringing the excluded and 'non-official' into juxtaposition with the official. In this essay I want to focus on the crucial transition from private to public discourse for women, and on the importance of the continuing dialogue between these two areas in feminist poetry. Part of my analysis will take the form of a comparison between a discourse designated 'feminine' by certain scientific discourses – the discourse of the hysteric (a victim of the bourgeois home who is not generally considered to be politically progressive) – and the work of a contemporary poet from Northern Ireland, Medbh McGuckian.[4]

In drawing an analogy between popular carnival and hysterical discourse I am wary of the difficulties in using the term 'hysterical' to refer to even quite a specific area of women's writing. One must continually ask, who speaks the name 'hysteric'? Bearing in mind the process by which the word serves to objectify and marginalise certain types of 'feminine' discourse, I want to look at texts which, precisely because they have lain so far outside official public norms, have been designated 'hysterical', not only by conservative theorists, but also by avant-garde critics such as Julia Kristeva. Since these texts are received as 'not quite literature', the imperative must be to investigate the most productive ways to use that position 'outside' the institution, not in order to be permanently disruptive, but in order to undo and remake that institution. As I hope to show, the constructive role of the 'hysterical' text will depend above all on the function which the work performs, both in relation to the writer's private life, and in bringing this private life into conflict with public norms.

Of central importance in any consideration of these questions is the status of popular festive forms within literature. For Bakhtin, in order for popular carnival to become politically effective it must enter the institution of literature. In *Rabelais and His World*, he argues that it is only in literature that popular festive forms can achieve the 'self-awareness' necessary for effective protest. Of carnival he says: 'its wide popular character, its radicalism and freedom, soberness and materiality were transferred from an almost elemental condition to a state of artistic awareness and purposefulness. In other words, medieval laughter became at the Renaissance stage of its development the expression of a new free and critical historical consciousness.'[5]

This concept of 'artistic awareness' is never fully theorised by Bakhtin, but what seems to be at stake is a juxtaposition of 'official' and 'non-official' modes of communication. In the final pages of the Rabelais book he relates the concept of 'awareness' to 'the victory over linguistic dogmatism' (p. 473), which is secured by the introduction of the vernacular into the category of 'great literature'. The power of carnival to turn things upside down is facilitated by bringing it into dialogic relation to official forms. Hence the mixing of popular and official languages which occurs in texts drawing on the vernacular as well as classical and medieval Latin brings an increased awareness of time and the *difference* between historical epochs. The dialogue between the languages 'suddenly disclosed how much of the old was dead and how much of the new was born' (p. 468). It is only by bringing the excluded and carnivalesque into the official realm in a single text that the concept of public discourse may be altered (so texts written solely in the vernacular would be too far outside the official realm to have an effect). It is Rabelais's ability to make use of official forms, including new forms of scientific knowledge, and bring them into dialogic relation with popular knowledge and 'festive' forms which can raise carnival to 'a higher level of ideological consciousness' (p. 473).[6] For in the Middle Ages carnival had been contained – centred in small pockets of activity in provincial towns, it lacked organisation. It was not in a position to 'dialogise' official forms of communication and organisation because, as Bakhtin points out, it remained 'strictly divided' from them:

> And so medieval culture of folk humour was fundamentally limited to these small islands of feasts and recreations. Official serious cultures existed beside them but strictly divided from the marketplace. The shoots of a new world outlook were sprouting, but they could not grow and flower as long as they were enclosed in the popular gaiety of recreation and banqueting, or in the fluid realm of familiar speech. In order to achieve this growth and flowering, laughter had to enter the world of great literature. (p. 96)

The opening up of the carnivalesque is ultimately achieved through literature,[7] but although Bakhtin stresses literature's power to communicate festive forms, to foster the protest that would otherwise remain contained in separate areas, he goes on to chart the narrowing of its potential through subsequent literary epochs. The ability to dialogise popular and official forms isn't the property of a particular text, but importantly depends on the type of institution into which it is inserted. So, and this is a point I shall return to, it's important not to look to individual texts by women to alter literary norms, abstracted from the need to control the way those texts are received.

Similarly contained, but this time within the private sphere of the bourgeois family rather than the public but provincial market-place, is the hysteric's protest incommunicable? The disruptive possibilities of hysteria and the 'hysterical' text have been debated within feminism, most notably in the discussion between Catherine Clément and Hélène Cixous in *The Newly Born Woman*, where they disagree about the hysteric's ability to 'break' the family mould. Here I want to relate this problem to the particular relationship to time and history which Bakhtin describes as the mark of carnival festivity, and ask: does the hysteric belong to the past? For Bakhtin, carnivalesque time looks to the past and the future. Unlike the official feast in which the link with time has become formal, and change and moments of crisis are relegated to the past, popular festive forms harness the 'timeliness' of past events in order to project a utopian time: 'Carnival was the true feast of time, the feast of becoming, change and renewal. It was hostile to all that was immortalised and completed' (p. 10). While the official feast looks to the past in order to reconfirm hierarchy, the return of the popular feast to the past ('the natural (cosmic) cycle' or 'biological or historic timeliness' (p. 9)) presages a moment of renewal. Like the mixing of languages in Rabelais, and this time outside the institution of literature, what seems to be valuable about carnival is its awareness of the discontinuity of history, or history as crisis.

There are two important questions concerning the hysteric's relationship to the past. Firstly, is she socially and historically bound to the Victorian era (in which case any abstraction in the form of a theory of the 'hysterical' text, or indeed, the whole of psychoanalytic practice would be called into question)? More specifically, is the hysteric bound to the past, personal and cultural, through reminiscence? In her cyclical return to the crises of her personal history, which she repeats in her symptoms, the hysteric may represent in miniature the relationship of popular festive forms to the past, yet her capacity for turning things 'upside-down' is contained within the family. The possible 'transgressive' nature of popular festive forms and hysterical discourse are connected not only in their similar relation to history, but also in their content. As Stallybrass and White point out, Freud's descriptions of the hysteric call on popular festive imagery: 'It is striking how the broken fragments of carnival, terrifying and disconnected, glide through the discourse of the hysteric' (p. 171). The carnival role of the grotesque body in mocking, degrading and inverting high culture has been displaced onto the psyche of the hysteric. Was the 'madness' of these Viennese women then the belated representation of popular carnival which had been suppressed? For Freud the repressed past survives in woman. He records in a footnote Frau Emmy von N.'s answer to an inquiry about her age: 'I am a woman of the last century.'[8]

But for Catherine Clément in *The Newly Born Woman*, the hysteric does not simply recall childhood events but represents in her symptoms and her discourse the repressed past of patriarchal history. The culture has a zone for what it excludes, which comprises those who are 'afflicted with a dangerous symbolic mobility. Dangerous for them because those are the people who are afflicted with what we call madness, anomaly, perversion, or whom we label, says Mauss, "neurotics, ecstatics, outsiders, carnies, drifters, jugglers, acrobats"' (p. 7). Stallybrass and White also stress the remembrance not only of a personal but also of a pantomimic past, as they analyse the hysteric in terms of carnival. They view hysteria both as a Victorian phenomenon, and as a displacement from previous history. As such it is simply the most recent manifestation of the bourgeoisie's contradictory relationship to the 'low' society which it has repressed. Since for them psychoanalysis, like the institution of art, corresponds to a sublimation of the social force of carnival into representation of carnival, the presence of an 'upside-down world' in the discourse of the hysteric is to be specifically linked to the bourgeoisie's attempt to define itself as a class in opposition to the social terrain of dirt, servants and sexuality. So, although the social force of carnival may have been displaced and fragmented, it retains a symbolic importance which is central to post-Renaissance culture. In the absence of social forms fitting to what they wish to express, hysterics attempt 'to produce their own by pastiche and parody in an effort to embody semiotically their distress' (p. 174). The hysteric's symptoms thus constitute a staging of the carnivalesque: 'Once noticed, it becomes apparent that there is a second narrative fragmented and marginalised, lodged within the emergent psychoanalytic discourse. It witnesses a complex interconnection between hints and scraps of parodic festive form and the body of the hysteric' (p. 174). Pantomime thus becomes the 'symptomatic locus' of the bourgeois imaginary as it attempts to represent the unconscious.

This historicised interpretation has a markedly different emphasis from Clément's feminist reading of the hysteric's 'reminiscence'. For her the hysteric, in her kinship with the witch and the sorceress (a kinship which Freud also notes), reinscribes the repression of women. Each figure, sorceress and hysteric, articulates the possibilities for protest available at different historical times. They are linked through their repetition of the crises of the women who came before them: the hysteric 'resumes and assumes the memories of the others' (p. 5). And it may be that the contemporary woman writer has been bequeathed the legacy of reminiscence left by the sorceress and hysteric. Just as Bakhtin saw popular festive forms enriched by their introduction into literature, the publication of texts which assume the memories of previous women's crises may be one way to open up the provincial, familial nature of the hysteric's protest. In this way Adrienne Rich dreams of a 'common language' that would draw together the transforming power of women separated by historical and social circumstance, asserting the identity of past and present not so that things should stay the same, but in order to show possibilities for the future.[9] The hope is that by creating a collective past, women will be able to break up the present. But if this is her legacy, how is it possible for the woman writer to make public the protest which in the case of the hysteric was contained within the bourgeois family, without merely becoming a spectacle for the male gaze? Moreover, *can* the past be a source of political change in the present? Clément asks, 'Do the abnormal ones – madmen, deviants, neurotics, drifters, jugglers, tumblers – anticipate the culture to come, repeat the past culture, or express a constantly present utopia?' (p. 8). In the same way we can ask of Bakhtin, what relationship can popular festivity have to the past which doesn't reconfirm hierarchy (like the official feast), and which can at the same time be effective in remaking public norms? The central difficulty concerns the discourse and representations of the hysteric, the power of anachronism. In *Origins of Psychoanalysis* Freud explains the process whereby 'anachronisms' live on in the psyche of the hysteric as a failure of translation. 'The memory behaves as though it were some current event', as the psychic force associated with the early traumatic event increases in its capacity to disrupt in the process of repression:

Each later transcription inhibits its predecessor and takes over the excitatory process from it. If the later transcription is lacking the excitation will be disposed of according to the psychological laws governing the earlier epoch and along the paths which were then accessible. Thus an anachronism remains: in a particular province fueros are still in force. Relics of the past still survive.[10]

The 'fuero' is an ancient Spanish provincial law. We could read Freud as saying that there has been insufficient centralisation in the 'state' of the hysteric. The crises of the past live on in a separate area of the psyche like the last vestiges of small-town marketplace carnival. When the crisis erupts it will have gathered force, yet the question remains of how to make public the disruptive potential of this experience of crisis so that it doesn't stay enclosed in the familial arena, since for Bakhtin the extended, protruding, secreting grotesque body was able to resist and destabilise the monumental, static, classical body precisely because of its *openness*.

Publicising the private

What power has the past to upset present cultural norms? The question hinges on the status of negativity, on the relationship between the excluded and the law, between, for Clément, the imaginary and symbolic. As Jane Gallop points out in her article 'Keys to Dora', it comes down to the relationship between public and private. Gallop plays on Freud's note to the Dora case, 'Open or shut is naturally not a matter of indifference', in order to ask whether the hysteric opens the family up or is closed by it.[11] Is her protest enclosed within the family, or does it have the power to alter the structure of the symbolic? Bakhtin notes the importance of the 'openness' of the grotesque body even after it has entered 'great literature', where the grotesque images become 'the means for the artistic and ideological expression of a mighty awareness of history and historic change, which appeared during the Renaissance' (pp. 24–5). But the grotesque spasms which play themselves out on the body of the hysteric are enclosed within the family, or the stage atmosphere of Charcot's hysterical spectacles at the Salpêtrière. If, as Bakhtin claims, the 'openness' of the grotesque images has been steadily denied since the Renaissance (so, for example, the Romantic grotesque becomes symbolic of individual isolation, separated from the material world), if the public sphere has been privatised, then the question is how can it be remade as public speech?[12] As I have noted, for Stallybrass and White the transgressive discourse of the hysteric has no power to change anything since it is part of the problem. The very conception of bourgeois individuality, they argue, has been created by a marginalisation and sublimation of the social force of carnival into individual psychic space, as the bourgeoisie attempt to differentiate themselves from the 'low' collectivity of the 'people'. Moreover, it is in the particular institutions of art and psychoanalysis that carnival lives on as the suppression of the material body of festivity leads to its return within symbolic discursive levels.[13] But while this historical thesis makes possible an illuminating narrative of post-Renaissance society, it overlooks the asymmetrical relation of women to literary and psychoanalytic practice.

Stallybrass and White identify the emergence of a notion of authorship with the beginnings of a relationship of observation and representation, instead of participation, between the subject and carnival; the author places himself above the scene of carnival and thereby transforms it into an object of representation (they instance Jonson's *Bartholomew Fair*). But even as he distances the 'low' carnivalesque activity and creates his identity as an author in opposition to it, it becomes all the more symbolically important in his writing: 'What is excluded at the overt level of identity formation is productive of new objects of desire' (p. 25). Thus the bourgeois subject has a 'dialogic' relation to carnival – the differentiation by which the subject creates his identity is dependent on disgust, but disgust in its turn bears the imprint of desire. So the hysteric's illness results from the Victorian middle-class suppression of the body. Hysteria, and Freud's discourse upon it, represent a '*psychic* irruption of *social* practices which had been suppressed' (p. 176). Here the importance of seeing carnival not simply as the underside of the symbolic order but as engaged in a dialogic relation with it becomes clear. The unconscious is not simply the repository of displaced popular carnival, but is constructed out of a fantasy relation of bourgeois ideology to carnival. Bakhtin, claim Stallybrass and White, wavers between a theory of the grotesque of carnival as oppositional, popular festivity which acts as a negation of the social symbolic order, and carnival as 'hybrid' – a mediation between high and low forms of culture rather than the Other of official culture. Emphasising the importance of the later theory, they argue that it is fruitless merely to positivise the various elements of carnival, to celebrate the body. In this respect, although it is clear that much of their theorising is indebted to Lacanian and Kristevan concepts, the authors are keen to distance themselves from what they argue is a dangerous tendency in theorists such as Kristeva and Foucault to analyse carnival in terms of its liberatory qualities. Celebratory claims for the power of the carnivalesque to undo hierarchies are merely a fetishising of the repressed, a repetition of the desire for lost domains which their book analyses as constitutive of bourgeois subjectivity. 'The bourgeoisie ... is perpetually rediscovering the carnivalesque as a radical source of transcendence', and it is simply misguided 'to associate the exhilarating sense of freedom which transgression affords with any necessary or automatic political progressiveness' (p. 201).

It is important therefore that the question of opening up the hysteric's protest isn't simply reduced to the issue of publicising or publishing a private language, since in those terms it would differ little from literary autobiography, leaving the relationship between the author and the carnival material unchanged. Nevertheless, bearing in mind the gendered nature of the literary and psychoanalytic institutions, women may have a different relationship to carnival, since, as Clément argues, they are both placed together in the zone of the anomalous. Thus the function which the literary work performs for the woman writer may differ in crucial ways from the need to maintain desiring distance from the popular realm which Stallybrass and White analyse as a defining characteristic of authorship. I want to deal with the precise ways in which this relationship might differ in a later section, and here turn instead to an alternative theory of bourgeois distancing, which stresses the importance of the male bourgeoisie's distancing of a specifically female and openly sexual 'low' realm.

In his book *Male Fantasies*, a psychoanalytic study of a group of officers of the Freikorps in Weimar Germany, Klaus Theweleit presents a different history of the creation of bourgeois identity.[14] He stresses the part played by a fantasy construction of womanhood in the evolution of a 'civilised' ego. As important as the 'self-distancing' behaviour by which the bourgeoisie separated themselves from the realm of dirt and servants (here, like Stallybrass and White, he follows Norbert Elias),[15] is the more specific fear of working-class female sexuality, crystallised in the figure of the 'Red Nurse'. Like Clément, Theweleit sees a connection between the figures of the witch and the hysteric, and twentieth-century male fantasies of female sexuality. His history is one of the persecution of female sexuality from burnings to private asylums – there is an internalisation of persecution concomitant with the movement from private to public sphere. For Theweleit, as for Irigaray, the 'unconscious' of bourgeois (and fascist) identity is a historically repressed femaleness. He therefore sees it as 'almost inevitable' that Freud would choose to investigate the psyches of hysterical women because, 'In the course of the repression carried out against women, those two things, the unconscious and femaleness, were so closely coupled together that they came to be seen as nearly identical' (p. 432).

The fantasies of the Freikorps men concerning the 'castrating rifle woman' and 'monstrous' proletarian woman seem to spring from a fear of the free circulation of working-class sexuality. Theweleit points out that the fantasies, though unconnected to women's actual behaviour, did have a bearing on the different sexual mores in working-class communities, notable for the 'conspicuous absence of any Christian bourgeois sexual ethic' (p. 141). The importance of this analysis for the discussion here lies in the soldier males' disgust at the *public* nature of the working-class women's protests and their unashamed displays of sexuality. It was this which inspired their murderous desire:

> The reality of working-class women didn't match the actual experience of soldier males, but it may well have fit in with the horror stories they were fed about erotic, aggressive, 'masculine' women. The war had freed working-class women from the housewife's role they had known beforehand. Forced to become sole providers for their families, many entered the factories. They had organized anti-hunger demonstrations and ransacked display windows. (p. 144)

This freely circulating body of the working-class woman would then be the antithesis of the closed body of the hysteric, contained within the family. But these two worlds are brought together in the figure of the servant girl – the one on the 'threshold' between the family and the world outside. Jane Gallop notes the 'murderous desire' for the servant girl on the part of the male bourgeoisie: 'As a threatening representative of the symbolic, the economic, the extra-familial, the maid must be both seduced (assimilated) and abandoned (expelled).'[16] In the mind of the male bourgeois there is a simple equation between the prostitute and the servant girl. (And Theweleit points out that they were often the same. In Vienna in 1926, seventy percent of registered prostitutes were either servants, unskilled workers or seamstresses. He notes: 'the typical master of the Wilhelmine bourgeois household thought that a kind of right to sexual access went along with the servant girls' (p. 165).) Crucially, of course, there is also an equation between the servant girl and the bourgeois woman. All these women are 'on the market' and any one can be substituted for any other. This is Dora's realisation, and the spur to her hysterical rebellion.[17] Hélène Cixous notes the importance of realising kinship with the other in the circuit of exchange where 'the servant girl is the repressed of the boss's wife' (p. 150). It may be that in order for public protest to be made, the bourgeois woman must realise that she is the same as the maid, for in the masculine economy the hysteric and the prostitute were always the same. In her history of hysteria, I. Veith charts a continuity in the accusation of excessive sexual needs in all these aberrant women, from the witch's copulation with the devil (curable by burning) to the hysteric's masturbation (curable by clitoridectomy). Even when such drastic measures weren't prescribed, Veith records the objections of a Dr Carter to the excessive use of the speculum in consultations with Victorian hysterical women. Frequent internal examination, he claimed, pandered to their worst instincts and placed them in the same category as prostitutes. Freud's 'discovery' of the sexual aetiology of neurosis can be read as the logical continuation of this diagnostic trend.[18]

But if it is the case that 'public' women become associated in male fantasy with the witch and the prostitute (as in the soldier males' fantasies of the proletarian women), how is it possible for women to protest publicly without feeding the network of disgust and desire described by Stallybrass and White, how can they become public on their own terms? The danger is that public woman (the woman who publishes) will merely perform the displaced abjection of the male bourgeoisie – her text will represent a place where the distance from carnivalesque content can be charted in the same moment as it is desired in the act of reading. In making public women's prostitution the writer will be taken for a prostitute herself (she 'sells herself' within the male institution). The poet Medbh McGuckian has made this connection explicit in discussing the difficulties of writing about a private life: 'I feel that you're going public – by writing the poem you're becoming a whore. You're selling your soul which is worse than any prostitution – in a sense you're vilifying your mind. I do feel that must be undertaken with the greatest possible fastidiousness.'[19] The difficulty is for the woman writer to utilise the myths which have been associated with her – to expose the history of her exclusion – without thereby 'making a spectacle' of herself.[20] The transgressive potential of women's writing hinges on the relationship between the excluded and the law. I have argued that for Bakhtin carnival must be brought into dialogue with official forms through the medium of literature, in order to be politically effective; analogously, the lawlessness of the witch, the hysteric and the proletarian woman must be brought within the public sphere, conforming to some extent with its norms, if it is to become a language which can engage politically with the 'official' language. At issue is the move from private production to public 'authorship'. Do women writers repeat the distancing of carnival content in the process of authoring which Stallybrass and White give as the constitutive moment of the institution of literature?

Although it may be valid to criticise modernism's 'transgression' as politically illusory, what this account omits is that authorship is gendered, and for women writers, who were never able to shore up their identity in the institution of literature, it may be precisely through access to representation that the sites of discourse could be altered. Shifted from public sphere to the bourgeois home, carnival ceases to be a site of actual struggle, but the conflicts of the modern private sphere may have generated a social force on to which the bodily energies of carnival have been displaced. Designated marginal to the dominant forms of culture, the attempt of many contemporary women writers to introduce the concerns of the private domestic sphere into the public discourse of literature entails a theoretical as well as a representational intervention, as it fuses the private (unofficial) side of women's narrative with the public (official literary) norm. So feminist poetry challenges the dominant literary canon by inscribing a different relationship to personal history, the body, the history of women's exclusion. In making a claim for the importance of the 'personal' and experiential nature of recent feminist poetry as a denial of distance, I am aware of the warning made most recently by Jan Montefiore against criticism of women's texts 'based on the assumption that what makes a poem valuable or interesting is its author's awareness of her own dilemma as a woman'.[21] Montefiore urges critics not to read poems for the way they show the writer to have been the emotional victim of patriarchy; rather it is important to be aware of what makes the poem *different* from autobiography. But conversely, the danger is a reading of feminist poetry which would repeat the canonical critical gesture which denies such 'personal' and experiential testimony its status as literature. The poetry is attempting to make an intervention on the level of acceptable representations, and any theoretical approach to feminist writing must allow it to retain its specificity as literature while being aware that at the same time it aims to change the sites of discourse. The challenge of feminist poetry is precisely a *literary* challenge, and only through that a political one; the text attempts to change the literary norm in formal ways, and through this the forms of cultural authority which it indirectly figures, as the literary canon comes to stand for the values of the dominant culture.[22]

But the ability of overtly feminist writing to remake public norms in this way is denied by theorists such as Julia Kristeva, for whom women's writing, precisely because of its position outside the dominant literary culture, is destined to remain always a negative, possessing no lever with which to prise open the realm of authoritative values. It is interesting therefore that Stallybrass and White criticise Kristeva for investing too much in literary transgression. For them, Kristeva 'confuses the projection of bourgeois desire with the destruction of its class identity' (p. 201). It is her simple positivisation of Bakhtinian carnival which means that she will only be able to alter representations rather than the sites of discourse. But what prevents Kristeva from entertaining radical subversion of the subject is her psychoanalytic orthodoxy; any text which privileges the semiotic without at the same time bolstering the law of the Father is psychotic. So transgression is no more than a cathartic outlet for the pre-oedipal in the repressed phallic subject. Transgression must accept 'another law', as she says in 'Word, dialogue, and novel', or it will be mere linguistic play.[23] Kristeva warns of the dangers for the woman writer, estranged from language: 'if no paternal "legitimation" comes along to dam up the inexhaustible non-symbolised impulse, she collapses into psychosis and suicide.'[24] With regard to women's writing, her emphasis on the need for the law means that she cannot see it as transgressive at all. Women's texts are too 'hysterical' to be truly disruptive: 'When a woman novelist does not produce a family of her own, she creates an imaginary story through which she constitutes an identity: narcissism is safe, the ego becomes eclipsed after freeing itself, purging itself of reminiscences. Freud's statement "the hysteric suffers mostly from reminiscence" sums up the large majority of novels produced by women.'[25]

So the question of whether the hysteric is contained or not, open or shut, is intimately connected to the question of reminiscence discussed earlier. In representing the past as symptom (which can have no efficacy), she seems destined to remain trapped by the past, rather than to offer a vision of the future. Turned the other way, the question concerns the possibility of entertaining a relationship to the past which isn't simply one of mastery. For Freud and Breuer in *Studies on Hysteria*, the successful cure of the hysteric involves a type of catharsis in which the repressed past (the initial trauma) is led into the light of rationality, and thus diffused. So, just as the persistence of memory is connected to repressed reaction, curing the hysteric may mean killing the past and its innovating force in the present. (Stallybrass and White note that Freud's early method involved reproducing grotesque material in comic form: 'When Frau Emmy can at last look at the "grotesque figures" and "laugh without a trace of fear", it is as if Freud had managed a singular restitution, salvaging the torn shreds of carnival from their phobic alienation in the bourgeois unconscious by making them once more the object of cathartic laughter' (p. 171). But such laughter can be read as the diffusion of the power to protest, a mastery of the psyche of the hysteric.)

Staging hysteria

If the personal and cultural past to which the hysteric is bound is to be effective it must be communicable, representing rather than represented. But if Theweleit is correct in interpreting the figures of mad and possessed women as male fantasies, in what way can they become productive images for women? In historical terms, Natalie Zemon Davies has shown how the image of the disorderly woman was able at certain times to widen behavioural patterns for women, sanctioning riots and political disobedience. There is a certain 'spillover into everyday life' from the inverted carnivalesque activity: thus women are shown ways to protest through 'mimicry' of the 'unruly' roles offered them.[26] The hysteric's reminiscence involves several types of repetition or mimicry.[27] Firstly there is what Stallybrass and White describe as a pantomime of carnival in the psyche, a repetition of social carnival in the unconscious (and, importantly, in the comic cathartic cure). Again, the hysteric's symptoms show a continuity with the past through repetition as symbol (Dora's facial neuralgia reproduces the slap she gives to Herr K). As Clément points out, it is this display of the past which gives the hysteric her power: 'That is how the hysteric, reputed to be incurable, sometimes – and more and more often – took on the role of a resistant heroine: the one whom psychoanalytic treatment would never be able to *reduce*' (p. 8). But this resistance can only act as a limit on the master discourse, especially since it is performed as a spectacle for the master. Mary Russo in her article 'Female grotesques: carnival and theory' examines the problems of female 'spectacle' in relation to hysteria. The staged photographs from the Salpêtrière 'can be read as double somatisations of the women patients whose historical performances were lost to themselves and recuperated into the medical science and medical discourse which maintain their oppressive hold on women'.

Bearing this in mind, Russo asks whether it is possible that the 'display' and 'stagings' of hysteria may be used to 'rig us up (for lack of the phallic term) into discourse'.[28] Is it possible that the recontextualisation of the discourse and representations of the hysteric may be able to overturn the master discourse, to turn the staged play upside-down? Luce Irigaray argues that it is in 'La Mystérique', where she encourages women to mime their hysterisation by the master: 'She is pure at last because she has pushed to extremes the repetition of this abjection, this revulsion, this horror to which she has been condemned, to which, mimetically, she had condemned herself.' Rather than a recontextualisation of the 'high' discourse in the realm of the 'low', as in carnival, this strategy involves a repetition of the woman's speculisation as object of the master discourse, but in a different context. Irigaray puts forward such 'subversive mimesis' as the only possible means for women to speak within patriarchal ideology. Parody takes place not in the way suggested by Bakhtin for the carnivalesque, which inverts the established hierarchy, but by representing the position of the 'low'. Irigaray asserts that women's capacity for resisting the patriarchal order stems not from an ability to take up a masculine subject position (since 'any theory of the subject is always appropriated by the masculine'), but from her ability to disrupt the subject/object split from her position as intractable object, insecure 'ground' of masculine speculations.

'Mimesis' entails taking up the role historically assigned to the feminine – Freud's 'masquerade of femininity'. Irigaray claims that in the reproduction of this role there always remains an excess, a part which is not accounted for in masculine speculations. She sees her task as the interpretation of that irreducible femininity which remains even when the speaker takes part in the masquerade.[29] But she leaves unanswered the important question of the speaker's intentions. Is it the speaker's consciousness that she is being subversive which makes her so, or is every statement by a woman within the masculine economy in fact subversive? Crucial in Irigaray's formulation is that the repetition would differ from the original spectacle in that it would no longer be performed for men. But it is difficult to see how such a 'new' context would be definable or recognisable. How would a truly transgressive hysteria differ from a recuperable one? The woman, Irigaray states, 'still subsists, otherwise and elsewhere than where she mimes so well what is asked of her. Because her own "self" remains foreign to the whole staging ... Her sex is heterogeneous to this whole economy of representation, but it is capable of interpreting that economy precisely because it has remained "outside".'[30] Can the representation of the self as a riddle in fact avoid mastery and masculine appropriation? Might it not instead reconfirm the Freudian thesis of female sexuality as a dark continent, i.e. precisely the scenario which encourages man to possess and conquer it?

For Irigaray the dreams and riddles of 'La Mystérique' are able to 'recast the roles that history has laid down for subject and object', but there is surely a danger that speaking in riddles, reproducing the discourse of the hysteric, will merely serve to make more complex the veils that are laid over the female. As Sarah Kofman argues, for Freud it was 'by virtue of her sexuality that woman is enigmatic, for sexuality is what constitutes the "great riddle" of life which accounts for the entire difference between men and women'. Female sexuality thus acquires a privileged status as the object of study; the secret of their sex is hidden by the 'shame' and 'modesty' which civilisation expects from them. Kofman describes Freud's investigation into female sexuality as a desire to uncover the whole story:

> Because woman does not have the right to speak, she stops being capable or desirous of speaking: she 'keeps' everything to herself, and creates an excess of mystery and obscurity as if to avenge herself, as if striving for mastery. Woman lacks sincerity, she dissimulates, transforms each word into an enigma, an indecipherable riddle. That is why the patient's narrative is always foreshortened, defective, disconnected, incomplete, lacking in 'links'.[31]

On the one hand, Irigaray would suggest that dissimulation, or covering up the 'truth', may be a means of subverting the existing order. On the other this veiling may differ little from traditional modesty. The male reader/subject is then drawn on by the mystery and disguise with which the object is veiled and spurred on to discover the 'truth' about the female, which in this guise differs little from the traditional 'dark continent' by which she has always been represented. The patient/woman's narrative is probed, opened up for the secrets it can tell about her sex. Here I want to look at two 'riddling' narratives, one author(is)ed by a man, one written and published by a woman, in order to ask if there is a difference when woman 'authors' herself.

The case histories presented by Freud and Breuer in which they document the importance of 'verbal utterance' in the cathartic cure of the hysteric are notable for the way the utterance itself is repressed. The hysteric's text is not present but represented by the texts of the male scientists. In his case history of Anna O, Breuer admires his patient's 'poetical compositions' but presents his own narrative as a substitute for them. He fills in the missing links in her 'defective narrative'. Moreover, the two narratives lead in opposite directions – while Anna O's narrative circles back to the previous year in its repetition of events, Breuer's narrative denies this cyclical movement, replacing it with a linear progression from the onset of the sickness, through a worsening of the symptoms after her father's death, to eventual cure. Unable to write her own diary (Breuer uses her mother's diary to 'check' her creations for accuracy), Anna O instead 'lived through the previous winter day by day'. Her 'poetry' consists of a personal documentation, its content the daily release of 'imaginative products' associated with the events of the day. Breuer describes how things have become 'stuck' inside her, which cause a diffusion of tension on release: 'She knew that after she had given utterance to her hallucinations, she would lose all her obstinacy, and what she described as her "energy".' The things which are stuck are the source of her energy, but Anna O is content at this point to have her energy diffused before an audience of one – so she is 'open' about her secrets (specifically she is open to Breuer in her phantom pregnancy), but closed to the world at the same time.[32]

McGuckian's poetry, by contrast, is enigmatically 'closed' to the reader in its syntactical difficulty, but widely available. McGuckian seems to be looking for a way to speak about women's experience which avoids being 'probed', a riddling discourse which will be public and at the same time distinctively different, disruptive of the normative codes of literary discourse. Her poetry has often been criticised for its obscurity, an enigmatic difficulty which is connected to a tendency to describe personal and political events through the metaphor of the female body. Whether the woman's body is open or closed is of crucial importance to McGuckian: 'open' during sex and pregnancy, is the body thereby closed off to other roles and modes of authority? The antithesis to the opened up body of the mother is the self-sufficient body of the Victorian maid or governess, who becomes symbolic in her poetry of 'single-mind-edness'. But this self-sufficiency is contained; like tulips which 'double-lock in tiers as whistle-tight'[33] against the intrusive rain, the Victorian woman is 'dry' and non-reproductive. McGuckian wants to find a way to connect these self-contained units, to link the separate histories of these women in order to make that history itself productive of new possibilities. And this entails the dangerous and ambivalent practice of being 'open'. 'I'm trying to make the dead women of Ireland, who I am the living memory of, I'm trying to give them articulation, if anything. In that sense I'm trying to make their lives not a total waste, that they didn't live in vain, that they have no record at all.' She undertakes this history writing through personal recordings of the 'poetry' of her everyday life. Like Anna O's compositions her poems constitute a diary – the poems are

> lies that are no longer true for what I am at the minute. They're like days in a diary which you've crossed out. But you're very involved with them when you need them – they seem so much waste. They've helped you through that day, and that's all they can do. And if they help anyone else who comes after you – you feel that they couldn't because no one else would possibly be in such a terrible state as you were.

The function of the poem is private (a private 'easing' similar to Anna O's compositions), yet once put into circulation the function alters as it bears witness to a private life. The poem 'Sabbath Park' is a battle over reminiscence – a struggle between stifling Protestant Victoriana and an attempt to carve out a space for female, Catholic creativity. Its analogue in the poet's life is when she moved into a large house in a once Protestant area of Belfast; in a gloss on the poem McGuckian has said, 'Louisa is the Victorian ghost who still inhabits the place, the Victorian novelist I sometimes feel tempted or frightened of lapsing into. I'm in battle with the house and my own history, the literary-political history of women, chastity or death.' Read thus the poem is one of affirmation, a celebration of growing strength due to battling with her own, her sex's and her country's history. Rather than attempt to achieve mastery of the past, like Anna O she goes backwards in order to go forwards. Putting into question the notion of history as a progression, her cyclical narrative returns to the hysterical crisis suffered by the Victorian woman, in order to investigate ways out. This entails reciprocity between the Protestant and Catholic women, so she puts 'faith' in a 'less official' entrance as she climbs into the past through the window of the house. She is the opposite of the law as she enters to take control of the house – childish and accidental she 'upsets' the obsolete world of Victoriana gestured towards in 'damask', 'lawn' and 'safari':

> Now, after a year misspent on the ragged
> Garden side of the door, I put faith
> In a less official entrance, the accidental
> Oblongs of the windows that I find
> Have neither catch nor pulley. Broody
> As a seven-months' child, I upset
> The obsolete drawing-room that still seems
> Affronted by people having just gone,
> By astonishing Louisa with my sonnets,
> Almost a hostage in the dream
> Of her mother's hands – that would leave them
> Scattered over their damask sofas after
> Some evening party, filled
> With the radiance of my fine lawn shirt.[34]

This introduction of modern confusion into the conventional femininity of the Victorian house is a byproduct of the speaker's search for her own mother, her own history. For the room she enters, like the mother, is both traditional and 'absent' or 'lost'. Like the Victorian woman she becomes 'almost' a hostage of Louisa's mother, but it is precisely because the house is dragging her 'into its age' that she is able to create. The malady is productive:

> I feel the swaggering beginnings
> Of a new poem flaring up, because the house
> Is dragging me into its age, the malady
> Of fireplaces crammed with flowers, even
> On a golden winter Sunday. No matter
> How hysterically the clouds swing out,
> They may not alter by one drop of rain
> The safari of the garden beds, or make
> Louisa's dress with its oyster-coloured overlay
> Of moss kidnap me kindly for a day,
> As though a second wife were sleeping
> Already in your clothes, the sewn
> Lilies near the ground growing downward.

The final lines effect a break with previous dead history – she will not be trapped by the reversed growth from the shroud of her embattled history. This is because, unlike Louisa and Anna O, she is able to make public the things which are 'stuck' inside her. The woman's psychic upset can be channelled through literature so that it may 'upset' social norms. An earlier poem, 'The seed picture', associates an enigmatic writing with the possibility of 'liberation'. McGuckian makes her portrait with seeds, her picture of Joanna will be able to grow with the body of the girl it represents:

> the clairvoyance
> Of seed work has opened up
> New spectrums of activity, beyond a second home.
> The seeds dictate their own vocabulary
> Their dusty colours capture
> More than we can plan.[35]

But this opening up is itself contained as the artist again goes backwards into the girl's history:

> Was it such self-indulgence to enclose her
> In the border of a grandmother's sampler,
> Bonding all the seeds in one continuous skin?

It is the connection with previously excluded history (the grandmother's needle-work) which creates that other 'transgressive' language which has its 'own vocabulary'. It is not simply an avant-garde practice but an attempt to open up the protests of the women of the past by seeing their similarity with the feminist protest of the present, just as Bakhtinian carnival brings together the crises of the past and present.

Of course one important consideration which I haven't touched on in this article is the necessity for this literary protest not simply to be contained in individual texts or works, but to be carried out within the framework of other attempts to alter the construction of the dominant literary institution. Developments such as feminist publishing houses are of crucial importance to this enterprise, because of the need to control the way texts are received and read, in order to prevent their objectification and marginalisation within the institution. It is in this respect that Bakhtin's warning that carnival became powerless when contained within texts which had lost the power to dialogise official forms, because of a narrowing of the literary institution, should act as a reminder against the tendency to celebrate the carnivalesque within specific texts.

In *The Female Malady*, Elaine Showalter warns against the dangers of a simple positivisation of women's madness, and the tendency to treat it as an archetypal form of protest when in fact it is a form of containment. And yet she draws a parallel rather than an opposition between the Victorian hysteric and the growing protest of the suffrage movement. Just as suffragettes in Holloway gaol were treated as hysterics (in the same way that Theweleit notes women protesters being treated as witches), so 'the elements of hunger, rebellion and rage latent in the phenomenon of female nervous disorder became explicit in the tactics of the suffrage campaigns'.[36] The suffragettes were able to utilise the link between female protest and madness, a link which was designed to exclude them further, in order to broadcast the contained protest of the hysteric. And so too a literature which draws on the female rebellion of the past may be able to bring it into conflict with official public patriarchal norms.

Notes

1 Peter Stallybrass and Allon White, *The Politics and Poetics of Transgression*, London and Ithaca, 1986; subsequent page references are given in the text.

2 Stallybrass and White implicitly acknowledge the politically progressive nature of women's relationship to transgression when they state, 'Only a challenge to the hierarchy of *sites* of discourse, which usually comes from groups and classes "situated" by the dominant in low or marginal positions, carries the promise of politically transformative power' (p. 201).

3 Hélène Cixous and Catherine Clément, *The Newly Born Woman*, trans. Betsy Wing, Manchester and Minneapolis, 1986; subsequent page references are given in the text.

4 Although I will be looking specifically at the work of McGuckian, my argument is a more general one; I mean it to hold for radical feminist poetry, and the poetry of female experience, such as work by Adrienne Rich, Audre Lorde, and Muriel Rukseyer.

5 Mikhail Bakhtin, *Rabelais and His World*, trans. Hélène Iswolsky, Cambridge, Mass., and London, 1968, p. 73; subsequent page references are given in the text.

6 See also p. 471: 'The influence of the centuries-old hidden linguistic dogmatism on human thought, and especially on artistic imagery, is of great importance. If the creative spirit lives on in one language only, or if several languages coexist but remain strictly divided without struggling for supremacy, it is impossible to overcome this dogmatism buried in the depths of linguistic consciousness. It is possible to place oneself outside one's own language only when an essential historic change occurs.'

7 Robert Young makes a similar point in relation to heteroglossia and the novel in 'Back to Bakhtin', *Cultural Critique*, 2, 1985–86, pp. 71–92. Young argues against critics who analyse carnival in terms of its 'social force' while neglecting its linguistic dimension, and emphasises Bakhtin's awareness of the need for the 'artistic organisation' of the ordinary languages of the people which takes place in the novel.

8 Sigmund Freud and Joseph Breuer, *Studies on Hysteria*, Pelican Freud Library, vol. 3, London, 1974, p. 107.

9 For poems by Rich memorialising female communities and the women of the past, see especially the volumes *The Dream of a Common Language*, New York, 1978, and *A Wild Patience Has Taken Me This Far*, New York, 1981.

10 Freud, *The Origins of Psychoanalysis*, New York, 1954, p. 175. Freud of course later rejected this theory of the traumatic inception of neurosis on his 'discovery' of infantile sexuality.

11 Jane Gallop, 'Keys to Dora', in Charles Bernheimer and Claire Kahane, eds, *In Dora's Case*, London, 1985, p. 204. See Freud, 'A case of hysteria', in *Case Histories I: Dora and Little Hans*, Pelican Freud Library, vol. 6, London, 1977, p. 102.

12 Several recent critiques of Habermas, notably by Nancy Fraser and Iris Marion Young, have stressed the importance for feminism and other resistance movements of including some notion of particularism, and values from the private sphere, in rational public discourse. Fraser suggests using the 'private' separate female community as a basis for the construction of a type of discourse which can then enter the public arena: 'separatism, while inadequate as a long-term political strategy, is in many cases a shorter-term necessity for women's physical, psychological and moral survival; and separatist communities have been the source of numerous reinterpretations of women's experience which have proved politically fruitful in contestation over the means of interpretation and communication' ('Habermas and gender', in Seyla Benhabib and Drucilla Cornell, eds, *Feminism as Critique*, Oxford, 1987, p. 54. See also Iris Marion Young's essay on the separation between private and public spheres, 'Impartiality and the civic public', *ibid.*, pp. 57–76).

13 But, as I have argued, for Bakhtin 'actual', nonliterary carnival is unorganised and politically ineffective.

14 Klaus Theweleit, *Male Fantasies*, Cambridge, 1987; subsequent page references are given in the text.

15 See Norbert Elias, *The Civilising Process*, vols. 1 and 2, New York, 1978 and 1982.

16 Gallop, 'Keys', p. 216. On the concept of 'threshold', see p. 215.

17 'No woman tolerates hearing (even if it is about the other woman), "My wife, a woman who is my woman, can be nothing". That is murder. So Dora, hearing it, knowing that the servant-girl had already heard it, sees woman, her mother, the maid, die, she sees woman massacred to make room for her. But she knows she will have her turn at being massacred. Her terrific reaction is to slap Mr. K' (Cixous and Clément, *The Newly Born Woman*, p. 153).

18 I. Veith, *Hysteria: The History of a Disease*, Chicago, 1965, p. 210. On

witches and burning, see also Keith Thomas, *Religion and the Decline of Magic*, London, 1971, pp. 435–86. On clitoridectomy (specifically Isaac Baker Brown's surgeries), see Elaine Showalter, *The Female Malady*, London, 1987, pp. 75–7; for Brown's own testimony, see Sheila Jeffreys, ed., *The Sexuality Debates*, London, 1987, pp. 11–42.

19 Interview of Medbh McGuckian by Clair Wills, Belfast, November 1986; subsequent prose quotations from McGuckian are taken from these interviews. Margaret Homans notes that it was considered scandalous in the early nineteenth century for a woman to write publicly: 'if she did, she was judged not as a writer but as a woman' (*Women Writers and Poetic Identity*, Princeton, 1980, p. 5). This tendency to look for a woman's sex in her words has of course continued.

20 Mary Russo, 'Female grotesques: carnival and theory', in Teresa de Lauretis, ed., *Feminist Studies/Critical Studies*, Basingstoke, 1988, p. 200.

21 Jan Montefiore, *Feminism and Poetry*, London, 1987, p. 5. This is a tendency which marks Sandra Gilbert and Susan Gubar's *The Madwoman in the Attic*. See also, for an argument aimed specifically at poetry, Alicia Suskin Ostriker's analysis of a 'line of feeling' traced through the history of women's poetry in *Stealing the Language*, Boston, 1986.

22 Extending the Russian Formalist idea of 'norm-breaking', John Frow provides an excellent account of the way in which literary norms come to 'stand for' dominant cultural norms: 'The literary canon acts as an exemplary mode of authority and comes to bear a heavy charge of value through which literature comes to "stand for" (though rarely *completely*) the whole realm of authoritative values' (*Marxism and Literary History*, Oxford, 1986, p. 128).

23 Julia Kristeva, 'Word, dialogue, and novel', in *Desire in Language*, ed. Leon S. Roudiez, trans. Thomas Gora, Alice Jardine and Leon S. Roudiez, New York, 1980, p. 71. Whereas for Frow the problem with Kristeva's concept of transgression is that it is not literary *enough*: 'the problem is that the notion of a social text does not allow us to discriminate between the ways in which different kinds of codes or discourse function in the literary text, and in particular to account for the literary code' (*Marxism*, p. 127).

24 Kristeva, *About Chinese Women*, New York, 1986, p. 41.

25 Kristeva, 'Oscillation between power and denial', in Elaine Marks and Isabelle de Courtivron, eds, *New French Feminisms*, Brighton and New York, 1981, p. 166.

26 Natalie Zemon Davies, *Society and Culture in Early Modern France*, London, 1975 (see especially pp. 124–51).

27 Veith notes the hysteric's aptitude for mimicry. Convulsive attacks in hysteria had become rare in Charcot's time, but when, because of lack of space, hysterics had to be housed with epileptic patients in the same wing at the Salpêtrière, they occurred frequently as mimicked epileptic fits (*Hysteria*, p. 230). See also, on the hysteric's 'histrionic' ability, Showalter, *The Female Malady*, pp. 152–4.

28 Russo, 'Female grotesques', p. 223. In some ways, of course, the language of the hysteric was never private, contained discourse, since it only became known and publicised as 'hysterical' through the official public discourse of

the scientist.

29 Luce Irigaray, 'La Mystérique', in *Speculum of the Other Woman*, Ithaca, 1985, pp. 191–202. See also in the same volume the sections 'A very black sexuality', pp. 66–73, and 'The avoidance of (masculine) hysteria', pp. 268–78.

30 Irigaray, *This Sex Which is Not One*, Ithaca, 1985, p. 152.

31 Sarah Kofman, *The Enigma of Woman*, Ithaca, 1985, pp. 36–7, 43.

32 Freud and Breuer, 'Fräulein Anna O', in *Studies*, pp. 74–102. Bertha Pappenheim was later to need both obstinacy and energy in her public reformist career.

33 McGuckian, 'Tulips', in *The Flower Master*, Oxford, 1982, p. 10.

34 McGuckian, 'Sabbath Park', in *Venus and the Rain*, Oxford, 1984, p. 54.

35 McGuckian, 'The seed picture', in *The Flower Master*, p. 23.

36 Showalter, *The Female Malady*, p. 162.

Brian Poole

From phenomenology to dialogue: Max Scheler's phenomenological tradition and Mikhail Bakhtin's development from 'Toward a philosophy of the act' to his study of Dostoevsky

Introduction

Rumour has it that Bakhtin scholars persist in adding water to the good wine. Witness the 'overuse and dilution' of Bakhtin's terms, the 'embarrassment we now feel upon the words "dialogue" or "carnival" dropped once too often in academic conversation'.[1] What we are serving up is losing its taste. One solution would be to examine Bakhtin's categories, and not just the terms. For, as many know, Bakhtin often uses a number of words to refer to a single phenomenon. But this leaves us with the problem of repetition. No matter what we say, we're still predicating Bakhtin's name. He wrote it all – earlier and better than anyone else. In the first edition of the present volume David Shepherd spoke of the 'tired gesture by which the Soviet theorist is burdened with the credit for having, either singlehandedly or with a little help from his friends, always already anticipated and surpassed the most significant theoretical trends of recent decades'.[2]

This is where the dilution begins. The problem Shepherd raised is how to escape the tautology of illuminating Bakhtin as the author of his own intellectual context. Bakhtin invented no new categories (few philosophers do). The development of his terminology lies in the sources he used. But errors in dating Bakhtin's texts complicate the vital question of Bakhtin's sources and his tradition. The 'anticipation' Bakhtin is credited with has impeded serious research and interpretation.

Bakhtin's own sources clarify his intentions. My goal is to unearth the sources of Bakhtin's phenomenology in his 'early works': 'Toward a philosophy of the act' and 'Author and hero in aesthetic activity'.[3] The influence of Max Scheler and his students in phenomenology provides the interpretive key. On the basis of internal evidence and archive materials I believe these 'early works' were composed in 1927. This assumption has consequences for the issue of Bakhtin's authorship of books by Voloshinov and Medvedev. It also suggests that Bakhtin's 'early works' are more closely related to the first edition of his study of Dostoevsky than we currently assume. The necessity of demonstrating my claims requires rather intensive quotation. I can only hope that the methodology and results of this paper will offer a humble contribution to the field.

Dating Scheler's influence on Bakhtin

Scheler's influence on Bakhtin is difficult to date. In the protocols of Bakhtin's interrogation on 28 December 1928, among his activities 'from 1924 to 1928' (a vague reference coinciding with his years in Leningrad) Bakhtin admitted that he had held two brief lectures (*referaty*) on Max Scheler:

> The first lecture was on confession. Confession, according to Scheler, is the revelation of one's self before an other which makes social ('word') that which had striven to its asocial and extraverbal border ('sin') and was an isolated, unlivedout foreign body in the inner life of the individual. The second lecture concerned resurrection. In brief: life is not resurrected for its own sake, but for the sake of the value which is revealed in it by love.[4]

This language appears to bridge the terminological gap separating Bakhtin's 'early works' from the first edition of his study of Dostoevsky. How close are they chronologically?

Dating Bakhtin's 'early works'

The dating of almost all of Bakhtin's works has seldom been an issue. It should be.[5] There are a number of arguments against dating Bakhtin's extant 'early texts' to a period prior to his arrival in Leningrad in 1924.[6] We cannot trust the author's memory. Bakhtin constructed his biography *post factum* to match his publications or his needs. The most reliable evidence concerning Bakhtin's early period is his correspondence with his best friend M. I. Kagan. Here Bakhtin refers to a study of the 'subject of ethics and the subject of law' which he 'began' in June 1921 and 'laid aside' some six months later (January 1922).[7]

This appears to date something. But:

1   There is *no* reason to suppose that Bakhtin is referring in this letter to the fragments we know as 'Toward a philosophy of the act' and/or 'Author and hero in aesthetic activity'; the plan of the former title extends well beyond the limits of a study of law and ethics (TPA, p. 54).

2   Bakhtin was repeatedly bedridden with an inflammation of the bone marrow in his leg (osteomyelitis); he never finished school for that reason. S. I. Kagan, Kagan's wife, believed Bakhtin was 'doomed' when she met him in Vitebsk in 1922.[8]

3   In 1922 Bakhtin also reported: 'I am now writing a work on Dostoevsky which I hope to finish *very soon*.'[9] Archive evidence *proves* that Bakhtin's study of Dostoevsky as we know it was still being *researched* in 1927. The material he collected during that year had a profound influence on the final product. If a work Bakhtin hopes to finish swiftly in 1922 is still evolving substantially in 1927, we must assume that his other texts could have passed through a similarly protracted evolution.

4   Pumpyanskii's notes from Bakhtin's lectures during 1924–25 indicate that Bakhtin was still developing the material for his early works.[10] Long gestation may be a characteristic of all Bakhtin's projects prior to the amputation of his leg; thereafter his health and productivity increased.

I turn now to the internal evidence.

The 'Scheler notebook'

In a large notebook (136 pages) compiled no earlier than late 1926, Bakhtin's notes for his study of Dostoevsky (a selection of quotations from works by Otto Kaus, Hans Prager, Askol'dov, Komarovich, Grossman and Engelhardt[11]) are prefaced by an overwhelming fifty-eight pages of excerpts from Scheler's *The Essence and Forms of Sympathy*.[12] The excerpts begin with three bibliographical references culled from the preface to the third edition of Scheler's work: Theodor Litt's *Individual and Society*;[13] Helmut Plessner and Frederik J. J. Buytendijk's essay 'The interpretation of mime expression';[14] and Viktor Emil von Gebsattel's essay 'The individual and his spectator'.[15] These titles not only illustrate the direction in which others were developing Scheler's ideas: they suggest a critical perspective from which Bakhtin found application for Scheler's ethical 'personalism' while writing 'Toward a philosophy of the act', 'Author and hero in aesthetic activity' and his study of Dostoevsky. These three bibliographical references appear together only in the Preface to the third edition of Scheler's *The Essence and Forms of Sympathy* (1926); since Scheler directs his readers' attention to the third edition of Litt's *Individual and Society* (Litt's 'Preface' is dated September 1926), I assume that Scheler's book appeared late in 1926 and reached Bakhtin no earlier than towards the end of that year. In what follows I shall demonstrate the relevance of this material for Bakhtin's 'early works' and his study of Dostoevsky. In view of the (current) impossibility of dating Bakhtin's early works external with evidence, only an analysis of the sources Bakhtin collected in 1926–27 and corresponding internal textual evidence can clarify Bakhtin's assimilation and application of Scheler's thought and phenomenological tradition. I shall return to the issue of dating Bakhtin's texts on *internal* evidence towards the end of this essay.

Bakhtin's reception of Max Scheler

In 1929 Bakhtin attributed to Scheler a prominent role in the theory of his study of Dostoevsky: 'At present, and on the terrain of idealism, the fundamental (*printsipal'naya*) critique of monologism as a specific Kantian form of idealism has begun. *Especially* noteworthy are the works of Max Scheler: *The Essence and Forms of Sympathy* (1926) and *Formalism in Ethics and Material Value-Ethics* (1921).'[16] The words 'especially noteworthy' tell us that Bakhtin's reception of Scheler must be seen primarily but not exclusively in relation to Scheler's two major successes, his study in ethics and his critique of theories of empathy.[17] These two immensely popular works justify Voloshinov's characterisation of Scheler as 'the most influential German philosopher of our time, the major representative of the direction of phenomenology'.[18]

Bakhtin's 'early works' contain a close application of the tradition of phenomenology inspired by Max Scheler; they thus remain critical of Husserl's transcendentalism and are not related to his egological intersubjectivity. The *systematic* correspondences with Scheler are overwhelming; but they have been largely overlooked. In 'Toward a philosophy of the act' Bakhtin combines a broad spectrum of concerns under an allusive, yet limited, philosophical framework and vocabulary. Here Bakhtin is both a critical and a programmatic thinker. At the centre of his programme is the act itself. The act is trenchantly rooted in the reciprocity of the 'I' and the 'other' (and not Buber's 'I' and 'Thou'). In 'Author and hero in aesthetic activity' Bakhtin speaks of the 'category of the other' (for instance, pp. 52, 53, 59). The 'emotional–volitional acts' Bakhtin discusses in 'Toward a philosophy of the act' engender an emphatic sense of 'participation' and 'participatory thinking', an alternative to the 'theoretism' dominating the philosophy of the turn of the century. Emotional–volitional acts are not primarily acts of cognition, but rather acts of lived co-experiencing. These conceptions are developed in a critique of empathy (*Einfühlung*), on the one hand, and in a critical review of theories of 'material' and 'formal' ethics, on the other. For many of Bakhtin's categories no sources have yet been found. True, Bakhtin never cites Scheler in 'Toward a philosophy of the act' and 'Author and hero in aesthetic activity'. And yet his critique of 'material and formal ethics' already contains the title of Scheler's mammoth study.[19]

Scheler's sympathetic feeling and the critique of *Einfühlung*

Aesthetic and psychological theories of empathy often err, according to Scheler, in that they do not take as their point of departure the person in his actions and volition, but the individual passive observer who, in his empathetic or sympathetic experience, merely *duplicates* that which appears to be contained in his observations. Genuine empathy, so Scheler claims, is an act expressing its own entirely personal ethical value. The theoretical demands on what Scheler calls 'sympathetic feeling' are particularly poignant because ethical considerations are subordinated to what appear to be aesthetic categories.

Scheler maintains that nothing is more misleading than the notion that 'co-experiencing' (there are many kinds) is in and of itself an ethical act. It is entirely possible, and even meaningful, to say 'I can imagine just how you feel but I don't have any sympathy for you': here the sense of how another feels 'remains in the sphere of cognition'.[20] The ability to feel precisely how someone else feels, if it were possible, would actually be bereft of any ethical value. For 'feeling with' or 'experiencing' in mimetic reproduction (*Nacherleben*) may also exclude any sense of participating (*Teilnehmen*).[21] Bakhtin noted in his synopsis of Scheler's study of sympathy: 'We feel the quality of another's suffering without co-suffering, we feel the quality of another's joy without co-enjoyment.'[22] Pages of Bakhtin's 'Toward a philosophy of the act' and 'Author and hero in aesthetic activity' are dedicated to the problems related to this phenomenon. Nevertheless, the ethical aspect Bakhtin refers to is far more elusive.

Scheler's distinctions clarify the issues. Four basic types of empathy are often conflated into a single category:[23]

1   The immediate co-feeling with one another (*Mit-einander-fühlen*) of one and the same occasion of joy or suffering. For example, a 'father and mother before the corpse of their beloved child'. They feel the same grief, and know that they do; but they do not feel one another's suffering objectively. Rather, they co-experience their commiseration with one another. 'There is no co-pain.' Their commiseration with one another is not the same as their own suffering. Such 'commiseration' expresses a 'value-content' never contained in mere sensory stimulation or physical feeling. It presupposes the existence of 'the highest form of love'.[24]

2   In this case once again suffering is not 'the cause' of empathy. All 'sympathy' contains the *intention* of feeling grief or joy upon the occasion of the experience of another; it is not simply a part of the objective judgement that the other suffers. It begins 'in the face of another's suffering' and is directed towards it. In sympathetic feeling with *someone else's* sense of suffering (e.g., '*your* child has died'), however, my sympathy and the other's grief are 'phenomenologically two distinct facts' and not one, as in the first case.[25]

3   The infection (*Ansteckung*) of feeling, its contagious spread, where the distinction between one's own feeling and another's is lost, as in the humorous atmosphere in a bar, where the spread of laughter itself 'infects' others, or the cry of terror that excites an atmosphere of horror undifferentiated by individual experience.[26] 'Genuine sympathy', factual 'participation', is the product of *both* the 'given existence of the feelings of another' *and* the 'value-content belonging to it in the very phenomenon of sympathy'.[27] The former cannot exist without the latter. Precisely the contrary is the case in infectious emotion. Here co-feeling is void of the ethical dimension expressed in genuine sympathy. Infectious emotional states can be observed in advanced forms of vital-biological life and they are comparable to the panic reaction of masses incited by contagious undifferentiated suggestion (Stalin!).

4   Finally, there are the various types of 'unitary feeling' (*Einsfühlung*[28]) which encompass 'the most primitive form of empathy';[29] they describe extreme cases of 'infection' or 'contagious feeling' and cases of total identification ('possession', total 'abandonment', hypnotic enchantment, *ecstasis*). Unitary feeling is manifest in primitive thought where objects in primitive consciousness do not merely represent another object, but are *experienced as* that object: it is evident in the experience of antique mystery cults where states of trance and ecstasy occur; it is apparent in hypnotic experience, where the differentiating function of the 'I' subsides as the individual is transported, through hypnotic suggestion, beyond his will and identity into a foreign object identification. 'Unitary feeling' often conveys the notion of being 'possessed' by a foreign power, possessed by a demon. Finally, unitary feeling can be observed in the more congenial identification of a child with an object.[30] The many ecstatic, mystic or pathological types of abandonment in unitary feeling are characteristic of a '*disposition lacking a distinction between "I" and "you"*'.[31] Scheler returns to the theme of 'distance' repeatedly, and this caught Bakhtin's attention. But first the forms of pathological identity must be traced.

Scheler distinguished, among the many forms of 'unitary feeling', two diametrically opposed types: the *idiopathic* (in which the 'I' subsumes under itself the 'I' of another) and the *heteropathic* (where the 'I' is so spellbound, captivated and 'carried away' that another's 'I' can ultimately take its place).[32] In Dostoevsky's *The Double* Golyadkin projects his own identity upon another after seeing his own reflection in a fountain (idiopathic). The hero of Gogol's *Diary of a Madman* is heteropathic: convinced that he is the King of Spain, his own identity is subsumed by this foreign identity. These two types of unitary feeling reflect pathological disruptions in intrapersonal relationships; they can be translated into various dialogic tensions using descriptive comparisons of the *distance* between the 'I' and the 'other', ranging from sympathetic empathy to pathological identification.

Many of Scheler's precise distinctions of forms of co-feeling are to be found in Bakhtin's early work. In this sense, Bakhtin's 'Toward a philosophy of the act' and 'Author and hero in aesthetic activity' form a catalogue of categories from the excerpts he collected reading Scheler and those who followed in his path. Bakhtin seizes upon and compresses complex phenomenological observations (usually, but not always, accurately). Thus, in 'Author and hero in aesthetic activity', the negative aspects of 'infection' are described as 'the *pathological* phenomenon of experiencing another's suffering as one's own', 'an *infection* with another's suffering, and nothing more' (AH, p. 26). Other difficult phenomena are abbreviated to an amusing minimum: 'The hero takes possession of the author', who 'cannot see the world of objects through any other eyes but those of the hero' (AH, p. 17). In Scheler's analysis this is the heteropathic form of unitary feeling. The alternative pathological relationship between author and hero also sounds familiar: 'The author takes possession of the hero'; 'the author's reflection is put into the soul or mouth of the hero' (AH, p. 20) – a clear case of Scheler's idiopathic form of unitary feeling.

What distinguishes sympathy from 'infection' and pathological unitary feeling is the intentional emotional act. The outstanding feature of any intentional act – and 'intentionality'[33] is a term used repeatedly in the first edition of Bakhtin's study of Dostoevsky – is its productivity, a feature of any cognitive or ethical act.[34] This is the basis of Scheler's critique of *Einfühlung*; and here Bakhtin follows him minutely. Thus Scheler criticises Lipps, who appears to confuse empathy with mere identification.[35] His argument is convincing. 'Whoever understands the fear of death of someone drowning', Scheler maintains, 'does not at all need to experience a real (though weakened) fear of death. This theory contradicts the phenomenological fact that in understanding we in no way experience what we have understood.'[36] This categorical distinction is reflected everywhere in Bakhtin's early work: 'My being afraid of my own death and my attraction to life as-an-abiding are essentially different in character from my being afraid of the death of another person, a person dear to me, and from striving to safeguard that other person's life' (AH, p. 104). In his application of Scheler's observation Bakhtin tarnishes somewhat the logical clarity of the very phenomenon his work is built on (my being afraid of death and my striving to safeguard another person's life are *already* 'different in character'). But the point remains clear: the distinction between mere co-feeling and Scheler's sympathy is the ethical intentionality expressed with reference to the other and the other's feelings (and not my own).

Real *sympathetic feeling* 'proclaims itself by virtue of the fact that it also takes account of the nature and existence of the other and his individuality in the object of commiseration or co-joy (*Mitfreude*)'.[37] This is the idea Bakhtin follows most tenaciously in his synopsis of Scheler's study of emotions. And precisely this aspect of Scheler's critique of *Einfühlung* is an essential part of Bakhtin's theory of 'Toward a philosophy of the act' and 'Author and hero' (AH, p. 26). Sympathetic 'commiseration', Bakhtin recorded, 'is suffering on account of the suffering of an other *as that other*. This "as the other" belongs in the phenomenological *factual reality* (*Tatbestand*). There is no reference to any sort of "unitary feeling" (*Einsfühlung*) or identification with the other or of my suffering with his suffering.'[38] In this 'category of the other' lies the key to Scheler's (and Bakhtin's) critique of empathy. Scheler's 'category of the other' – fundamental to both of Bakhtin's 'early works' – also provides the buttress for Bakhtin's critical remarks on Husserl's phenomenology. Bakhtin's criticism of Husserl's egological phenomenology is clearly expressed in a remark in 'Author and hero': 'idealism is a phenomenology of my experience of myself, but not of my experience of the other' (p. 110). Bakhtin's 'Author and hero in aesthetic activity' is, of course, a treatise against idealism *and* Husserl's transcendental phenomenology.

The overwhelming import of Scheler's study is conveyed in Bakhtin's 'category of the other' and its ethical role in sympathy and co-suffering: 'My suffering, my fear for myself, my joy are profoundly different from my compassion or suffering with the other, rejoicing with the other, and fearing *for* the other – whence the difference in principle in the way these feelings are *ethically* qualified' (AH, p. 48; my italics). But only in Scheler's work can we learn to appreciate the full ethical dimensions of these observations. To this central equation Bakhtin will add the 'uniqueness of place' in the experience of 'co-being' and the position of 'being located outside': 'The other's co-experienced suffering is a completely new ontic formation that I alone actualise inwardly from my *unique place outside* the other' (AH, p. 103; my italics). In what follows I review the sources of these terms. But there is still more to discover about Bakhtin in Scheler's works.

Bakhtin's application of Scheler's theory of distance

Scheler began his critique of empathy by asking the question: what would be the sense of my feeling the pain of someone else who is suffering? The precondition for sympathetic empathy and for understanding is the *distance* between my emotions or ideas and the emotions or ideas of the other, a distance which makes participation both compelling and productive – and necessary. In a passage

Bakhtin copied and emphatically scored in the margins of his synopsis, Scheler explained his reasons for rejecting 'monistic' theories of empathy which presuppose that empathy is the duplication of the emotional experience of one individual in another: 'Decisive is the fact that, in genuine sympathy, the *"distance" between the persons and their own consciousnesses* as well as their *consciousness of differentiatedness* . . . remains.'[39] Scheler claims that such 'distance' provides the basis for genuine 'communication'.[40] 'Indeed', Scheler elaborates, 'in communication it is essential that we understand the communicated content first and foremost as the experience of the one doing the communication, and furthermore that we, in understanding this experience, co-experience the communicated content as simultaneously coming from the other'.[41] In yet another passage Bakhtin highlighted in the margins of his synopsis, Scheler hypothesises: 'Without a certain self-consciousness and feeling of self-esteem, which is not first and foremost deduced from one's impression upon others but is initial, one cannot live ethically.'[42] Here again Scheler explicitly relates both '*self*conscious and *self*esteem as well as the independent life of the individual' – the 'prerequisites of genuine sympathy' – with the 'experienced "distance" from the other'.[43] In these observations Scheler draws attention to the path leading from his phenomenological critique of empathy to an ethically informed theory of communication which he himself did not traverse.

Bakhtin did. In the development of the ethical import of the concept of polyphony, 'distance' is the hinge upon which everything phenomenologically observable swings. The analytical categories used to describe narrative reveal an intersubjective plane of interaction upon which the author's characters appear to have a consciousness distinct from the author himself: they lie at a distance, have a position of their own. Distance allows them to speak in their own 'voice', to utter their own 'word'. Dostoevsky, according to Bakhtin, 'was capable of representing someone else's idea, preserving its full capacity to signify as an idea, while at the same time also preserving a *distance*, neither confirming the idea nor merging it with his own expressed ideology.'[44] The revision of Engelhardt's view of Dostoevsky's heroes as 'ideologists' (Bakhtin's synopsis of Engelhardt's essay is in the 'Scheler notebook') begins by applying Scheler's spatial metaphor to qualify the distinctiveness of the 'consciousness' of author and hero as the 'artistic dominant governing the construction of a character' (*PDP*, p. 50). This principle distinguishes not only fiction from biography, but also Dostoevsky's novels *per se* from those of other authors who, like Turgenev and

Tolstoy, coalesce with or express '*directly, without distance*' (*PDP*, p. 84; Bakhtin's italics) the consciousness of their heroes:

> Self-consciousness, as the artistic dominant in the construction of the hero's image, is by itself sufficient to break down the mono-logic unity of an artistic world – but only on condition that the hero, as self-consciousness, is really represented and not merely expressed, that is, does not fuse with the author, does not become the mouthpiece for his voice; only on condition, consequently, that accents of the hero's self-consciousness are really objectified and that the work itself achieves a distance between the hero and the author. (*PDP*, p. 51)

The emphatic sense of 'dialogue' and linguistic terminology in general are largely absent in Bakhtin's 'Author and hero in aesthetic activity' and 'Toward a philosophy of the act'. By contrast, the influence of Scheler in these works is conspicuous. The fact is important. In the course of Bakhtin's development we observe a continuous 'thickening' of terminology arising out of a phenomenological approach to literature, to which Bakhtin later added a linguistic dimension (and for which Voloshinov furnished certain inspiration). Thus Bakhtin wrote: 'To preserve distance in the presence of an intense semantic bond is no simple matter. But distance is an integral part of the author's design, for it alone guarantees genuine objectivity in the representation of a character' (*PDP*, p. 64).

The varieties of 'distance' in Bakhtin's narrative theory

There are other literary sources at work in Bakhtin's study of Dostoevsky which show the continuity of Bakhtin's development from his 'early' fragments up to 1929 and beyond. Bakhtin encountered the expression 'polyphonic dialogue' in Ernst Hirt's study *The Formal Laws of Epic, Dramatic and Lyrical Literature*.[45] I mention Hirt here to demonstrate the help Bakhtin's sources offer in defining his terminology. In his discussion of the 'inner form' of epic Hirt refers to the 'cosmic distance' of the epic poet *vis-à-vis* the earth, a perspective of 'infinite' removal, 'extraterrestrial'.[46] The point of view (*Standpunkt*) of the novelist is, by comparison, flexible, a key to the compositional principles of the author. The novelist's 'irony, floating over everything, orders the values nearer to or further from the essential'; the authorial position intervenes in the plot of the novel, adding a controlled 'relativisation of the events' manifest in adjectives, scenic description, reflections and emotional outpourings.[47] In contrast to the epic 'cosmic distance', the novel offers us an 'earthly point of view', a 'perspective' characterised by Hirt as 'human' and 'psychological'; 'space' and 'time' are alternatively 'continuous' or 'dense', the 'place and hour are empirically real'.[48]

Here, in the orbit of another source, 'distance' obtains an entirely different, a *negative,* meaning – without endangering in the least the ethical and, by extension, narrativistic significance of 'distance' in Bakhtin's study of Dostoevsky. Bakhtin used this concept of distance to distinguish epic and novelistic narrative perspective in his historical overview of the rise of the novel; thereafter he celebrated 'proximity' in his study of Rabelais. The two seemingly contradictory theories of distance peacefully cooperate in the second edition of Bakhtin's study of Dostoevsky and deepen considerably the approach to the problems of narrating consciousness, on the one hand, and narrative perspective, on the other.

Without knowledge of the sources, the historical origins and the various functions of the categories 'polyphonic dialogue', 'monologue' and 'distance' recede into a Protean nightmare of oscillating meaning. Only a historical review of the evolution of these categories in conjunction with Bakhtin's sources provides clarification. Already in the second half of the nineteenth century the German novelist and critic Otto Ludwig had pointed out that the words in a soliloquy of a single figure on the stage may seem so affected by the presence of those offstage that his monologue sounds to us like polyphonic dialogue. The phenomenon is more than an illusion. For it shows consciousness anticipating, provoking, remonstrating – acting *as if* in dialogue with others. Acting as if in Scheler's world of the other. By giving aesthetic preference to 'dialogic' monologue, to the polyphonic tensions of dialogic interaction in a single individual's speech, Otto Ludwig and Ernst Hirt anticipated Bakhtin's tastes – but not his *phenomenological analysis* and his critique of epistemology.

Nicolai Hartmann's theory of being outside

Scheler pointed to the psychophysical indifference of the person which cannot be understood as a thing located within the body itself. The Marburg philosopher Nicolai Hartmann (1882–1950) developed this concept and other concepts from Scheler's *Formalism in Ethics and Material Value-Ethics.* Thus, despite Hartmann's occasional critical remark, Scheler praised highly both Hartmann's

Foundations of a Metaphysics of Cognition and (1921) and his *Ethics* (1926).[49]

The language of Hartmann's analysis is the result of an alternative approach to the phenomenology of perception, closer to Scheler, light-years from Husserl. Hartmann worked towards a solution for the central antimony of 'immanence philosophy' arising from historical theories of perception which, since Descartes, sharply distinguished between the *res extensa* and the *res cogitans*. In the wake of Kant's Copernican revolution, German philosophy and particularly neo-Kantian idealism had given theoretical priority to the perceiving subject, isolated, locked within its own consciousness.[50] The radical isolation of the subject in consciousness is masked, of course, by creating of the particular a universal: 'consciousness in general' displaces the apparent plurality and particularity of beings.

The principle of 'immanence philosophy' is easily explained: all we can know is restricted to the content of our consciousness. Sensory data are deceptive. Like Leibniz's monads, we have no windows. Hartmann, a former student of the Marburg school (and somewhat embittered by the influence of its negative reputation upon his career[51]), pointed to Cohen's *Logic of Pure Reason* as an extreme form of 'scientistic' idealism caught in this very antimony.[52]

The historically positive role of idealism is not to be scoffed at. (Bakhtin, well aware of the issues, remained an idealist.) The idealist premiss avoids the sensualist fallacy: the erroneous notion that the stimulation of the senses is tantamount to consciousness, to cognition of that which stimulates our senses.[53] But transcendental idealism responds to the problem of sensory perception by isolating the subject within the content of its own consciousness. In 'immanence philosophy' only thought is objective, but that objectivity seems to be of limited value for cognition since, 'despite all the objectivity of thought (*des Gedachten*), consciousness does not escape from that iron ring, the circle of thought (*Zirkel des Denkens*)'.[54] Hartmann's intention is to break through this 'isolation', to unearth and describe another relation between subject and object.[55]

Hartmann believes there is more to cognition than is apparent in the subject–object relation. Consciousness and the subject are not identical. If consciousness (or thought) cannot escape the isolation within its own content, this does not mean that the *subject* is contained within consciousness alone. The object remains transcendent to the consciousness of the subject, but Hartmann suggests that the subject steps outside itself (*aus sich heraustreten*) in order to obtain a cognitive picture of that which lies beyond it.[56] 'This *being outside itself of the subject (Aussersichsein des Subjekts)* in the cognitive function is the puzzle.'[57]

The 'being outside itself' of the subject is a rather 'unsharp image' for a 'complexly structured relation'.[58] Hartmann claims that the isolation of the consciousness actually pertains only to the *content* which consciousness 'has' *(Haben)* and not to the gnoseological process of grasping *(Erfassen)* new determinations; this process reveals the subject's movement beyond the sphere of consciousness into the transcendent sphere of the object and the *returning* movement of the subject back to consciousness with its 'transcendent determinations' which consciousness thus receives from beyond itself.[59] As a content of the consciousness these determinations represent only a mediate picture of what is beyond the 'I'; but what they represent nevertheless bears a relationship to what is represented. Cognition begins, however, with the *return* of the subject (Bakhtin's 'consummation'). In Hartmann's language: 'The subject thus cannot "grip" the object without leaving itself (transcending itself); but it cannot be conscious of what has been grasped without being back again in its own sphere. Thus the cognitive function may be represented in a tripartite act: as a *going outside,* a *being outside the self* and a *return* of the subject to itself.'[60]

Again and again Bakhtin combines this structure of cognition with Scheler's categories ('sympathetic feeling', 'distance', the 'category of the other') to form an ethically and aesthetically relevant intersubjective theory of perception. Bakhtin overloads the ethical sense of return and consummation in aesthetic activity; but the ethical sense of 'distance' and 'sympathy' explain why he does so. Thus my sympathetic 'projection of myself'[61] into another who is suffering 'must be followed by a *return* into myself, a *return* to my place outside the suffering person, for only from this place can the material derived from my projecting myself into the other be rendered meaningful ethically, cognitively, or aesthetically' (AH, p. 26).

There can be no doubt that in his 'early works' Bakhtin is operating in a philosophical tradition combining Scheler and Hartmann. In his *Ethics* (1926) Hartmann devoted a subchapter of his work to 'empathy' and 'return', to 'feeling into' and 'feeling back' *(Einfühlung und Rückeinfühlung).*[62] Extending the implications of his cognitive theory, which posit the return of the subject to itself as a necessary factor of cognition (the consummation, as it were, of the cognitive operation), Hartmann writes here: 'if we wish to

maintain the category of empathy, ... we cannot avoid the consequence that feeling into (*Einfühlung*) must be accompanied by an
equally primary and significant feeling back (*Rückeinfühlung*). Only
in the reciprocal activity of both may the *consciousness of a moral inner
world* appear.'[63] Hartmann also uses Schelerian categories of the 'I
for myself' and 'I for the other' in his *Ethics*.[64] Is this a fortuitous
coincidence? Scheler praised Hartmann's *Ethics* in the Preface to his
study of sympathy. Why didn't Bakhtin record the title, date and
publisher in his notebook along with those of Litt, Plessner and
Gebsattel? Because at that time (1926–27) he had read it already!
And his study of Hartmann's *Ethics* may be documented in
Bakhtin's 'early works'. Without Hartmann's category of the
'return', Bakhtin perceives in empathy merely a form of Scheler's
'unitary feeling' ('infection') bereft of ethical value. Bakhtin states
quite categorically: 'Aesthetic activity proper actually begins at the
point when we return to our own place outside the suffering
person' (AH, p. 26).

Hartmann refers to the subject's 'being outside itself' spatially
as its own individual 'eccentric *position*'.[65] This eccentricity has of
course no relationship to religious *ecstasis*. Nor is the subject's
'being outside itself' a theory of subjectivism, despite the fact that
Hartmann begins with the intrasubjective, the *individual* cognitive
experience. The combination of Hartmann's theory with Scheler's
views on sympathy renders the multiple functions of Bakhtin's use
of the category of the 'location outside' plausible.

But why do I mention Hartmann here? He's not in the notebook. M. I. Kagan studied phenomenology with Nicolai Hartmann
and Georg Misch in Marburg in 1914. In the mid-1920s Kagan
himself speaks of 'being located outside' in an unpublished fragment
on the 'spheres of being'. The illusion of Bakhtin's original categories is the ignorance of their sources. The result: a loss of their
philosophical integrity. We may be thankful that Bakhtin wasn't
just an 'original'.

Bakhtin beyond 1927

We've been looking at Bakhtin for years. But we've scarcely begun
to see him in his own philosophical horizon. We've been trying to
feel our way into Bakhtin's texts. It's time for a *return*. For without
the *distance* necessary for understanding, the sympathetic views of
Bakhtin's work and life resemble pathological forms of identification or projection. There are heteropathic interpretations of

Bakhtin, where Bakhtin wears the face we give him. There are idio-pathic readings of Bakhtin, where Bakhtin is the other we wish for ourselves. The lack of distance between author and hero is at times reflected in the collapse of philological principles.

We have missed the drama of Bakhtin's life by creating an author who didn't care about publications ('several lost books') and academic degrees. We've swallowed the legends – hook, line and sinker. Yet already in the early 1920s Bakhtin was struggling to gain access to an academic world for which he was formally unqualified. Whereas Kagan complained of the adventurists in the academic environment, Bakhtin became one: 'Alas, we, too, must become somewhat adventurists. What can be done if there is no other way to act? We shall begin with the adventure in order to transform it into something more solid and fundamental.'[66] There is no reason to separate Bakhtin's 'solid and fundamental achievement' from his adventurism. He did not study at a university – whether in Odessa or in St Petersburg. He was not a trained classicist. There is not a single Greek or Latin word in Bakhtin's published works that cannot be identified by referring to his excerpts of (largely German) secondary literature. In order to survive Bakhtin 'literally composed his early biography' on the basis of his brother's life (who did study in Petersburg).[67] In another example, recently discovered, Bakhtin assumed the biography of his best friend, M. I. Kagan: he changed the date of his birth and claimed that, from 1910 to 1912, he had studied for four semesters at the University of Marburg and one semester at the University of Berlin.[68] Bakhtin was the Svistonov of his Leningrad milieu.[69]

Bakhtin, (co-)author of a theory of non-coincidence, had a hardy appetite for the biography of the other. Why? With an irreg-ular income, he may simply have been hungry. But he did not devour his colleagues' publications. And he could not have written them. These are claims Bakhtin himself never made in print or in personal correspondence. Others do that for him. In a letter to V. Kozhinov in 1961 Bakhtin wrote:

> The books *Formal Method in Literary Scholarship* and *Marxism and the Philosophy of Language* are well known to me. V. N. Voloshinov and P. N. Medvedev are my deceased friends. In the period of the creation of these books we worked in very close creative contact. Moreover, the foundation of these books and my work on Dostoevsky is a common conception of language and speech production.

Bakhtin explicitly acknowledges here that this 'in no way reduces the independence and originality of each of these books'.[70] Kozhinov adds a footnote: Bakhtin admitted before his death that the works were 'almost completely' written by him.[71] Assuming that to be true, Bakhtin also 'admitted' in a recorded interview with Duvakin that he studied philosophy and classics at two universities and graduated before the Revolution.[72] According to Kozhinov, Bakhtin lied throughout this long account of his years as a student. 'There are no grounds', he says, 'to maintain that Bakhtin finished school (*Gymnasium*).'[73] So we believe him when we want to? And call him a liar when we don't? We must refer to internal evidence and objective evidence. Bakhtin spoke of a *common background*. Who was first in what department?

Internal evidence and archive documents suggest that Bakhtin's 'early works' were written perhaps as late as 1927. They cannot be dated earlier than 1924. Thus if we choose to remain optimistic (supposing that the young author studied Scheler's work on two occasions), there can be no question that Bakhtin's early works make extensive use of material which appeared only in the second edition of Scheler's critique of empathy, published late in 1923.[74] According to extant synopses dating from 1927, when he worked intensively on his study of Dostoevsky, Bakhtin was still without sources for his *linguistic dialogism*.[75] He had, however, already developed a phenomenological method, both more complex and more anthropologically convincing than existing Humboldtian theories of language, which focus upon the relationship between language and consciousness to the detriment of other sensory experience.[76]

Enter Voloshinov. Beginning in 1925 Voloshinov studied at the Russian Association of Scientific Research Institutes for Material, Artistic and Verbal Culture. There can be no doubt that he was highly respected by his colleagues.[77] From 1925 to 1928 Voloshinov received formal training as a linguist. One of his advisers was L. P. Yakubinskii, author of the first study in Russian dedicated exclusively to dialogic speech.[78] And one of the first studies Voloshinov encountered was of course Spitzer's 300-page study of dialogue.[79] Spitzer's descriptions of the tensions between depersonalisation and adaptation (*Entpersönlichung–Anpassung*) in dialogue form a natural complement to the tensions Bakhtin unearthed in phenomenology.[80]

Similarities between Bakhtin's and Voloshinov's language and works are explainable. We know Voloshinov read Scheler already in 1925. It is not, therefore, surprising that his texts contain elements of personalism to be found also in Bakhtin's work.[81] There is no need to suggest that Voloshinov's personalism reflects what Bakhtin 'most fruitfully passed on to his friends and collaborators'.[82] According to the existing documents, Voloshinov was the first to study Scheler. In any case, the naive belief that serious philosophers simply dream up their systems reflects the sophomoric side of Bakhtin studies. Scheler's personalism predates the entire school by at least a decade. Bakhtin and Voloshinov have sources; but here the contrasts are considerable. Whereas in 1929 Bakhtin quotes Scheler as the pivotal figure between monologism and dialogism, Voloshinov points to Ernst Cassirer a year earlier as the philosopher who, upon the foundation of human consciousness, moves linguistics beyond both neo-Kantianism and transcendental phenomenology.[83] With this preference Voloshinov anticipates Bakhtin's later development. In his study 'Forms of time and of the chronotope' (1938–40) Bakhtin, writing in an analytical framework indebted to Cassirer, refers to Scheler as a 'not strictly scientific thinker'.[84]

Linguistic dialogism has *philosophical* sources which can identified and dated. Cassirer was one important source. Among the members of the 'Bakhtin Circle', who all specialised in the field, Voloshinov was the first to plagiarise Cassirer.[85] He continued to do so throughout his publications. Even in his later, most Marxist, phase we find Voloshinov returning to the lessons rooted in linguistic idealism. The unidentified motto for his essay 'Literary stylistics' (1930) is a quotation of a quotation from Cassirer's work (written by Ludwig Noiré).[86] Some would prefer to assume that Voloshinov read the book. But Voloshinov's analysis here of the 'stages' of human history (the magic stage, totemism, the cosmic period) and his interpretation of the 'hand' as 'man's first word', opening the 'pathway to civilization', is extracted from the second volume of Cassirer's *Philosophy of Symbolic Forms*.[87] The examples are legion. Where does this begin?

In 'Discourse in life and discourse in poetry' (1926) Voloshinov refers to the manner in which certain languages, particularly the Japanese, indicate social status with lexical and grammatical 'etiquettes'; he cites Wilhelm von Humboldt's *Kawi-Werk* and Hoffmann's *Japanische Sprachlehre* (1877).[88] (I'm sure someone has credited Bakhtin with studying Japanese on this basis.) In the first volume of Cassirer's *Philosophy of Symbolic Forms* we find in a single footnote the same two works quoted with the same page numbers. We also find Voloshinov's argument.[89] Voloshinov thus tells us (by not telling us) that Cassirer is a source for more than footnotes. Like Scheler's name, missing in Bakhtin's 'early texts', Voloshinov is too close to Cassirer to consider him a mere subtext of his own. We thus move into a context that Voloshinov is assimilating as he writes. In his analysis of the 'inclusive and exclusive' forms of the pronoun 'we' in Australian languages, and in his observations on the 'grammatical forms which are used in strict dependence on the rank of the hero of the utterance' in Japanese, Voloshinov solicits Cassirer's theory and evidence to illuminate how 'purely grammatical forms are able to convey even more flexibly nuances of the social interrelationship between the speakers and the differentiated degrees of their intimacy'.[90] These aspects represent for Voloshinov not just a 'question of grammar', but a 'question of style'. Yet the 'principles of changing style' are themselves 'dependent upon a change of social value' which may be glimpsed in the utterance itself.[91] The 'degree of intimacy of author and hero' is reflected here in *sociolinguistic* categories. These appear for the first time only in Bakhtin's work during the latter half of the 1930s. The moment Bakhtin had read Cassirer, the evidence of his influence abounded.[92] Bakhtin did not write Voloshinov's works.

Voloshinov was also the first to note the applications of *dialogic linguistics* to the study of Dostoevsky.[93] It is likely that Bakhtin's own selection of sources reflect a debt to Voloshinov's research. One notebook in the Bakhtin archive, dated 1926, contains excerpts copied by Bakhtin's *wife* from works by Askol'dov, Komarovich, Vinogradov, Skaftimov, Gizetti, Vossler, and Shpet, excerpts which actually appear in print in Voloshinov's study of the philosophy of language.[94] The name of the owner of the notebook has been meticulously scratched off the cover. How did Bakhtin and his wife survive *materially* during the 1920s? Bakhtin's wife excerpted scores of books for Bakhtin during the 1920s. On one of the notebooks she wrote: 'Misha's material'. Why? Because she also worked for Voloshinov, who had an income and could afford to help his friend?[95] That is, of course, pure speculation.

Despite our sympathies, we shall never understand Bakhtin without a clearer image of his sources and the context within which he developed intellectually. The sources of his 'early works' also reveal how Bakhtin went beyond them in one central issue: in his phenomenological interpretation of narrative. There is a philosophical depth and integrity to Bakhtin's thought often decimated by romantic projections, far-fetched associations and juvenile piety for the man himself. Like any great thinker, Bakhtin is always standing on someone else's shoulders. Rooted in Scheler's observations, Bakhtin moves beyond both him and Hartmann, defining, in the form of a question, the principles of a pioneering narrative theory. Bakhtin asks 'whether (1) the author/beholder's aesthetic activity is co-experiencing with the hero that tends ultimately toward both of them coinciding, and (2) whether form can be understood from within the hero, as an expression of his life – an expression that tends ultimately toward an adequate *self*-expression of that life' (AH, p. 72). Bakhtin learned from Scheler: distance provides the key. But Scheler never dreamed of narratology. Bakhtin asks revolutionary questions: 'To what extent does verbal art have to do with the spatial form of the hero and his world?' (AH, p. 92). The lessons he learned from Scheler and Hartmann helped to provide the answer, but not the question itself.

In 1923 Oskar Walzel (an important author for Voloshinov, Medvedev and Bakhtin) observed that 'the word "phenomenology" resounds everywhere in connection with the arts'. 'Unfortunately', he added, 'Husserl and Scheler have not at all shown us how art can be examined phenomenologically.'[96] This was the subject Bakhtin addressed in his 'early works'. And it was also the field in which he made the largest contribution. The ideas developed in Bakhtin's early works and applied to Dostoevsky in 1929 inaugurate a truly innovative approach to narrative with anthropological and sociological implications still in need of development. A full analysis of Bakhtin's background will dispel the many myths surrounding Bakhtin's life; but it will also assure him his *own* place in the history of that and other subjects.

Notes

1 See Caryl Emerson, 'Keeping the self intact during the culture wars: a centennial essay for Mikhail Bakhtin', *New Literary History*, XXVII: 1, 1996, p. 107.

2 David Shepherd, 'Bakhtin and the reader', in Ken Hirschkop and David Shepherd, eds, *Bakhtin and Cultural Theory*, Manchester, 1989, p. 91.

3 The English translations of these texts are: *Toward a Philosophy of the Act*, trans. Vadim Liapunov, Austin, Texas, 1994; 'Author and hero in aesthetic activity', in *Art and Answerability: Early Philosophical Essays by M. M. Bakhtin*, ed. Michael Holquist and Vadim Liapunov, trans. Vadim Liapunov and Kenneth Brostrom, Austin, Texas, 1990, pp. 4–208. References to these essays will be provided in the text as TPA and AH respectively, followed by the relevant page number.

4 The entire protocol is quoted in S. S. Konkin and L. S. Konkina, *Mikhail*

Bakhtin, Saransk, 1993, pp. 181–5, here p. 183.

5 Most of the dates are off by at least two years. Generous guesswork dominates the procedures. And most texts were recast for publication.

6 Bakhtin's 'Toward a philosophy of the act' is dated 1919–21 by Michael Holquist and 1920-24 by S. G. Bocharov. See Holquist's 'Foreword' and Bocharov's 'Introduction to the Russian edition' in TPA, pp. viii and xxiii respectively.

7 Letters from M. M. Bakhtin to M. I. Kagan, one from late 1921, one from January 1922, published by Kagan's daughter Yu. M. Kagan in 'O starykh bumagakh iz semeinogo arkhiva (M. M. Bakhtin i M. I. Kagan)', *Dialog Karnaval Khronotop*, 1, 1992, pp. 71, 72.

8 Interview with S. I. Kagan, June 1993.

9 M. M. Bakhtin to M. I. Kagan, January 1922 (my italics), in Yu. M. Kagan, 'O starykh bumagakh', p. 72.

10 See N. I. Nikolaev, ed., 'Lektsii i vystupleniya M. M. Bakhtina 1924–1925 gg. v zapisyakh L. V. Pumpyanskogo' ('Lectures and interventions by M. M. Bakhtin in 1924–1925, from notes by L. V. Pumpyanskii'), in L. A. Gogotishvili and P. S. Gurevich, eds, *M. M. Bakhtin kak filosof*, Moscow, 1992, pp. 221–52.

11 Some of the quotations noted in this notebook appear in *Problemy tvorchestva Dostoevskogo* (Leningrad, 1929), the first edition of Bakhtin's *Problems of Dostoevsky's Poetics*.

12 Bakhtin uses the third edition of *Wesen und Formen der Sympathie* (Bonn, 1926). The excerpts contain subsequent highlighting in the margins. None of the Russian works Bakhtin excerpted were treated in such detail. This alone suggests that, quantitively, Scheler is the central *philosophical* source for Bakhtin's study of Dostoevsky.

13 Theodor Litt, *Individuum und Gesellschaft*, 3rd edn, Leipzig and Berlin, 1926.

14 H. Plessner and F. Buytenijk, 'Deutung des mimischen Ausdrucks', *Philosophischer Anzeiger*, I, 1925, Bonn (1925–26), pp. 72–126.

15 V. E. von Gebsattel, 'Der Einzelne und sein Zuschauer', first published in *Zeitschrift für Pathopsychologie*, II: 1. Heft, and reprinted in V. E. von Gebsattel, *Prolegomena zu einer medizinischen Anthropologie*, Berlin and Göttingen, 1954, pp. 237–69 (I quote from the latter edition).

16 Bakhtin, *Problemy tvorchestva Dostoevskogo*, p. 78 (my italics). Bakhtin's note was not included in the second edition of his study of Dostoevsky and thus does not appear in the English translation.

17 The former, *Der Formalismus in der Ethik und die materiale Wertethik* (*Formalism in Ethics and Material Value-Ethics*), Halle, 1921, was originally published in Husserl's *Jahrbuch für Philosophie und phänomenologische Forschung* in two volumes (1913, 1916). The latter was originally published (in shorter form) in 1913 under the title *Zur Phänomenologie der Sympathiegefühle* (*Towards a Phenomenology of Sympathetic Feelings*), Halle.

18 V. N. Voloshinov, *Freudianism: A Marxist Critique*, ed. I. R. Titunik and Neal Bruss, trans. I. R. Titunik, New York, 1976, p. 13. Voloshinov cites Scheler's *Zur Phänomenologie der Sympathiegefühle* (i.e. the earlier edition of the work) and *Vom Ewigen im Menschen*, Leipzig, 1920. Bakhtin read the

latter of these two works. His treatment of repentance (*pokayanie*) is closely related to Scheler's 'Reue und Wiedergeburt' ('Repentance and rebirth', 1917) in *Vom Ewigen im Menschen*. Voloshinov's appreciation of Scheler's thought in 1927 is in no way unusual for the period. Heidegger, a former student of Husserl, dedicated his study of Kant to Scheler; in 1928, on the occasion of Scheler's death, Heidegger wrote: 'Max Scheler was . . . the strongest philosophical force in contemporary Germany, no, in contemporary Europe and even in current philosophy in general' (Heidegger, *Gesamtausgabe*, Bd. 26, Frankfurt/Main, 1978, p. 62ff).

19 Vadim Liapunov chose to translate the words *material'naya etika* as 'content ethics' (TPA, pp. 22ff., 92n69), although he acknowledged that the German equivalents of Bakhtin's terms are *materiale und formale Ethik*. This is the subject of Scheler's *Formalism in Ethics and Material Value-Ethics*. The translation leads away from the sources.

20 Scheler, *Wesen und Formen der Sympathie*, p. 5.

21 Scheler, *Wesen und Formen der Sympathie*, p. 5.

22 Bakhtin, Synopsis of Scheler, 'Scheler notebook' (Bakhtin Archive), MS 2; Scheler, *Wesen und Formen der Sympathie*, p. 5n1. Here Bakhtin noted the title of Edith Stein's dissertation, *Neues über Einfühlung* (Freiburg, 1917), one of the most incisive critiques of *Einfühlung* from a phenomenological perspective available at the time.

23 Scheler, *Wesen und Formen der Sympathie*, p. 9.

24 Scheler, *Wesen und Formen der Sympathie*, pp. 9–10.

25 Scheler, *Wesen und Formen der Sympathie*, p. 10.

26 Scheler, *Wesen und Formen der Sympathie*, pp. 12–13.

27 Scheler, *Wesen und Formen der Sympathie*, p. 11.

28 The German word *Einsfühlung* means literally 'one-feeling' in contrast to *Einfühlung* or 'feeling into'. Bakhtin uses the expression 'pure empathising' in TPA, p. 15 and *passim*.

29 Scheler, *Wesen und Formen der Sympathie*, p. x.

30 Scheler, *Wesen und Formen der Sympathie*, pp. 17–31.

31 Scheler, *Wesen und Formen der Sympathie*, p. 20 (my italics).

32 Scheler, *Wesen und Formen der Sympathie*, p. 17. The difference is one of (extreme) projection or identification.

33 The Russian publishers of the second edition of Bakhtin's study of Dostoevsky insisted that the author remove the 'idealism'; the reference to Scheler (see note 11 above) and the category of intentionality were thus removed.

34 Scheler speaks of 'original (*ursprüngliches*) intentional feeling' which is essentially 'feeling of values' and therefore distinct from sensual feeling, but also distinct from Husserl's use of intentionality (*Der Formalismus in der Ethik*, pp. 270-1). Such feeling is manifest in 'spontaneous acts' in distinction to (mechanically) reactive acts. Here feeling is not the feeling of sensual stimulation, but the intentional act of empathy (for example) manifest in a commiserating glance, a smile of solidarity, etc. On the role of the body in co-feeling as an expressive semiotic system (*Zeichensystem*) with an intentional character, see *Der Formalismus in der Ethik*, pp. 353ff. The body is, in this case, not primarily a receptor (as it was for the sensualists), but

an expressive, almost linguistic unity.
35 Bakhtin, Synopsis of Scheler, MS 2; Scheler, *Wesen und Formen der Sympathie*, p. 17.
36 Scheler, *Wesen und Formen der Sympathie*, p. 8.
37 Scheler, *Wesen und Formen der Sympathie*, p. 43.
38 Bakhtin, Synopsis of Scheler, MS 3–4; Scheler, *Wesen und Formen der Sympathie*, p. 40.
39 Bakhtin, Synopsis of Scheler, MS 8–9; Scheler, *Wesen und Formen der Sympathie*, p. 75 (my italics).
40 Scheler, *Wesen und Formen der Sympathie*, p. 285.
41 Scheler, *Wesen und Formen der Sympathie*, p. 286.
42 Bakhtin, Synopsis of Scheler, MS 8; Scheler, *Wesen und Formen der Sympathie*, p. 50.
43 Scheler, *Wesen und Formen der Sympathie*, p. 49 (Scheler's italics).
44 Mikhail Bakhtin, *Problems of Dostoevsky's Poetics*, trans. Caryl Emerson, Manchester, 1984, p. 85. Further references will be given in the text as *PDP* followed by the page number.
45 Ernst Hirt, *Das Formgesetz der epischen, dramatischen und lyrischen Dichtung*, Leipzig and Berlin, 1923, p. 130. Hirt is quoting the term from Otto Ludwig (1813–65), German novelist and author of an astonishingly insightful series of articles on novelistic narrative and dramatic theory. It is comforting for Shakespeare scholars working with Bakhtin's terminology to note that Ludwig elaborated his theory of *polyphonischer Dialog* in his *Shakespeare-Studien* (posthum., 1871). Ludwig's role in narrative and dramatic theory in Germany was noted by Gustav Freytag, Käte Friedemann, Oskar Walzel and (among the Russian Formalists) Boris Eikhenbaum. Hirt develops the conception of polyphonic dialogue particularly with regard to drama, although he noted some interesting facets of polyphony in speech.
46 Hirt, *Das Formgesetz*, p. 53.
47 Hirt, *Das Formgesetz*, p. 53. See Bakhtin's synopsis (in total 71 pages, here MS 19).
48 Hirt, *Das Formgesetz*, p. 57 (Bakhtin's synopsis, MS 20). The influence of Hirt's study is manifest in 'Author and hero in aesthetic activity' (a subject I cannot enter into here). Incidentally, while extracting material from Hirt's work and from other sources Bakhtin never pauses to note references to and discussions of Lukács's *Theory of the Novel*. Bakhtin's purported plan to translate Lukács's essay is a myth.
49 See Scheler, *Wesen und Formen der Sympathie*, pp. 78, 247; *Formalismus in der Ethik*, pp. 19–23.
50 See Stephan Pietrowicz's study of Helmut Plessner, *Genese und System seines philosophisch-anthropologischen Denkens*, Freiburg and Munich, 1992, pp. 55–7, 62, for a review of the historical problems which Hartmann and Plessner confronted in their early works.
51 See Ulrich Sieg, *Aufstieg und Niedergang des Marburger Neukantianismus*, Würzburg, 1994, pp. 316–28.
52 Hartmann, *Grundzüge einer Metaphysik der Erkenntnis*, Berlin and Leipzig, 1926, p. 288.

53 Cohen provides a classic formulation of the vagaries of sensualism in his *Kants Theorie der Erfahrung*, 3rd edn, Berlin, 1918, pp. 60–70. See Helmut Plessner, *Grundlinien einer Ästhesiologie des Geistes* (1923) in *Gesammelte Schriften*, Bd. I, Frankfurt/Main, 1980, pp. 53, 55.

54 Hartmann, *Grundzüge einer Metaphysik der Erkenntnis*, p. 49.

55 Hartmann, *Grundzüge einer Metaphysik der Erkenntnis*, pp. 75, 263, 278.

56 Hartmann, *Grundzüge einer Metaphysik der Erkenntnis*, p. 262.

57 Hartmann, *Grundzüge einer Metaphysik der Erkenntnis*, p. 49 (Hartmann's italics).

58 Hartmann, *Grundzüge einer Metaphysik der Erkenntnis*, p. 264.

59 Hartmann, *Grundzüge einer Metaphysik der Erkenntnis*, p. 262.

60 Hartmann, *Grundzüge einer Metaphysik der Erkenntnis*, p. 37 (my italics). In German the last words here read: *Heraustreten, Aussersichsein und in sich Zurückkehren des Subjekts*.

61 There are two aesthetic theories which Scheler (and Bakhtin) attack: the projective theory and the theory of identification; both posit that what one acquires from the object was somehow already there. Bakhtin's use here of the word 'projective' would appear to be a lapse into erroneous or outmoded aesthetics. But the word here represents Hartmann's category of 'stepping outside', which is really his addition to Scheler's model of the psychophysical indifference of the psyche.

62 Hartmann, *Ethik*, 4, Auflage, Berlin, 1962 [1926], chapter 8, section d, pp. 76–8. But in contrast to Scheler and Litt, Hartmann remains largely upon an egological foundation: 'One's own feeling of the "I" is and remains the foundation for the feeling of the "you"' (p. 79).

63 Hartmann, *Ethik*, p. 77 (my italics).

64 Hartmann, *Ethik*, p. 450 and *passim*.

65 Hartmann, *Grundzüge einer Metaphysik der Erkenntnis*, p. 159 (my italics).

66 Letter from M. M. Bakhtin to M. I. Kagan, March 1921, in Yu. M. Kagan, 'O starykh bumagakh', p. 68.

67 See N. A. Pan'kov's wonderful archive research, 'Zagadki rannego perioda', *Dialog Karnaval Khronotop*, 1, 1993, p. 76.

68 See A. G. Lisov and E. G. Trusova, 'Replika po povodu avtobiografi-cheskogo mifotvorchestva', *Dialog Karnaval Khronotop*, 3, 1996, pp. 161–6. The documents of Bakhtin's uneven attendance at school, meticulously collected and commented on by V. I. Laptun and N. A. Pan'kov, reveal that in 1910 Bakhtin was certainly not at the University of Marburg, but rather in the third grade of the gymnasium in Vilnius (where neither he nor his brother studied Greek, but rather Latin, French and German); in 1912 (then in Odessa) Bakhtin was just entering his fifth year of the gymnasium. In 1912 the evidence of Bakhtin's school education disappears. Even if all had gone well, Bakhtin would not have graduated from the gymnasium prior to 1916. Thus Bakhtin could not possibly have received more than two years of university education prior to his arrival in Nevel' in 1918; see Laptun, 'K "Biografii M. M. Bakhtina"', *Dialog Karnaval Khronotop*, 1, 1993, pp. 67–73, and Pan'kov, 'Zagadki'.

69 Konstantin Vaginov's novel *Works and Days of Svistonov* (Leningrad, 1929) portrays an author who steals the biographies of his friends and acquain-

tances in order to incorporate them into his fiction; once fixed in Svistonov's fictional world, their fate is sealed. For some years now Voloshinov and Medvedev have suffered a comparable annihilation in the extent to which Bakhtin's name has assimilated their works. Bakhtin himself (and/or Voloshinov) appears in masked form in Vaginov's *Satyr's Song* (Leningrad, 1928). On Vaginov's *Svistonov* see David Shepherd, 'Discrowning the writer: Konstantin Vaginov', in his remarkable study *Beyond Metafiction: Self-Consciousness in Soviet Literature*, Oxford, 1992, pp. 90–121.

70 Letter from M. M. Bakhtin to V. Kozhinov (10 January 1961), in 'Iz pisem M. M. Bakhtina', *Moskva*, 12, 1992, p. 176.

71 V. Kozhinov, 'Iz pisem M. M. Bakhtina', p. 176n.

72 See Brian Poole, 'Introduction', in M. M. Bakhtin and V. D. Duvakin, *Conversations*, ed. and trans. Brian Poole, Austin, Texas, forthcoming.

73 The interview was published in *Vestnik Rossiiskoi akademii nauk*, LXV: 11, 1995, p. 989.

74 Bakhtin often studied valuable works on more than one occasion. Thus he created a detailed synopsis of Georg Misch's *Geschichte der Autobiographie*, Bd. 1, Leipzig, 1907, on two occasions, the first largely in German, the second, containing the material from the first, largely in Russian. The final text emerges in Bakhtin's study of 'ancient biography and autobiography' in the essay 'Forms of time and of the chronotope in the novel', published in *The Dialogic Imagination* (ed. Michael Holquist, trans. Caryl Emerson and Michael Holquist, Austin, Texas, 1981, pp. 130–46); a section which is almost entirely dependent upon Misch.

75 We must remain agnostic on the question of Bakhtin's essay 'The problem of content, material and form in verbal art', which is conspicuously close to Medvedev's work. I cannot comment on the extent to which this text was prepared for publication by the author in the 1970s; there appear to be no manuscripts reflecting Bakhtin's work on it (Bakhtin's materials for all his other publications are more or less extant). The essay obviously belongs to a common context. But was the author, interested in writing on 'the subject of ethics and the subject of law' in 1922, qualified immediately upon arrival in Leningrad in 1924 to upstage his professionally trained colleagues? And if the text was indeed prepared for publication in 1924, why did it not appear in any number of journals in 1925 or 1926? We need a dated manuscript.

76 Both Bakhtin and Voloshinov find in Cassirer's work an exception to this reservation.

77 N. Pan'kov has published Voloshinov's university records, with a short Introduction, as 'Mifologema Voloshinova (neskol'ko zamechanii kak by na polyakh arkhivnykh materialov)' and 'Lichnoe delo V. N. Voloshinova' in *Dialog Karnaval Khronotop*, 2, 1995, pp. 66–99.

78 See L. P. Yakubinskii's dialogic analysis of a passage from Dostoevsky's *Journal*, 'O dialogicheskoi rechi', *Russkaya rech'*, 1, 1923, pp. 124–7.

79 Leo Spitzer, *Italienische Umgangssprache*, Bonn and Leipzig, 1922. In 1923 Yakubinskii claimed in his own essay that he knew of no publications 'dedicated to dialogue' ('O dialogicheskoi rechi', §16). But V. V.

Vinogradov pointed to Spitzer's study in his own research on dialogue; see the chapter on grimaces of dialogue (*Grimasy dialoga*) in Vinogradov's *O poezii Akhmatovoi (stilisticheskie nabroski)*, Leningrad, 1925.

80 Bakhtin cites Spitzer on p. 194 of *Problems of Dostoevsky's Poetics*, but he is still quoting him on p. 197 (cf. the term *Gegenrede*).

81 Voloshinov's remark on Scheler in his article 'On the other side of the social' (1925; reprinted in Valentin Voloshinov, *Filosofiya i sotsiologiya gumanitarnykh nauk*, St Petersburg, 1995, pp. 25–58) is critical (see p. 26). Nevertheless, Scheler's personalism is apparent in 'Discourse in life and discourse in poetry' (1926), in *Bakhtin School Papers*, Russian Poetics in Translation No. 10, ed. Ann Shukman, Oxford, 1983, pp. 5–30.

82 Ann Shukman, 'Introduction', in *Bakhtin School Papers*, p. 4.

83 In recently published materials for his study *Marxism and the Philosophy of Language* Voloshinov makes this point quite clearly. Between the 'realism of the phenomenologists' (note the meaning: *universalia sunt realia*) and the 'conceptualism of the Neo-Kantians' Voloshinov identifies a 'third realm' which – like Scheler for Bakhtin, 'on the terrain of idealism' – reaches beyond both schools of thought, since the 'symbolic form' itself 'is common to both fields of cultural creation, uniting them'. 'That is the systematic position of the word' which Voloshinov finds in Cassirer's 'Neo-Kantian' *Philosophy of Symbolic Forms* (*Die Philosophie der symbolischen Formen*, 3 vols, Berlin, 1923–29). Here, Cassirer's neo-Kantianism cannot be understood as the old bully monologism, for Voloshinov adds: 'Precisely on the terrain of the philosophy of language the scientism and logism of the Marburg school and the abstract ethicism of the Freiburg school are presently being surmounted.' The passages are cited from the 'Plan and some leading thoughts of the work *Marxism and the Philosophy of Language*, published in 'Lichnoe delo V. N. Voloshinova', p. 87. Compare Voloshinov, *Marxism and the Philosophy of Language*, trans. Ladislav Matejka and I. R. Titunik, New York, 1973, p. 11n1.

84 M. M. Bakhtin, 'Forms of time and of the chronotope in the novel', pp. 99, 251.

85 As I have shown elsewhere, about five running pages of Bakhtin's study *Rabelais and His World* (including an almost full-page verbatim quotation) stem from Cassirer's study of Renaissance philosophy (*Individuum und Kosmos in der Philosophie der Renaissance*, Leipzig and Berlin, 1927), a work which Bakhtin does not cite; quotations from Cassirer's *Philosophy of Symbolic Forms* also appear in Bakhtin's study of Rabelais. The archive evidence demonstrates Bakhtin's productive and systematic development of Cassirer's thought on a number of issues. See my essay 'Bakhtin and Cassirer: the philosophical origins of Bakhtin's carnival messianism' in *South Atlantic Quarterly*, XCVII: 3–4, 1998, pp. 537–78.

86 Voloshinov, 'Literary stylistics', in *Bakhtin School Papers*, p. 93: 'Language and the life of reason have resulted from cooperative activity directed towards the achievement of a common goal, from the primeval labor of our ancestors.' See Cassirer, *Die Philosophie der symbolischen Formen*, Bd. I, Berlin, 1923, p. 259.

87 Voloshinov, 'Literary stylistics', pp. 97–9. See Cassirer, *Die Philosophie der*

symbolischen Formen, Bd. II, Berlin, 1925, p. 257.

88 Voloshinov, 'Discourse in life and discourse in poetry', pp. 22, 30n8.

89 Cassirer, *Die Philosophie der symbolischen Formen*, Bd. I, p. 216. For the paragraph discussing the various 'inclusive' and 'exclusive' uses of the pronoun 'we' on the following page of Voloshinov's text and the footnote referring to Matthews's *Aboriginal Languages of Victoria*, see Cassirer, Bd. I, p. 209. Voloshinov never cites Cassirer in this essay.

90 Voloshinov, 'Discourse in life and discourse in poetry', pp. 22–3.

91 Voloshinov, 'Discourse in life and discourse in poetry', p. 22.

92 Bakhtin cited Cassirer in the manuscript of his study of 'Discourse in the novel', but the references were removed from the text when it was prepared for publication.

93 Voloshinov, 'Discourse in life and discourse in poetry', p. 25. Compare Bakhtin, 'Author and hero in aesthetic activity', pp. 146, 172.

94 The notebook is dated 1926 on the cover, but includes material from Gustav Shpet published in 1927 (thus obviously begun in 1926).

95 The covers of many notebooks are missing.

96 Oskar Walzel, *Gehalt und Gestalt*, Berlin, 1923, p. 325.

David Shepherd

Bakhtin and the reader

What a recent book calls 'the return of the reader' is hardly a sensational event – the reader has been back with us for long enough now to make further welcoming receptions unnecessary. Indeed, it would seem that this familiar figure never really left, but lingered even in the unlikeliest of places: Elizabeth Freund has argued that, although the reader was 'banished by doctrinal fiat' from the most notorious of Anglo-American critical schools this century, 'a suppressed and unacknowledged reader-oriented criticism' was crucially constitutive of the whole project of New Criticism.[1] However, despite the sheer volume of reader-oriented work, the bewildering multiplicity of guises assumed in it by the reader means that questions about how best to theorise the concept are still being asked and still worth asking. And, as is clear from some of the other contributions to this volume, the issue of how the reader might best take advantage of her/his widely acknowledged importance has lost none of its urgency.

To bring Bakhtin to bear is to risk seeming to rehearse the tired gesture by which the Soviet theorist is burdened with the credit for having, either singlehandedly or with a little help from his friends, always already anticipated and surpassed the most significant theoretical trends of recent decades. But in fact there is no theory of reading or the reader to be plucked ready-formed from the diverse Bakhtinian legacy. Bakhtin does, it is true, make numerous references to readers and their importance. But their systematic cataloguing would be of little value: neither in isolation nor taken together will such references yield worthwhile insights unless they are approached critically from the standpoint of Bakhtin's broader theories of discourse. The purpose of this essay is thus a two-fold and modest one: to pinpoint those aspects of Bakhtin's work which seem most relevant and useful to a reader-oriented project, and to place these aspects alongside and against some of the best known reader-oriented theories, illuminating their aporias and indicating possible new directions.

It is that most frequently exegetised of Bakhtin's texts, 'Discourse in the novel', which provides our starting point. In this elaboration of the concept of dialogism, Bakhtin continually refers, with characteristic terminological largesse, to reader, listener, understander, and varying combinations of the three which suggest that, for the purposes of this particular essay, they are essentially interchangeable. And if the definition of dialogism itself begs numerous questions, the same is even truer of this shady reader. What he is *not* is clear enough – he is opposed to the 'passive listener' assumed, from the standpoint of traditional stylistics, to lie beyond the self-sufficient, 'closed authorial monologue' which is the literary work.[2] His role is one of 'active understanding' enabling the dialogic encounter of historically determinate utterances, each of which not only takes account of what has already been said about its object, but is also always oriented towards and shaped by an anticipated response. Although Bakhtin here describes the process in terms of spoken rather than written language, he does go on to contend that such an orientation towards their reader is characteristic of Tolstoy's works:

> Active understanding ..., by bringing what is being understood within the new horizon of the understander, establishes a number of complex interrelations, consonances and dissonances with what is being understood, enriches it with new moments. It is precisely this kind of understanding that the speaker takes account of. Therefore his orientation towards the listener is an orientation towards the particular horizon, the particular world of the listener, it introduces completely new moments into his discourse: what takes place here is an interaction of different contexts, different points of view, different horizons, different expressively accented systems, different social 'languages'. The speaker seeks to orient his discourse with its own determining horizon within the alien horizon of the understander and enters into dialogic relations with moments of that horizon. The speaker penetrates the alien horizon of the listener, constructs his utterance on alien territory, against his, the listener's, apperceptive background. (DN, p. 95/282)

The similarities between this and other theoretical readers are striking – the terms 'horizon' and 'apperceptive background', for example, recall the familiar categories of 'horizon of expectations'

(Jauss) or 'literary competence' (Culler). Indeed, Allon White has characterised dialogism as 'a kind of reader-oriented self-consciousness' which 'can be compared to the effect created in discourse by the "implicit reader" spoken of by Wolfgang Iser', so that 'Bakhtin thus anticipated much of the current German thinking about reception'.[3] But this evaluation of the possible relationship between Bakhtin and German reception theorists does not lie easily with White's overall emphasis on the sociolinguistic import of Bakhtin's theory. At first sight, Iser's 'implied reader' does have much in common with the Bakhtinian listener: his contribution to the meaning of literary texts is apparently one of 'active understanding' without which textual signification is impossible. Iser informs us that the term 'incorporates both the prestructuring of the potential meaning by the text, and the reader's actualisation of this potential through the reading process'.[4] But this formulation of the implied reader's constitutive powers begins the ineluctable process by which he is made to relinquish them. Even as he encounters and fills the various 'blanks' and 'vacancies' in the text – an activity without which the text cannot possess wholly determinate meanings – Iser's reader must remain constantly mindful of what at one stage is referred to as the 'ultimate meaning' of the text.[5] The traditional dominance of the 'prestructuring of the potential meaning', despite all appearances to the contrary, goes essentially unchallenged, and the text's apparent indeterminacies emerge as just another aspect of its comforting, all-embracing determinacy. The problem is, as Robert Holub has pointed out in his often devastatingly incisive account of German reception theory, that 'Iser wants ... a way to account for the reader's presence without having to deal with real or empirical readers.'[6] When he says 'the literary text enables its readers to transcend the limitations of their own real-life situation', Iser signals most clearly his profound discomfort with any notion of readership which might actually make a difference, might question the capacity of literature 'from Homer right through to the present day' to exercise its transcendent charm on successive generations of essentially unchanging readers. Hardly surprising, then, that when he does escape his ambivalent existence as both real being and textual function, the implied reader should come to represent 'a transcendental model which makes it possible for the structured effects of literary texts to be described'.[7] Ultimately it is difficult to understand why he should be called a reader at all.

Interestingly, in a piece written in the 1970s, Bakhtin is witheringly dismissive of such an approach:

Contemporary literary scholars (the majority of them Structuralists) usually define a listener who is immanent in the work as an all-understanding ideal listener ... This, of course, is neither an *empirical* listener nor a psychological idea, an image of the listener in the soul of the author. It is an abstract ideological formulation ... In this understanding the ideal listener is essentially a mirror image of the author, replicates him. He cannot introduce anything of his own, anything new, into the ideally understood work or into the ideally complete plan of the author. He is in the same time and space as the author or, rather, like the author he is outside time and space (as is any abstract ideal formulation), and therefore he cannot be *another* or other for the author, he cannot have any *surplus* that is determined by his otherness.[8]

It is possible to see the (implied) reader in 'Discourse in the novel' as trapped in this Iserian limbo between supposed activity and actual passivity only if, as is all too often the case, dialogism is uncritically accepted as a description of the immanent characteristics of a certain generically defined type of text (the novel). Bakhtin's opposition of novelistic language to poetic, his account of the history of the novel as the history of a genre, and his descriptions of the features of hybridisation, stylisation, parody, and so forth which mark discourse as novelistic – all may seem strongly to suggest that the dialogic character of language is something inherent in it, something fundamentally intratextual. The reader–listener–understander of 'Discourse in the novel' would thus be reduced to, at best, a metaphor for the productive playing out of stylistic tensions. However, the constant sliding throughout the essay between speaking and writing, listener and reader, although it leads to a certain theoretical fuzziness, actually goes hand in hand with an unremitting emphasis on the dependence of dialogism on a context which is crucially *not* intratextual, but external to the enclosure of the text: 'every word smells of the context or contexts in which it has lived its socially intense life, all words and forms are inhabited by intentions' (DN, p. 106/293). As Ken Hirschkop has written, 'the dependence of textual meaning on social situation is by now an accepted Bakhtinian axiom. But the full import of this relational definition of meaning is often evaded'. One of the most enabling insights of radical Bakhtin criticism is the recognition that dialogism and its antonym monologism are not inherent characteristics of particular types of (literary) discourse, that 'meaning lies neither in text nor content but in the relation between them ... dialogism and monologism are not different kinds of texts, but different kinds of intertextual configuration'.[9] Bakhtin's account of the novel and dialogism, even as it seemingly accepts and bolsters the self-sufficiency of 'literature', insistently gestures to a world outside it; and as the intratextual gives way to the intertextual, it is possible to glimpse a reader no longer threatened by Iserian redundancy. 'Discourse in the novel' ends with a discussion of the 'reaccentuation' of novelistic characters and languages, their acquisition of different resonance and meaning in different contexts. This comes about because

> in the changed dialogue of languages of the age the language of the image begins to sound in a different way, for it is illuminated differently, is perceived against a different dialogising background ...
>
> There is no gross infringement of the author's will in reaccentuations of this kind. The process can be said to take place *in the image itself*, and not only in the changed conditions of perception. These conditions have only actualised in the image a potential already present in it (at the same time, it is true, weakening others). It can be claimed with some justification that in one respect the image has been better understood and heard than before. In any case, a certain misunderstanding is here combined with a new, deepened understanding. (DN, p. 231/240)

In this passage we see Bakhtin struggling to negotiate the same difficulties which were to defeat Iser in his attempts to theorise the relationship between stable or determinate textual meaning and the variable or indeterminate supplement required to complete it. There is a strong attachment, evinced elsewhere in the essay, to the notion of authorial authority over textual meaning, and a concomitant reluctance to confront the implications for this authority of a fully theorised notion of reception. Hence, perhaps, the striking absence of any mention of a reader, and the predominant use of the passive voice to describe the process and effects of reaccentuation. At the very moment when it would seem most apt to reintroduce it, the notion of 'active understanding' as a constitutive moment of dialogism is nowhere to be seen. Instead we have the familiar Bakhtinian image of the 'dialogising background', with all its disturbing connotations of passivity and secondariness. However, the suggestion that reaccentuations subsequent to the text's production are somehow always already inscribed in the text, for all that it seems to go hand in hand with this apparent move away from the centrality of active understanding, in fact offers, as we shall shortly see, a way of going beyond the somewhat restrictive dichotomy of determinacy and indeterminacy.

The theorist whose work comes most readily to mind in relation to Bakhtin's notion of active understanding is Stanley Fish, scourge of the literary-critical profession and imperious adversary of Wolfgang Iser. Fish tackles the problem with panache, grandly dismissing the opposition of determinacy and indeterminacy, arguing instead that 'determinacy and decidability are always available not, however, because of the constraints imposed by language or the world – that is, by entities independent of context – but because of the constraints built into the context or contexts in which we find ourselves operating.'[10] The most important 'contexts' for Fish are his notorious 'interpretive communities', through which he can seemingly account for just about any eventuality:

> Interpretive communities are made up of those who share interpretive strategies not for reading (in the conventional sense) but for writing texts, for constituting their properties and assigning their intentions. In other words, these strategies exist prior to the act of reading and therefore determine the shape of what is read rather than, as is usually assumed, the other way round ... [This] explains why there are disagreements and why they can be debated in a principled way: not because of a stability in texts, but because of a stability in the makeup of interpretive communities and therefore in the opposing positions they make possible. Of course this position is always temporary (unlike the longed for and timeless stability of the text). (p. 171)

The interpretive community seems to represent a space in which reading as 'active understanding' can proceed apace, and stand revealed as the only condition of possibility of textual meaning: texts mean anything at all only when they are read, and what they mean depends entirely on the shared values of those reading them. Variations in meaning are accounted for by processes of negotiation and attempts at persuasion carried out by members of interpretive communities with different shared ideas about what the meaning of a given text is. It is possible for one person to persuade another over to his way of thinking because people share enough common ideas about what does and does not make sense to allow decisions to be made about the acceptability or unacceptability of this or that interpretation. (Fish describes in detail how this process works in his final chapter, 'Demonstration vs. persuasion: two models of critical activity'.)

But there is something distinctly fishy about this model of dialogue between reader and text, and reader and reader. Its witty advocacy of communal interpretive strategies and values cannot mask the disabling absence of any convincing explanation of how exactly the interpretive community comes to be constituted. Although he does speak of 'the power of social and institutional circumstances to establish norms of behaviour' (p. 371), Fish's contexts are as a rule 'situational' rather than social or historical. It is enough that interpretive communities can be pointed to as existing: if Fish's logic is followed through, their workings and pervasiveness are such that they can neither not exist nor have ever not existed. Furthermore, the operations of inter-communal persuasion are such as to preclude any meaningful notion of crisis or conflict, or even of the most rudimentary kind of change. Hence the paradox by which, in taking issue with Iser's distinction between determinate and indeterminate textual meaning, Fish is able to argue that Iser is wrong precisely because it is possible for him to be right: 'It is just that the distinction itself is an assumption which, when it informs an act of literary description, will *produce* the phenomena it purports to describe.'[11] William Ray has characterised well just how Fish's reader is for ever doomed to move, like the Vatican, from one state of certainty to the next: 'Fish's reader knows no anguish, can provoke no change in himself. Theoretically capable of persuading others, he can never outflank the beliefs of the institutions that define him; he can trigger no revolutions: the discipline will always have already understood, assimilated, indeed produced, any arguments for its realignment he might generate.'[12] Thus when Fish himself poses the question of what implications his argument has for literary criticism as traditionally practised, he breezily answers 'none whatsoever' (p. 370). Everything must remain the same because, even when there is an apparently radical shift, the new circumstances and their underlying assumptions following from this shift will be based on the same type of consensus as informed the old.

So interpretive communities, despite their apparent promise of providing a framework for understanding the historical and institutional factors in the activity of reading, turn out to be little more than a mirror image of the very ahistorical textual determinacy they are supposed to supersede. But, rather than succumbing to the powerful temptation to dismiss Fish as too clever by half, it is worth returning to Bakhtin for possible ways of giving Fish's model some of the rigour it so perversely eschews. It is not difficult to understand why Bakhtin should have been more reluctant than Fish to abandon notions of textual meaning not wholly dependent on the shared predispositions of readers. If the text has a determining role in the way it is read, this is because the socially and historically inscribed meanings of its constitutive utterances are never forgotten:

> There is neither a first nor a last word and there are no limits to the dialogic context (it extends into the boundless past and the boundless future). Even *past* meanings, that is, meanings born in the dialogue of past ages, can never be stable (finalised, ended once and for all) – they will always change (be renewed) in the process of subsequent, future development of the dialogue. At any moment in the development of the dialogue there are immense, boundless masses of forgotten contextual meanings, but at certain moments of the dialogue's subsequent development along the way they are recalled and invigorated in renewed form (in a new context).[13]

The contrast between Bakhtin and Fish emerges particularly starkly in the light of Fish's rather slippery formulation of the same problem: '[Words] always and only mean one thing, although that one thing is not always the same. The one thing they mean will be a function of the shape language *already has* when we come upon it in a situation, and it is the knowledge that is the content of being in a situation that will have stabilised it' (p. 275). The constitutive tension, the historically conflictual dynamic of discourse insisted on by Bakhtin is reduced by Fish to the stasis of an ill-defined situationality. Bakhtin, it will be recalled, speaks in 'Discourse in the novel' of a process of 'reaccentuation' '*in the image itself*, and not only in the changed conditions of perception'. The later text provides a timely reminder that 'the image itself' is not an originary instance, free from the tensions of dialogism until its insertion into it during reading, but *already* contextual, *already* dialogic. We should not be misled by the word 'itself', so often used in criticism to signal the essential nature of something, stripped of extraneous accretions: for Bakhtin the image can be itself only because, as an utterance, it cannot exist without these 'accretions', without context, which cannot satisfactorily be described as either secondary or primary with regard to the textual 'image'. Thus Bakhtin's position is not, as might appear from the earlier quotation from 'Discourse in the novel', that all possible future meanings are always already inscribed in a text from the very moment of its production, but rather that a text continues to bear the marks of its past historical engagements which, as well as being open to recontextualisation, must also place some limit on the nature and degree of that recontextualisation. Determinate meaning exists to the extent that the production of meaning is contextual, and contexts are not freely interchangeable or, *pace* Fish, wholly encompassed by the historical moment of a given interpretive community. If the activity of reading is based on dialogic relations between reader and text, and text and context, then these are relations which have a past as well as a present. A simple opposition of determinacy and indeterminacy is ultimately inadequate as a means of theorising this immensely complex position.

As for the reader/critic who engages in this activity, for Bakhtin the most important thing is the concrete social and historical milieu in which s/he operates. The alternative to the reader-as-textual-function criticised by the late Bakhtin is to be found in one of the disputed texts of the 1920s. Although it refers specifically to Formalist theories of the nature of sound in poetry, the following passage from Medvedev/Bakhtin's *The Formal Method* possesses much broader significance for the general problem of readership:

> The work is a part of social reality, not of nature ... The sound cannot be understood within the bounds of the individual organism or of nature.
>
> Therefore, the problem of the signifying sound and its organisation is connected with the problem of the social audience, with the problem of the mutual orientation of the speaker and the listener, and the hierarchical distance between them. The resonance of the signifying sound is different, depending on the character of the social interaction of people, of which the given sound is an element. The social audience is constitutive to the signifying sound and its organisation.[14]

What all this would seem to suggest, then, is that the meaning of a text will change as it is read in new contexts by always historically and socially situated readers who will always bring to it (shared) presuppositions about, among other things, the nature of literature, literary meaning, aesthetic value and so on, and may in turn find these presuppositions being modified in the process of their dialogic encounter with the text. However, it is important never to lose sight of the fact that the character of the text–reader encounter is dialogic: if the meanings of the text are indissociable from the reader's active understanding, then that understanding in its turn must strictly speaking be equally indissociable from the encounter with the text, must be precisely context-specific. In other words, the dialogic act of reading is disruptive of the seemingly fixed positions of text and reader; these positions cannot come through the dialogic encounter unchanged because they do not pre-exist it. Difficult though this may be, it is important not to lapse into what John Frow calls an 'assumption of entities fully constituted prior to the textual process'.[15]

There are further consequential differences in the ways Fish and Bakhtin treat the *effects* of readers' positioning. Fish refers in the subtitle of his major work on the subject to 'the authority of interpretive communities'. The authority of a given community, and that of the interpretations it puts forward, is for Fish something essentially suasive, not coercive. Criticism is 'a matter (endlessly negotiated) of persuasion' in a world where 'political and persuasive means ... are the same thing' (pp. 17, 16). Authority derives from powers of argument, and is therefore always open to challenge ('negotiation') by superior powers. This is all part and parcel of Fish's closed, crisis-free world of enduring consensus and certainties, and sounds reassuringly polite and gentlemanly. But, as Elizabeth Freund pertinently remarks in the conclusion to her chapter on Fish, 'Fish's position so far has refused to face up to the ways in which the authority of interpretive communities might become grimly coercive. The salutary curb on subjectivity, without a corresponding curb on the authority of consensual norms, remains troubling. The appeal to the imperialism of agreement can chill the spines of readers whose experience of the community is less happily benign than Fish assumes.'[16]

Authority in Bakhtin, by contrast, is something altogether 'less happily benign', has a more recognisable and often more sinister character. Against the dialogical production of meaning within a socially stratified and historically developing language there operate forces of centralisation which seek to restrict the range of intertextual relations, to curtail and constrain the subversive proliferation and dispersal of meaning, to assert the congruence of word and single meaning. As usual in Bakhtin, these forces have several names – monoglossia, monologism, authoritarian or authoritative discourse, the language of poetry and epic. But just as dialogism cannot be reduced to an essence of novelistic language, so monologism cannot be explained away as a property of non-novelistic or 'poetic' texts. Perhaps even more explicitly than for dialogism, Bakhtin insists on the social, historical and political contextuality of monologism: 'the authoritarian word demands our unconditional acknowledgement, and not at all a free mastering and assimilation ... It is indissociably fused with authority – political power, an institution, a personality – and stands or falls together with it. It is impossible to divide it, to agree with one thing, accept another, but not entirely, and to reject totally a third' (DN, p. 156/343). However unelaborated Bakhtin's evocation of authority, it profoundly unsettles any idea that Fish's endlessly negotiated persuasion is always and everywhere the order of the day.[17] Bakhtin's work demonstrates an acute understanding of just how naively idealistic it would be to assume that in any dialogue, literary-critical or otherwise, all contributions carry equal weight. Some voices are louder than others, even if they are not the ones articulating the most elegantly convincing arguments. That Bakhtin should have been so aware of the possible true meanings of discursive authority is hardly surprising. 'Discourse in the novel' was written in 1934, the year in which Socialist Realism was declared the officially sanctioned 'method' for Soviet literature and art in general; the monologic, restrictive understanding of the term as a simple synonym for 'Party-mindedness' was not long in following.[18] This was symptomatic of a more generalised process whereby the Stalinist state gathered to itself the right of first and last word on all matters of import. In the cultural sphere this meant not only an insistence on 'portrayal of reality in its revolutionary development', a goal whose posts were constantly changed to accompanying declarations of its immutability. It also set in train a project (one which continued well beyond the Stalin years) of establishing, often with peculiarly unsubtle authority, definitively monologic intertextual relations between past and present cultural artefacts and the context allotted to them. Thus Socialist Realism acquired precursors in the literature of the 1920s and earlier; Soviet literature in general became the organic continuation of the enduring literary 'heritage' of the nineteenth century, thanks in particular to the mediating and transitional role of key writers such as Gorky; Soviet culture, although 'multinational' to the extent that it contained elements of the culture of all the constituent nations of the Soviet Union, was at the same time to be a unified whole; and the notion of 'popular' or 'mass culture' was to acquire an unremittingly negative resonance. The cost of the imposition of this rigid set of relations by a state for which politics was so often more than a matter of mere persuasion was, as is well enough known, a high one in terms of lives and of squandered cultural opportunities.

What happened to culture in general and literature in particular under Stalin and afterwards is a grim and stark illustration of what critical authority can mean; there are many now silent witnesses of the consequences of trying to draw the monologic voice of the Stalinist state into dialogic interchange.

No doubt many would argue that this is all a grotesque anomaly, that the role of politics and ideology in matters literary and cultural in the West is negligible by comparison, that Stanley Fish is by no means wrong to associate authority in the production of stable, determinate textual meaning with the free give and take of mutual persuasion in a mercifully pluralist academy rather than with the brutal ukases of state centralism. But of course the conflation of the absence of 'Stalinist' politics with the absence of politics in general is in itself a profoundly political gesture which cannot conceal the discernible similarities between, for example, Soviet and Western notions of tradition and national cultural heritage and their importance of the practices of criticism: as well as on coercion, Stalinist politics relied on notions of tradition, 'Russianness' and so on whose appeal was enormously powerful, not to say persuasive. And arguments about the politics of literature and culture are by no means unknown even within our own more homely institutions. What is important at this point is that when Bakhtin is introduced into the specific area of reader-oriented theory, this brings us ineluctably to acknowledge those questions of politics and ideology which are bracketed out, consciously or otherwise, by theorists such as Iser and Fish. Iser's notion of readerly activity is never allowed to develop enough for its accompanying politics to be examined. Fish, for all that he recognises the political undisinterestedness of the activities of his interpretive communities, defines that quality within unacceptably narrow confines; the authority of his arguments rests upon a principled refusal to inquire what, outside the walls of the academy, might underpin them.[19]

An approach to the reader through Bakhtin thus leads irresistibly beyond the confines of a putative self-contained encounter between an individual person and an individual text – from the 'microcosm of response' to the 'macrocosm of reception', to borrow the terms of Robert Holub's contrast between the two doyens of German reception theory, Iser and Hans Robert Jauss (p. 83). Indeed, from a Bakhtinian viewpoint, Jauss's project of re-theorising literary history, discredited in Germany, in order to realise what he saw as its potential as a 'challenge to literary theory', seems the most promising of the most frequently anthologised reading theories of recent years. Jauss took as his starting point the idea that 'literature and art only obtain a history that has the character of a process when the succession of works is mediated not only through the producing subject but also through the consuming subject – through the interaction of author and public'.[20] His principal means of achieving this integration of aesthetic reception and history was to be his 'horizon of expectations'; but, just as Iser's implied reader was to prove disablingly nebulous, so Jauss's key concept fell prey to a debilitating lack of rigour. Robert Holub conveys well just how difficult it is to pin down: 'The trouble with Jauss's use of the term "horizon" is that it is so vaguely defined ... "Horizon of expectations" would appear to refer to an intersubjective system or structure of expectations, a "system of references" or a mind-set that a hypothetical individual might bring to any text' (p. 59). Holub here suggests that the horizon of expectations is a property of a text's reader or readers, in line with Jauss's assertion that 'The coherence of literature as an event is primarily mediated in the horizon of expectations of the literary experience of contemporary and later readers, critics, and authors' (p. 22). However, at other times the horizon of expectations is referred to as a property of the text: 'the horizon of expectations of a work allows one to determine its artistic character by the kind and the degree of its influence on a presupposed audience' (p. 25). This ties in with what Jauss promisingly calls the 'dialogical character of the literary work' (p. 21) – a formulation emphasising an apparent similarity with the Bakhtinian approach to reception and its refusal to privilege either text or context. This double-edged conception of the horizon of expectations might actually be very productive, but its potential remains sadly unrealised. Jauss's orientation towards the extra-textual is short-lived as, in seeking to find a way of 'objectifying' the horizon of expectations for a given work, he looks for evidence in the first place to the very text whose reception he intends it to account for. This is an inevitable consequence of his strict hierarchisation of the horizons of expectation: 'the meaning of a work is always constituted anew, is a result of a coincidence of two factors: the horizon of expectations (or *primary code*) implied by the work and the horizon of experience (or *secondary code*) supplied by the receiver.' In thus reinstituting a traditional primacy of the text, Jauss puts himself in a position where he is unable to follow through the full implications of his notion of the dialogic character of texts. His description of the encounter of text and reader as 'a game of questions and answers', in which the text has most of the questions *and* the answers, is redolent of a notion of dialo*gue* stripped of the complexity and dynamic tension which make Bakhtinian dialog*ism* so productive and valuable – a dialogue between two pre-existent, stable entities.[21] So, although he says that 'the interpreter must bring his own experience into play, since the past horizon of old and new forms, problems and solutions, is only recognizable in its further mediation, within the present horizon of the received work' (p. 34), Jauss effectively disqualifies the 'experience' of the 'interpreter' as soon as he has recognised it and takes refuge in the very enclosure of purely literary history he set out to rupture. His characterisation of 'literary' texts takes on an inevitably familiar resonance: 'Literary works differ from purely historical documents precisely because they do more than simply document a particular time, and remain "speaking" to the extent that they attempt to solve problems of form or content, and so extend far beyond the silent relics of the past.'[22] Jauss fails to carry through the challenge, which he began by calling for, to the notion of literature as an autonomous entity independent and transcendent of history. Although he makes great play of 'that properly *socially formative* function that belongs to literature' (p. 45), he all too quickly loses sight of the fact that the concept of literature is also socially *formed*, that its social and historical reception is, as Bakhtin points out, one of its key constitutive moments.[23]

Thus, brought to bear on some of the best known reader-oriented theories, Bakhtin insistently requires the restoration of an often excluded history, and focuses attention on 'the relations of discourse and power' which Jane Tompkins, at the conclusion of her survey of reading as a historically specific activity, identifies as the proper concern of criticism.[24] The question immediately begged by this, however, is whether there is anything peculiarly Bakhtinian about such an emphasis, which can be said to subtend many of the best known 'alternative' critical projects of recent years. Within the narrower field of reading theory, a good deal of work has been done on 'institutional' factors, understood as more than just those at work within the literary-critical academy – factors such as the mechanisms and institutions of publication and distribution of books, including those producing and policing the division between 'high' and 'popular' literature, or the potential of feminism to transform entrenched notions of reception.[25] These are precisely the kind of factors to which, as we have already seen, Bakhtin more often than not refers only in passing, or whose relevance to his model of discourse he leaves largely implicit. Nevertheless, this does not automatically diminish Bakhtin's potential contribution to such approaches – a point confirmed if we look briefly at the place occupied by Bakhtin, whether explicitly or implicitly, in the work on questions of reception and reading done in recent years by Tony Bennett.

In *Formalism and Marxism* Bennett addresses the Jaussian theme of literary history, in particular the Russian Formalist model to which the German theorist is extensively and openly indebted. He focuses on the critique, in *The Formal Method*, of the Formalists' notion of a fundamentally closed literary system whose dynamic is independent of history in the broader sense, and elaborates on this by showing how the Rabelais book reveals the dependence of a text's 'literary' qualities on 'the different political and ideological conjunctures which the text enters into during the course of its historical existence'.[26] He thus arrives, through Bakhtin, at precisely the kind of formulation of the problem to which Jauss comes tantalisingly close before infuriatingly shying away from its full implications. Bennett's subsequent work on 'reading formations' represents an attempt to examine these questions of reception more closely, to specify more precisely the conditions under which texts enter such conjunctures; a reading formation ('a set of intersecting discourses which productively activate a given body of texts and the relations between them in a specific way') might well be described as an 'interpretive community' understood in proper relation to institutional and political factors not exhausted by the narrowly academic parameters to which Stanley Fish confines himself. It is striking that, although he refers at one point to Voloshinov's *Marxism and the Philosophy of Language*, Bennett makes no explicit mention of Bakhtin in his discussion of the relationship between texts and reading formations. Had he done so he might have avoided the lapse into a Fish-like nihilism which leads him, in quite properly questioning the auratic status of 'the text itself', to state bluntly that the text 'has no meanings which can be traduced'.[27] On the other hand, elsewhere Bennett, again without explicit reference to Bakhtin, defines the reading formation squarely in the spirit of dialogic understanding of text–context relations: 'The concept of reading formation ... is an attempt to think context as a set of discursive and intertextual determinations, operating on material and institutional supports, which bear in upon a text not just externally, from the outside in, but internally, shaping it – in the historically concrete forms in which it is available as a text-to-be-read – from the inside out.'[28] The difficulty of maintaining this purchase on the dialogic relation of text and context which Bakhtin

so insistently requires is at no point underestimated by Bennett –
hence, perhaps, the extensive refining of the concept of reading
formations and the understandable scarcity of examples illustrating
how they can be seen to operate. Hence, too, his refreshingly frank
admission in the earlier article that he is not really very sure of what
the practical consequences of his rethinking of text–context relations might be.[29]

And indeed, it is far from easy to know exactly where or how
to begin to use a Bakhtinian theory of reading. More precisely, to
return to the title of this article, it is perhaps not immediately
obvious what a theorist as complex, contradictory or just plain difficult as Bakhtin can do for a 'reader' – a reader such as a student in
a 'literature' (or perhaps 'cultural studies') course where there *is* a
text in the class, a reader with a more or less vague sense of his/her
own empirical pre-constitutedness, and a probably greater sense of
the reality of a 'text-to-be-read' which stubbornly resists immediate
interrogation of its ontological status. My contention (largely
untried, and so tentative and speculative) would be that in such a
situation the most immediately useful aspect of Bakhtin is precisely
that close attention to the features of texts which has so often led
to his being used in a markedly conservative way. Bakhtinian
textual analysis, if predicated on a proper, thorough understanding
of dialogism and the utterance, offers possibilities of working 'from
the inside out' in such a way that the very difficulties of 'active
understanding' can become a means of making explicit the conditions of possibility of that understanding and of past understandings
of the text – that is, of grasping the untenability, celebrated time
and again by Bakhtin, of a too stark opposition of 'inside' and
'outside', 'text' and 'context' so often initially challenged but ultimately reinstated by other theorists of reading.

Notes

1 Elizabeth Freund, *The Return of the Reader: Reader-Response Criticism*,
London and New York, 1987, p. 42.
2 Mikhail Bakhtin, 'Slovo v romane', in *Voprosy literatury i estetiki*, Moscow,
1975, p. 87; English translation in Bakhtin, 'Discourse in the novel', in *The
Dialogic Imagination*, ed. Michael Holquist, trans. Caryl Emerson and
Michael Holquist, Austin, 1981, p. 274. Since I find the Emerson and
Holquist version of the passages from 'Discourse in the novel' cited in this
essay somewhat wordy and imprecise, I have used my own, very substan-
tially different, translations; subsequent references are given in the text as
DN, followed firstly by the page number for the original Russian, then by

that for the Emerson/Holquist translation.

3 Allon White, 'Bakhtin, sociolinguistics and deconstruction', in Frank Gloversmith, ed., *The Theory of Reading*, Brighton and Totowa, NJ, 1984, pp. 128, 129.

4 Wolfgang Iser, *The Implied Reader: Patterns of Communication in Prose Fiction from Bunyan to Beckett*, Baltimore and London, 1974, p. xii.

5 Iser, *The Act of Reading: A Theory of Aesthetic Response*, Baltimore and London, 1978, p. 98.

6 Robert Holub, *Reception Theory: A Critical Introduction*, London and New York, 1984, p. 84; subsequent page references are given in the text.

7 Iser, *The Act*, pp. 79, 227, 38.

8 Bakhtin, 'Toward a methodology for the human sciences', in *Speech Genres and Other Late Essays*, ed. Caryl Emerson and Michael Holquist, trans. Vern W. McGee, p. 165 (translation slightly modified).

9 Ken Hirschkop, 'The domestication of M. M. Bakhtin', *Essays in Poetics*, XI: 1, 1986, pp. 80, 81. There is no room here to go into the full significance of this formulation. The potential it confers upon Bakhtin's texts as tools of cultural, as opposed to merely literary analysis, is explored in Hirschkop's 'Bakhtin, discourse and democracy', *New Left Review*, 160, 1986, pp. 92–113.

10 Stanley Fish, *Is There a Text in This Class? The Authority of Interpretive Communities,* Cambridge, Mass., and London, 1980, p. 268; subsequent page references given in the text for quotations from Fish are to this work.

11 Fish, 'Why no one's afraid of Wolfgang Iser', *Diacritics*, XI: 1, 1987, p. 7, quoted in Holub, *Reception Theory*, p. 103. Holub gives a good critical account of the Fish–Iser debate (pp. 101–6); see also Freund, *The Return*, pp. 148–51.

12 William Ray, *Literary Meaning: From Phenomenology to Deconstruction*, Oxford, 1984, p. 169.

13 Bakhtin, 'Toward a methodology', p. 170.

14 P. N. Medvedev, *The Formal Method in Literary Scholarship: A Critical Introduction to Sociological Poetics*, trans. Albert J. Wehrle, Baltimore and London, 1978, p. 102 (translation modified).

15 John Frow, *Marxism and Literary History*, Oxford, 1986, p. 183.

16 Freund, *The Return*, pp. 110–11.

17 On the frequent paucity in Bakhtin of detailed discussion of institutional factors, and the difficulties this can cause, see Frow, *Marxism*, pp. 98–9, and Hirschkop, 'Dialogism as a challenge to literary criticism', in Catriona Kelly, Michael Makin and David Shepherd, eds, *Discontinuous Discourses in Modern Russian Literature*, London and New York, 1989, pp. 27–35.

18 The simplistic but widespread idea that Socialist Realism was from the very beginning imposed by force on a community of writers and artists almost universally hostile to it has been cogently challenged in a recent important study: Régine Robin's refreshingly subtle and discriminating *Le Réalisme socialiste: une esthétique impossible*, Paris, 1986, offers a closely argued account of the complex beginnings and troubled development of the concept.

19 Richard Wortman presents a devastating analysis of Fish's failure to escape

from 'a literary world, separate from society, that is an invention of the literary mind' in his attempt to account for changes in the accepted reading of Books XI and XII of *Paradise Lost*: see Fish, 'Transmuting the lump: *Paradise Lost*, 1942–1982', and Wortman, 'Epilogue: history and literature', in Gary Saul Morson, ed., *Literature and History: Theoretical Problems and Russian Case Studies*, Stanford, 1986, pp. 33–56 and 275–93 (p. 286).

20 Hans Robert Jauss, 'Literary history as a challenge to literary theory', in *Toward an Aesthetic of Reception*, trans. Timothy Bahti, Brighton, 1982, p. 15; subsequent page references given in the text for quotations from Jauss are to this article.

21 Jauss, 'Esthétique de la réception et communication littéraire', in Zoran Konstantinović, Manfred Naumann and Hans Robert Jauss, eds, *Literary Communication and Reception (Proceedings of the IXth Congress of the International Comparative Literature Association)*, Innsbruck, 1980, pp. 15 (my italics), 16. The possible significance of Bakhtin's work for an aesthetic of reception was not lost on Jauss: see Andrei Corbea, 'L'Esthétique de la réception comme théorie du dialogue', *Cahiers roumains d'études littéraires*, 3, 1986, pp. 21–30. Corbea's account of Jauss's description of aesthetic pleasure in terms of alterity and self-Other dialogue (pp. 25–6) suggests that Jauss's un-Bakhtinian understanding of dialogue may result in part from a failure to distinguish sufficiently between the position taken by Bakhtin in 'Author and hero in aesthetic activity' and that taken in 'Discourse in the novel' (on the differences between these positions, see Ann Jefferson's contribution to this volume, pp. 212–14).

22 Jauss, 'History of art and pragmatic history', in *Toward an Aesthetic*, p. 69.

23 On Jauss's failure to break out of the enclosure of literary history, see also Holub, *Reception Theory*, pp. 53–82; Manon Brunet, 'Pour une esthétique de la production de la réception', *Etudes françaises*, XIX: 3, 1983, pp. 65–82; and Rita Schober, 'Réception et historicité de la littérature', *Revue des sciences humaines*, LX: 189, 1983, pp. 7–20.

24 Jane P. Tompkins, 'The reader in history: the changing shape of literary response', in Tompkins, ed., *Reader-Response Criticism: From Formalism to Post-Structuralism*, Baltimore and London, 1980, p. 226.

25 For details of the kind of sociological approach called for by the East German Manfred Naumann (see his 'Remarques sur la réception littéraire en tant qu'événement historique et social', in Konstantinović, Naumann and Jauss, eds, *Literary Communication and Reception*, pp. 27–33) and attempted in the GDR, see Holub, *Reception Theory*, pp. 128–46. Peter Humm *et al.*, eds, *Popular Fictions: Essays in Literature and History*, London and New York, 1986, addresses the division between 'high' and 'popular', and contains several contributions which deal with the institutional factors affecting the reception of texts: see especially Graham Holderness, 'Agincourt 1944: readings in the Shakespeare myth', pp. 173–95, and Paul O'Flinn, 'Production and reproduction: the case of *Frankenstein*', pp. 196–221. Finally, a wide range of approaches to questions of reception from the standpoint of gender is to be found in Elizabeth A. Flynn and Patrocinio P. Schweikart, eds, *Gender and Reading: Essays on Readers, Texts and Contexts*, Baltimore and London, 1986 (Schweikart's contribution,

'Reading ourselves: toward a feminist theory of reading', pp. 31–62, raises a number of important issues, including the need to overcome the common tendency to over-privilege one of text or context at the expense of the other).

26 Tony Bennett, *Formalism and Marxism*, London and New York, 1979, p. 92. It is perhaps worth noting here that Bakhtin's own versions of literary history are characteristically non-uniform, and emphasise the fruitlessness of any attempt to view Bakhtin's work in terms of over-arching coherence: as often, for Bakhtin to be of use here it is necessary to turn certain aspects of his thinking against others. Thus, as Joan DeJean has pointed out, whereas the Rabelais book denies literary history its traditional autonomy, the study of Dostoevsky seems to do the opposite and validate a more 'purely literary history' ('Bakhtin and/in history', in Benjamin A. Stolz, Lubomir Doležel and I. R. Titunik, eds, *Language and Literary Theory*, Ann Arbor, 1984, p. 235). And elsewhere Bakhtin speaks of the qualitatively different transcendent 'great time' (*bol'shoe vremya*) inhabited by valuable cultural products – most notably, and perhaps most disarmingly, at the end of the passage quoted above (p. 97) about the limitlessness of dialogic context: see also his 'Response to a question from the *Novy Mir* editorial staff', in *Speech Genres*, pp. 1–7.

27 Bennett, 'Texts, readers, reading formations', *Literature and History*, XI, 1983, pp. 216, 224.

28 Bennett, 'Texts in history: the determinations of readings and their texts', in Derek Attridge, Geoff Bennington and Robert Young, eds, *Post-Structuralism and the Question of History*, Cambridge &c., 1987, p. 72. There is a more explicit indebtedness to Bakhtin in John Frow's elaboration of a politics of reading which is in many ways close to that of Bennett: see the final chapter of *Marxism and Literary History*.

29 See Bennett, 'Texts, readers', p. 223.

Nancy Glazener

Dialogic subversion: Bakhtin, the novel and Gertrude Stein

Feminists have readily enlisted Bakhtin's writings for the project of replacing the patriarchal account of individualistic literary creation with a politicised account of the social production of literature. Bakhtin's own work is not markedly feminist: he wrote mainly about canonical male authors, flirted with *auteur* theories of literary creation, and was conspicuously silent about feminism and the social effects of gender difference.[1] Nevertheless, his combination of linguistic theory, narratology and cultural analysis meshes appealingly with materialist and post-structuralist currents in contemporary literary studies, and it appears to be hospitable to the inclusion of gender as an additional, significant social and discursive category. Bakhtin derives the heteroglossia of literary discourses – their multiplicity and their tendentious interaction – ultimately from the stratification of social life, in which different social groups create distinctive discourses from their common language; as a result, the meaning of a word is always a function of its torque, of its being turned to incommensurate purposes by speakers who use it in different discourses. Likewise, these discourses, products of discrete but inextricable social formations, depend so much on their interrelationship for their intelligibility that they are ultimately significant only in relation to the entire complex of language use. Discourses cannot be tailored semantically to the expressive intentions of an individual without betraying the social fabric from which they have been cut.

Thus, from a feminist point of view, Bakhtin's project has at least two major attractions. First, his assertion that literature represents a struggle among socio-ideological languages unsettles the patriarchal myth that there could be a language of truth transcending relations of power and desire. Second, Bakhtin's insistence that words and discourses have socially differential significance implies that linguistic and literary forms are necessarily shaped by the gender relations that structure society. In Bakhtin's conception of the utterance, language always registers not only the subjectivities of its speaker and its intended addressee but also the historical traces of the repeated and varying appropriations of words by individuals who are socially constituted. The concept of the subjectively-defined utterance ensures that for as long as gender has a share in the social constitution of subjectivity, part of every utterance's social intelligibility will derive from its orientation toward gender.

Fiction transforms social discourses in the course of representing them, so that they do not transparently reflect their social origins but are (at least) doubly ideologised. If one extrapolates from Bakhtin's theories, gender might be imagined to enter fictional texts in several ways: as an object of represented discourse (through discussions of maleness and femaleness, either in the abstract or as embodied in characters); as an actual or imaged subjectivity that inflects discourse (due to the genders of author, characters, and audience); or as a structuring discursive absence in the text. In any of these cases, the problematic of gender inhabits the texts with a polemical force that might be superficially downplayed or denied, but that has the potential to be elaborated. 'Every age re-accentuates in its own way the works of its most immediate past', Bakhtin writes, thereby opening the way for feminists to sift the novels of patriarchy for evidence of the effects that women's oppression, suppression, exclusion, co-option and – more optimistically – successful cultural activity have had on literary production.[2]

In light of Bakhtin's convergence, at this general level, with feminist analysis, I would like to examine more carefully two of his theories that have been most eagerly adopted by feminists. I hope to convey that Bakhtin's interrelated ideas about the subversiveness of the dialogic novel and its carnivalesque origins, though valuable and provocative, cannot be appropriated for feminism without revision and re-contextualisation. Bakhtin's concept of the carnivalesque function of the novel closely resembles some feminist conceptions of the feminine as an anarchic, somehow inherently subversive force. I hope in the first half of my essay to consider the extent to which such a purely symbolic subversive force can be credited with effectively disrupting the official categories that confer and contain meaning, and to propose a way of mediating between what I will designate the essentialist and reflexive conceptions of such disruptive forces. I will also suggest that only a more complicated understanding of the revisions and accommodations that accompany any apparent subversion can enable relatively disempowered groups like women to appraise their political successes and defeats accurately.

Although, in Bakhtin's theories, no one controls language and meaning securely – since all are continually being reconstituted and resisted by the only media through which they can produce meaning – feminists assert that some subjects, including women, are more distorted and constrained than others by the languages available to them. To investigate the compatibility between Bakhtin's ideas about language and literature and some of the concerns of twentieth-century feminism, I will use some of Bakhtin's own methods of discursive analysis in the second half of this essay to examine Gertrude Stein's subversion of classic realism. Stein's version of realism reveals the particular estrangements from language and divisions of subjectivity suffered by women in a specific historical and ideological milieu, and it implies an understanding of the ideological status of novelistic discourses different from – and illuminating for – Bakhtin's.

Underlying both sections of this essay is my proposal that the concept of the anarchically disruptive, diffusely subversive Other, which parts of Bakhtin's work and certain strains of feminist theory have endorsed, is more mystifying than enlightening, and that it tends to overshadow the analysis of particular strategies for ideological contention and subversion. Strategies like Stein's, though meaningful and effective, are historically delimited, inextricable from their circumstances of production, and calculated rather than anarchic. Indeed, the historicist methods provided by Bakhtin himself in other parts of his theory and by other kinds of feminist analysis can lead to the discovery of these strategies. Subversion never accomplishes a clean break or an unambiguous negation, and cultural analysts, feminist and other, ought to avoid oversimplifying the process and effects of subversion without giving up substantive political critique.

Dialogic ideologies in the novel

Bakthin defines the novel as an intermingling of discourses, unified by the author's significant orchestration but none the less preserving their ideological discreteness. The novel typically foregrounds the social differentiation of these discourses by embodying them in characters who occupy distinct social worlds; it stages their interaction through the confrontations of characters, and usually it sets them against a narrator's diverse and socially significant modes of description, explanation, and judgement as well.[3] Furthermore, these incommensurate discourses are not only represented, they are themselves the means for representing the world of the novel. Between the poles of complete objectification (a language portrayed as a dead thing, worthy of satire but in no way productive) and reverential transmission (the mode by which authoritative discourses are conveyed), novelistic discourses are dialogic, speaking to each other and to the author (conceived of as an intentional position, not an expressive subjectivity).[4]

In so far as Bakhtin historicises the novel and assigns a comparative value to it, however, the concept becomes unstable. Bakhtin sometimes describes the novel as a genre distinct from the epic, the drama, or poetry, emphasising the power of novels to open into ongoing history (in contrast with the bounded world of epic) and to subvert official or high discourses by relativising them (in contrast with the monoglossia he ascribes to drama and poetry). But at other times he suggests that only one kind of novel conforms to this definition – the heteroglossic, dialogic novel, exemplified by Dostoevsky – whereas other texts that he also identifies as novels are more monologic and epical, and not at all subversive. Bakhtin's conception of the novel uneasily promotes several claims: the roots of the novel in ancient serio-comic genres and in the carnivalesque modes of popular discourse in the Renaissance; the novel's early (pre-nineteenth-century) association with low genres (DN, p. 379); the novel's formal capacity to represent heteroglossia; and the potential within the novel form for differing degrees of ideological conformity or enforcement.

To some extent, these claims can be organised around two issues. The first concerns the historical intelligibility of the novel's subversiveness: Bakhtin tries to endow the novel with a subversive potential derived from its inscription, through its ancestry, with (lower-)class identity and class resistance.[5] The second concerns the somewhat dehistoricised formal capacity of the modern novel to relativise the official discourses of its own day (even though some novels, Bakhtin concedes, reinforce them). The novel would therefore seem to be subversive partly because of a value or complex of values that it represents and partly because of its capacity to bracket as discourses and thereby undermine whatever values the official (presumably oppressive) regime espouses. The novel's historical associations seem to become part of its identity or being in the first version, whereas in the second version the novel serves as Other to dominant discourses, as a threatening projection of the lacunae in their own identities. Therefore, these two dimensions might be formulated as the essentialist and the reflexive understandings of the novel, respectively.[6]

Julia Kristeva insists that the carnivalesque relativising Bakhtin promotes is always the transgression of a law on behalf of '*another* law'; otherwise, it would be irresponsible and irrelevant linguistic play.[7] And Bakhtin himself, in emphasising the addressivity of the word (its orientation towards its speaker and its audience), would also seem to imply that any subversion takes place along a specific vector, on behalf of a specific speaking position. Yet his main accounts of the novel in 'Discourse in the novel' and *Problems of Dostoevsky's Poetics* tend to obscure this implication. His study of Rabelais (one of the novel's important predecessors) is, however, explicit about the value that Rabelais's central representational mode, the carnivalesque, promotes: it is the body, considered as a slighted partner in meaning.

Carnival subversion, as Bakhtin describes it in *Rabelais and His World*, is directed against an official language that would deny the body, the cyclical nature of human life, and the triumph of the species over the death of the individual. Bakhtin holds the carnivalesque to be an antidote not only to a particular dominant meaning but also, more profoundly, to a particular *form* of meaning: the abstracted, disembodied concept of meaning that the Platonic philosophical tradition has favoured. Carnival laughter is not an abstract negation, a bracketing 'not-x'. It undermines official language in the Renaissance by mocking it, em-bawdying it, and re-connecting it to the life cycle: 'Negation in popular-festival imagery has never an abstract logical character. It is always something obvious, tangible. That which stands behind negation is by no means nothingness but the "other side" of that which is denied, the carnivalesque upside down.'[8]

Carnival laughter challenges traditional concepts of logic and identity. It is ambivalent in that it affirms and denies at once, diminishing the individual but re-ennobling him or her through the medium of the collectivity; it expresses 'the point of view of the whole' on the whole, not private ridicule (p. 416). In addition to its oral genres, which are characterised by hyperbolic praise and abuse, its principal manifestation is the masquerade, in which masks destabilise identities in general and masked surrogates for high figures are ritually degraded and deprived of their official identities. Bakhtin proposes that these sexual or scatological humiliations defy official-dom's pretences to personal power and reassert the power of the metaphorical body of the people, the life cycle that transcends the individual.

The subversion of essentialising, abstract, unitary meaning on behalf of the body holds obvious attractions for feminism, which may be said to have taken the part of the body in several ways. Feminists have asserted the body's role in meaning (in shaping the voice, in providing the spatial modelling for the conceptualisation of the world, in the materiality of the sign). They have also called attention to the ways in which women play the part of the body for male subjectivity, being identified not only with both eerie and celebratory conceptions of reproduction but also with the threatening potential for the body to become a corpse and silence the mind. And they have investigated the reduction of the body to part-objects: to the objectified female erogenous zones, and to the having or not-having of a penis (misconstrued as the Phallus, a signifier of privilege, rather than as a mere bodily organ among others) which becomes symbolically overwritten as gender identity.[9] In the course of creating an abstracted, primarily mental version of subjectivity, Western culture has projected many aspects of the body on to its margins: not only on to women, but also on to the lower classes (Bakhtin's popular culture of pre-capitalism, the proletariat of capitalism) and on to outsiders it deems exotic and Other.[10] Women, like these other groups, have an interest in integrating the body's semantic and organic aspects in order to free themselves from *embodying* the body, symbolically, for their culture(s).

But the myth Bakhtin derives from Rabelais of a larger-than-life folk body, the emblem of material-based class consciousness for the people, raises more problems than it solves for feminists. Even aside from the fact that the 'symbolic, broad meaning' (p. 301) of the carnivalesque body cannot be unmarked by gender – so that women's participation in this myth, historically and figuratively, is problematised[11] – Bakhtin's concept of the carnivalesque folk-body harks back to a golden age in which 'the people' were clearly separate from official culture and therefore capable of making their critique from a conceptually pure 'outside'. Not only could there be no analogous myth of an outside for women; materialist understandings of culture preclude the possibility of any class stratification that is not maintained by the interrelations of classes. Although Bakhtin elsewhere suggests that true understanding from outside (exotopy, *vnenakhodimost'*) must be preceded by a moment of identification, and although he recognises that Rabelais himself participated in both high and low culture, he seems at moments to espouse an ideologically mystified, nostalgic, and historically suspect conception of the lower classes as a monolithically subversive force. At best, his account may be considered to elide the political, economic, and ideological interrelation of the 'high' and the 'low' and the historical proofs of the marketplace genres' subversiveness for heuristic purposes.[12]

But apart from Bakhtin's claims about its social origins, the concept of carnivalesque provides a useful gloss not only on the semantics of the body in Rabelais's text but also on subsequent shifts in the semantic range of the represented body. As Bakhtin describes it, the modern individual body comprehends both the sublimated (sentimentalised, abstracted) and the degraded (shameful, inert) conceptions of the body in privatised forms. The degraded conception of the body, however, no longer possesses the capacity to enrich the abstracted one because it has been privatised: whereas shit metaphorically attributed to the collective body of the people could symbolise the life cycle and the fertility of decay, personal shit is merely the detritus of individuals whose lives are separate and ephemeral (pp. 301–2). But even though most social forms of carnival have betrayed their popular origins by being (like the body) institutionalised or privatised, some literary traces of carnival forms survive in their true ambivalence: the 'genres of reduced laughter – humour, irony, sarcasm' (p. 120); the literary types of the rogue, the clown and the fool, who unsettle identities by parodying them; and the novel's tendency – derived from carnivalesque ridicule – to interanimate and relativise discourses. In each of these cases, the carnivalesque that Bakhtin originally imagined to exist outside official discourses persists only the form of an 'in between', an interstitial and relativising relationship to other meanings and identities.

Bakhtin's critique of the artificial opposition between meaning and the body that obtains in modernity by no means implies that this binary can be restored, through combination or synthesis, to some semblance of an original totality.[13] The sundering into body and meaning does not divide a whole into halves that may be reconnected, any more than the sublimated and degraded versions of the body could be joined to produce an undistorted whole. In this respect, Bakhtin's attempt to subvert the categories of meaning and identity greatly resembles the project of deconstruction, which de-naturalises binary oppositions by showing that their terms do not cohere. Deconstruction exposes the ways in which binary terms develop in response to each other and in response to the very category of meaning itself; it suggests that the stable definitions abstracted from words, and submitted to logical analysis, are in fact misleading generalisations that occlude the textual and semantic specificity of the differing usages of a word. Bakhtin's emphasis on the primacy of the utterance – the discursively, historically, and subjectively specific use of language – leads to a similar conclusion about the fraudulence of abstracted definitional categories. Yet an advantage of Bakhtin's approach over deconstruction lies in its greater emphasis on the (socio-)historical and subjective, or intentional, constitution of language.[14] At this juncture, where the social practices of individuals are transmitting and refracting discursive traditions, ideology can be grasped not as a seamless system but as a dynamic and temporal interrelation of utterances.

Because of its emphasis on the intersubjectivity of the utterance, Bakhtin's work reminds us that any attempt at purely semantic subversion addresses itself to another utterance: a particular deployment of a category of meaning that is itself in the process of historical becoming. The logical negation or linguistic transgression of a conceptual category may or may not affect the disposition of power that it justifies or conceals within specific utterances; however, such an assault may probe the digestive power and resilience of the dominant ideologies. In this light, carnivalesque literary form (the grotesque rejoining of separated and transformed categories) and content (the semantic elaboration of biology) can be understood as inextricable and vital protests against the specious separation of form from content, body from meaning – though not as literary encodings of an effective political protest. But even though the carnivalesque's literary and semantic subversion may have exerted a transformative ideological pressure on the dominant discourses it opposed, some of its effects seem to have escaped its original purpose. It was anti-individualist, to the extent that individualism imposes an abstracted and alienating concept of insular personhood. But it also drew upon the concept of organicism – aligning itself with humanism – as an alternative to the abstraction and repression promoted by officialdom, and organicism was subsequently institutionalised under less liberating auspices.

For by the time of Dostoevsky, authoritarian asceticism had given way to an organic version of liberal individualism within dominant political, scientific and literary discourses. The body had by no means been re-integrated with meaning, but a fascination with the body as a site of interchange between the individual and the environment had set in.[15] The new dominant ideology figured the individual as an organic whole whose transactions with the environment were *free*, in at least three senses: intentional, unfettered by significant collective obligations, and without subjective impact or 'cost' for the individual. As a result of this ideological transformation, the embodiment of Dostoevsky's characters mainly signifies their individuation, not their corporeal existence; Bakhtin does not emphasise the subversiveness of folk-tradition and bawdy laughter in discussing the novels of Dostoevsky. Instead, he locates Dostoevsky's importance in his depiction of characters who are ideologues – who interact with each other, who attempt to persuade each other, who represent certain values for each other. The dialogic novel of Dostoevsky implicitly criticises the *laissez-faire* relations among individuals in a market society by emphasising the mutual constitution of selves and the grounding of subjectivity in ideologically significant languages. This literary imaging of other languages and other persons as engaged and engaging subjectivities – however abstract and mystified their very mode of individuation might be – complicates the model of free human interaction promoted by classical economics. In other words, by the time of Dostoevsky the dominant ideology had come to incorporate certain elements of the carnivalesque forms that Rabelais and others had deployed against it, so that Dostoevsky's counter-hegemonic stance was significantly and appropriately different from that of Rabelais.

Viewed in conjunction, Bakhtin's discussions of Rabelais and Dostoevsky amount to neither an empirical account of the novel's history and form, nor a manifesto about what the novel should become. Rather, Bakhtin uncovers the ideological range of the novel genre we have inherited as a function of its past, and its history might best be understood as the accumulation of a repertory rather than as a linear development.[16] The novel does not simply espouse the values of the body deriving from the carnivalesque, but neither is it a value-free form that relativises all discourses indiscriminately. The heritage of the carnivalesque provides the novel with a set of specific strategies for relativising the discourses it portrays, strategies such as their incarnation in vividly embodied and concretely situated characters and the juxtaposition of discourses marked as high and low, inner and outer. These strategies lend themselves to the purposes of specific historical critiques with varying degrees of receptiveness.[17] Thus, the novel cannot be considered inherently (historically or formally) subversive, but neither is the novel as a genre a politically neutral vehicle for ideology.

The novel's potential to be oppositional without being merely reflexive, qualified by the individual novel's capacity to enforce or undermine dominant ideologies, affords a useful metaphor for conceiving of female identity as a range of particular relationships – subversive or affirmative – to an historically mutating power structure.[18] The example of the novel suggests that the history of women's oppression and resistance by no means guarantees subversiveness to female identity, whether that subversiveness is construed essentially (as the promotion of female values) or reflexively (as the conceptual bracketings of masculinity and phallicism represented by French feminist theories about the transgressive multiplicity of the female genitals and of female *jouissance*).[19] Nevertheless, the concept of 'woman' as an historically produced but ultimately rhetorical identity provides one useful way to reconcile feminist agency in sociopolitical life with the impossibility of essentialised female identity. From a feminist point of view, 'woman' must be disunified as a conceptual category and disavowed as an essential object of knowledge; but women must continue to be recognised as structuring sites, objects, and Others of utterance.[20]

Furthermore, a dialogic and historicised conception of subversion – exemplified by the interaction between the carnivalesque and the discourse of individualism – points to the need for women to redefine themselves continually and polemically due to official culture's propensity to re-annex the values that it has projected, in distorted form, on to its Others.[21] The patriarchal structure whose oppressions feminists combat is always changing, and the terms of feminist attempts at refutation and subversion must respond to these changes. For example, the growing attention paid by the media in recent years to the phenomenon of the 'sensitive man' and in general to men's capacity for nurturance – traditionally a feminine function – by no means implies that feminism has begun to work itself out of a job. On the contrary, feminists must investigate the shifts in political power and redefinitions of socioeconomic allegiances that have made this ideological accommodation possible (and *advantageous*) without its having wrought or reflected a significant change in the general socioeconomic position of women. Just as carnivalesque organicism proved susceptible to drastic reinterpretation, any value that women espouse for oppositional purposes can be not only 'double-voiced' but duplicitous, especially if it originated in the distorted projections and repressions of patriarchy (DN, p. 324).

Ideology as the vanishing-point of dialogue: the case of Gertrude Stein

Bakhtin's dialogic encounter with Dostoevsky's novels led him to develop a celebratory, heroic version of the discursive possibilities for interchange between self-conscious ideologues depicted in Dostoevsky's novels. Locating these ideological discourses in individuals also preserves individual agency. Despite the profound innovations of Dostoevsky's novels, however, the aspects of them that Bakhtin extols mainly fall within the practice of realism, the novelistic mode that predominated in the late nineteenth century: individual accountability was, after all, the byword of realism, even though it was typically understood as a matter of personal ethics rather than of existential authenticity. Therefore, I would like to consider Bakhtin's theory of the novel in the light of one of the stories from Stein's *Three Lives* (1909), a text on the cusp between realist and modernist conceptions of the novel. I claim it as a novelised form because of its engagement with the novelistic tradition and its foregrounded representation of incommensurate discourses; I do not intend to deny any distinction between the short story and the novel by this tactic. Stein's 'The gentle Lena' does not exemplify Bakhtin's theory of the novel but rather serves as an instructive rejoinder to it.

Stein's *Three Lives* undertakes the narration of ordinary, inarticulate lives. This is the problem of Western realism *par excellence* – something many critics have failed to take into account when they have contrasted Stein's attention to the lives of the lowly with a high-culture or patriarchal literary ideal of the heroic or event-filled literary life; the fascination with the ordinary experiences of ordinary people had, in fact, already overtaken Anglo-American prose fiction by the late nineteenth century. The significant innovation of Stein's *Three Lives* was not its subject-matter (which was inspired by Flaubert's *Trois Contes*) but its abandonment of one of the most significant chronotopic characteristics of realism: the time of decision-making and self-awareness.[22]

Classic realism had replaced heroic action with heroic subjectivity by representing the self-consciousness of characters, a textual space of reflection that seemed to endow them with a human potential greater than their circumstances.[23] George Eliot neatly articulated this solution in 1857 while enlisting the reader's sympathies for her ordinary characters: '[T]hese commonplace people – many of them – bear a conscience, and have felt the sublime prompting to do the painful right; they have their unspoken sorrows, and their sacred joys ... Nay, is there not a pathos in their very insignificance – in our comparison of their dim and narrow existence with the glorious possibilities of that human nature which they share?'[24] Elaborating this human nature became one of the primary concerns of classic realism, accomplished by a narrator who bore the burden of ideology by undertaking to account for the *representativeness* of every action, the illustrative or explanatory value that distinguished it from mere contingency. As a result of this emphasis on typicality, the reader's identification with characters was supposed to take place on a level of common human nature that transcended circumstances. The characters into whose subjectivities the narrator dips try to make generalisations about human nature from their experience, and in turn to apply those rules ethically; this space of ethical reflection is the main token of subjectivity within realism.

In contrast to the play of induction and deduction in the classic realist novel, Stein's narrator and characters in 'The gentle Lena' – the third of her *Three Lives* – seem to be remarkably opaque, slow-witted, and cautious about generalisations. The characters are not ideologues (as in Dostoevsky, and to a lesser extent in typically realist novels), and neither is the narrator an ideologue (as in most realist novels). There is no space of reflection or decision-making, except for the barest reference to what Lena feels or knows on a few rare occasions. It would, in fact, be hard to *characterise* either the narrator's relationship to Lena or our own, precisely because of the narrator's refusal to signal in her own discourse either Lena's subjectivity (with which we could identify) or her secure objectification (which we could pity).

This ambiguity within the representation of Lena appears most strikingly in the narrator's references to 'Poor Lena'. The repetition of the phrase (like many repetitions in Stein) renders it suspect, opening up a casual use of language that could pass for cliché to a more discriminating attention. Furthermore, the phrase is ironised by Mrs Haydon's having warned her daughter Mathilda that 'she [Mathilda] knew her cousin Lena was poor and Mathilda must be good to poor people'.[25] Since Mrs Haydon's perception of Lena as poor allows her to manipulate Lena, and since her daughter Mathilda's perception of Lena as poor contributes to Mathilda's contempt for her, we are made to see that pity for Poor Lena by no means implies sympathy with her.

It is important to differentiate the way in which Stein destabilises her narration from the kind of ultimately stable irony that

Bakhtin describes in 'Discourse in the novel' as grounding the 'hybrid construction(s)' in a Dickens novel (DN, p. 304). Bakhtin's examples from *Little Dorrit* show how the narrative double-accenting of certain 'official–ceremonial' languages and languages of public opinion expose 'the hypocrisy and greed of common opinion' (DN, p. 307). One of his examples is the narrator's voicing of the general awe at a sumptuous dinner given by Mr Merdle, the climax being, '*O, what a wonderful man this Merdle, what a great man, what a master man, how blessedly and enviably endowed* – in one word, what a rich man!' Bakhtin explains, 'The whole point here is to expose the real basis for such glorification, which is to unmask the chorus' hypocrisy: "wonderful", "great"', "master", "endowed" can all be replaced by the single word rich ... The ceremonial emphasis on glorification is complicated by a second emphasis that is indignant, ironic, and this is the one that ultimately predominates in the final unmasking words of the sentence' (DN, p. 304).

Despite the complexity of the sentence's multi-addressivity (the people's address to each other and to Mr Merdle, the narrator's address to us), the italicised words in the quotation are stably ironised. The truth of social esteem, we see, is money and the self-interested relation of the have-nots to the haves. The false discourse of virtue is made to undermine itself for the sake of some unexhibited (in this example) *true* discourse of virtue. Indeed, Bakhtin's own references to 'greed' and 'hypocrisy' partake of this language of individual virtue. Hypocrisy in particular – a concept that permeates the nineteenth-century realist novel – presupposes an essential moral character that a represented individual attempts to deny, conceal or prettify. This judgement of hypocrisy is possible, in fact, only because the narrator stabilises moral judgement – whether of individual characters or of the straw man, public opinion – through authorial evaluation, or through the presentation of non-public episodes that seem to illustrate a character's most private and therefore most fundamental nature.

The lack of interiority in Stein's 'The gentle Lena' takes the story out of the realm of individual virtue or hypocrisy: similarly, its problematisation of discourses is not usually governed by classic irony. Aside from these innovations, Stein's parodic revision of realism is most apparent in the travesty of the central marriage plot. Lena, the main character, is a German immigrant who is happily established as a servant in the United States when the story begins. Overwhelmed by the machinations of her aunt and Herman Kreder's mother, Lena and Herman submit to being married. But their submission is not enough for their relatives, who try to convince them to *want* to get married. Herman's sister, to whom he flees on the date first set for his wedding, tries to graft a language of bashful sexuality on to the situation: '"I'd be awful ashamed Herman, to really have a brother didn't have spirit enough to get married, when a girl is just dying for to have him"' (p. 266). Herman's father also offers him a language for his situation: '... [S]aying you would get married to a girl and she got everything all ready, that was a bargain just like one you make in business and Herman he had made it, and now Herman he would just have to do it ...' (p. 263).

Similarly, Mrs Haydon, Lena's aunt, tries to present Lena with a narrative of Herman as a good catch, only to be irritated by Lena's incomprehension:

> 'Answer me, Lena, don't you like Herman Kreder? He is a fine young fellow, almost too good for you, Lena, when you stand there so stupid and don't make no answer. There ain't many poor girls that get the chance you got now to get married.'
> 'Why, I do anything you say, Aunt Mathilda. Yes, I like him. He don't say much to me, but I guess he is a good man, and I do anything you say for me to do.' (pp. 252–3)

What Mrs Haydon is asking of Lena is what Herman's sister and father are asking of him: for the couple to assume ideology, not simply to be subjected to it. Discourses of passion, of honour and of economic advantage are presented to Herman and Lena, discourses that would have them assume responsibility for their marriage. Their refusal to assume these discourses, to express anything but passive obedience, functions in some ways like the fool's polemical incomprehension of convention described by Bakhtin.[26] But they are not tricksters who gleefully elude fixed identities. Rather, they are estranged from the languages available to them.

Not all of the discourses of realism have been unsettled, though. For example, Stein's description of Lena's cousin Mathilda is couched in terms of moral evaluations (evaluations not thematised by the subsequent narrative, in contrast to realist practice) that are naturalised by being figured in Mathilda's body, as well as by being omnisciently pronounced: 'Mathilda was an overgrown, slow, flabby, blonde, stupid, fat girl, just beginning as a woman; thick in her speech and dull and simple in her mind, and very jealous of all her family and of other girls, and proud that she could have good dresses and new hats and learn music, and hating very badly to have a cousin who was a common servant' (p. 248). And Lena herself is given an aesthetic–sensual value in the opening of the story, a trace of romanticisation in the description of her voice being 'as awakening, as soothing, and as appealing, as a delicate soft breeze in midday, summer' (p. 239). Integral character is preserved; however, the use of repeated epithets – in addition to 'poor Lena', there are the 'good German cook' and the 'pleasant, unexacting mistress' – calls attention to the formulaic quality underlying any representation of stable identity in fiction.

Nevertheless, the narrative omniscience inherited from classic realism allows Stein to expose two factors in the constitution of identity that classic realism excludes: the unconscious and the impingement of ideology on the individual. Forgoing classic realist examinations of Lena's interiority (replications of her thoughts), the narrator none the less tells us what Lena does not feel, does not know, or does not know she feels. 'Lena did not really know that she did not like it' in Germany, we are told (p. 246). 'Lena would have liked much better to spend her Sundays with the girls she always sat with' than at Mrs Haydon's (p. 247). 'She did not know that she was only happy with the other quicker girls, she always sat with in the park' (p. 248). Lena 'did not ask if she would like being married any better' than being a servant (p. 254). Once Lena has been established in the Kreder home, 'nobody ever noticed much what Lena wanted, and she never really knew herself what she needed' (p. 269). The effacement of Lena's subjectivity is presented as her estrangement from her feelings and especially from her desires; in order to highlight the way in which other people's utterances appear to Lena as alienating imperatives, the narrator must assure us that Lena has suppressed unconscious desires, even a suppressed capacity *to* desire.

The attempts to appropriate or exclude desire in the story are mediated by the discourse of the *propre*: the relation between propriety and property governing society's demand that the self and its desires be contained and managed as a prerequisite for the individual's being awarded self-ownership.[27] Desire, in its unmanaged form, threatens to disrupt the *propre*: 'Herman all his life never wanted anything so badly, that he would really make a struggle against any one to get it. Herman all his life only wanted to live regular and quiet, and not talk much and to do the same way every day like every other with his working' (p. 271). The implicit opposition between orderly living and desire in this remark has in fact been developed by the story that precedes 'The gentle Lena' in *Three Lives*, in which the title character Melanctha's belief in a 'wisdom' that results from wandering (wandering that is accorded sexual, anti-domestic overtones) is contrasted with Jeff Campbell's endorsement of '"living regular and not having new ways all the time just to get excitement"' (p. 167). 'The good Anna' similarly highlights the efforts of Anna to manage other people, to 'put things in their place' (p. 39), to create orderly households and also to uphold her 'firm old world sense of what was the right way for a girl to do' (p. 24). If the good Anna practises a somewhat empowering (but also self-destructive) internalisation of the *propre*, and if Melanctha and Jeff articulate a struggle between the body's meaning-ful desires and the *propre*, then Lena might exemplify a body's passive and abject acquiescence to the ideological imperative of domestic reproduction that the discourse of the *propre* mediates. Bakhtin writes that in Dostoevsky's novels, '*a specific sum total of ideas, thoughts, and words is passed through several unmerged voices, sounding differently in each*'. But whereas Dostoevsky's method reveals '*the fully signifying word*', the word enriched by repetition, each rendition of the *propre* in Stein's text elaborates its deadening monologism and especially its capacity to set female subjectivity at odds with the female body.[28]

After Lena becomes pregnant, her old friend the 'good German cook' mourns the extent to which she has '"let [herself] go"' (p. 272) – failing to assume the *propre* in two senses. But Herman, in contrast, has found something to desire: 'It was new for Herman Kreder really to be wanting something, but Herman wanted strongly now to be a father, and he wanted badly that his baby should be a boy and healthy' (p. 275). Herman eventually takes upon himself the perpetuation of the *propre* in domestic life: 'He more and more took all the care of their three children. He saw to their eating right and their washing, and he dressed them every morning, and he taught them the right way to do things...' (p. 278). Whereas Herman assumes the discourse of the *propre*, channelling his desire into his role as *paterfamilias*, Lena increasingly loses concern for the body that she very clearly does not control. After the third child, Lena 'did not seem to notice very much when they [the babies] hurt her, and she never seemed to feel very much now about anything that happened to her' (p. 278). When her last child is born dead, Lena dies, too, and 'nobody knew just how it had happened to her' (p. 279). Herman subsequently becomes both father and mother, not only assuming Lena's function but also acquiring her personal adjective 'gentle' for himself and the children (pp. 278, 279) – a sinister dispersion of her identity.

Ideology functions in this text as the limits of what can be known, felt, and thought. It is not a positive discourse, embodied in an ideologue who can be refuted (as in Dostoevsky) or represented by the narrator in the inter-arrangement of discourses. Like the carnivalesque understanding of negation, ideology is not simply the abstract opposite of what is said but is rather the obverse, the implicated Other, of what is said. Experienced individually as an unconscious (Lena's failure to feel), it becomes socially intelligible according to what is unspeakable and thereby unthinkable: the unspeakable challenges to the *status quo* or the unspeakable assumptions that make the *status quo* possible. That Lena might have some desire that cannot be channelled into the domestic reproduction of society is unthinkable in the first sense; that Lena's death was the handy disposal of a body that had served its (others') purpose, not an unforeseeable contingency whose cause or logic 'nobody knew', is unthinkable in the second sense.

In contrast to Bakhtin's celebration of the festival of meanings (in which every one 'will have its homecoming')[29] and the liberation of the individual from monologic definitions, Stein's 'The gentle Lena' demonstrates language's potential to appropriate an individual repressively. Working from the realist depiction of characters as liberal and self-constituted individuals, Stein depicts an epistemological gap within the individual between feeling and knowledge that corresponds to the individualised, Freudian unconscious. And working from the realist ironisation of the discourses of common sense, common knowledge, and social propriety, Stein points to a new understanding of the ideological status of these discourses, inhering not in their interested concealment of some deeper truth (as in the hypocritical discourses of classic realism) or in their forthright articulation of existential relations, but rather in their limits, in their suppressions of knowledge and inquiry, and in their ability to obscure the possibility of counter-discourse.

In particular, Stein exposes the contradiction between the form of subjectivity implied by dominant social discourses (of romance, of honour, of economic negotiation) and the desires of the body (especially the female body) that those discourses attempt to order and manage. She exposes the access women have to this form of subjectivity as a kind of self-negation in 'The good Anna', even though the alternative represented by Lena's passive resistance by no means corresponds to a *'joyful relativity'*[30] or creative marginality. The text shows how ideology can function, not by being manipulated consciously by its beneficiaries (since the manipulators, Mrs Haydon and Mrs Kreder, are equally subject to the ideologies that they transmit), but by being internalised and embodied in the desires of the subject (as in Herman's upsurging of paternal desire).

Stein's feminist–modernist response to realism (which I am construing as a response to Bakhtin as well) raises disturbing questions. For example, does the narrator's stabilising knowledge of Lena's feelings have sinister implications in a culture in which women are too often spoken for? And doesn't the representation of a woman whose only choices are between self-alienating acquiescence to society's demands and inarticulate, equally self-alienating resistance to them reinscribe the futility of women's struggling against patriarchal discourses? It seems important, in considering these questions, to remember that Stein's text is not an assertion: not an authoritative answer, not a conclusive allegory in which Lena stands for all women within patriarchal societies. The story interrelates the ideological discourse of the *propre* and the twin projects of biological and ideological reproduction by demonstrating that ideology's discursive power to exclude or encode unconscious desires; it is not a model of all ideology's necessary functioning.

Stein's story hints at the kind of accommodation that Bakhtin's theories might productively make for some modernist novels, construed as an alternative (though not an equivalent) to the Dostoevskian way of representing ideology. And a Bakhtinian reading of 'The gentle Lena' reveals that the story's undeniable subversion of certain aspects of realism – a subversion that highlights the oppression of women in private life but that engages other literary and cultural issues besides feminism as well – is neither a bracketing and unimplicated negation of realism, nor a simple exposure of the ways in which classic realism occludes 'essential' truths about female experience. Rather, Stein's text squarely addresses realism as a polyphonic but ideologically specific artistic practice that has been shaped by the interests of patriarchy, and must be adapted to the purposes of feminism. This dialogic engagement with realism allows her to create a supple narrative that is both a version (a loyal, but not identical, repetition) and a subversion (a critical version, a version that lurks beneath the surface of realism) of the realist marriage plot, and it aptly dramatises the dialogic relation that every subversion maintains to its opponent.[31]

Notes

1 Bakhtin holds certain conservatively humanist views of literature: he values the coherence and mastery of authorial intentions, 'great time' as the test of the work of art's richness, and the organic unity of the work. Those of us who encountered these concepts within New Criticism or reverentially biographical forms of thematic criticism may sense a contradiction between post-structuralist Bakhtin and humanist Bakhtin; the tension between his aesthetics of organic containment and politics of hegemonic conflict deserves further attention. Nevertheless, it is certain that Bakhtin's emphasis on the social constructedness of authors and artworks disavows the transcendental overtones that claims about intentionality and artistic unity have acquired in twentieth-century Anglo-American criticism.

2 Mikhail Bakhtin, 'Discourse in the novel', in *The Dialogic Imagination*, ed. Michael Holquist, trans. Caryl Emerson and Michael Holquist, Austin, Texas, 1981, p. 421; subsequent references are given in the text as DN, followed by page number.

3 Varied generic definitions of the novel appear throughout Bakhtin's work; they are not all transparently in agreement, as I suggest below. The versions I privilege are most fully articulated in 'Discourse in the novel'.

4 Bakhtin, 'From the prehistory of novelistic discourse', in *The Dialogic Imagination*, pp. 44–5.

5 Bakhtin, 'From the prehistory', p. 50.

6 The complexity of Bakhtin's ideas about the novel might also be reduced to a conflation of description with prescription; this is to some extent Tzvetan Todorov's claim in *Mikhail Bakhtin: The Dialogical Principle*, trans. Wlad Godzich, Manchester and Minneapolis, 1984, p. 90. In general, however, the latter version of the two I propose – the novel as relativising technique – has predominated in criticism on Bakhtin, obscuring his careful attention to typologies of novel subgenres and other marks of formal and historical specificity within the novel. Katerina Clark and Michael Holquist, for example, state that 'Bakhtin assigns the term "novel" to whatever form of expression within a given literary system reveals the limits of that system as inadequate, imposed, or arbitrary' – a statement which reflects only Bakhtin's most extreme claims about the novel's powers of parodic critique and renewal (*Mikhail Bakhtin*, Cambridge, Mass., and London, 1984, p. 276).

7 Julia Kristeva, 'Word, dialogue, and novel', in *Desire in Language*, ed. Leon S. Roudiez, trans. Thomas Gora, Alice Jardine and Leon S. Roudiez, New York, 1980, p. 71.

8 Bakhtin, *Rabelais and His World*, trans. Hélène Iswolsky, Cambridge, Mass., and London, 1968, p. 410; subsequent page references are given in the text.

9 For a sample of the formulations by feminists, mainly working out of a psychoanalytic tradition, that have governed many Anglo-American treatments of the relationship between meaning and the body, see Elaine Marks and Isabelle de Courtivron, eds, *New French Feminisms*, Brighton and New York, 1981.

10 Peter Stallybrass and Allon White describe the further consolidation of this 'sublimated public body' as a specifically bourgeois phenomenon. Their revisionist reading of Bakhtin as the foundation for the study of the social constitution and interrelation of 'high' and 'low' has powerfully influenced my own reading of Bakhtin and subversion (*The Politics and Poetics of Transgression*, London and Ithaca, 1986, p. 93).

11 A detailed reading of the valences of gender in Bakhtin's reading of Rabelais is beyond the scope of this essay; however, it is significant that most of Bakhtin's attempts to explain away any personal misogyny in Rabelais's references to women merely reinscribe the symbolic subjectivity in the text. Wayne Booth also addresses the issue of misogyny in Bakhtin's reading of Rabelais, but he implies (construing misogyny as a personal rather than a symbolic offence) that the somewhat democratic inclusion of women's point of view in the text would have solved the problem ('Freedom of interpretation', in Gary Saul Morson, ed., *Bakhtin: Essays and Dialogues on His Work*, Chicago and London, 1986, p. 165).

12 Bakhtin's ideas on 'exotopy' or 'outsidedness' appear in 'Author and hero in aesthetic activity' ('Avtor i geroi v esteticheskoi deyatel'nosti'); they are referred to by Todorov in *Mikhail Bakhtin*, p. 99. See also Ann Jefferson's contribution to this volume, especially pp. 202–8.

   In deriving the carnivalesque as a literary phenomenon from the social practices of the marketplace, Bakhtin hypothesises a closer relationship between literary forms and socio-economic realities than he elsewhere deems defensible; see Todorov, *Mikhail Bakhtin*, p. 58. Moreover, some of Bakhtin's interpreters have suggested that he may have indulged in the myth of the subversive folk for polemical purposes, as a veiled critique of monoglossic Stalinism or as an antidote to sterile, overly abstract readings of Rabelais's work (see Clark and Holquist, *Mikhail Bakhtin*, pp. 295–320, and Richard M. Berrong, *Rabelais and Bakhtin: Popular Culture in 'Gargantua and Pantagruel'*, Lincoln, Nebraska and London, 1986, p. 107 and *passim*). On the problematic subversiveness of carnivals, fairs, and markets, see Stallybrass and White, *The Politics*, especially pp. 15–18.

13 Feminists who hold certain values (nurturance, sharing, an orientation toward processes, caretaking of the body and the living space) to be essentially female and worthy of being emphasised over the falsely dominant male values (aggression, competition, goal-orientation, abstraction and intellection) succumb to this belief that the sexes possess complementary sets of 'essential' possibilities for human self-realisation. Similarly, any attempt to synthesise the sexes into an androgynous whole merely reinscribes the distortions of the categories themselves.

14 On the relationship between Bakhtin's theories and deconstruction, see Juliet Flower MacCannell, 'The temporality of textuality: Bakhtin and Derrida', *Modern Language Notes*, C: 5, 1985, pp. 968–88; Graham Pechey, 'Bakhtin, Marxism and post-structuralism', in Francis Barker *et al.*, eds, *Literature, Politics and Theory: Papers from the Essex Conference, 1976–1984*, London and New York, 1986, pp. 104–25; and Allon White, 'Bakhtin, sociolinguistics and deconstruction', in Frank Gloversmith, ed., *The Theory of Reading*, Brighton and Totowa, NJ, 1984, p. 133.

Derrida repeatedly emphasises the historicity of the sign and the scene of writing, but the tendency of deconstructive readings thus far has been to undo terms as verbal-conceptual abstractions within the context of intellectual history, at what Bakhtin would call their 'semantic heights' (DN, p. 284).

15 The sublimated interchanges of the body became the object of faculty psychology, which considered the link between cognition and bodily perception in an abstracted form; they also emerged as pathos to be managed in the literature of romanticism and realism. Similarly, the degraded body was posited by Darwinism and naturalism. In these conceptions, the body was thematised as a link to generation and mortality, but only on an individual level.

16 Bakhtin explicitly compares generic tradition to a language in *Problems of Dostoevsky's Poetics*, ed. and trans. Caryl Emerson, Manchester and Minneapolis, 1984, p. 159.

17 For example, nineteenth-century Anglo-American novels readily juxtaposed inner and outer views of character in order to expose individual dissimulation and hypocrisy, but such critiques were always in danger of being reduced to *ad hominem* judgements rather than evaluations of broader social systems.

18 The relationship between women and the novel exceeds mere analogy because of the historical intersection of women's and the novel's concern for the revaluation of the body. Diane Price Herndl also addresses this relationship in the context of theories of feminine writing in 'The dilemmas of a feminine dia-logic' (paper read in the session 'Toward a Theory of Feminist Dialogics' at the 1987 convention of the Modern Language Association).

19 For an elaboration of these theories, see especially the selections by Luce Irigaray, Hélène Cixous, and Julia Kristeva in Marks and de Courtivron, eds, *New French Feminisms*, as well as Kristeva's 'The novel as polylogue', in *Desire in Language*.

20 This double imperative was formulated at least as early as 1974 by Kristeva and restated at least as recently as 1985 by Toril Moi. It is worth considering repeatedly because all the resolutions so far proposed to it, to my knowledge, take the form of imperatives, barely grasped metaphors, or necessarily abstract analogies. Discovering a viable articulation of female identity for the post-structuralist era is, arguably, the most urgent task of feminism at this time, and in the meantime every new approach to the problem renders it slightly more conceivable. See Kristeva, 'Women can never be defined', in Marks and de Courtivron, eds, *New French Feminisms*, p. 137, and Toril Moi, *Sexual/Textual Politics: Feminist Literary Theory*, London and New York, 1985, p. 13.

21 Stallybrass and White argue convincingly that transgressive mining of its own symbolic margins is characteristic of the bourgeoisie: transgression can be 'a powerful ritual or symbolic practice whereby the dominant squanders its symbolic capital so as to get in touch with the fields of desire which it denied itself as the price paid for its political power' (*The Politics*, p. 201). But their account does not address the peculiar position of women who (if

they are bourgeois) can be both dominant and marginal.

22 The time of ethical reflection that I describe could be considered a further, specialised development of '*psychological time*', which Bakhtin describes as an innovation of the novel of ordeal; it seems to me to be a distinctive chronotopic hallmark of realism (Bakhtin, 'The *Bildungsroman* and its significance in the history of realism', in *Speech Genres and Other Late Essays*, ed. Caryl Emerson and Michael Holquist, trans. Vern W. McGee, Austin, Texas, 1986, p. 15).

23 Catherine Belsey persuasively elaborates a politicised account of the concept of 'classic realism' in *Critical Practice*, London and New York, 1980, especially chapters 3 and 4.

24 George Eliot, *Scenes of Clerical Life*, ed. David Lodge, New York, 1982, pp. 80–1.

25 Gertrude Stein, *Three Lives*, New York, [n.d., reprint of 1909 edition], p. 249; subsequent page references are given in the text.

26 See Bakhtin, 'Forms of time and of the chronotope in the novel: notes toward a historical poetics', in *The Dialogic Imagination*, p. 164.

27 The French word *propre* can convey not only the sense of 'propriety' but also of 'one's own' (possessions or self) and connects etymologically to 'property'; this significant linkage between bodily conduct, public respectability, ownership, and subjectivity was pointed out by Derrida in 'La Parole soufflée', in *Writing and Difference*, trans. Alan Bass, London and Henley, 1978, p. 183.

28 Bakhtin, *Problems*, pp. 265–6 (Bakhtin's italics).

29 Bakhtin, 'Toward a methodology for the human sciences', in *Speech Genres*, p. 170.

30 Bakhtin, *Problems*, p. 124.

31 Consultations with Paul Foster have been invaluable to me in preparing this essay.

Tony Crowley

Bakhtin and the history of the language

> Historians have constantly impressed upon us that speech is no
> mere verbalisation of conflicts and systems of domination, but that
> it is the very object of man's conflicts. (Foucault)

One of the most remarkable facts about the history of the language
as a field of academic research in recent years has been its tenacious
resistance to modern theoretical work. This is surprising given the
centrality of questions of language and history in modern theory. It
is all the more surprising given the enormous theoretical and speculative foundations of the discipline of historical linguistics in the
nineteenth century – ranging from anthropological to geological
concerns – of which the history of the language was a sub-branch.
Yet it is none the less true that the sort of debates which have
dominated literary studies have had no place in the history of the
language. One pertinent, if historically odd reason for such an omis-
sion is that the field has been characterised by a rigorous adherence
to the Saussurean division between what is properly internal and
external to the study of language. According to this division internal linguistics was to concentrate on the formal relations between
units within a system; external linguistics on the relations between
language and race, languages and political history, language and
institutions and so on.[1] The result of the division was a field of study
largely devoted to formal linguistic inquiry with only minor, and
certainly untheorised, attention paid to questions of what was
termed 'style'.

However, with the shifts which have taken place within
modern theory itself a new situation has developed. The theoretical
drift away from the more arid types of formalism to what can be
described as more discursive and, both implicity and explicitly,

political forms of critique has had deep effects. Across fields such as linguistics, literary criticism, philosophy and historiography, there has been a significant appreciation of the social constitution of their objects and the political implications of the methods of treatment of such objects. A key set of texts in this shift has been those of Bakhtin, whose influence, it seems, continues to grow apace. Yet if such influence in these fields has been significant, not least in the production of an historical self-consciousness, it is ironic that these texts have had almost no influence in the field in which their importance seems obvious. For like that of the other major theorists, Bakhtin's work has been resolutely ignored in the history of the language, despite the fact that this work seems to offer a number of crucial insights which open up new directions in the field. His theoretical and historical treatment of forms of discourse appears to provide the foundations for bridging the gap between the internal and external approaches – or if not bridging the gap, then exposing the division as theoretically untenable and regressive. The importance of this is that if the gap were to be bridged, or exposed as a false division, the field would be radically altered in terms of both its methodology and its aims. Therefore the aim of this essay will be to explore precisely such a possibility by considering the relevance of Bakhtin to the field of study entitled the history of the language.

The key concepts

It is possible, and indeed his translators frequently do it, to draw up a glossary of the key Bakhtinian terms. If such a glossary were to be compiled with particular reference to those terms relevant to the study of the history of the language then it would necessarily include the coupling of dialogism and monologism along with monoglossia (*odnoyazychie*), polyglossia (*mnogoyazychie*), and heteroglossia (*raznorechie*). Therefore in considering the utility of these terms to the field under consideration it will be necessary first to ascertain the ways in which Bakhtin uses them in his own analyses. The two terms dialogism and monologism are evidently central to his work and yet, as Ken Hirschkop has noted, they are terms whose function alters across his texts.[2] The change can be characterised as the politicisation of philosophical concepts, and takes place between the early and later texts. In the early use these terms refer to opposed 'world-views', one of which (monologism) is superseded by the other in an ethical and teleological progression. In their later use, however, the terms are employed in at least three distinct ways. First, to refer to the historical forces which are in conflict in discourse: dialogical versus monological forces. Second, to the effects brought about by the conflict: monological or dialogical forms of discourse. Third, to the nature of the conflict itself: given that the forces are always in conflict, the form which dominates at any one time has to engage in constant dialogical re-negotiation with the other in order to retain its position. This development from a static view of opposition to the perception of active historical conflict is crucial, since its stress on dialogical struggle as the foundation of all forms of discourse allows for the relation between particular dialogical and monological forms to be theorised from an historical perspective. They can thus be viewed as the results of precise social struggles in which their status and position are always at stake. This in turn means that, rather than an ethical and teleological viewpoint, these terms now embody a political mode of analysis which facilitates not simply readings of past formations of discourse, but the possibilities of interpreting and changing those discursive forms which dominate our present.

The general principle to be abstracted from this theoretical politicisation is that all forms of discourse – from the smallest units to the national language and beyond – are shot through with social and historical conflict. With regard to the history of the language this is a revolutionary principle, since it threatens to deconstruct the rigid polarisation of interests which had been its fundamental tenet. For rather than privileging internal over external concerns, Bakhtin's premiss means that such a hierarchy would be reversed; but more than this, it would also mean that those forces which had been thought of as not properly belonging to the field would now be viewed as constituting it. The complex relations between, for example, languages and political history are taken in the Bakhtinian perspective to embody the conflict of social forces which will produce particular discursive forms, effects and representations. For the history of the language, if this view were taken seriously, this would mean that its static conception of language, in which any particular language moves through evolutionary stages of being, would have to be replaced by the view which saw the very concept of *a* language as already the result of particular social conflicts. The field would then have to be more concerned not only with questions of history and struggle but with a self-conscious reflection of the role of the field in such struggles. It is this which has been so markedly absent from the field as yet, and this which is necessary for the field to give an adequate account of its object.

If dialogism–monologism are key themes in Bakhtin's work in general, then monoglossia, polyglossia, and heteroglossia would seem to have particular importance for the history of the language. Yet these terms also shift their signification in his texts, and it is likewise important to distinguish their differing uses. In one set of uses, mirroring the static conception of opposed forces set out in the early dialogic–monologic pairing, these terms referred to stages in the historical being of language. Monoglossia therefore would be the primary state of being of a language which reflected directly the self-enclosed 'world-view' of its speakers. Homeric Greek might be cited as such a monoglossic form, since it signalled its blindness to difference and desire for purity in its division of the world into Hellenes and Barbaroi (Greek speakers and the rest). Such a form is represented as self-sufficient and self-originating and approaches a theological status which is typified in Socrates' claim in *Cratylus* when he refers to the language 'in which the Gods must clearly be supposed to call things by their right and natural names'.[3] Another example of the monoglossic language might be Anglo-Saxon, since it too was often represented as the purest form of a particular language. In this representation it was the 'true English' before it was bastardised in its miscegenation with the Norman French.

According to the same teleological and ethical order presented earlier, monoglossia is superseded by polyglossia when the self-sufficient language becomes conscious for the first time of otherness. In *Cratylus* such otherness is already perceptible in Socrates' references to geographic, historical, social and gender-related variation which needs to be suppressed, by way of the *etumos logos*, in order to recover the divine language of truth. However, once the perception of differences has entered then the self-enclosed Ptolemaic language becomes irreversibly transformed into the open Galilean set of languages in a variety of relations with one another. Latin would play the role of polyglossia to the Greek monoglossia since Latin came into existence aware of itself as precisely not self-sufficient but derived at least in part from its Greek forebear. In such a shift the absolute confidence of self-origination is relativised by the acute awareness of historical roots and therefore dependence.

The final stage in the schema occurs when polyglossia is supplanted by heteroglossia and both internal and external differences are uncovered. In this stage of being a language drops the absolute and relative unity characteristic of its former stages and thus reveals the full dialogic and heteroglot reality of its pluralistic character:

... the internal stratification of any single language into social dialects, characteristic group behaviour, professional jargons, general languages, languages of generations and age groups, tendentious languages, languages of the authorities, of various circles and of passing fashions, languages that serve the specific socio-political purposes of the day, even of the hour ...[4]

At this stage any positing of unity becomes a transparent fiction by which the complex inter-relational differences of all these languages is suppressed.

The teleological and ethical tone which accompanies this schema is one which Bakhtin never quite manages to lose. For it is always and everywhere the case that dialogism is preferable to monologism and heteroglossia to monoglossia. The validity of this view will be challenged later, but first it is necessary to demonstrate the limitations of such a view and the attempts made by Bakhtin to overcome them. For Bakhtin it is clearly the case that polyglossia and heteroglossia are ethically superior to monoglossia, since in the transformation from the earlier to the later stages, 'Language is transformed from the absolute dogma it had been within the narrow framework of a sealed-off and impermeable monoglossia into a working hypothesis for comprehending and expressing reality ... Only polyglossia fully frees consciousness from the tyranny of its own language and its own myth of language.'[5] In this transformation the forces of liberation are victorious in their conflict with those of narrow dogmatism, and yet if such a view is followed to its (teleo-)logical conclusion then it can only follow that we live today in a world in which the forces of linguistic liberation have triumphed. It is an argument made by Bakhtin when he argues that we too live in a world which is beyond monoglossia:

> We live, write, and speak today in a world of free and democratised language; the complex and multi-leveled hierarchy of discourses, forms, images, styles and linguistic consciousnesses was swept away by the linguistic revolutions of the Renaissance. European *literary* languages – French, German, English – came into being while this hierarchy was in process of being destroyed ... For this reason these new languages provided only very modest space for parody: these languages hardly knew, and now do not know at all, sacred words ... (PND, p. 71)

Such optimism could only be brought about by rigid adherence to a teleological schema whose accuracy would be disproved by one quick glance at the historical conditions which actually prevail in our world. However, it is at this point that the shift which took place in the use of the dialogism–monologism pairing has further relevance. For under the influence of the politicised conception of those terms, the relations between monoglossia, polyglossia and heteroglossia appear very differently. Rather than seeing these terms as referring to opposed stages of linguistic being in an irreversible teleology, the politicised view sees them as forms and representations of language brought about by social and historical conflicts. Monoglossia, in such a view, would be the product of the dialogical struggle between opposing tendencies, and although it achieves a certain stability its status could never be absolute: 'It must not be forgotten that monoglossia is always in essence relative. After all, one's own language is never a single language: in it there are always survivals of the past and a potential for other-languaged-ness ...' (PND, p. 66). Monoglossia is now a result of historical circumstances which can be altered rather than a primary, pure stage of language. Its representation as a version of the pure Adamic language in which world and word meet is the result of the desire for purity rather than historical accuracy.

Once this shift had been made, the impossibility of monoglossia (and in consequence polyglossia and heteroglossia) as actual stages of linguistic being led to the crucial, axiomatic statement on the processes of historical becoming in language: 'Thus at any given moment of its historical existence, language is heteroglot from top to bottom: it represents the co-existence of socio-ideological contradictions between the present and the past, between differing socio-ideological groups in the present, between tendencies, schools, circles and so forth ...' (DN, p. 291). In the same sense in which dialogism can refer to both a form of discourse and the founding principle of all such forms, heteroglossia is also one of the historical representations of a language as well as its grounding characteristic. From this the importance of the historical, conflictual nature of all discourse is apparent, and it is this which is of greatest significance for the historian of language.

The conflict of opposing tendencies is characterised by Bakhtin as the perpetual dialogic struggle between centripetal forces whose aim is to centralise and unify, and centrifugal forces whose purpose is to decentralise. The crucial point is that in their struggle the relations between such forces will differ in their forms and effects at different historical periods. At one time, and under specific historical conditions, centripetal forces will organise a certain form of discourse as the centralised, unified, authoritative form, and thus monoglossia and monologism will be effected. At another the centrifugal forces will be victorious and any such attempts at unity will become impossible. All forms of discourse and representations of language become dialogised in this process as effects whose forms are created by the particular historical arrangements of the opposed forces at any one time.

An example of such a discursive representation, and one with particular relevance for the history of the language, is the 'unitary language'. This is not, as it is represented in the title 'the history of the language', a historical fact waiting to be discovered, but a discursive form which has to be fought for: 'Unitary language constitutes the theoretical expression of the historical processes of linguistic unification and centralisation, an expression of the centripetal forces of language. A unitary language is not something given (*dan*) but is always in essence posited (*zadan*)' (DN, p. 270). Both the formal unity which it has, and the cultural unity whose purpose it serves, are the effects of massive centralising forces overcoming heteroglot differences. The sites of such struggles, ranging in Bakhtin's account from Aristotelian poetics to Indo-European philology, are the fields in which such significant discursive effects are achieved.

This brief account of Bakhtin's work has concentrated upon the important transformation of the central concepts and their consequent relevance for historians of the language. The shift is crucial in that it focuses attention on the various institutionalised sites of struggle in which the competing forces meet, and so enables historians to trace the battle lines of the conflict and the complex relations by which discursive effects and power are inter-related. There are, however, problems with such an account which specifically involve the level of abstraction at which such concepts are deployed, the lack of historical specificity, and a consequent failure to lose entirely the ethical and teleological tone which was attached to the early use of these concepts. These problems in turn mean that the specific questions of the relations between discourse and power are not fully answered. In the rest of this essay, therefore, the aim will be to give a sketch of one period of historical struggle between centripetal and centrifugal forces in order to develop the possibilities of their use and to tackle the problem of historical specificity. The site of conflict will be the history of the language in late nineteenth-century Britain and its desired object, the 'standard language'.

The formation of the unitary language

The history of the language as a distinct field of study with major cultural significance first appeared institutionally in mid to late nine-teenth-century Britain. Taking as its object a concept already inscribed in the politics of centripetalisation, *the* language, this field was at the heart of a number of important cultural debates. In their work on language the linguistic historians produced texts and read-ings whose effects across a whole range of discourses were a necessary part of the process of establishing cultural hegemony. In particular the concept of the 'standard language', and the uses to which it was put, was one of the central factors in this hegemony, and its role will be examined later. First it will be necessary to point to the discursive and political effects of the new field of study.

Bakhtin's argument claimed that linguistics, stylistics and the philosophy of language had been major centralising forces in the history of cultural formations whose method had consisted of seeking for unity in the face of diversity. Such methodology focused upon both formal unity, by means of the identification and stabili-sation of common linguistic features and their uses, and cultural unity, by means of an ordering of certain cultural functions of discourse and language. The attempt to forge unity took may forms: 'The victory of one reigning language (dialect) over the others, the supplanting of languages, their enslavement, the process of illumi-nating them with the True Word, the incorporation of barbarians and lower social strata into a unitary language of culture and truth ...' (DN, p. 271). The double-edged nature of unifying processes is significant in the task of achieving hegemonic rule in that it not only seeks the centralisation and solidification of grammatical or cultural forms but also insists at the same time that the cultural significance of such forms be centralised and solidified. Without the successful fulfilment of both tasks hegemonic rule in this area cannot be assured.

If the politicised version of Bakhtin's scheme is followed then it becomes clear that the nineteenth-century linguistic historians were engaged in a major way in the dialogic struggle between centripetal and centrifugal forces. However, as will be demon-strated, it is apparent that their work was not simply a form of centralisation which excluded diversity, since it is something of an oversimplification in Bakhtin's account to suggest that a form of discourse is simply either monologic or dialogic, or a language only monoglossic, polyglossic, or heteroglossic. What is striking about the work of the linguistic historians and its role in this respect is that, as in any effective hegemony, the forms with which they worked, and the representations which they effected, are protean. They change to meet the historical requirements of hegemonic rule, which are in turn dictated by the levels of resistance, necessities of inclusion, patterns of exclusion and so on. It is for this reason that the language is figured sometimes as a monoglossia, at others a polyglossia, and yet others a heteroglossia. The particular situation in which a representation is to be deployed dictates the form of the representation.

The social aims revealed in the texts produced within this field, to whose end representations were formulated, were principally three: national unity, social unity, and unity of political purpose in the imperialist project. Taking the first of these aims, one of the most overt demands of any group making a claim for itself as a nation in the nineteenth century was to claim a monoglot language and history as its own. The monoglot language had the function of marking off the nation's citizens from all others and binding them together in a fictional national equality, since it appear not to recognise either internal or external otherness – though in fact it will be argued later that it did precisely this. According to one linguistic historian language was the perfect instrument to reflect deep structural unity: 'It is evident therefore that unity of speech is essential to the unity of a people. Community of language is a stronger bond than identity of religion or government, and contemporaneous nations of one speech, however formally separated by differences of creed or of political organisation, are essentially one in culture, one in tendency, one in influence.'[6] In such a reading the unity of the monoglot language can operate as a guarantor of the depth of true cultural unification in the face of superstructural division. Against opposed political forces, however, such unity might well have been shattered if it had not been posited upon the basis of a seamless continuity of the present and past which seemed to offer further evidence of the durability of the nation. Writing of the education of the English schoolboy, one linguist made this representation of the language:

> Perhaps the next important step, is that his eyes should be opened to the Unity of English, that in English literature there is an unbroken succession of authors from the reign of Alfred to that of Victoria, and that the language which we speak *now* is absolutely *one* in its essence, with the language that was spoken in the days when the English first invaded the island and defeated and overwhelmed its British inhabitants.[7]

The eradication of linguistic difference in this example takes the form of a banishment of historical alterity in favour of a unified and radically synchronic system. Its effect is to suppress questions of change by pitting them against the posited depth of cultural unity enshrined in the language.

If the unity of the nation was seen as a question of ensuring the stable security of its self-definition, then the question of social unity took a distinct but related form. For once national unity had been posited there then remained the task of erecting a mythical form of equality in the area of citizenship. Here too the representations of language were important, since in such depictions the language became the cipher for those qualities of liberality, decency and freedom which were also held to be characteristic features of British society. Moreover precisely the same qualities were attributed to the language and its speakers, and thus on the question of word-borrowing one linguist was able to comment that 'the English language, like the English people, is always ready to offer hospitality to all peaceful foreigners – words or human beings – that will land and settle within her coasts'.[8] The language was to be revered sacramentally, 'worthy of our holiest and never-ceasing devotion', on the grounds that 'it will bear to future ages the sentiments of a free, generous, and singularly energetic race of men'.[9] This absolute symmetry of values shared by English speakers, their language, and the society in which they lived, was a common representation in a number of different discourses. Perhaps one of the most interesting and durable was that which saw this symmetry as stemming precisely from the fact that all three members of this holy trinity were held to be free from fixed rules which would constrict them. All three are gloriously irregular and unconstitutional in any precise sense of the term, and so the English language '... is like the English constitution, and perhaps also the English church, full of inconsistencies and anomalies, yet flourishing in defiance of theory. It is like the English nation, the most oddly governed in the world, but withal the most loyal, orderly and free.'[10]

These discursive representations had a specific role in the achievement of cultural hegemony in this period in its predication of a nation at one with its past, present and future, and which had arranged for itself the best of all possible social orders. It was a united, organic order in which liberality, consensus and freedom were the guiding principles. The forces of centripetalisation, however, were not confined to a united language internal to the British state, since the historical situation demanded rather more.

The consolidation of Britain as the imperial state required the extension of the monoglot language beyond the national boundaries until English became that frequently desired object, 'the world language'. The imperial language sought to extend its domain over the whole world: 'That language too is rapidly becoming the great medium of civilisation, the language of law and literature to the Hindoo, of commerce to the African, of religion to the scattered islanders of the Pacific. The range of its influence, even at the present day, is greater than ever was that of the Greek, the Latin, or the Arabic, and the circle widens daily.'[11] Outstripping other empires in the reach of its ambition, the imperial language was represented as carrying its liberal and decent qualities on to the world stage in order to take its rightful place: 'English is emphatically the language of commerce, of civilisation, of social and religious freedom, of progressive intelligence, and of an active catholic philanthropy; and beyond any tongue ever used by man, it is of right the cosmopolite speech.'[12] Such properly ordained linguistic domination meant of course that the 'cherished and sanctified institutions of its native soil' which were borne along with the language would be transmitted to those regions which fell under its sway. One linguist felt that this would eventually bring about a linguistic and cultural order in which the world would be 'circled by the accents of Milton and Shakespeare'. He concluded that this argued for 'a splendid and novel experiment in modern society', in which English would be the monoglossic language 'so predominant over all others as to reduce them in comparison to the proportion of provincial dialects'.[13]

The importance of such representations of the language is the historical confirmation of Bakhtin's assertions about the study of language. Such representations indicate the force of centripetalising tendencies in the formation of cultural unity as they are set against the historical differences of the past (in stressing national continuity), the present (in praising the liberality of the social order), and the future (in the promise of world domination). They are crucial in the processes of hegemonic dissemination in working towards a suspension of major differences in favour of minimal but durable unity and commonality.

Such are the general characteristics of the discursive and political effects of the new field of study in its early period. For a more specific analysis of such effects it will be necessary to turn to the actual material engagements of the field in the cultural debates of the period. The major project undertaken within the field of the history of the language was the recording of the unitary 'standard language', a term recorded as having been coined in the 1858 *Proposal* for the *New/Oxford English Dictionary*. The context for the coinage was the debate about what was to be included within the dictionary, a debate which in the very fact that it took place at all ruled out the possibility of the 'standard language' pre-existing its appearance in the dictionary. The lexicographers argued that the language did exist as a fact to be recorded by asserting that 'as soon as a standard language has been formed, which in England was the case after the Reformation, the lexicographer is bound to deal with that alone'.[14] In fact the arguments about whether there was such a standard form had raged for well over a century and a half, its *locus classicus* being Locke's extension of his arguments in favour of social stability to language, particularly in his warnings of the dangers of formal and semantic instability which so preoccupied the eighteenth century. For the nineteenth-century British historians, however, the 'standard language' was not a pre-existing fact – despite their theoretical protestations – but a unifying concept which gathered the materials upon which they had to work into an organised and delimited object. It was to become an object fully determined and centripetalised in the *Proposal* for the dictionary, the guidelines for its editors (the 'Canones Lexicographici'), and the eventual text itself. Moreover, it was to be not simply an object possessed of internal unity but one which also carried significant external centripetalising force.

The formulation of 'standard English' as a set of determinate linguistic forms and meanings can be traced in the texts of the history of the language and can be characterised as a form of monoglossia. The *Proposal* itself set out the monoglossic intentions of the lexicographers which were indicated by five principal delimitations: to ascertain the vocabulary by recording 'every word in the literature of the language'; to privilege writing over speech by professing to 'admit as authorities all English books'; to set the limits of English by marking off the historical point at which the language originated; to illustrate the meaning of the terms of the language; and finally, to settle their etymological history.[15] The purpose of these delimitations was to enable the recording of the 'standard language', which in this early use clearly refers to the literary language. In this task the monoglossia which is constructed is only relative since the historians were well aware of both the arbitrariness of their delimitations and the historical other-languagedness of English. However, in its centralising and authoritative influence even this relative monoglossia was highly important.

That such a monoglossia was theorised and constructed at this time is a problem if the early Bakhtinian use of the term is followed, since he had claimed that with the Renaissance and its consequences the national European languages had become polyglossic. If the later use of the term is followed, however, the problem disappears and the formation of such a monoglossia is explicable in terms of the conflict of opposing forces. In fact its appearance is related to those many other practices of centralisation and unification which occurred in nineteenth-century Britain. The processes of urbanisation and the consequent erection of national yet centralised forms of authority in institutions such as the police force, bureaucratic government and elementary education are parallel to the task of the linguistic historians in their own field. For the monoglossic standard literary language had a quite specific role to play in the formation of hegemony, since it offered a means of disciplining citizens with the purpose of ensuring that they took up only certain positions within the social order. The standard literary language, to be learnt in the novel forms of elementary education which appeared contemporaneously with it, was related to the requirements of an advanced technological form of capitalism, and in particular the need for a literate workforce. The linguistic historians, as with their professional counterparts in government, education and the police, to name a few of the organising agencies, were engaged in centralising and unifying work which had a clear relation to certain forms of power, since they provided the theoretical justification and the material exemplification of a certain form of 'standardised' literacy. This is not to attack such an effect, but to indicate its cultural significance and its implication with a number of other discursive practices.[16]

However, the relations between a monoglossic form and its discursive effects are perhaps most evident when considering a later development of the use of the term 'standard English'. In the later use it referred not to the literary language but to the language of the literate; if in the first use of the term it had referred to a linguistic 'fact', then in its later use a social fact became the basis of its definition: 'Standard English, like Standard French, is now a class dialect more than a local dialect: it is the language of the educated all over Great Britain.'[17] Its later Oxford English Dictionary definition gave it to mean 'a variety of the English language which is spoken (with modifications, individual or local), by the generality of the cultured people in Great Britain'. In this sense of the term the relations of the monoglossic 'standard language' to forms of discursive power are explicit: the monoglossic form is simply that of the powerful, the best, the educated, the cultured, of Great Britain. All other usage is relegated to the dialectal, provincial, rustic, and poor forms of the language.

The consolidation of 'standard English' as the monoglossic form spoken by the great and the good is a process which continues throughout the nineteenth and early twentieth centuries. Its effects on non-standard speakers were evident, since, as one observer of the urban proletariat argued when speaking in terms of liberal identification: 'always noisy, we rarely speak, always resonant with the din of many voiced existence, we never reach that level of ordered articulate utterance: never attain a language that the world beyond can hear'.[18] It is a silencing which appears to lend weight to Bakhtin's claims for the powerful blindness and exclusion brought about by monoglossia and its monologic forms. And yet, as the politicised version of these concepts indicates, it never can be the case that such forms triumph absolutely to bring about the silencing of the excluded other. Instead it is necessary to recall that such a victory is relative and determined by the historical situation. Rather than a total exclusion, the monoglossic 'standard language' and the processes by which it was disseminated brought about a precise pattern of inclusion which placed its subjects in certain positions and hierarchical relationships. The monoglossic form did not exclude differences but hierarchised them: posited as the central form, it then had ranged around it dialectal, class, gender and race-related differences in an inferior relation to its own powerful status. It was not blind to, but in a keen dialogical relation with, the heteroglot reality of the languages of a modernised society. It did not refuse difference but marked itself off as the form which could not be used by certain speakers, whilst at the same time damning their own speech as inferior. This is exemplified in the evidence provided by a non-standard speaker:

> This will be understood by a case of which I was told in a parish in Dorset, where the lady of the house had taken a little boy into day-service, though he went home to sleep ... the lady began to correct his bad English, as she thought his Dorset was; and, at last, he said to her weeping 'There now. If you do meake me talk so fine as that, they'll laef at me at hwome zoo that I can't bide there'.[19]

The silencing which certain observers perceive does not in fact take place; what occurs rather is the production of hesitancy, a faltering with words felt to be alien and difficult, and a sense of shame and inferiority when meeting with social and linguistic 'superiors'.

The task embodied in the erection of a monoglossic form in such circumstances, characterised by both formal and cultural unity, is the legitimation of a particular system of power relations. This takes place by the formation of an appearance of equality which in fact masks a hierarchy and which brings about the sacramentalisation of the authoritative words of which monoglossia is composed. These words, and the genres to which they belong, are forms whose authority attends them and which brook no argument. Or at least they strive for that end; for the important historical lesson is that such authority is not absolute but merely gathers to itself the appearance of finality and incontestability. For the spring of dialogism never runs dry, heteroglossia is always ranged against monoglossia, and carnival lies just beneath the surface. The observer who had previously noted the silence of the working class elsewhere notes their noisy entry into the forbidden territory:

> We gazed at them in startled amazement. Whence did they all come, these creatures with strange antics and manners, these denizens of another universe of being? ... They drifted through the streets hoarsely cheering, breaking into irritating laughter, singing quaint militant melodies ... As the darkness drew on they relapsed more and more into bizarre and barbaric revelry. Where they whispered, now they shouted, where they had pushed apologetically, now they shoved and collisioned and charged. They blew trumpets, hit each other with bladders; they tickled passers-by with feathers; they embraced ladies in the streets, laughing generally and boisterously. Later the drink got into them, and they reeled and struck, and swore; walking and leaping and blaspheming God.[20]

It is not silencing which has taken place, as this observer had previously claimed, but a denial of forms of discourse and power which would permit anything other than carnivalesque mayhem.

This short account of the way in which a monoglossic form of the language can be constructed to a particular end supports Bakhtin's claim for the constant struggle which takes place in discourse. Yet there are problems with his argument. For if the conflict which characterises social life is resolved in one way then monoglossic and monologic forms dominate, the word of the father is the last word, and authoritative discourse appears to be the only form permitted. If the conflict is resolved in another way, however ... then what? At this point there is a genuine problem in Bakhtin's work which centres on the difficulty of what it is that is to oppose monoglossia and monologism. For surely in modernised and differentiated societies certain forms of unity and organisation are necessary? Without them it is impossible to see how social life could be conducted. But if this is so then it must mean that there will be a necessary suspension of absolute heteroglossia in favour of unifying tendencies at particular levels. In Bakhtin's work, however, such a suspension does not seem conceivable, and instead an authoritarian form of monoglossia faces an ineffectively pluralist heteroglossia in a sterile binary opposition. Such an opposition clearly needs to be avoided, and the means of getting around it lies in taking the later politicised concepts which Bakhtin had articulated to their logical conclusions by stressing the importance of the historical context of the relations between the differing forms of discourse. Only then can they be evaluated politically, and it is this that needs to be explored by a consideration of specific historical examples.

Political contexts

It is clear that forms and representations of discourse and language play crucial roles in the operations of hegemony briefly considered above. Yet what is most significant from the perspective of those who are attempting to understand and change hegemonic rule as currently constituted is that such roles are not fixed but plastic. This is to argue that Bakhtin's stress on the differing relations between the concepts articulated in the politicised version of his histories of discourse is correct. Yet it is also clear that his preference for heteroglossia and dialogism, typified in his extravagant claims for novelistic discourse, needs to be challenged. This challenge has to read his work against itself by arguing that if the forms of discourse and language, and the roles they play, *are* dependent upon their historical and political contexts, then it is possible that in certain contexts a preference for heteroglossia and dialogism would be politically regressive. If monoglossia and monologism are not essentially absolute static forms then it is possible that they could play an important role in the struggle against certain authoritarian forms rather than reinforcing them. The question is this: if the ruling forces can adapt monoglossic, polyglossic, and heteroglossic forms and representations to their own purposes, then why cannot the forces which oppose them do likewise?

In order to answer this question both theoretically and with regard to empirical evidence, it is necessary to turn to another historical philologist whose work was also concerned with the connections between discourse and power. Gramsci commented in one of his *Prison Notebooks*: 'Every time the question of language surfaces, in one way or another, it means that a series of other problems are coming to the fore: the formation and enlargement of the governing class, the need to establish more intimate and secure relationships between the governing groups and the national-popular mass, in other words to reorganise the cultural hegemony.'[21] Gramsci's stress on the importance of language in the formation of cultural hegemony is essentially a political theorisation of Bakhtin's more elliptical assertions. For Gramsci, however, the importance of language lay not merely in this area but in the fact that at a more abstract level it functioned as a paradigm for the operations of social change and the achievement of hegemony. Thus it was at one and the same time involved in political practice and a blueprint for it. As Franco Lo Piparo has argued in *Lingua Intellettuali Egemonia in Gramsci*, the concept of hegemony was derived at least in part from the work of the 'spatial linguists' at Turin, and in particular from the work of Gramsci's supervisor for his thesis in historical linguistics, Matteo Giulio Bartoli.[22] Essentially the argument of the 'spatial linguists' was that linguistic change was brought about by the effect of the prestigious speech community's language in its contact with the languages of non-dominant neighbouring speech groups. Rather than by means of direct imposition, the 'spatial linguists' saw change as being effected by the operation of prestige on the one hand, and active consent to change on the other. Thus the spread of any particular linguistic feature, as it passed from the dominant community through to its subordinates, would be brought about by consent rather than coercion and would eventually become universal. If this argument as to the formation of Gramsci's concept of hegemony is correct then the importance of language to his work is central, for not only does it operate as the marker of social conflict, it also functions as the model for the means by which such conflicts are broached and resolved.

Given the central role ascribed to language, it is no surprise to find that Gramsci asserts implicitly the necessity of a language programme for any group which aspires to cultural hegemony. However, and it is at this point that his work takes a theoretical and practical line distinct from that of Bakhtin, Gramsci's argument is that in the historical and political conjuncture in which he was located, rather than arguing for heteroglossia, what was required was precisely the organising force of a monoglossia. If Bakhtin, faced with the increasing centralisation and brutal forms of unity engendered by Stalinism, had argued for the importance of diversity and pluralism, Gramsci, faced with a divided and multi-factional national-popular mass, stressed the need for unity. His argument in favour of a unitary language was based on the difficulties of organising an illiterate mass in a society in which literacy was largely the prerogative of the governing class. The argument is a useful reminder of the need to historicise theoretical debates:

> If one starts from the assumption of centralising what already exists in a diffused, scattered but inorganic and incoherent state, it seems obvious that an opposition on principle is not rational. On the contrary it is rational to collaborate practically and willingly to welcome everything that may serve to create a common national language, the non-existence of which creates friction particularly in the popular masses among whom local particularisms and phenomena of a narrow and provincial mentality are more tenacious than is believed. (p. 182)

In this historical situation a preference for heteroglossia over monoglossia would be a reactionary stance, given that it would serve only to heighten the differences which exist to prevent necessary forms of unity. In a situation in which a linguistic hierarchy exists, a refusal to work for common and unified forms is tantamount to support for an unjust distribution of power. If that refusal to intervene institutionally is based on an abstract rather than historical evaluation of monoglossia and heteroglossia, then what in effect is brought about is a denial of access to the forms by which organisation can take place: 'In practice the national-popular mass is excluded from learning the educated language, since the highest level of the ruling class, which traditionally speaks standard Italian, passes it from generation to generation, through a slow progress that ... continues for the rest of one's life' (p. 187). Gramsci's assertion that 'the "question of the language" has always been an aspect of the political struggle' can be seen to be analogous to many of the arguments proposed by Bakhtin. The difference, however, is that Gramsci pushes Bakhtin's arguments to the limits by refusing to attach any ethical overtones to them. For Gramsci, unlike Bakhtin, it is the historical situation which will enable the cultural activist to evaluate which are to be the required forms of discourse and language. Thus, although Bakhtin's preference for heteroglossia is correct when analysing the formation of the 'standard language' and its role in the cultural hegemony of Britain, it is correct only in regard to this particular historical conjuncture. The repressive and centralising forms of unity demanded by the imperialist state offer an example of a monoglossic language, and monoglossic forms of discourse, which need to be resisted by the privileging of heteroglossia and dialogism. But the diffuse and politically disorganised situation of Italy, in which lack of forms of unity amongst the national-popular mass served the interests of the governing class, requires a quite different analysis.

The fate of nations which have managed to escape from colonial rule and the historical complexities involved in such processes serve as further counter-examples to Bakhtin's preferences and again stress the need for historical specificity in the analysis of such situations. The preference for pluralism and difference may well be a laudable one: but history demonstrates that forms of unity and organisation may be a prerequisite before such an achievement can be attained. One example of a nation which defeated its colonial masters in a revolutionary struggle, and for which the question of the language was important, was America. After the War of Independence an important cultural task for the newly liberated people was the necessity of constructing a monoglossic 'federal English' by which they would at once mark themselves off as distinct from their former masters and posit themselves as a united federal nation. As one of the most famous of the linguists involved in this task, Noah Webster, argued in 1789,

> We have therefore the fairest opportunity of establishing a national language, and of giving it uniformity and perspicacity, in North America, that ever presented itself to mankind. Now is the time to begin the plan. The minds of the Americans are roused by the events of a revolution; the necessity of organising the political body and of forming constitutions that shall secure freedom and property, has called all the faculties of the mind into exertion; and the danger of losing the benefits of independence has disposed every man to embrace any scheme that shall tend, in its future operation, to reconcile the people of America to one another, and weaken the prejudices which oppose a cordial union.[23]

In this role the language was to act precisely as an abnegator of the differences which prevented union; in such a role, at such a time, its monoglossic function was radical rather than conservative. (In the altered historical circumstances of the present, of course, the relations between, and the political nature of, the centripetal and centrifugal forces has changed.)

Perhaps the most interesting example of the way in which the cultural functions of monoglossia and heteroglossia change historically is provided by Britain's oldest and last colony: Ireland. In early twentieth-century Ireland the English language served as a monoglossic language which, blind to the political differences which beset it in its use in Ireland, attempted to silence Irish aspirations for an independent national identity while at the same time ramming home the triumphalist position of the imperialists. This was the historical situation within which Joyce's texts were written and against which they were set. The familiar scene in *A Portrait of the Artist as a Young Man* in which the English Dean of Studies and Stephen discuss the propriety of the word 'tundish' is a good illustration of the social conflict embodied in discourse as it entails questions of political, literary and cultural identity. It is a debate which ends in silence for Stephen as he feels himself to be beyond the pale of the monologic tradition embodied in the Dean's 'best English': 'The language which we are speaking is his before it is mine. How different are the words *home*, *Christ*, *ale*, *master*, on his lips and on mine! I cannot speak or write these words without unrest of spirit. His language, so familiar and so foreign, will always be for me an acquired speech. I have not made or accepted its words. My voice holds them at bay. My soul frets in the shadow of his language.'[24] The monoglot language, at once familiar and foreign, necessary but felt to be alien, carries with it the force and violence of colonial oppression. It does not produce absolute silence but presents the colonial subject with a problem to which there appears to be no answer: how to engage in discourse without, in using the oppressor's language, reinforcing one's own dispossession.

The answer Joyce provided in this war with monoglossia and monologism was to pit against these forces absolute heteroglossia and dialogism. At the end of the 'Oxen of the Sun' chapter of *Ulysses* Joyce terminates what appears to be an account of the seamless development of the unitary language posited by linguistic historians with this:

> Waiting guvnor? Most deciduously. Bet your boots on. Stunned like seeing as how no shiners is acoming. Underconstumble? He's got the chink *ad lib*. Seed near free poun on un a spell ago a said war hisn. Us come right in on your invite, see? Up to you, matey. Out with the rof. Two bar and a wing. You larn that off of they there Frenchy bilks? Won't wash here for nuts nohow. Like chile velly solly. Ise de cutest colour coon down our side. Gawds teruth, Chawley. We are nae fou. We're nae tha fou. Au resevoir, Moosoo. Tanks you.[25]

Against seamless unity Joyce posits various forms of poly- and heteroglossic difference. Against the teleological arrogance of a literary tradition sure of its beginning and end Joyce undertakes an act of massive usurpation by placing himself as its culminating, triumphant master. Already in this extract from *Ulysses* we can read the language of *Finnegans Wake*. It is the language of absolute heteroglossia which explodes the very possibility of *a* (determinate) language by insisting on the intertextuality of all linguistic forms. It is likewise the language of absolute dialogism since, as even its title demonstrates, it is the language in which no form has only one meaning and all questions have at least two answers. Against the striving for purity characteristic of monoglossia and monologism and typified by that desperate search for the *etumos logos*, Joyce sets *Finnegans Wake* and the 'abnihilisation of the etym'.[26]

In this sense then Joyce enacted a form of political and cultural national self-assertion by attacking and resisting the colonial monoglossic language and its monologic traditions. The radical tools which he employed in this task were the heteroglot differences which had been suppressed or ranked as inferior. However, in what may be termed, optimistically, post-colonial Ireland (semi-post-colonial Ireland might be more apt), a new historical situation has arisen which requires a different cultural analysis. Again this is relevant to the development and use of Bakhtin's concepts, since it reveals how a distinct historical conjuncture, and one which has been formed within fifty years of Joyce's act of rebellion, will dictate what attitude is to be taken to forms of language and discourse. The linguistic situation in contemporary Ireland is complex: in the Republic of Ireland the official language of the state is Gaelic, though most people use a form of English (Hiberno-English) in their everyday interaction. In Northern Ireland, a separate state still under direct British rule, the dominant form is Ulster English (also known as Ulster Scots), while there are also small but growing numbers of Irish republicans who attempt to use only Gaelic for their everyday purposes. The linguistic complexities of the situation are perhaps mirrored only by its political difficulties, in particular the sustained urban guerrilla war which provides the backdrop for intricate and apparently intractable political view-points. Given the difficulties of the linguistic and political situation, it is not surprising that cultural activists have sought for forms which might engender unity at the expense of differences seen to be destructive and harmful. Thus the poet and cultural critic Tom Paulin has recently appealed for a 'federal concept of Irish English' modelled on Webster's 'federal English'. Such a monoglossic form would be a major radical step in Irish politics and culture since it would be tantamount to ignoring the border which currently divides Northern Ireland from Eire. It would lead, it is claimed, to an ideal cultural unity:

> Thus in Ireland there would exist three fully-fledged languages – Irish, Ulster Scots and Irish English. Irish and Ulster Scots would be preserved and nourished, while Irish English would be a form of modern English which draws on Irish, the Yola and Fingallian dialects, Ulster Scots, Elizabethan English, Hiberno-English, British-English and American-English. A confident concept of Irish English would substantially increase the vocabulary and this would invigorate the written language. A language that lives lithely on the tongue ought to be capable of becoming the flexible written instrument of a complete cultural idea.[27]

The role of language in the formation of cultural unity such as that aspired to here can only be undertaken by a language which has a certain level of stability and confident unity. It would necessarily be a monoglossic language which, though aware of its historical indebtedness to other languages, would be sure of a central place in a unified culture. In such an historical development the role of the monoglossic language would again be radical and progressive rather than narrow and dogmatic.

The force of these examples is not to discredit the validity of Bakhtin's theoretical distinctions but to demonstrate the necessity of developing them further in order to increase their utility for theories of discourse. The examples serve to show how the highly abstract and ethical evaluation which attaches to these concepts in Bakhtin's work is an impediment which can only be eradicated by specific historical analyses which take into account the relative state of the different forces. This has significant implications for the history of the language since it means that the field, while necessarily employing these concepts, will have to do so in a way which demonstrates a clear view of the historical and political contexts to which they are related. In turn this reveals the central significance of the question of power and its distribution. For although Bakhtin is correct in arguing that there is a constant conflict of centralising and decentralising forces in discourse, it sometimes appears as though this conflict takes place without historical cause and to little historical effect, save that of producing fresh discursive conflict. However, as the examples above demonstrate, the struggle between dialogism and monologism, and that between monoglossia, polyglossia and heteroglossia, is not simply a conflict of discursive tendencies and effects but a conflict in which what is at stake are precisely forms of power and their distribution. The political status of any particular form of discourse or representation of language cannot be decided in advance, since they depend on the historically specific forms of power which they engender. It is this that both historians of language and Bakhtin scholars will need to recall.

Notes

1 The Saussurean division is formulated in the *Course in General Linguistics*, Introduction, chapter 5.
2 See Ken Hirschkop, 'Bakhtin, discourse and democracy', *New Left Review*, 160, 1986, pp. 93–5.
3 *Cratylus* 391e, in *The Dialogues of Plato, vol. 3: Timaeus and other Dialogues*, trans. B. Jowett, London, 1970, p. 138.
4 Mikhail Bakhtin, 'Discourse in the novel', in *The Dialogic Imagination*, ed. Michael Holquist, trans. Caryl Emerson and Michael Holquist, Austin, Texas, 1981, pp. 262–3; subsequent references are given in the text as DN, followed by page number.
5 Bakhtin, 'From the prehistory of novelistic discourse', in *The Dialogic Imagination*, p. 61; subsequent references are given in the text as PND, followed by page number.
6 G. P. Marsh, *Lectures on the English Language*, New York, 1860, p. 221.
7 W. W. Skeat, *Questions for Examination in English Literature*, Cambridge, 1873, p. xii.
8 J. Meiklejohn, *The English Language: Its Grammar, History and Literature*, London, 1886, p. 279.
9 Rev. M. Harrison, *The Rise, Progress and Present Structure of the English Language*, London, 1848, p. 378.
10 G. C. Swayne, 'Characteristics of language', *Blackwoods Edinburgh Magazine*, March 1862, p. 368.
11 E. Guest, *A History of English Rhythms*, 2nd edn, London, 1882, p. 703.
12 Marsh, *Lectures*, p. 23.
13 T. Watts, 'On the probable future position of the English language', *Proceedings of the Philological Society*, IV, 1850, p. 214.
14 *Proposal for the Publication of A New English Dictionary*, London, 1858, p. 3.
15 The principal aims are set out on pp. 2–8 of the *Proposal*.
16 For a historical account of processes of centralisation in this period, see Gareth Stedman Jones's *Languages of Class*, Cambridge, 1983. For work which concentrates on the deployment of particular forms of language and literacy and their relation to the prevailing political contexts in French history, see R. Balibar, *Les Français fictifs: le rapport des styles littéraires au français national*, Paris, 1974, and R. Balibar and D. Laporte, *Le Français*

national: constitution de la langue nationale commune à l'époque de la révolution démocratique bourgeoise, Paris, 1974.

17 H. Sweet, *Sounds English*, Oxford, 1908, p. 7.
18 C. F. G. Masterman, *From the Abyss*, London, 1908, p. 25.
19 W. Barnes, *A Glossary of the Dorset Dialect*, Dorchester, 1885, pp. 34–5.
20 Masterman, *From the Abyss*, p. 3.
21 Antonio Gramsci, *Selections from Cultural Writings*, London, 1985, pp. 183–4; subsequent page references are given in the text.
22 See Franco Lo Piparo, *Lingua Intellettuali Egemonia in Gramsci*, Bari, 1979.
23 Noah Webster, *Dissertations on the English Language*, Boston, 1789, p. 36.
24 James Joyce, *A Portrait of the Artist as a Young Man*, Harmondsworth, 1960, p. 189.
25 Joyce, *Ulysses*, Harmondsworth, 1986, p. 347.
26 Joyce, *Finnegans Wake*, London, 1971, p. 353.
27 Tom Paulin, 'A new look at the language question', in *Ireland and the English Crisis*, Newcastle upon Tyne, 1984, p. 191.

Ann Jefferson

Bodymatters: self and Other in Bakhtin, Sartre and Barthes

I borrow the title of this essay from a British television programme whose underlying premiss is that the body matters primarily as a mechanism whose functioning the programme sets out to exhibit and explain. Human physiology is turned into a spectacle for our admiration and edification, and we are implicitly led to believe that all it takes to achieve psychological and social equilibrium is a proper recognition and management of the needs and workings of the human frame: *mens sana in corpore sano*. But the physiological *corpus* extolled by the TV is not the one that any of the writers discussed in this essay would be prepared to recognise as their own. Indeed Sartre and Barthes both explicitly disown such a body, and they do so in the first instance because it does not correspond to the form in which human subjects actually experience their own bodies. Moreover, they also dissociate themselves from physiological conceptions of the body because it is not physiology that figures in the intersubjective relations without which neither psychology nor sociality would be conceivable. The body matters in the work of the three writers I shall be exploring – Mikhail Bakhtin, Jean-Paul Sartre and Roland Barthes – because it proves to be indispensable both to the undoing and to the salvation of all our dealings with others. In one way or another all three give the lie to the notion propounded by our libertarian culture that repression can be undone by a freeing of the body and a proselytising dissemination of knowledge about its workings. Far from being a self-sufficient mechanism, the body in their conception is treated as the site and focus of a whole variety of problems and conflicts.

There are several reasons for discussing these three writers together. In addition to the fact that they are all theorists of the body in their own right, there is a measure of cross-fertilisation between them: Sartre's allusion to Bakhtin in one of his last interviews puts an intriguing gloss on the striking similarities between them on a number of key issues.[1] And as for Barthes, as Annette Lavers argues so persuasively, he has an undeniably Sartrian streak; this is made particularly explicit in his *dédicace* to *Camera Lucida* which he presents as a homage to Sartre's *L'Imaginaire*.[2] But the chief reason is that they all see self–Other relations in the same underlying terms: quite simply, these relations are determined by the fact that one does not see oneself as one is seen by others, and this difference in perspective turns on the body. More specifically, since the body is what others see but what the subject does not, the subject becomes dependent upon the Other in a way that ultimately makes the body the focus of a power struggle with far-reaching ramifications. Thus, in one way or another all three writers take issue with the popular claim that the body is free and self-determining: it is not and cannot be so because it is subject to the grip and grasp of the gaze of the Other.[3]

Taking these three writers together makes it possible to construct a sequence of argument that begins in the early 1920s with Bakhtin, proceeds via the Sartre of *Being and Nothingness*, returns to the Bakhtin of the 1930s and ends with the late work of Barthes in the 1970s, up to and including *Camera Lucida*. In a sense all I am proposing to do here is to offer an exposition of the ideas of these thinkers on the topic in hand (the body in self–Other relations), and, by presenting these ideas in a quasi-narrative sequence, make of them a sort of relay of argument and counterargument, problems and solutions. At the very least, I hope to show that there has been a continuing and long-standing debate around this issue, even if the participants themselves have not all always been aware of each other and their alternative positions. And, somewhat more ambitiously, if a little more tentatively, I shall also be seeking to explore the implications for literature and writing that are raised by this issue. The rather mystifying inclusion of the body on the recent literary-theoretical agenda may in part be explained in terms of the argument whose history it is my more modest aim to document.

Bakhtin – the body as gift

I shall begin at the chronological beginning of my sequence of ideas – which is also the point where relations between self and Other are presented in their simplest and sweetest light – with Bakhtin's early essay 'Author and hero in aesthetic activity'. Written between 1920 and 1924, it is only the second recorded item in Bakhtin's voluminous output, and precedes the well-known Rabelais study (which I shall be discussing below) by nearly twenty years.[4]

In this essay Bakhtin sees life largely in terms of the literary metaphors of 'author' and 'hero'. The relations between self and Other are viewed as equivalent to those between hero and author. This is because the self is always 'authored' or created by the Other/author (the near-homophony in English is a nice bonus for Bakhtin's association of the two terms). The identity of the subject–hero is dependent upon the creative activity of the Other; and, in particular, what is authored by the Other, the thing that makes the subject a hero, is the body. Self is placed in relation to Other via the body because the body is not a self-sufficient entity: 'the body is not something self-sufficient: it needs the *other*, needs his recognition and his form-giving activity' (p. 51/51). Without the Other the body has neither shape nor form because the self has no direct or coherent access to it.

The self (subject) experiences himself and the world quite differently from the way in which he is experienced and perceived by others, and this difference is centred on his body.[5] The subject's position in the world is determined by his body, and it is from its vantage point that his gaze embraces a world which he sees as if from a frontier: 'I am situated on the boundary, as it were, of the world I see. In plastic and pictorial terms, I am not connatural with it' (p. 30/28). The Other, however, has a perspective on the subject that enables him both to see the external body that constitutes the subject's vantage point on the world, and also to see that body as part of that world. This is a perspective that is at once radically different from that of the subject, yet also serves to complete it.

There are other differences too, which also have the body as their focus: living his body from the inside, the self experiences his external body (the one the Other sees and authors) as a series of 'scattered fragments, scraps, dangling on the string of my inner sensation of myself' (p. 30/28). Self and Other are divided by the fact that what is for one sensation and fragment is for the Other object and whole, and it is this unbridgeable difference in experience that both opposes self to Other, and yet simultaneously creates the dependency of self upon Other. Bakhtin repeatedly emphasises the significance of the author's 'outsidedness' (his necessary otherness) in relation to the object of his authoring. The Other relates to the self by building on that difference – not by attempting to relive the subject's sensations, but by creating external shape and form for the subject's body. This is why the Other is an Author.

Essentially this authoring is an act of *gathering*. The author gathers together all the parts of the body that escape the subject's own visual field ('his head, his face and its expression' [p. 25/23]), and then places the resultant entity in the world where for the author (but not, of course, for the hero) the body appears as an object amongst other objects. In short, he transforms the dispersed-ness of the subject's experience into the assembled whole that makes him a hero. Thus self–Other relations are essentially active and productive: something is produced (rather than merely being revealed), and furthermore that production is construed primarily as an aesthetic one. For Bakhtin it is the

> author's fundamental, *aesthetically productive* [my italics] relationship to the hero ... It is a relationship in which the author occupies an intently maintained position *outside* (*vnenakhodimost'*) the hero with respect to every constituent feature of the hero ... And this being-outside in relation to the hero enables the author (1) to collect and concentrate *all* of the hero, who, from within himself, is diffused and dispersed ...; (2) to collect the hero and his life and to complete him to the point where he forms a whole by supplying all those moments which are inaccessible to the hero himself from within himself (such as a full outward image, an exterior, a background behind his back, his relation to the event of death and the absolute future, etc.). (pp. 17–18/14)

Artistic activity 'saves' the subject from his limitations (the limitations of his perspective on himself and on the world) and from his fragmentation. Part of the 'sweetness' of Bakhtin's version of self–Other relations in this essay comes from the fact that the subject doesn't appear to be unduly bothered that the price of his 'salvation' is this dependence upon his author. (It's perhaps also worth drawing attention to another aspect of Bakhtin's optimism, namely the fact that the aesthetic is synonymous with the construction of coherence and wholes: this is a view which we will not find endorsed either by the later Bakhtin or by Barthes.)

The author's production of the hero is not just an aesthetic act, it is also an act of love. Relations between author and hero are conceived as entirely happy and loving relations in which the subject–hero receives the whole that the author makes of him as a gift offered by the (author–)lover to his (hero–)beloved. Love is the culmination – or even the condition – of the aesthetic: 'Only love can be aesthetically productive.'[6] Bakhtin's love is a strikingly one-

way process in which the author–lover is the active partner and the
beloved–hero his passive counterpart. Bakhtin speaks of them as
two 'souls' or two 'activities' of which 'one of these lives and experiences its own life and has become *passive* for the other, which
actively shapes and sings the first' (p. 113/120, my italics). Bakhtin
makes it clear that the beloved's passivity (tellingly defined as 'feminine') is absolutely essential for the success of the authorial activity
and its construction of the physical form of the beloved. But it is
only the thoroughly undialectical nature of these relations that
makes possible such amorous harmony.

This non-dialectic basis of self–Other relations is indirectly
confirmed by the instances of a number of possible hiccups in the
system mentioned – though not seriously explored – by Bakhtin.
Briefly stated, problems may arise when the hero doesn't like the
authorial 'judgement' that has been passed on him; when he inter-
nalises an image of his external self; when desire brings the two
partners too close; or when the hero's death is acknowledged as a
part of the picture the author creates of him. In the first three cases,
there is, in one way or another, a blurring of the active and passive
roles whose clear demarcation is so necessary for the proper functioning of the aesthetic–loving system. If the hero becomes
dissatisfied with his physical appearance (i.e. the authorial judgement – the two are synonymous), the result is a kind of authoring
of the author by the hero: 'Vexation and a certain resentment, with
which our dissatisfaction about our own exterior may combine, *give
body to this other – the possible author of our own exterior*' (p. 35/33, my
italics). Frustration produces a kind of turning of the tables on the
author, and the hero assumes a doubly active role; first as author in
his own right, and second in his response to his author/Other which
becomes frankly aggressive: 'Distrust of him, hatred, a desire to
annihilate him become possible' (p. 35/33). This unloving activity
on the part of the oxymoronic hero–author has an authoring effect
of its own, and it is the hero's very resistance to the authorial
portrait of himself that engenders a 'heroic' version of the author:
'In trying to fight against another's [the author's] potential, compre-
hensively formative evaluation, I [the hero] consolidate it to the
point of giving it self-subsistence, almost to the point where it
becomes a person localized in being' (p. 35/33). When the hero
takes issue with the author over who or what he is, then their roles
are not only reversed but also blurred in such a way as to change
the whole principle on which their relations function. Bakhtin
himself fails to pursue the implications of heroic frustration as far as

this, but had he done so he would have found himself working with a concept very like the *dialogic*, which is in essence a mode of conflict (rather than sweetness and light) where (because) all subjects have (at least in principle) equal right of say.

The second of Bakhtin's hiccups – where the external image is fatally internalised by the subject – involves the same crossing of the demarcation line. The implied assumption in Bakhtin's discussion of the author's dealings with his hero is that the hero will not take any active interest in the gift which the author makes of him and to him. Loving relations require a thoroughgoing naivety on the part of the beloved; for instance, the beloved cannot have access to his own beauty (p. 51/51): beauty is always and only in the eye of the beholder. The case that Bakhtin cites is not one that in the first instance involves the hero's own sense of identity, but it can be extrapolated from the purely sporting example described by Bakhtin:

> Thus, when one has to perform a difficult and risky jump, it is extremely dangerous to follow the movement of one's own feet: one has to collect oneself from within and to calculate one's own movements – again from within. The first rule of any sport: look directly *ahead* of yourself, not *at* yourself ...
>
> The external image or configuration of an action and its external, intuitable relation to the objects of the outside world are never given to the performer of the action himself ... (p. 45/44–5).

Looking (at yourself) while you leap is a highly dangerous thing to do, and on the figurative plane the effects of such self-regarding attitudes can be just as devastating, because they empty acts of their substance and purpose, and *action* is, significantly, turned into *play* or *gesture* (p. 46/46). It is fatal – both to leaping and to any seriousness of purpose – for the hero–subject to adopt an authorial perspective on himself, and the system only works as long as each (but particularly the hero) keeps to his allotted role. If the implications of this example had been pursued any further by Bakhtin he might have come up with something like Sartre's idea of *mauvaise foi* which entails precisely this internalising of such external images. (Bakhtin's emphasis on the word gesture (*geste* in French) may by now have suggested Sartre to anyone who hadn't already anticipated that this was where the argument was heading.[7]) That Bakhtin failed to get as far as the sort of problem implied by *mauvaise foi* can be attributed quite clearly to the absence of any dialectic in Bakhtin's view of self–Other relations. *Mauvaise foi* is an inevitable component of the Sartrian scenario because of his assumption that self and Other are in a relation of reciprocity; for Bakhtin, by contrast, sporting injuries and the occasional lapse into *geste* are mere accidents in a system in which such things are not programmed to happen.

The confusions wrought by desire in the Bakhtinian scenario constitute another variant of the demarcation issue. The problem with desire in a context where self–Other relations are conceived as relations created by an 'outsided' authoring of the human subject is that it brings the two parties too close together. The body of the hero (and remember that his body is the basis of his construction as hero) simply disintegrates on contact with the Other, and becomes indistinguishable from that of the author as subject: 'the other's outer body [here the body of the hero] disintegrates and becomes merely a constituent in my own *inner* body' (p. 52/51). Desire places the two parties on the same side of the boundary, or rather destroys the distance that makes it possible to construct boundaries in the first place, and it must ultimately be for this reason that: 'By itself, it [the sexual approach to the Other's body] is incapable of developing form-giving plastic–pictorial energies, i.e., it is incapable of giving form to the body as a determinate external entity that is finished and self-contained' (pp. 51–2/51).

The final problematic aspect of Bakhtin's self–Other system can be extrapolated from his remarks about the hero's death. Bakhtin points out that the completedness of the author's 'plastic–pictorial' image of the hero implicitly entails the hero's death; for the authorial picture to be truly complete, the hero must be as if dead, which, says Bakhtin, is tantamount to saying that 'death is the form of the aesthetic consummation of an individual' (p. 122/131). This introduces an entirely new dimension to the authored version of the hero's incarnation: 'Throughout the entire course of an embodied hero's life, one can hear the tones of a requiem' (p. 123/131). The lover's gift rings a death-knell for his beloved.

Bakhtin finds his way out of this unhappy state of affairs by saying that the hero's death will be transformed by art: 'In art, however, this lived-out life is saved, justified, and consummated in eternal memory' (p. 123/131). This is a solution that is very much of its time (the 1920s – think of Proust, for example), and it implies an astonishing acquiescence on the part of the hero. Either the hero remains unaware of the death predicted by the 'tones of a requiem' accompanying his incarnation as hero, just as he was of his beauty;

or else, in living his incarnation as an immolation upon the altar of art, he consents to his own death. Bakhtin would seem to have carried the logic of his system to its ultimate extreme: for what he is saying is that the hero's passivity has no limits and cannot be galvanised even by the prospect of his own extinction. This is an outcome that one cannot imagine many heroes confronting without some wish to revolt, for on these terms the hero would have every reason to refuse the gift of his incarnation, to refuse to play the role of hero, and to demand that the demarcation line that constitutes his role as hero be crossed or simply erased.

I have dwelt on these examples not only because they provide the basis for a critique of the ideas Bakhtin puts forward in the 'Author and hero' essay, but also because they pave the way both to a more *dialogic* conception of intersubjectivity and to Sartre – which, as I hope to demonstrate, in some senses amounts to the same thing. In addition, what the move on to Sartre will also permit is a proper consideration of the role that language plays in self–Other relations, even if the literary dimension (so central in the metaphors of Bakhtin's discussion) ceases for the time being to be a significant part of the issue.

Sartre and the body as theft

In formal terms Sartre's scenario is very similar to Bakhtin's: the subject's position in the world is determined by his physical location in it, and the view he has on that world is the one provided by the vantage point that is his body. He shares with Bakhtin's subject the very limited perspective on his own body which in *Being and Nothingness* Sartre neatly defines as the 'point of view on which he has no point of view'. This limitation means that the Other, like Bakhtin's author, is in a position to perceive him (the subject) as he himself cannot – as an object amongst objects in a meaningful rela- tion to the world – that is to say, to give him flesh and identity. Sartre corroborates Bakhtin in maintaining that it is the body that makes possible the subject's incarnation by the Other: 'I exist for myself as a body known by the Other.'[8] But in spite of the close structural similarity of the situation described by both Sartre and Bakhtin, there is a profound contrast in the evaluation that each of them makes of it.

Whereas in Bakhtin the author/Other's incarnation of the hero/subject is a loving and aesthetically motivated gift, in Sartre this incarnation (which he calls an image) is a negation (p. 228), a theft (p. 225), an alienation (p. 263), an enslavement (p. 267); it represents danger (p. 268); it brings shame (p. 261) and fear (p. 259), and is the harbinger of death – 'the death of my possibilities' (p. 271). The Other lets loose a catalogue of irremediable catastrophes for the subject; and even love itself in Sartre proves to be just one of the necessarily antagonistic modes in which self relates to Other.

The difference between these two evaluations of what is fundamentally the same situation can be explained by the fact that Sartre's subject is much more alive than is Bakhtin's to the content of the Other's authoring (although Sartre does not use this word), and his knowledge of this content obliges him to make some kind of response to it. Sartre's subject cannot sit passively upon his pedestal, or naively busy himself with living a life whose celebration in the eyes of the Other has no effects upon that life.

Significantly, there is never any question that the image of the subject created by the Other might be inaccurate: shame, rage, fear (and the occasional instance of pride) are marks of the subject's recognition of the validity of that image. The role of the Other is to reveal the truth of the subject to himself: 'With the appearance of the Other's look I experience the revelation of my being-as-object' (p. 351). This 'being-as-object' cannot be denied or disowned by the subject, as is shown by Sartre's famous *voyeur* scenario. In Sartre's dramatic illustration of this aspect of self–Other relations he has a jealous subject peeping through a key-hole. The jealousy is something that the subject *is*, but not something that he knows. Such knowledge can only be acquired through the intermediary of the Other. For the subject, the sound of footsteps in the corridor is enough to indicate the presence of an Other who instantly transforms his (the subject's) perception of himself and reveals to him his jealousy. The *in flagrante* quality of the scene serves to support the implication that the verdict is incontrovertible: there is no denying the subject's jealousy because he is caught red-handed being jealous.

Yet true as it is, the verdict, like all verdicts, is alienating; the subject is divided from himself by the image of himself that comes from the Other. He is, but also is not what the Other reveals him to be, and shame, rage and fear are as much a sign of the subject's alienation from what he is as they are an index of his recognition of what he is. 'The person [in this case the jealous person] is presented to consciousness *in so far as the person is an object for the Other*' (p. 260). This means that his identity lies in the hands of the Other:

'all of a sudden I [this is the subject speaking] am conscious of myself *as escaping myself . . . in that I have my foundation outside myself.* I am for myself only as I am a pure reference to the Other' (p. 260, my italics). The Other's image is at once a completion of the kind we encountered in Bakhtin's authoring of the hero, and yet also a theft, a loss; giving here proves to be a form of taking. In particular what is taken from the subject is his sense of mastery: as subject he has to concede that '*I am no longer master of the situation*' (p. 265). The Other's image of the subject's *ego* has an authority which deprives the subject of any authoring capacity of his own. Sartre's 'hero' (to describe him in Bakhtin's terminology for a moment) is keenly aware not only of what is being done to him in his incarnation by the Other, but of the price that he has to pay for its implementation, namely the loss of any active role. Being a hero in Sartre's world is not a gift bestowed by the loving attentions of the Other, but evidence of a loss of mastery. The subject only becomes a hero because the Other has contrived to strip him of his status as author.

Passivity and activity are not so unquestionably distinct as they are in Bakhtin: in Sartre passivity (in the subject) is the result of a privation of activity; and (the Other's) activity is the means whereby he brings that privation about. Consequently, passivity is something to be resisted, and resisted through a struggle for active mastery. The result is that self–Other relations are a perpetual see-saw on which neither party can ever achieve permanent ascendancy over the other. The site of this struggle is the body, because it is through the body that one becomes vulnerable to the Other: 'My body is there not only as the point of view which I am but again as a point of view on which are actually brought to bear points of view which I could never take; my body escapes me on all sides. This means first that this ensemble of *senses*, which themselves cannot be apprehended, is given as apprehended elsewhere and by others' (p. 352). The subject is vulnerable to the Other on two counts: in the first place, as Sartre is saying here, he cannot control the image or interpretation that his body constitutes in the eyes of the Other. And in the second place, the Other is liable to reduce the subject to being a mere object, *only* a body, thus denying what Sartre calls the subject's transcendence. For Sartre one is both one's body and more than one's body. One 'exists one's body', as Sartre puts it (p. 351), and at the same time goes beyond it.

It is this going beyond which the Other's construction negates; the Other reduces one's existence to mere 'facticity': 'to the extent that I am conscious of existing for the Other I apprehend my own facticity ... The shock of the encounter with the Other is for me a revelation in emptiness of the existence of my body outside as an in-itself for the Other' (pp. 351-2). For Sartre this revelation is experienced by the subject as a terrible degradation whose humiliations are compounded by Sartre's implicit gendering of the situation. In the existential world transcendence tends to be presented in masculine terms, facticity in feminine ones. The concepts of 'active' and 'passive' already carry a latent set of connotations that link activity with masculinity and passivity with femininity, but the material qualities of facticity specifically associate it with the feminine.[9] The intervention of the Other, then, brings the subject low by depriving him not only of his transcendence but also of his masculinity. There are parallels here with Bakhtin's gendering of author and hero, but the passivity of Bakhtin's hero was so extreme that he appeared oblivious or indifferent even to the implied threat to his virility brought by his authored condition. However, I shall leave the feminist strand in my argument hanging for the time being in order to return to a different aspect of the conflict constituted by self–Other relations as described by Sartre.

I say 'as described by Sartre', but what I have been seeking to demonstrate is that the Sartrian scheme merely makes explicit the conflicts and problems which are bound to be thrown up in the view of self–Other relations which he shares with the early Bakhtin. In Bakhtin they remain latent and only surface on the margins of the argument as unfortunate but supposedly incidental exceptions to the basic optimistic rule. Sartre offers a full descriptive account of what is broadly the same situation, and shows that Bakhtin's exceptions *are* the rule. But it is to Bakhtin that one has to return for an understanding of the nature of the power that self and Other each lay claim to, as well as for an indication of a possible way out of the dilemma.

In Sartre power is automatically granted to the Other; his very presence guarantees him an ascendancy which the subject then seeks to wrest from him in order to appropriate it for himself. But it cannot just be his apparent priority that gives the Other the whip hand in the confrontations in which the subject encounters him. The power which holds the subject in thrall cannot be ascribed to the simple *fiat* of the Other's imaging of that subject; the authority of the image constructed by the Other derives from his implicit recourse to the superior authority that is language.

Sartre does not linger on the linguistic implication of the question because his largely individualist view of human experience and human relations prevents him from taking on board their full discursive extent. Nevertheless, the following claim opens up a whole new dimension to the problem:

> Language is not a phenomenon added on to being-for-others. It *is* originally being-for-others; that is, it is the fact that a subjectivity experiences itself as an object for the Other ... [Language] is already given in the recognition of the Other. I *am* language. By the sole fact that whatever I may do, my acts freely conceived and executed, my projects launched toward my possibilities have outside of them a meaning which escapes me and which I experience. (p. 372).

Dialogism is exactly this: for in self–Other relations the subject is translated into linguistic terms over which he has no control and whose meaning is inevitably determined by the Other. At this point, therefore, Bakhtin comes back into the argument – no longer as the author of 'Author and hero' (no pun intended), but as the theorist of dialogism. It might be going too far to suggest that Bakhtin himself could have written the following, but the author of *Problems of Dostoevsky's Poetics* and of 'Discourse in the novel' would have appreciated (and I can't help thinking wholly endorsed) every word of the following lines from Sartre:

> the 'meaning' of my expressions always escapes me. I never know exactly if I signify what I wish to signify ... For lack of knowing what I actually express for the Other, I constitute my language as an incomplete phenomenon of flight outside myself. As soon as I express myself, I can only guess at the meaning of what I express – *i.e.* the meaning of what I am – since in this perspective to express and to be are one. *The Other is always there, present and experienced as the one who gives to language its meaning.* (pp. 373–4, my italics)

The self is constituted by the language of the Other which draws its power from the simple fact that it is language. It is not actually the otherness of the Other that gives him priority in the confrontation between self and Other, but language. It is precisely this linguistic priority that gives the constructions that the Other places on the subject the force of their conviction. The subject's awareness that the Other has access to a language that lies beyond his (the subject's) control exemplifies precisely what Bakhtin means by dialogism.[10] If relations between self and Other can be conceived of as dialogic, then Bakhtin's concept of dialogism could be taken as an implicit acknowledgement on his part that the scenario of 'Author and hero in aesthetic activity' does have its darker side, and that author and hero are linked as much by the kind of conflict described by Sartre as by the love adduced by the early Bakhtin.[11]

Once the relationship between self and Other has been set up in the terms that I have been outlining, there is no real possibility of any exit from it.[12] Sartre's galvanising of Bakhtin's hero into a more active role only compounds the problems inadvertently raised by Bakhtin, so that every form of human relations proves to be merely one of two equally unsatisfactory alternatives. As Sartre says at the end of his discussion of the various manifestations of 'concrete relations with Others' (love, language and masochism on the one hand, and indifference, desire, hatred and sadism on the other):

> ceaselessly tossed from being-a-look to being-looked-at, falling from one to the other in alternate revolutions, we are always, no matter what attitude is adopted, in a state of instability in relation to the Other ... and we shall never place ourselves concretely on a plane where the recognition of the Other's freedom would involve the Other's recognition of our freedom. The Other is on principle inapprehensible; he flees me when I seek him and possesses me when I flee him. (p. 408)

The recognition of the role of language in the situation exacerbates it still further because the weight of the linguistic system seems to remove all possibility of any individual initiative as a means of getting out of the dilemma.

However, the factor that both Sartre and the Bakhtin of 'Author and hero' overlook is that they are limiting themselves to seeing things entirely in terms of *representation*. Or at least, while they acknowledge that what they are propounding takes representation as its basis, they do so very fleetingly and without pausing to consider whether there might not be an issue here worth exploring at greater length. Bakhtin mentions in passing that the distance he establishes between author and hero makes the activity of representation the key to the relations that exist between the two protagonists: 'a word that comes closer to expressing the actual aesthetic event adequately is the term ... *izobizazhenie* in Russian, or imaging forth. This term shifts the center of gravity from the hero to the aesthetically active *subiectum* – the author (pp. 80/83–4). The underlying determination of the situation is ultimately attributable to the fact that it is conceived in terms of a representation: the author acquires his status through his authoring of a representation of which the hero is both object and passive recipient.

Equally for Sartre, the effect of the gaze of the Other is to produce an image of the subject which he may experience as an inadequate representation, but which is none the less precisely that, a representation.[13] The subject may suffer from the representation constructed by the Other, but his responses – be they evasive or aggressive – still show him to be thinking in terms of representation. Either he longs for a better, more adequate representation of himself, or he retaliates by making the Other the object of his own representation.

But the later Bakhtin – the Bakhtin who theorises carnival in the Dostoevsky and particularly the Rabelais book – demonstrates that there is another world outside and beyond representation. And in this other world, self–Other relations do not have to involve the ascendancy of one protagonist over another, because they do not have to be restricted to the roles that representation entails (notably author, object and recipient). Crucially, what carnival reveals is that relations of representation can be reconstituted as relations of participation, or at the very least that the specular basis of classical representation can be transformed into one which implies an involvement with representation, its objects and its recipients. For the sake of simplicity I shall use the term 'representation' for the former and 'participation' for the latter.

Carnival: representation versus participation

Bakhtin and many of his commentators have tended to portray carnival as a kind of Renaissance Eden from which modern bourgeois man has fallen into representation in a one-way historical process. But I shall be arguing here that carnival is also a concept and a practice which comprise an alternative to – rather than just a predecessor of – representation.

Peter Stallybrass and Allon White have shown that there is nothing that inherently protects carnival from its potential vulnerability to an observing gaze. Its participants can always be transformed from active and equal subjects into the objects of a representation constructed by an author who chooses to place himself above or beyond the scene of carnival.[14] In fact authoring is by its very nature a decarnivalising activity, for the authorial perspective and the demarcations between observer and participants

are against the whole spirit of carnival. Carnival 'does not acknowledge any distinction between actors and spectators ... Carnival is
not a spectacle seen by the people; they live in it and everyone
participates because its very idea embraces all the people.'[15] The
unattainable equality between subjects whose absence is so
lamented by Sartre in his scheme of things proves, all of a sudden,
to be the cornerstone of Bakhtin's carnival. This indicates, first, that
carnival does indeed create a different order of human relations
from those constructed by and associated with representation, and
second, that carnival may therefore constitute some kind of a solution to the *impasse* of representation. Indeed, Sartre may be trying
to grope his way towards some such idea in the post-script to his
discussion of 'concrete relations with Others', where he addresses
the issue of the togetherness implied in *'Mitsein'*. But he makes no
real headway with the idea because he is unable to conceive of a
'we' except as a variation on the basic representational schema, that
is to say as either 'co-spectator' or collective object of the gaze of
the Other.

One index of the difference between representation and carnival is the thoroughgoing difference in construction of the body that
is involved. The represented body is roughly what Bakhtin in
Rabelais and His World calls the 'classical body': a completed entity
sealed off both from the world which is its context and from other
bodies. In the 'Author and hero' essay the author's function is to
'gather' the fragments through which the subject experiences
himself into a completed whole, the whole which simultaneously
constitutes him as a hero. Similarly, in Sartre the subject may be
split, but only in the sense that he is alienated from the being that
he is for the Other – not in the sense that the image produced by
the Other is not complete. (The problem is even – perhaps – that
the image is *too* complete: the subject's anguish comes from the way
that jealousy is 'added' to his sense of himself through the intervention of the gaze of the Other.) The corollary of this image of the
body as whole and complete is its isolation. In the Rabelais book
Bakhtin speaks of the 'atomisation' of the being in this conception
(p. 24), and comments on the way that in its expression as realism
'boundaries' are drawn between bodies and objects (and thus
between body and body) and serve to 'complete each individual
outside the link with the ultimate whole' (p. 53).

The carnival body – or what Bakhtin calls the body of
'grotesque realism' – is quite different. It loses its individual definition and is collectivised at a transindividual level:

> In grotesque realism ... the bodily element is deeply positive. It is presented not in a private, egotistic form, severed from the other spheres of life, but as something universal, representing all the people ... [T]his is not the body and its physiology in the modern sense of these words, because it is not individualised. The material bodily principle is contained not in the biological individual, not in the bourgeois ego, but in the people, a people who are constantly growing and renewed. (p. 19)

The 'bodily element' (it becomes difficult to speak of 'the body' in the context of carnival) is epitomised by events and activities in which boundaries between bodies, and between bodies and the world, are at their most obscured and eroded: birth, death, copulation, defecation, eating, etc.

At the same time the individual body is frankly dismembered into a series of focal points through which or from which bodies make contact with what lies outside them. The carnival body is a collectivised jumble of protruberances and orifices: bellies, noses, breasts, buttocks, assorted genitalia, mouths, guts, and so on, in which what belongs to whom is both irrelevant and impossible to determine. It is a body whose character is best expressed by the 'senile pregnant hags' in the terracotta collection which Bakhtin discusses. In these figurines is combined 'a senile, decaying and deformed flesh with the flesh of new life, conceived but as yet unformed' (pp. 25–6). (The figures point to an aspect of the corporeal that neither the earlier Bakhtin nor Sartre had addressed in their consideration of the body and its relation to the Other, namely pregnancy.) And at the same time they also suggest a completely different evaluation of factors that they did consider: death, the feminine, and degradation in general (death and woman constituting particular forms of degradation). Death in the collective body of the people is not the unmitigated disaster that it was for both Bakhtin's hero (who was 'saved' only by the art of the author), and for Sartre's subject (whose experience of the death-in-life of the gaze of the Other was so destructive of his own possibilities). In the blurring of boundaries that accompanies death, death and life become indistinguishable: 'Death and death throes, labor and childbirth are intimately interwoven' (p. 151).

Equally, the evaluation of woman in carnival is completely transformed. In his association of the feminine and facticity Sartre is continuing what Bakhtin here calls the ascetic tradition of medieval Christianity which saw woman as 'the *incarnation* of sin, the temptation of the *flesh*' (p. 240, my italics). But carnival derives from a

quite other tradition, the popular one, which puts an entirely different value on flesh, and in particular on the flesh of 'the material
bodily lower stratum':

> The popular tradition is in no way hostile to woman and does not
> approach her negatively. In this tradition [as indeed in the other]
> woman is essentially related to the material bodily lower stratum;
> she is the incarnation of this stratum that degrades and regenerates
> simultaneously. She is ambivalent. She debases, brings down to
> earth, lends a bodily substance to things, and destroys; but, first of
> all, she is the principle that gives birth. (p. 240)

The destructive/regenerative quality of woman here is exactly the
quality which characterises carnival in general, and as such its
degradations bring joy rather than the dreadful humiliation suffered
by Sartre's subject in his experience of his own facticity. If Sartre's
subject is brought low by his objectivation as flesh this ought – at
least in the carnival world-view it ought – to be a matter of rejoicing rather than the *malaise*, shame, rage or fear that constitute the
Sartrian response. In all forms of grotesque realism things are
'degrade[d], br[ought] down to earth, their subject [turned] into
flesh'. And the laughter associated with carnival is singled out by
Bakhtin as being particularly effective in 'degrading' and 'material-
ising' (p. 20). In other words, the process which in the context of
representation creates a terrible trauma for the Sartrian subject is
turned around and re-evaluated to become an enabling and regen-
erative one in the context of carnival.

Finally, these differences may be summarised in an opposition
between the finished and the unfinished: the body of Bakhtin's
hero, like the body of Sartre's subject, in short, the body of representation is a *finished* construction, whereas the body of carnival and
the grotesque is by definition *un*finished. In so far as the grotesque
body has identifiable shape (comprising its various protruberances
and orifices), that shape serves primarily to draw attention to the
unfinished processes of becoming and regeneration, as it does so
typically for Bakhtin in the figure of the senile, pregnant hag. This
is essentially what carnival is about. The distinction contained in the
two kinds of body is thus ultimately one between process and
product: carnival is a process, representation makes a product.

Comparing and contrasting representation and carnival has
yielded a picture of quite precise parallels and inversions, suggesting the existence of underlying structural similarities which enable
one to see how each might succeed in gaining purchase on the

other. As I have already said, the story is usually told so as to suggest that representation undoes and betrays carnival, sealing up the body's orifices, removing its 'protruberances and its offshoots', smoothing out its 'convexities', and moving it away from the thresholds at which the body either enters or leaves life (i.e. birth and death) (p. 29), so that representation is presented as a repression of carnival, as something which necessarily follows rather than precedes it.[16] Nevertheless, in Bakhtin's occasional glimpses of the broader historical view, he does seem to be implying that there has been a series of cultural shifts between something like representation and something like carnival: the literary and artistic canon of antiquity was focused on the 'classical body' that I have associated with specular representation, in contrast to which he cites Doric comedy, '"satyric"' drama, Sicilian comic forms, Aristophanes and other writings of 'nonclassic' antiquity as an alternative perspective (p. 31). Similarly, he contrasts the Renaissance and its (carnivalesque) view of the body with the body as it appears in the canons of the Middle Ages, thus establishing a chronology in which carnival follows rather than precedes representation. What the motor behind this sequence is Bakhtin doesn't say, but it would be fairly extraordinary if carnival did not succeed on some occasions in actively ousting representation rather than leaving the initiative permanently with the classicism that supports specular representation.

To get some idea of how it might be possible for carnival to turn the tables on representation in this way, I propose to conclude by raising the – perhaps – unlikely-looking question of reading. I do so because in his discussion of reading Roland Barthes seems to be sketching out an exemplary strategy for using carnival as a means of resisting representation, and moreover to be making the body the linchpin of the whole enterprise.

Barthes and the body in the text

The relevance of carnival to reading is not immediately obvious in Bakhtin's own account of carnival but there is, nevertheless, a glancing acknowledgement of its role in his brief synopsis of the history of Rabelais's reception in France in and after the Renaissance period. What Bakhtin is seeking to demonstrate here is that with the passing of the carnival era, reading Rabelais became more or less impossible: La Bruyère in the age of classicism, for example, could see him only as an irreconcilable combination of genius and obscenity; Voltaire in his Enlightenment context was able to appreciate in Rabelais only what he saw as overt satire, and found the rest simply unintelligible; and while the Romantics were more attuned than their predecessors to the grotesque in Rabelais, they (most notably Victor Hugo) could see laughter only in a negative and destructive light. As for the moderns, their positivist bent restricts them to a mere assembling of scholarly material. In the age of representation Rabelais becomes unreadable to an audience which had lost contact with the 'tradition of popular–festive laughter' that informed Rabelais's work: 'The authentic and common interpretation of Rabelaisian images was lost, together with the tradition that had produced them' (p. 115). In other words, to read Rabelais aright you have to place him back in his carnival context. But significantly, the question that Bakhtin does not address is whether the *manner* in which one reads Rabelais's carnivalesque text will be affected by its carnivalesque context. This is because underlying Bakhtin's discussion of Rabelais is an assumption that – even in his own terms – is a kind of self-contradiction: namely, that Rabelais's text is a *representation of carnival*. In the perspective of Bakhtin's discussion, Rabelais is deemed to be making a spectacle of carnival[17] which only those who understand what carnival is can properly interpret; but it is an understanding and an interpretation that is ultimately conceived in a representational mould. The question one should ask – and it is the question that I believe Barthes is trying to answer – is: what if Rabelais's carnival extended to the reading of Rabelais himself?

However, before going any further I should also explain how reading fits into an argument that began with self–Other relations and the relation of those relations to the body. It fits – or at least it fits in Barthes – because the reading strategy he is seeking to promote is a response to a problem created by the existence of the Other and by the effects that the Other has on the subject. Barthes's conception of the Other is a sort of mixture of Sartrian antagonisms and Bakhtinian dialogism: that is to say, while he would seem to be adopting a broadly Sartrian view of self–Other relations, he picks up Sartre's cue about the linguistic dimension of these relations and recasts them as a problem of discourse. This is how he does it.

Like Sartre, Barthes is exquisitely sensitive to the hold that the Other has over the subject through his ability to represent the body of the subject. As he says in *Roland Barthes*: 'You are the only one who can never see yourself except as an image ...: even and especially for your body, you are condemned to the repertoire of its images [à l'imaginaire]' – that is to say, condemned to a repertoire that lies in the hands of the Other.[18] The situation takes one of its most extreme and painful forms in the experience of being photographed as Barthes describes it in *Camera Lucida*: 'I feel that the Photograph creates my body or mortifies it, according to its caprice.'[19] In other words, photography performs the Sartrian trick of transforming 'subject into object'. But this transformation is above all a linguistic one because effectively what it does is to translate the subject into the terms of the *doxa*, the *déjà-dit* (the already-said), the platitudes of public opinion. The Other constitutes a threat to the Barthesian subject not because he (the Other) has the whip hand in a Sartrian single-handed combat of self–Other relations, but because it is through the Other that the subject falls prey to a representation that constructs him in terms of the stereotype. The Barthesian subject is alienated not merely by becoming an image in the eyes of the Other but through this assimilation into the *doxa*.

The problem thus becomes explicitly a dialogic one in that the conflict between self and Other is conceived ultimately as a conflict of discourses. The Barthesian subject's experience of the Other is painful because it reveals to him (the subject) the prior existence of the *doxa*, a discourse which precedes him and to which he is supremely vulnerable. He cannot fight his way out of the tyranny of the *doxa* by adopting or asserting an alternative discourse of his own; he can do so only through a certain *practice* of language which Barthes calls writing and whose effectiveness depends on its being precisely that – a practice – rather than a particular characterisable style.

In this practice the body's relation to language is altered from being the object of its representation to becoming the support and condition of a certain linguistic activity. Or as Barthes rather elliptically puts it, 'Writing proceeds through the body [L'écriture passe par le corps]' (*RB*, p. 80). When the body sides with the subject, then it becomes possible to counter the finished and static representations of the *doxa*, a discourse which Barthes describes as being without a body, even if it takes the body as its object.[20] A *doxa* is no longer a *doxa* if it is no longer finished and complete, if its structures are opened up. The body is a kind of wild-card that slides and also creates slide – like Barthes's own use of the word, 'floating, never *pigeon-holed*, always *atopic*' (*RB*, p. 133). The body is 'the principle of all structuration' and as such opens up the way for a politics directed against the *doxa*: 'If I managed to talk politics *with my own body*, I should make out of the most banal of (discursive) structures a structuration' (*RB*, p. 175).

There is something distinctly carnivalesque involved in Barthes's use of the body here: it is not the object of a representation, and it is committed to process and practice rather than being defined as a product. There are a number of other aspects of Barthes's use of the body that confirm this impression. The body first makes a substantial and serious appearance in Barthes's work in association with the rather unserious topic of pleasure in *The Pleasure of the Text* (and as a consequence has been an aspect of Barthes's thinking that some critics have been unable to take at all seriously).[21] The pleasure of *jouissance* is a bodily pleasure and is much closer to the joyful corporeality of carnival than to the humiliations of facticity that are thrown up by Sartrian desire. Also, the Barthesian body is a dismembered body: it is only as fragment and fetish that it interests and excites. The body that gives pleasure is 'split into fetish objects, into erotic sites', not a whole body.[22] Similarly, Barthes is drawn by the body's ability to blur boundaries. For Barthes an erogenous zone is one between two borders (the gap between jeans and sweater), or as he says in *The Pleasure of the Text*, 'Is not the most erotic portion of a body *where the garment gapes?* ... It is intermittence ... which is erotic' (*PT*, pp. 9–10). It is precisely this lifting or questioning of boundaries that is carnivalesque.

What is also carnivalesque is the sliding between bodies that my own listing of the carnivalesque in Barthes has illustrated: it began with a focus on the subject's use of his own body in practice, structuration and the pleasures of *jouissance*, but pleasure also entails a drift that links the body of the subject to other bodies, bodies that give pleasure as fetish and as fragments of erogenous intermittence. And it is at this point that we can at last begin to home in on the question of reading. For in Barthes it seems to be the carnivalesque features of the body that enable self–Other relations to be altered from the fundamentally Sartrian form that is associated with their dependence upon the *doxa* to something more positive and enabling. And this shift is best exemplified for him in the processes of reading and writing. When these are operating as Barthes would ideally wish them to, both body and text are carnivalised, and there finally ceases to be any distinction between subject and object, spectator and representation, distinctions that are entailed by the order of the *doxa*.

Representation is abolished as the body comes out of the frame within which representation seeks to confine it. This abolition is the effect of what Barthes calls *figuration*. Figuration is everything that representation is not: 'Figuration is the way in which the erotic body appears ... in the profile of the text' (*PT*, pp. 55–6), creating an erotic rather than a specular relationship with its recipient. In representation, by contrast, any desire that there is remains firmly on the diegetic plane: 'such desire never leaves the frame, the picture; it circulates among the characters; if it has a recipient, that recipient remains interior to the fiction'. And Barthes concludes: 'That's what representation is: when nothing emerges, when nothing leaps out of the frame: of the picture, the book, the screen' (*PT*, p. 57). The leap out of the frame that is figuration creates a connection between bodies which completely transforms the relations between what would otherwise be the subject and object of a representation.

Self–Other relations in Barthes have been recast from those that exist between author and hero, between the subject and the object of a representation, to those that exist between a writer and his reader, a reader and a text. The Other is stripped of his authorial potential by a subject who conceives of his other (with a small 'o', perhaps to distinguish him from the Sartrian one) as the recipient rather than the represented object of his text. In the process reading too is carnivalised.

The key to the Barthesian carnival is what he begins by calling, in an essay by the same title, 'the third meaning', and which in *Camera Lucida* he calls the *punctum*. In the earlier essay he makes the connection with carnival quite explicit when he writes: 'the obtuse meaning [another term for the 'third meaning'] ... belongs to the family of puns, jokes, useless exertions; indifferent to moral or aesthetic categories (the trivial, the futile, the artificial, the parodic), *it sides with the carnival aspect of things* [*il est du côté du carnaval*]'.[23] Being 'du côté du carnaval' means that the third meaning bursts out of the frame, and this puts reading itself on the side of carnival as well.[24] In *Camera Lucida* Barthes works his way towards an understanding of the *punctum* not by trying to describe what the *punctum* is, but by describing its effects. The presence of a *punctum* in a photograph triggers 'tiny jubilations' in its reader, 'an internal agitation' which in French he also calls 'une fête'.[25] It sets the reader in motion, casts him loose; in short, it launches him into carnival.

The value of this readerly 'fête' for Barthes is primarily in its capacity to counter the *doxa* and open up representations. The 'obtuse meaning' is an active resistance to the pre-established and pre-existing *doxa*. It 'disturbs' the representational discourse that is metalanguage, it 'baffles' [and] subverts ... the entire practice of meaning'.[26] It is a kink in the order of representation, the bug in its system. It shows, in a word, what carnival can do to representation, that carnival is not the passive victim of the predations of representation, that it can fight back.

It should, nevertheless, be admitted that Barthes's 'fête' does not restore the full-blooded Renaissance carnival that Bakhtin describes in Rabelais. In the first place, Barthes's is a very ungregarious carnival in which the subject discovers the singularity of his own body rather than the collective embrace of the people.[27] And in so far as the whole thrust of the Barthesian carnival is designed to disengage the subject from the *doxa* (which is the language of the public, the masses) it could be seen as an attempt to positively extricate the subject from any collective (linguistic) embrace. Equally, the tone of Barthes's carnival is one of elegy (self-confessedly so in the case of *Camera Lucida*), and not that of the uproarious epic exemplified in Rabelais. But for all that it is still carnival. And it does still counter the nefarious effects of representation.

There does, however, remain a question about the efficacy of Barthes's largely literary solution as it might apply both to the personal and to the political sphere. Does Barthes's carnival of reading offer solutions to the problem of how to live in the face of the Other (a question which might pose itself for a woman)? Or to the problem of how to counter politically the politically undesirable constructions of the Other (a question which might pose itself for a feminist)? Stallybrass and White argue that the transgressions of modernism and its successors (amongst whom one must surely number Barthes) are in political terms purely illusory because 'Only a challenge to the hierarchy of the *sites* of discourse ... carries the promise of politically transformative power'.[28] And indeed, Barthes himself seems to acknowledge something of the kind when he suggests that the political effects of his strategy of structuration are quite likely to go unnoticed: 'The problem is to know if the political apparatus would recognise for very long this way of escaping the militant banality by thrusting into it ... my own unique body' (*RB*, p. 175).

It would seem that the problem of self–Other relations is at once solved and re-opened by the explicit inclusion of language and literature into the frame of reference. For the early Bakhtin (who, it will be remembered, excludes any serious consideration of language from his discussion), literature offers a unique and highly efficacious solution to self–Other relations – but this is a solution that is offered before there is any real problem. The significance of literature is most evident in the metaphors that Bakhtin uses in his discussion, and their justification is provided by the fact that he is proposing aesthetic activity as the model for self–Other relations. With Sartre, for whom these relations can only be construed as problematic, the possibility of a solution to the see-saw of power relations between self and Other is fairly decisively removed when language is added into the balance. In enlarging the scope of the problem through the inclusion of the linguistic dimension Sartre shows the scales to be unavoidably tipped in favour of the Other. At this stage of Sartre's argument literature is neither here nor there.

The implicit synonymy between the carnivalesque and the novelistic in Bakhtin is explicitly developed by Barthes in his festival of reading. But in providing a convincing way out of the dilemmas posed by Sartre in a sphere that was apparently expanded to include language, Barthes paradoxically pays the price of a dramatic reduction in the scope of the arena in which the battles are now fought and won. His lonely carnival of reading may have dissolved the antagonisms between the subject and his Other, but it has done so through a tactics of subversion that is liable to escape the attention of that Other, particularly in its overtly political guise. So that the feminist and even the plain old human subject living out her/his life is unlikely to be able to extend the solution from the purely literary domain, in the manner that the early Bakhtin took for granted.

The difficulty seems to rest on this paradoxical expansion and reduction of the sphere of the literary. On the one hand the field has been enlarged by modernism, and (especially) its successors from the dimensions of the classical work to the infinitely extensible text, and within this text solutions to the problem of the Other have been found. But at the same time, there has been a parallel trivialising of the literary precisely, perhaps, on the part of the Other. It would appear that he (the Other) may have escaped the stratagems that the carnivalesque subject has been trying to coopt him into, and simply removed himself to his traditional and powerful distance. From this distance his gaze can operate in the way that Sartre describes so well, and simply constitutes literature as what he will – trivial or whatever. Literature may provide the arena for a solution for self–Other relations, but it is one which is unable to determine how it in turn may be determined. Literature cannot provide the means for a solution unless it is empowered by the Other to do so, since it is caught up in the very problematic for which it seemed – momentarily – to have provided the solution.[29]

Notes

1 Interview with Michel Contat and Michel Rybalka in *Le Monde*, 14 May 1971, pp. 17 and 20–1. Sartre mentions having recently read the Dostoevsky book, but is somewhat dismissive of it as an example of the 'new formalism' which, he says, 'does not lead anywhere' (p. 21). Bakhtin alluded to Sartre with tantalising brevity in a couple of later interviews. In one he refers to the polyphonic qualities of Sartre's fiction, but finds that although there is a lot of Dostoevsky in Sartre, it is 'profounder' in Camus ('O polifonichnosti romanov Dostoevskogo', *Rossiya*, 2, 1975, pp. 189–98). In the other he mentions Sartre as a 'brilliant' example of the thinker as distinct from the philosopher or sage (see Maya Kaganskaya, 'Shutovskoi khorovod', *Sintaksis*, 12, 1984, pp. 139–90).

2 See Annette Lavers, *Roland Barthes: Structuralism and After*, London, 1982.

3 When I speak of the Other here I shall be using the word largely in the sense shared by the three writers under discussion, borrowing from Sartre the capitalisation that designates his special role. There are, I am aware, psychoanalytic dimensions to the problem which I shall not be pursuing.

4 Mikhail Bakhtin, 'Avtor i geroi v esteticheskoi deyatel'nosti', in *Estetika slovesnogo tvorchestva*, 2nd edn, Moscow, 1986, pp. 9–191. For the place of this essay in Bakhtin's work, see the bibliography of his writings in Katerina Clark and Michael Holquist, *Mikhail Bakhtin*, Cambridge, Mass., and London, 1984, pp. 353–6. Clark and Holquist discuss this essay in their chapter devoted to 'The architectonics of answerability', which they see as laying the groundwork for all that followed in Bakhtin's thought. Vadim Liapunov's English translation of the essay, used here, is found in *Art and Answerability: Early Philosophical Essays by M. M. Bakhtin*, ed. Michael Holquist and Vadim Liapunov, trans. Vadim Liapunov and Kenneth Brostrom, Austin, Texas, 1990, pp. 4–208. Since the first appearance of the present essay, an earlier section of 'Author and hero' has appeared in Russian (it is also translated in the above cited volume). Page references for the quotations from 'Author and hero' are given in the text, the first number referring to the Russian edition, the second to Liapunov's English translation. In these and all subsequent quotations italics are the authors' own unless otherwise indicated.

5 I shall be using the masculine pronoun in referring to the subject. In this context *she* is not strictly interchangeable with *he*, since the topic of the body in self–Other relations entails quite particular (cultural and political) problems for the female subject. Any gendering of the situation raises issues which, regrettably, are not directly confronted by any of the authors in question. There will be more discussion of the feminine dimension of the problem below.

6 Bakhtin, [Untitled], ed. S. G. Bocharov, in *Den' poezii 1984*, Moscow, 1985, p. 130, quoted in Ann Shukman, 'Reading Bakhtin with a stiff upper lip', *Scottish Slavonic Review*, 6, 1986, p. 123.

7 Holquist and Clark mention the similarities (and one of the differences) between Bakhtin and Sartre in their chapter devoted to 'Author and hero', but these are only fleeting (if suggestive) allusions whose implications I am seeking to draw out here (*Mikhail Bakhtin*, pp. 63–94).

8 Jean-Paul Sartre, *Being and Nothingness* (1943), trans. Hazel Barnes, London, 1957, p. 351; subsequent page references are given in the text.

9 For further discussion of this see Toril Moi, 'Existentialism and feminism: the rhetoric of biology in *The Second Sex*', *Oxford Literary Review*, VIII: 1–2, 1986, pp. 88–95.

10 For a short-hand definition one could do worse than refer to that given by Michael Holquist in the appendix to *The Dialogic Imagination*: 'Dialogism is the characteristic epistemological mode of a world dominated by heteroglossia. Everything means, is understood, as part of a greater whole – there is a constant interaction between meanings, all of which have the potential of conditioning others. Which will affect the other, how it will do so and in what degree is what is actually settled at the moment of utterance. The dialogic imperative is mandated by the preexistence of the language world relative to any of its current inhabitants' (Glossary, in Bakhtin, *The Dialogic Imagination*, ed. Michael Holquist, trans. Caryl Emerson and Michael Holquist, Austin, Texas, 1981, p. 426).

11 Ann Shukman points out – quite rightly – that the 'radical change in Bakhtin's approach to the problems of personal interrelationship came in the mid-Twenties when language entered his purview and henceforth was treated as the main bonding element between the self and the world of others' ('Reading Bakhtin', p. 123). By contrast, Tzvetan Todorov's discussion of the importance of 'alterity' in 'Author and hero' fails, I think, to follow through fully the implications of the linguistic dimension of self–Other relations, and for this reason somewhat misrepresents Bakhtin's 'philosophical anthropology' (see *Mikhail Bakhtin: The Dialogical Principle*, trans. Wlad Godzich, Manchester and Minneapolis, 1984, pp. 94–112).

12 Sartre's most thorough – and also his gloomiest – exploration of self–Other relations in the theatre, *Huis clos* (the play in which he uses the famous phrase 'Hell is other people'), has as its English title *No Exit*.

13 'Objectivation is a radical metamorphosis. Even if I could see myself clearly and distinctly as an object, what I should see would not be an adequate *representation* of what I am in myself and for myself' (p. 273, my italics).

14 See especially the last part of the discussion of 'Authorship in the eighteenth century' and the account of the city in Peter Stallybrass and Allon White, *The Politics and Poetics of Transgression*, London and Ithaca, 1986, pp. 118–24 and 125–48. It is, of course, enormously relevant to my own argument that Stallybrass and White identify the emergence of the notion of authorship with that of a relationship of observation and representation between subject and carnival, instead of one of participation. They also rightly contest the view that carnival was exclusively a feature of the

Renaissance, and their account is designed to show, among other things, that carnival has been displaced and fragmented, but not lost or destroyed, by post-Renaissance culture. A final accolade for their study: Stallybrass and White are rare among Bakhtin commentators in their understanding of how far the ramifications associated with the body extend.

15 Bakhtin, *Rabelais and His World*, trans. Hélène Iswolsky, Cambridge, Mass., and London, 1968, p. 7; subsequent page references are given in the text.

16 This is also the implication behind the account of Stallybrass and White, who in effect have written a history of the way in which the bourgeoisie, authorship and its concomitant representational strategies have been constituted through the carving out of a differentiating distance from the phenomenon that is carnival. In other words, while they describe representation's relation to carnival, they don't have much to say about carnival's relation to representation.

17 Rather as Ben Jonson does in *Bartholomew Fair*. See Stallybrass and White, *The Politics*, pp. 61–79.

18 Roland Barthes, *Roland Barthes* (1975), trans. Richard Howard, London, 1977; subsequent references are given in the text as *RB*, followed by page number. There is a telling (and no doubt deliberate) echo of Sartre in Barthes's comment that 'the image system [l'imaginaire] is the very thing over which others have an advantage [cela même sur quoi les autres ont barre]' (*RB*, p. 82). The term 'l'imaginaire' is adopted, but also adapted, by Barthes from Sartre as much as it is derived from Lacan's Imaginary. More telling is the 'avoir barre'; it echoes the following sentence from *Being and Nothingness*, which sums up the basic problem in Sartrian relations between self and Other: 'And as the Other's existence reveals to me the being which I am without my being able either to appropriate that being or even to conceive it, this existence will motivate two opposed attitudes: First – the Other *looks* at me and as such he holds the secret of my being, he knows what I *am*. Thus the profound meaning of my being is outside of me, imprisoned in an absence. The Other has the advantage over me [*autrui a barre sur moi*, my italics]' (p. 363).

19 Barthes, *Camera Lucida* (1980), trans. Richard Howard, London, 1982, p. 11. In this context, I should mention another telling echo in Barthes, this time from Bakhtin's 'Author and hero': describing his own experience of his body in the two forms of migraine and sensuality, Barthes writes, 'my body is not a hero' (*RB*, p. 60). (This is not, of course, an echo in the strict sense of the word, since dates of publication rule out any possibility of influence.)

20 'The stereotype is that emplacement of discourse *where the body is missing*, where one is sure the body is not' (*RB*, p. 90).

21 This is especially true of Jonathan Culler in his otherwise exemplarily illuminating *Barthes*, London, 1983. Culler is highly suspicious of Barthes's appeal to his body in the later work, which he regards as a symptom of an underlying regression in Barthes's thought. He accuses Barthes of introducing a latent mystification that makes the body the repository of 'Nature' as an ideal truth. While Culler acknowledges the strategic function of the

body in Barthes, I think he underestimates the significance of such a strategy. He might also have been a little less dismissive of it had he paused to consider (as I am seeking to do) the extent of the intellectual tradition and the sheer weight of the arguments that lie behind the strategy. See especially chapter 8.

22 Barthes, *The Pleasure of the Text* (1973), trans. Richard Miller, London, 1976, p. 56; subsequent references are given in the text as *PT*, followed by page number. Barthes is actually talking about the text as body here, but I shall be returning to the question of the bodily fragment at greater length in my discussion of Barthes's *punctum*.

23 Barthes, 'The third meaning' (1970), in *The Responsibility of Forms*, trans. Richard Howard, Oxford, 1986, p. 44 (my italics).

24 Barthes is actually talking about Eisenstein in this essay, and the discussion of the *punctum* in *Camera Lucida* is about photography, but I think it is in the spirit of Barthes's thinking to use 'reading' as a term to cover the experience of seeing a film and looking at a photograph as well as what is normally understood by the word.

25 Barthes, *Camera Lucida*, pp. 16, 19. Howard translates 'une fête' as 'an excitement', a choice of word which fails to capture the carnivalesque connotations of the original.

26 Barthes, 'The third meaning', pp. 55, 56.

27 E.g. in *Roland Barthes*, where Barthes writes of the way that migraines and sensuality serve to 'individuate my own body' (*RB*, p. 60).

28 Stallybrass and White, *The Politics*, p. 201.

29 I am indebted for inspiration and advice, intellectual as well as bibliographical, to Ken Hirschkop, Mike Holland, Rhiannon Goldthorpe, David Shepherd and Elizabeth Wright.

Terry Eagleton

Bakhtin, Schopenhauer, Kundera

Few modern critical concepts have proved more fertile and suggestive, more productively polymorphous, than the Bakhtinian notion
of carnival. Indeed it would be a brave critic nowadays who did not
at least reverently tip his or her hat in the direction of the concept,
when the topic comes up. It is a seriously limiting comment on the
work of a critic as superb as the late Paul de Man that it is almost
impossible to imagine him being in the least enthused by the idea.
In the austere, humourless, astringently negative world of a de
Man, none of the emphases we customarily associate with carnival
– a certain pleasurable grossness, a plebeian crudity, knockabout
iconoclasm and orgiastic delight – would seem to have the least
place, as they might in some sense in the worlds of F. R. Leavis and
William Empson. The bulging, grotesque, excessively replete
subjects of carnival could only, one feels, appear as repellently
logocentric, obscenely over-present, to the tragic, sober, emptied
subjecthood of de Man's criticism. There is absolutely no feel in de
Man, as there in an Empson, for the vulgar health of the senses, of
all that follows from our most banal, biological insertion into the
world. For all his epistemological scepticism, there is little sense of
an intellect which has come to doubt its own sovereignty by
glimpsing itself, with a cackle of derisive laughter, from the standpoint of the guts or genitals. De Man's daring subversions of reason
remain impeccably academic affairs, rendered more in the tones of
northern European high seriousness than southern European high
spirits. Perhaps de Man should be praised rather than censured for
his puritan resistance to such scandalous carryings on, for the ruth-
lessness with which he expels the human body from his discourse.
For the concept of carnival, looked at in another light, may be little
more than the intellectual's guilty dues to the populace, the soul's

blood money to the body; what is truly unseemly, indecent even, is the apparent eagerness of deans, chaired professors and presidents of learned societies to tumble from their offices into the streets, monstrous papier mâché phalluses fixed in place. Perhaps the remorselessly anti-sentimentalising de Man had sniffed all this out, punitive Fury of bad faith that he was, and was prepared to sit soberly at his desk rather than to risk appearing dishonest, which is not the same as being afraid of appearing ridiculous.

In *Beyond Good and Evil*, Nietzsche opposes 'the stupidity of moral indignation' to what he calls a 'philosophical sense of humour'. 'Cynicism', he remarks, 'is the only form in which common souls come close to honesty; and the higher man must prick up his ears at every cynicism, whether coarse or refined, and congratulate himself whenever a buffoon without shame or a scientific satyr speaks out in his presence.' Whenever anyone speaks 'badly but not ill' of human beings, as bellies with two needs and a head with one, crudely deflating metaphysical solemnities, then 'the lover of knowledge should listen carefully, and with diligence'. The *buffo* and the satyr, Nietzsche laments, are strangers to the ponderous German spirit, lacking as it does 'the liberating scorn of a wind that makes everything healthy by making everything *run!*'[1] If Bakhtin is the *buffo*, then Marx and Brecht might be proposed as the scientific satyrs, as scornful in their own ways as Nietzsche of high Germanic seriousness. To trace some of the roots of Nietzsche's preoccupation with the body in the work of Schopenhauer, however, is to be rather less persuaded of its spontaneous blessedness – to turn this somatic cynicism on the body itself. It is a striking thought that, had Arthur Schopenhauer not studied medicine and physiology as a university student, the course of Western philosophy, all the way from Nietzsche's praise for the *buffo* to Jean-François Lyotard's points of libidinal intensity, might have been different. No thinker has been more attentive to the body than Schopenhauer, and none less the dupe of its seductive immediacies. Yet it is from Schopenhauer's coarsely materialist meditations on the pharynx and the larynx, on cramps, convulsions, epilepsy, tetanus and hydrophobia, that Nietzsche will derive some of his own affirmations of bodily life; and all that solemn, archaic nineteenth-century discourse of Man in terms of the ganglions and lumbar regions, which survives at least as long as Lawrence, then forms the hinterland for some of our contemporary eulogists of physicality, which includes the exponents of carnival.

Schopenhauer is quite unembarrassed to detect his celebrated

Will, that blindly persistent desire at the root of all phenomena, in yawning, sneezing and vomiting, in jerkings and twitchings of various kinds, and seems wholly oblivious of the bathos with which his language can veer without warning in the space of a few pages from high-flown reflections on free will to the structure of the spinal cord or the excrescences of the caterpillar. There is a kind of Bakhtinian bathos or Brechtian *plumpes Denken* about this sudden swooping from *Geist* to genitalia, from the oracular to the orificial, which in Bakhtin's hands at least is a political weapon against ruling-class idealism's paranoid fear of the flesh. With Schopenhauer it is less a question of political revolt than of a kind of thumping cracker-barrel crassness, as when he solemnly illustrates the conflict between body and intellect by pointing out that people find it hard to walk and talk at the same time: 'For as soon as their brain has to link a few ideas together, it no longer has as much force left over as is required to keep the legs in motion through the motor nerves.'[2] Elsewhere, Schopenhauer suggests that a short stature and neck are especially favourable to genius, 'because on the shorter path the blood reaches the brain with more energy' (p. 393). All of this vulgar literalism is a kind of theoretical posture in itself, a sardonic smack at high-toned Hegelianism from one who, though a full-blooded metaphysician himself, regards Hegel as a supreme charlatan and most philosophy except Plato, Kant and himself as a lot of hot air. Crotchety, arrogant and cantankerous, a scathing Juvenilian satirist who professes to believe that Germans need their long words because it gives their slow minds more time to think, Schopenhauer's work reveals a carnivalesque coupling of the imposing and the commonplace evident in his very name.

Indeed incongruity becomes in Schopenhauer's hands the basis for a full-blown theory of comedy which is not without relevance to the work of Bakhtin. The ludicrous, so Schopenhauer argues, springs from the paradoxical subsumption of an object under a concept in other ways heterogeneous to it, so that an Adorno-like insistence on the non-identity of object and concept can come to explain why it is that animals cannot laugh. Humour, in this speciously generalising view, is by and large high words and low meanings, and so like Schopenhauer's own philosophy has an ironic or dialogical structure. This is in itself, however, profoundly ironic, since the discrepancy between percept and concept which occasions the release of laughter is exactly that disjuncture between experience and intellect, or will and representation, which lies at the very core of Schopenhauer's disgusted view of humanity. The inner structure of this bleakest of visions is thus the structure of a joke. Schopenhauer's comic theory is here strikingly close to Freud:

> [Perception] is the medium of the present, of enjoyment and cheerfulness; moreover it is not associated with any exertion. With thinking the opposite holds good; it is the second power of knowledge, whose exercise always requires some, often considerable exertion; and it is the concepts of thinking that are so often opposed to the satisfaction of our immediate desires, since, as the medium of the past, of the future, and of what is serious, they act as the vehicle of our fears, our regrets, and all our cares. It must therefore be delightful for us to see this strict, untiring, and most troublesome governess, our faculty of reason, for once convicted of inadequacy. Therefore on this account the mien or appearance of laughter is very closely related to that of joy. (p. 98)

Comedy is the will's mocking, malicious revenge on the representation, the strike of the Schopenhauerian id against the Hegelian super-ego; but this source of hilarity is also, curiously, the root of our utter hopelessness. For reason, that crude, blundering servant of the voracious, imperious will, is always pathetic false consciousness, a mere reflex of desire which believes itself absurdly to present the world just as it is. Concepts, in that familiar brand of nineteenth-century irrationalism not wholly irrelevant to the world of a Bakhtin, cannot cling to the rich intricacies of experience but appear as maladroit as a surgeon in boxing gloves.

If humour and hopelessness lie so close together, it is because human existence for Schopenhauer is less grand tragedy than squalid farce. Writhing in the toils of the implacable will, driven on by a relentless appetite they idealise, men and women are less tragic protagonists than pitiably obtuse. The most fitting emblem of the human enterprise is the shovel-pawed mole: 'to dig strenuously with its enormous shovel-paws is the business of its whole life; permanent night surrounds it ... What does it attain by this course of life that is full of trouble and devoid of pleasure? Nourishment and procreation, that is, only the means for continuing and beginning again in the new individual the same melancholy course' (pp. 353–4). Nothing could be more obvious to Schopenhauer than the fact that it would be infinitely preferable if the world did not exist at all, that the whole project is a ghastly mistake which ought long ago to have been called off, and that only some crazed idealism could possibly believe the pleasures of human existence to outweigh its pains. Only the most blatant self-delusion – values, ideas, the rest of that pointless paraphernalia – could blind individuals to this laughably self-evident truth. It is hard for Schopenhauer to restrain a burst of hysterical laughter at the sight of this pompously self-important race, gripped by a remorseless will-to-live which is secretly quite indifferent to any of them, piously convinced of their own supreme value, scrambling over each other in the earnest pursuit of some goal which will turn instantly to ashes in their mouths. There is no grand *telos* to this 'battleground of tormented and agonised beings', only 'momentary gratification, fleeting pleasure conditioned by wants, much and long suffering, constant struggle, *bellum omnium*, everything a hunter and everything hunted, pressure, want, need and anxiety, shrieking and howling; and this goes on *in saecula saeculorum* or until once again the crust of the planet breaks' (p. 354). If Hegel is the ultimate high-minded mystifier of bourgeois civil society, Schopenhauer is the *buffo* who mouths the truths of the marketplace.

There is something amusing about the very relentlessness of this Schopenhauerian gloom, a perpetual grousing with all the monotonous, mechanical repetition of the very condition it denounces. If comedy for Schopenhauer involves subsuming objects to inappropriate concepts, then this is ironically true of his own pessimism, which stamps everything with its own inexorable colour and so has the funniness of all monomania. The monological has its own unwitting humour, of which the dialogical knows nothing. Any such obsessive conversion of difference to identity is bound to be comic, however tragic the actual outlook. To see no difference between roasting a leg of lamb and roasting a baby, to view both as mere indifferent expressions of the metaphysical will, is as risible as mistaking one's left foot for the notion of natural justice. In another sense, however, Schopenhauer's intense pessimism is not in the least outrageous – is, indeed, no more than the sober realism he himself considers it to be. Absurdly one-sided though this viewpoint may be, it is a fact that throughout class history the fate of the great majority of men and women has been one of suffering and fruitless toil. The dominant narrative of history to date has been one of carnage, wretchedness and oppression; and any Bakhtinian celebration which has not in some sense gone through this belief and emerged somewhere on the other side is politically futile. Moral virtue has never flourished as the decisive force in any historical society, other than briefly and untypically. The monotonous driving forces of history have indeed been enmity, appetite and dominion (the Schopenhauerian Will); and the scandal of that sordid heritage is that it is indeed possible to ask of the lives of innumerable individuals whether they would not in fact have been better off dead. Liberal humanists have the option of either denying this truth, or acknowledging it but hoping that, for some obscure reason, the future might turn out rather better. Such pious wishful thinking is unlikely to withstand the coarse cackle of a Schopenhauerian materialism. There is absolutely no reason why the future should turn out any better than the past, unless there are *reasons* why the past has been as atrocious as it has. If the reason is simply that there is an unsavoury as well as a magnificent side to human nature, then it is hard to explain, on the simple law of averages, why the unsavoury side has apparently dominated almost every political culture to date. Part of the explanatory power of historical materialism is its provision of good reasons for why the past has taken the form it has, and its resolute opposition to all vacuous moralistic hope. Those liberal humanists who have now enlisted the joyous, carnivalesque Bakhtin to their cause need perhaps to explain rather more rigorously than they do why the experience represented by carnival is, historically speaking, so utterly untypical. Unless the carnivalesque body is confronted by that bitter, negative, travestying style of a carnivalesque thought which is the philosophy of Schopenhauer, it is difficult to see how it signifies any substantial advance on a commonplace sentimental populism, of a kind attractive to academics.

The confrontation between those two kinds of body is perhaps nowhere so graphically demonstrated as in the fiction of Milan Kundera. His novel *The Unbearable Lightness of Being* sees an intolerable lightness and frailty in anything unique, as though anything which happens only once might as well have not happened at all. *Einmal ist keinmal.* If history can be dissolved into pure difference, then it suffers a massive haemorrhage of meaning, because past events only happen once, they fail to take firm root in our lives and can be expunged from memory, having about them the ineradicable aura of pure accident. The past thus perpetually threatens to dissolve beneath the heel of the present, and this plays straight into the hands of the totalitarian state, adept as it is at airbrushing disgraced politicians out of photographs. What imbues persons and events with unique value, then, is precisely what renders them insubstantial, and Kundera's writing is deeply gripped by this sense of sickening ontological precariousness. It contrasts in this sense with the writing of most of our current fetishists of difference. Pure difference for Kundera cannot be valuable, for value is a relational term; but the paradox is that repetition is an enemy of value too, since the more a thing is repeated the more it tends to fade into meaninglessness.

The point where difference and identity converge most undecidably for Kundera is in the body and sexuality. For sexual love links the unrepeatable experience of a particular, unique relationship with the ceaselessly repetitive, tediously predictable character of the bodily drives. What might be thought to be most deviant, stimulating, shockingly unconventional – a sexual orgy – turns out in the novel in question to be hilariously comic in its endless mechanical repetitions, the supposed singularity of erotic love uproariously repeated in a wilderness of mirrors, each individuated body mockingly mimicking the next. Kundera recognises the profound comedy of repetition, which is one reason why sex is usually the funniest part of his novels; his laughter is that release of libidinal energy which comes from momentarily decathecting the utterly self-identical love object, the magnificent *non-pareil*, in the moment of wry recognition that we all share a common biology. The traditional name of this emancipatory moment is, of course, the carnivalesque, that aggressive onslaught on the fetishism of difference which ruthlessly, liberatingly reduces back all such metaphysical singularities to the solidarity of the flesh.

Kundera's attitude to such emancipation, however, is a good deal more ambiguous and dialectical than that of some official exponents of carnivalesque affirmation. For how is one to use this fleshly solidarity of the species as a demystifying force while avoiding that brutal erasure of difference which is Stalinist uniformity? How to stay faithful to the positive political therapy of carnival without lapsing into biologistic cynicism, or, as Kundera himself might put it, crossing over that hair-thin border which distinguishes 'angelic' meaning from the demonic cackle of meaninglessness? Reproduction, in every sense of the word, may be a source of liberatory humour, which is no doubt one thing Marx meant by suggesting that all tragic events repeated themselves as farce; but the farce in question can be destructive as well as redemptive, which was another of Marx's meanings. The bureaucratic state for Kundera is itself a contradictory amalgam of romantic idealism and cynical materialism: if its discourse is the pure *kitsch* of high-flown sentiment (more evident perhaps these days in the USA than the Soviet Union), its practices render individual bodies and events indifferently exchangeable. The political problem is then to know how to subvert the state's lying romantic idealism without lapsing into a version of its own lethal levelling. One must remember here that for Kundera the image of ungainly naked bodies crowded into a single space, repeating one another endlessly, suggests not only the hilarity of the sexual orgy but the concentration camp.

Every time something is repeated, it loses part of its meaning; the unique, on the other hand, is a romantic illusion. This contradiction in Kundera can be rephrased as a tension between too much meaning and too little. A political order in which everything is oppressively meaningful buckles under its own weight: this is the realm which Kundera names the 'angelic', an intolerable existence since a degree of non-meaning is essential for our lives. The demonic exists to puncture this stifling logocentrism: it is the laughter which arises from things being suddenly deprived of their familiar meanings, a kind of estrangement effect akin to Heidegger's broken hammer, and which a monstrous proliferation of the supposedly singular, as in the sexual orgy, can bring about. Such meaninglessness may be a blessed moment of release, a temporary respite from the world's tyrannical, compulsive legibility in which we slip serenely into the abyss of silence. The demonic is thus closely associated in Kundera with the death drive, a spasm of deconstructive mockery which, like carnival, is never far from the cemetery. But that is enough to remind us that this blessed meaninglessness is by no means wholly to be celebrated. It has about it a malicious, implacable violence, the pure negativity of a Satanic cynicism. Carnival releases us from the terrorism of excessive significance, multiplying and so levelling meanings; but as such it is never far from Schopenhauer's grossly somatic vision of empty futility. Kundera is, I think, right to associate evil, or the demonic, with a radical loss of meaning. Evil, unlike simple immorality, is not hostile or indifferent to particular values but to the whole idea of value as such. It is driven to incredulous mocking laughter, like the compassionate Schopenhauer, by the sheer deceitful hollowness of human beings' pathetic belief that there is ever anything more than facts, than the body, and like Iago relieves the intolerable frustration of this cynicism by reaping malicious delight from destroying value wherever it finds it. This is why evil is traditionally conceived of as radically motiveless: it is not this or that delusion of value which drives it to despair but just a faith in value as such. One of the most unthinkable aspects of the concentration camps is that they were quite unnecessary. It is significance as such that the demonic finds an insupportable scandal; and it is therefore, as Kundera well sees, a tempting lure for the opponents of angelic–authoritarian order, who will be led by it to their doom. The savage irony of the demonic is that it finally dismantles the antithesis of the angels only to conflate the whole of reality together in a levelling not far from the angels' own. Bodies are indifferently interchangeable for both Stalinism and carnival, transgression prized by both revolutionary and cynic. The liberal humanist prizes uniqueness and difference, and supports a bourgeois order which has time for nothing but exchange value.

Just as we are precariously positioned by our very bodiliness on some indeterminate frontier between sameness and difference, biology and history, so for Kundera we must seek to position ourselves on some wellnigh invisible border between too much meaning and too little, embracing all that the angels reject – 'shit' is the blunt term Kundera gives to the angelically unacceptable – without settling for that sheer shitlike amorphousness which is Stalinism, nihilism, the demonic or (to add a term about which the Eastern European exile is curiously silent) the levelling exchanges of the capitalist marketplace. Happiness is the yearning for repetition, but repetition is what fatally erodes it; the male sexual drive, rather like the authoritarian states of both East and West, is cripplingly divided between a romantic idealism of the uniquely particular (the wife, the permanent mistress) and a promiscuous exchangeability of bodies. *Kitsch* is the name Kundera gives to all 'shitless' discourse, all idealising disavowal of that fundamental meaninglessness which belongs to our biological condition. In the realm of *kitsch*, the dictatorship of the heart reigns supreme: *kitsch* is all smiles and cheers, relentlessly beaming and euphoric like an aerobics class, marching merrily onward to the future shouting 'long live life!' The Gulag, Kundera comments, is the septic tank *kitsch* uses to dispose of its refuse. If the authoritarian state cannot be opposed by romantic idealism, it is because it actually has a monopoly of it; and this is one reason why Kundera's own critique is inevitably bent back towards a materialism of the body very close to the Bakhtinian notion of carnival. But the endless couplings and exchanges of the carnivalesque body are also terrifyingly close to what is worst about modern political regimes; and there is thus no way in which Kundera can uncritically celebrate some romantic image of plebeian riot. Those who can no longer tolerate shitless discourse are always likely to end up in the shit, boomeranging from angels to devils, pitched helplessly from one metaphysical pole to another. Those who find hierarchies, divisions and distinctions rather too oppressively elitist, too smugly rational, might prefer instead some release of bodies and actions to the same level, of the kind that Schopenhauer describes at one point: 'To enter at the age of five a cotton-spinning or other factory, and from then on to sit there every day first ten, then twelve, and finally fourteen hours, and perform the same mechanical work, is to purchase dearly the pleasure of drawing breath' (p. 578). It is hard to know how much necessary non-meaning, how much free-wheeling contingency, can be embraced by any system of meaning without it collapsing into the demonic. 'We insist that everything must have meaning', writes Vincent Descombes,

> otherwise nothing would have meaning. But there is an alternative hypothesis. Certain defects in meaning are perhaps to be welcomed at the same time as certain defects in the intelligence of meaning are to be deplored. It could be a misfortune to find meaning in everything, for it would then become impossible to understand a meaning in this or in that. Here then is an alternative hypothesis: It is not the case that everything has meaning which claims it, otherwise nothing could claim to have meaning.[3]

A situation where everything is meaningful is certainly oppressive: the logical extreme of such an attitude is paranoia, a condition in which reality becomes so pervasively, ominously meaningful that its slightest fragments operate as signs in some sinisterly coherent text. Kundera tells the story in *The Book of Laughter and Forgetting* of a Czech being sick in the middle of Prague, not long after the Soviet invasion of the country. Another Czech wanders up to him, shakes his head and says: 'I know just what you mean.'

Derek Parfit argues in his *Reasons and Persons* that what differentiates human beings from one another is just not significant enough a basis on which to build an ethics. Or, one might add, a politics. It is ironic that radicals must spend as much time as they do emphasising the vital distinctions of class, nation, gender and race to a political antagonist who can afford to ignore them, since none of these distinctions is in the end very important, and the only political strategy likely to dismantle the oppressions they involve is one which is aware of this truth. It is not only tragic but farcical that biological differences of race and gender should have been made the basis of whole systems of brutal dehumanisation, since no serious theoretical defence of their significance has ever been, or can be, advanced. It is not true that there is any isolable, identifiable condition known as 'being Irish', 'being female', 'being Jewish'. Being

Irish, female or Jewish may most certainly, in specific social terms and places, be associated with highly particular ways of feeling, ways of feeling which may even be peculiar and exclusive to such appellations; but nobody has yet brought off the difficult epistemological trick of peering into themselves and discovering, by introspection, an isolable state of being, independent of all other determinations, which simply was a matter of being one of these things. They are not, in this sense, *identities* at all, any more than 'being human' is. Radical political strategies, of the kind one imagines Bakhtin would have approved, need continually to adjust the tension between the urgent angelic significance of such oppressed subject-positions, and that kind of demonic cynicism which would reduce them to sheer amorphousness. The interesting point about Bakhtinian carnival, in this respect, is that it at once cavalierly suppresses hierarchies and distinctions, recalling us to a common creatureliness not irrelevant to an age gravely threatened with common biological extinction, and at the same time does so as part of a politically specific, sharply differentiated, combatively one-sided practice – that of the lower classes, who incarnate some utopian 'common humanity' at the very moment they unmask their rulers' liberal-minded ideology of 'common social interests' for the shitless, self-interested rhetoric it is. Much of the critical discourse by which Bakhtin has currently been appropriated would seem to me, in Kundera's precise meaning, strikingly shitless – the demonic cackle raised to the service of an angelic ideology. It is very hard to believe that Bakhtin spilt so much ink just to inform us that we should listen attentively to one another, treat each other as whole persons, be prepared to be corrected and interrupted, realise that life is an endless unfinished process, that too much dogma makes you narrow-minded, that nobody has a monopoly of the truth and that life is so much richer than any of our little ideas about it. He was not, after all, George Eliot or E. M. Forster or a liberal Democrat. Those who believe that 'being human' is indeed an identifiable condition of being, whereas being female or Irish is of course not, can no doubt reap solace from parts of Bakhtin's writing, but will need to engage in a fair bit of rewriting elsewhere. Schopenhauer certainly believed in a common human condition; it is just that he also believed that this was the problem, not the answer. It may be that, as a concept, carnival has fought its way through the demystifying pessimism of a Schopenhauer and the dialectical ambivalences of a Kundera, to emerge somewhere on the other side; but this is a hypothesis to be demonstrated rather than assumed.

Notes

1   F. Nietzsche, *Beyond Good and Evil*, Harmondsworth, 1979, pp. 40, 42.
2   A. Schopenhauer, *The World as Will and Representation*, vol. 2, trans. E. F. J. Payne, New York, 1969, p. 284; subsequent page references are given in the text.
3   Vincent Descombes, *Objects of All Sorts*, Oxford, 1986, pp. 15–16.

Carol Adlam

Critical work on the Bakhtin Circle: a new bibliographical essay

In his 1989 bibliographical overview of critical English-language material on the Bakhtin Circle, which the present essay both partially duplicates and supplements, Ken Hirschkop predicted turbulence ahead: the 'snowball' of material, he wrote, was gathering such momentum that it was on the point of becoming an 'avalanche'. The accuracy of Hirschkop's prognosis is indisputable: in the English-speaking academic world alone there has been a veritable cavalcade of work bearing the marks of assimilation and application of Bakhtinian tenets, while in Bakhtin's homeland, particularly since the 1990s, Russian academic criticism has been similarly inundated. While the necessarily delicate and demanding task of sifting the layers of this so fundamentally transfigured academic terrain was begun early (Karpunov *et al.*, 1989; Sadouski and Thomson 1983; Shukman 1978), it is now the case that the history of the runaway expansion of Bakhtinian thought has itself become a salient constitutive feature of Bakhtin studies, with increasing discussion of the processes and consequences of such a singular phenomenon (Adlam 1997a; Emerson 1997; Lähteenmäki 1998; for an early example see Hirschkop 1986). The task of this essay, however, must be considerably less refined: functioning rather more as a snow-plough than as a sensitive instrument for the evaluation of minute shifts in the critical topography, it will clear some paths to expose something of the lie of the land, and, in its focus on the Russian- as well as English-language material both before and since Hirschkop's original article (which dealt exclusively with Anglophone material), will perhaps uncover some bodies of work which might otherwise remain buried under linguistic as well as disciplinary snowdrifts.

The inescapable selectivity such an approach entails may be

mitigated by the existence of several major scholarly bibliographic resources elsewhere which are devoted exclusively to Bakhtin studies. The online Bakhtin Centre Analytical Database, produced by the Bakhtin Centre at the University of Sheffield, holds details of over 3,500 pieces of work (see bibliography for details); and the journal *Dialogism* (1998), also produced under the aegis of the Bakhtin Centre, is to take up the bibliographical baton from the long-running, almost entirely bibliographically-oriented, Canadian journal of Bakhtin studies *The Bakhtin Newsletter* (1983–96). The latter's final issue, edited by Lee and Thomson (1996), and entitled 'Bakhtin around the world', contains a wealth of information about the reception of Bakhtin in countries other than England and America, such as Australia (Fielder 1996), Israel (Ginsburg 1996), Japan (Kuwano 1996), and Poland (Żyłko 1996), as well as analyses of the reception of specific Bakhtinian concepts (Shepherd 1996). The Anglo-American and British reception has been reviewed by Brandist (1995) and Hitchcock (1996), while an emergent attention to the interpretation of Bakhtin by the 'other' is also evident in cross-national discussions. The most prominent of these is a growing exchange regarding discrepancies of views between scholars in Russia and scholars from, largely, Anglophone Western countries. (For examples of such 'bilateral' discussions see Emerson 1992, 1996; Jaireth 1995; Makhlin 1993, 1995b; Osovskii 1994; and Yurchenko 1995. For an example of a direct exchange of views see Makhlin and Morson 1991, followed by Perlina 1997 and Morson 1997.)

Indications of the frequently considerable divergences between Russian and Western interpretations quickly revealed themselves at the first sustained public encounter between Russian and Western Bakhtin scholars, the Seventh International Bakhtin Conference at the University of Manchester in 1991. Shepherd's account (1993b) of this confrontation reveals the extent to which Bakhtin's work was extensively and variously interpreted in accordance with the chief theoretical allegiances of the representatives of the two national and geographic 'camps', and documents the significant misprisions of the 'other' which took place as a result. While it may be no surprise that the Russian encounter with Bakhtin has been no less, if differently, mediated by politicised factors than the Western one – with its own complex history of mediating and, at times, obfuscating factors informing the processes of reception – this should not diminish the significance of this meeting of worlds, since neither Russian nor Western scholars can now refer to

impregnable barriers of information (if not, with still some quali-
fication, movement) as justification for viewing the work of their
counterparts as unknowably, homogeneously 'other'. Indeed, for
all the evident divergence of approach, there appears increasingly
to be a basic agreement of sorts on the vital importance of extensive research into Bakhtin's philosophical and theoretical
influences.

While the European and Anglophone post-structuralist atmosphere into which Bakhtin was first introduced in the West left its
several tenacious marks in the drive to textual and semiotic application to follow, an attention to Bakhtin's personal historical and
intellectual contexts was not absent even in the early years of
Anglophone reception (see, most notably, the highly influential
monographs by Clark and Holquist 1984 and Morson and Emerson
1990). More sustained consideration of this, however, has taken
place in the West only after the years of *perestroika*, and consequently, one might argue, as a product of the ongoing exposure to
the work of Russian Bakhtin scholars in particular (see Poole 1994,
1997, 1998; Tihanov 1997a, 1997b; and the Bakhtin Centre's electronic project 'The Russian and European Contexts of the Bakhtin
Circle').

In Russia, this task has been facilitated by the publication of a
large amount of archival material over recent years. First-person
accounts of Bakhtin's life by those who had met him in his later
years (Bocharov 1993a, 1993b; Broitman 1990; Estifeeva 1995;
Konkin 1996; Kozhinov 1988, 1992) have been supplemented by
the publication of various sets of correspondence with Bakhtin
(Bakhtin 1992a, 1992b; Kagan 1992; Turbin 1991; Yudina 1993).
This material contains, along with more substantive information,
such anecdotal snippets as Bakhtin's fondness for Chaplin films; his
belief that he had last been incarnated in sixteenth-century
Germany; and his claim that his cat was a descendant of Egyptian
temple cats – a claim made on the grounds of its deafness (see,
respectively, Vulis 1993; Zdol'nikov, 1993; Kozhinov 1996). Such
publications also contain material pertaining to professional and
scholarly matters, including details of Bakhtin's agreement in 1961
with Giulio Einaudi for the first publication in Italian translation of
Problemy poetiki Dostoevskogo (*Problems of Dostoevsky's Poetics*) by
the Italian publishing house Einaudi (Strada 1997); his intentions
to give a series of lectures on music (Yudina 1993); the lengthy
transcript of his dissertation defence (Pan'kov 1993); and a transcript of lectures on Kantian philosophy and religion delivered by

Bakhtin to his famous philosophical seminar in 1924–25 (Nikolaev 1992). These and other *varia* have been published in several journals, but most noticeably through the efforts of the prolific quarterly journal *Dialog Karnaval Khronotop* (*Dialogue Carnival Chronotope*). The first issue of the journal *Nevel'skii sbornik* (*The Nevel' Miscellany*), which includes newspaper articles documenting Bakhtin's participation, while in Nevel', in public debates on such topics as 'God and socialism' (Maksimovskaya 1996), also promises much of interest. Likely to be even more pertinent to the current re-evaluation of Bakhtin's own circumstances, both personal and historical, is the publication of a series of lengthy interviews with Bakhtin conducted in the 1970s by Viktor Duvakin, which cover his life and career from his family and student days to the time of interview (Duvakin 1996). In addition, the Russian Academy of Sciences' much-anticipated project of a seven-volume *Sobranie sochinenii* (*Collected Works*), under the general editorship of Sergei Bocharov, has been launched recently with the publication of an extensively-annotated 700-page tome subtitled *Raboty 1940-kh–nachala 1960-kh godov* (*Works from the 1940s to the Beginning of the 1960s*) (Bakhtin 1996). This, the fifth of the projected seven volumes, contains a great deal of previously unpublished material from Bakhtin's archive, including substantial notes on 'Problema rechevykh zhanrov' ('The problem of speech genres'), material previously published piecemeal or otherwise bowdlerised, and such new material as pieces on Flaubert, Mayakovskii, sentimentalism, satire, and much more. The editors' priority is to publish all Bakhtin's works *as they are* in the archive: this alone promises to make *The Collected Works* the focus of considerable debate and reassessment, and, consequently, one of the most significant events in Bakhtin scholarship for some time to come.

Although there may be some interval between this publication and its accompanying volumes, and the translation of (at least) the previously untranslated material therein, we may nevertheless speculate with some justification that the planned seventh volume, *Raboty 'kruga Bakhtina'* (*Works of the 'Bakhtin Circle'*), indicates the emergence of a certain consensus with regard to the constitution of the Bakhtin corpus. The question of the authorship of the texts first published under the names of Medvedev and Voloshinov has provoked heated argument since the early 1970s, when a footnote in an article by Ivanov (1973) stated that Bakhtin was the texts' true author. Anecdotal testimony has since accumulated from those who had direct dealings with Bakhtin, to the effect that he was responsible, in varying degrees, for the works in question. Such testimony is offered, most notably, by Bocharov (1993a), Broitman (1990), Clark and Holquist (1986), Kozhinov (1977), and Wehrle (1978). One of the few Russian critics to reject the claims for Bakhtin's authorship of the texts published under Medvedev's name is Yurii Medvedev (1992), while Pan'kov (1995), in an introduction to a selection of administrative documents belonging to Voloshinov, further deepens the mystery by noting that the hand-written 'author's summary' and 'plan' for the book *Marksizm i filosofiya yazyka* (*Marxism and the Philosophy of Language*) contained therein, and dated 1928, are written in neither Voloshinov's nor Bakhtin's hand, but in that of an unknown third party. An earlier survey by Osovskii (1992) evaluates in detail the arguments and evidence offered, consolidating the general agreement in Russia with his conclusion that the publication of the works under others' names may be explained by either expediency (Bakhtin could not get his works published at the time), altruism (Bakhtin wished to assist his friends' professional and/or financial standing, as in the case of Kanaev) or philosophical experiment (Bakhtin transposed his concepts of 'masks', 'alibis' and 'participative creation' to his real-life situation). In the West, Bakhtin's authorship has most notably been challenged by Godzich (1985) and Titunik (1984, 1986), although, in the absence of conclusive evidence either way, such researchers as Perlina (1983, 1989), Shukman (1983) and Todorov (1985) have undertaken comparative stylistic and lexical analyses in order to argue that Bakhtin had some part in the writing of these 'disputed' or 'deutero-canonical' texts.

The stakes in this debate were raised in the mid-1990s as a direct consequence of the aftermath of the collapse of the legal infrastructure of the former Soviet Union, whereby an already vulnerable copyright law could, with a degree of impunity, be bypassed (particularly if publication took place outside the territory of the Russian Federation, as was the case with the publication in Kiev (by the Next publishing house) of a collection of Bakhtin's early works entitled *Raboty 1920-kh godov* (*Works from the 1920s*), and *Problemy tvorchestva/poetiki Dostoevskogo* (*Problems of Dostoevsky's Art/Problems of Dostoevsky's Poetics*) (Bakhtin 1994a, 1994b), under the editorship of O. V. Garun. Bocharov, Kozhinov, and Melikhova (1994), the executors of Bakhtin's estate, protested that the publication in this series of the unauthorised edition of *Problemy tvorchestva Dostoevskogo* (*Problems of Dostoevsky's Art*) in particular was 'piratical'. A slightly earlier publication in Moscow of a series entitled 'Bakhtin under a mask' also resulted in a debate in *Dialog Karnaval Khronotop*, in which a piece by Ivanov and Kozhinov, who stood by their claims for Bakhtin's authorship, was pitted against a letter to the editors from Medvedev (1995). This letter is both poignant and noteworthy: poignant in Medvedev's defence of his father's memory, and noteworthy in scholarly terms, in so far as Medvedev claims that his father's archive contains article drafts substantially similar to the published version of *The Formal Method in Literary Scholarship*. Furthermore, Yurii Medvedev draws attention away from the lexical content of the book, instead urging consideration of its contextual and circumstantial impetus. Such an approach corresponds, however unintentionally, with the 'solution' offered by Makhlin (1996c) in the Foreword to one of the latest volumes of the 'Bakhtin under a mask' series (a collection of essays by Kanaev, Medvedev and Voloshinov, in this instance indicatively subtitled 'Bakhtin half-masked'). Cutting through the Gordian knot, Makhlin suggests that, while it would appear probable that Bakhtin participated in some way in the creation of the texts therein, the truly salient 'masks' which we should strive to put aside are those imposed upon Bakhtin by later interpreters, impelled by allegiances created by their own critical and theoretical circumstances. Renfrew (1997b) also has advanced this argument, in relation to both the disputed texts and the broader field of Bakhtin's influence.

This 'bio-bibliographical' debate in Russia is clearly imbricated with the ongoing enquiry into specific theoretical allegiances and precursors of the Bakhtin Circle, in which investigation into their philosophical antecedents and contemporaries is increasingly regarded as a prerequisite to an adequate understanding of key Bakhtinian tenets. While some Western scholars have undertaken research into, for example, aspects of Bakhtin's historicism, the main impetus has come from Russian scholars, for whom Bakhtin is almost entirely a philosopher, if – and this too is increasingly seen as important – an unconventional one. While it is a moot point whether the relatively recent Russian awareness of the initial post-structuralist Western terms of response to Bakhtin has been a reactively formative influence in the Russian view of Bakhtin as philosopher, it is also possible, as argued by Jaireth (1995), that another source of this view of Bakhtin may be a late- or post-Soviet reluctance to align Bakhtin with a form of 'science', a word which held dubious connotations after decades of Marxist–

Leninist discourse. However, the more persuasive arguments advanced in favour of viewing Bakhtin as a 'thinker', as he described himself, are to be found in the ongoing research into Bakhtin's own Russian and European (notably German) intellectual influences. Collections edited by Aleksandrova and Breikin (1992), Gogotishvili and Gurevich (1992), Isupov *et al.* (1991), and Konkin *et al.* (1992) all testify to this recent direction in Russian scholarship, supported by archive materials which, for instance, illuminate Bakhtin's relation to the Marburg School and the Nevel' school (Gushchina 1995; Makhlin 1996b; Nikolaev 1991). In particular, such researchers as Bonetskaya (1993) and Makhlin (1988, 1991, 1995a, 1996a) have been instrumental in instigating debate on the philosophical origins and significance of Bakhtin's concept of dialogue. Makhlin is also the author of a monograph (1995, 1997) which comprises an exploration of Bakhtin's links with such 'philosophers of dialogue' as Martin Buber and Franz Rosenzweig, and he is the editor of conference proceedings dating from 1993, the keynote of which constitutes a debate over the respective weight of Bakhtin's philosophical and literary contributions to the humanities (1994). Various collections of articles, such as that edited by Gabinskii *et al.* (1994), also discuss Bakhtin as an epistemic philosopher, as does Bibler (1991). Two more recent monographs (Peshkov 1996; Smirnov 1996) engage with Bakhtinian thought in order to further, in the former's case, purely philosophical investigations and, in the latter's, research into philosophical anthropology, while monographs by Mihailovic (1997) and Coates (1999) examine the theological aspect of his work.

Anglophone Western research has, as I have already mentioned, taken a rather different direction, with efforts made only relatively recently to locate Bakhtin within contemporaneous philosophical tendencies (with reference to Nietzsche, for example, see Curtis 1986; Erdinast-Vulcan, 1994, 1995; and with reference to Kant, see Godzich 1991). Much of this realignment of Bakhtin is predicated on a rejection of the theoretical circumstances of Bakhtin's introduction to the West (largely credited to Kristeva: see Cavanagh 1993) from the early 1970s onwards. In those early days, Bakhtin was given an enthusiastic welcome for ostensibly both anticipating and providing the means for a resolution of the impasses of structuralism and post-structuralism, either from a position of 'late formalism' (see Morson 1978; Todorov 1977) or as a proto-structuralist (Pomorska 1968). This led to later exploration of apparent contiguities with theorists of the Prague school (see Danow 1986; Holquist 1985). With increasing acquaintance with the complexity of Bakhtin's intellectual contexts, however, some (e.g. Morson 1991) have qualified their earlier identifications of Bakhtin, while others (e.g. Kuyundzhich 1990; Rutland 1990) have been more eager to locate Bakhtin within the fields of both 'post-structuralism' and 'post-modernism'. Recently, and largely in Russia, the question of Bakhtin's affiliations with the Formalists has been reactivated (Nikolaev 1991, 1996; Shaitanov 1994; 1996). Shaitanov, for instance, proposes that the Bakhtin Circle's polemic with the Formalists was an expedient stratagem which concealed a fundamental common affiliation with Veselovskii.

In addition, a significant number of researchers challenged the post-Kristevan deconstructionist approach to Bakhtin (Eagleton 1981; Erdinast-Vulcan 1995; MacCannell 1985), and, in the late 1980s, there emerged the suggestion that an excessive emphasis on Bakhtin as textual theorist vitiated the sociological–cultural implications of his work. The indivisibility of these two aspects of Bakhtinian thought led Williams (1986), following Bennett's more restricted argument (1979), to present the work of the Bakhtin Circle as a touchstone for an emerging materialist cultural theory. Similar arguments were proposed by Frow (1986), Godzich (1985) and Walton (1981), while LaCapra (1983) and, most notably, Stallybrass and White (1986), have argued that Bakhtin's work demands a sustained and theorised attention to forms of historical materialism. The Marxian basis of these arguments has more recently been extended in monographs by Bernard-Donals (1994), and Gardiner (1992). Such scholars as Pechey have been particularly instrumental in sustaining this area of investigation: Pechey's earlier work explores the relation of the Bakhtin Circle to Formalism and Marxism (1980; 1986), while his more recent research investigates cultural materialism in the context of post-colonialism (1987; 1990; 1994; 1997). Similar work relating specifically to issues of postcolonial discourse has in addition been undertaken by Hale (1994) and Wesling (1993), following Clifford (1983) and Crapanzano (1985).

Indicative of the ways in which Bakhtinian thought potentially enables the study of various fields of discourse, in particular the discourse of the 'other', is the growing area of feminist Bakhtinian analysis. The initial stimulus for this field, which first emerged in the early 1980s, was provided by Booth's 1982 discussion of Bakhtin's evasion of the issue of misogyny in Rabelais. Russo (1986) also responded to *Rabelais and His World*, while Cerquiglini

(1986) drew on both *Rabelais and His World* and 'Discourse in the novel' to produce an analysis of the ways in which gender informs medieval texts. From the late 1980s onwards there was a notable increase of interest in the subject (see Díaz-Diocaretz 1989a, 1989b, 1989c; Hadjukowski-Ahmed 1990; O'Connor 1990). Bauer's was the first book-length study to explore the viability of a reader-based feminist dialogical criticism (1988), and this was later extended in Bauer and McKinstry's edited collection (1991), in which several essays advocated a circumspect optimism with regard to the application of Bakhtinian thought to feminist research (see, for example, Herndl 1991). A specifically literary approach to the subject was explored in the later collection edited by Hohne and Wussow (1994), while Castellanos is one of an increasing number of researchers to extend Bakhtin's potential through the discussion of specific texts, in this case in a book-length study of Charlotte Brontë (1995). The popularity of such extensions of Bakhtin in Anglophone criticism is a by-product of the impact of feminism in the humanities generally, but it should come as little surprise that the only piece to date by a researcher seemingly of Russian provenance to discuss Bakhtin in relation to gender issues (here, women's writing) engages with Bakhtin on only the most superficially formalist of levels (Ivanova 1993). The effect of this piece is further undercut by its juxtaposition with Emerson's brisk critique of feminist extensions of Bakhtinian thought in the same 1993 collection.

Such explorations of Bakhtin's contributions to literary criticism are to be found elsewhere, where his contributions to genre theory, and to discourse analysis and linguistic research, are discussed. For example, the tension between the materialist and formalist aspects of his work is reflected frequently in comparative studies of Bakhtin and other theorists of the novel (Aucouturier 1983; Poole 1994). Bakhtin's relationship with Lukács is one such area of investigation (see Jha 1985; Kovács 1980; Tihanov 1997a, 1997b). There have been other 'discourse-based' investigations into, for example, the contributions of the Bakhtin Circle to the field of linguistics. This area of research was initiated early on by Presnyakov (1978), who discussed Bakhtin and Potebnya, and broadened by Grigor'ev (1979) and, later, by Sokolyansky (1993) – both of whom discuss the relation of the Bakhtin Circle to Vinokur – and Ponzio (1993, 1994). In the field of textual analysis, Bakhtin is brought to bear in specialised monographs on such authors as Christa Wolf and Virginia Woolf (Herrmann 1989), Shakespeare (Hall 1995), Joyce (Kershner 1989) and Dostoevsky (Morson 1981), and is also applied in monographs concerning such bodies of writing as Gothic literature (Howard 1994), metafiction in the Soviet era (Shepherd 1992) and Russian Soviet fiction (Booker and Juraga 1995). While the categories of carnival, dialogism, chronotope and so on have been deployed in ways too various and with regard to subjects too numerous to attempt to rehearse here (on carnival, for example, see, most notably, Berrong 1986 and Kinser 1990), the overall viability of these concepts is at least suggested by their extension into such branches of the 'non-literary' arts as drama (Cunliffe 1993; Joki 1993), film (Stam 1989) and the visual arts (Haynes 1995).

The late 1980s saw a growth also of introductory and explanatory material devoted purely to Bakhtin and the Bakhtin Circle. Clark and Holquist (1984) and Todorov (1984) provided the earliest such works, which were highly determinative of the reception of Bakhtin in the West, as was Morson and Emerson's 1990 monograph. There have been no comprehensive English-language presentations of Bakhtin's life and work since these publications: however, their singular position may well be challenged by Hirschkop's 1999 monograph. There now exist important introductory texts by Danow (1991), Holquist (1990), and most recently Vice (1997), as well as several readers edited by Dentith (1995), Morris (1994) and Osovskii (1995). There is now a remarkable number of essays and articles gathered under the sign of Bakhtin, occasionally by individual authors (Lodge 1990, 1995; Pearce 1994), though more frequently in the form of collections of articles by various scholars. The earliest examples of such in the Anglophone critical world were edited by Díaz-Diocaretz (1989a), Morson and Emerson (1989), Barsky and Holquist (1990), Thomson (1990) and Shepherd (1993a). More recent collections include Thomson and Dua (1995), Mandelker (1996), Adlam et al. (1997b), Renfrew (1997a), Brandist and Tihanov (2000), as well as journal special issues edited by Hitchcock (1998) and by the San Diego Bakhtin Circle (2000). Thematic collections have also appeared, on medieval textual scholarship (edited by Farrell 1995) and, more recently, on rhetoric (edited by Farmer 1998) and on Shakespeare and carnival (edited by Knowles 1998). In Russia, conference proceedings and special issues of journals devoted to the Bakhtin Circle are frequently released, particularly since Bakhtin's centenary year in 1995, including collections and journals edited by Bezmenova (1991), Eremeev et al. (1989; 1992), Gershkovich and Khatchaturov (1996), Gorbanov (1990), Kuyundzhich et al. (see *Bakhtinskii sbornik* 1, 1990 and 2, 1991), Isupov et al. (1995), Voronina et al. (1995) and Makhlin (1994).

References

Adlam, Carol, 1997a. 'In the name of Bakhtin: appropriation and expropriation in recent Russian and Western Bakhtin studies', in Renfrew 1997b, pp. 75–90.

Adlam, Carol, Rachel Falconer, Alastair Renfrew and Vitalii Makhlin, eds, 1997b. *Face to Face: Bakhtin in Russia and the West*, Sheffield.

Akimov, Vladimir and Yurii Medvedev, 1994. 'Ne maski, a litsa: Bakhtin v labirinte' ('Not masks but faces: Bakhtin in the labyrinth'), *Segodnya*, 82: 4 May, p. 10.

Aleksandrova, R. I. and O. V. Breikin, eds, 1992. *Filosofiya M.M. Bakhtina i etika sovremennogo mira* (*The philosophy of Mikhail Bakhtin and the ethics of the contemporary world*), Saransk.

Aucouturier, Michel, 1983. 'The history of the novel in Russia in the 1930s: Lukács and Bakhtin', in J. Garrard, ed., *The Russian Novel from Pushkin to Pasternak*, New Haven, pp. 229–40.

Bakhtin, M. M., 1996. *Sobranie sochinenii. Tom 5. Raboty 1940-kh–nachala 1960-kh godov* (*Collected works, Vol. 5: Works from the 1940s to the Beginning of the 1960s*), Moscow.

Bakhtin, M. M., 1994a. *Problemy tvorchestva/poetiki Dostoevskogo* (*Problems of Dostoevsky's Art/Problems of Dostoevsky's Poetics*), Kiev.

Bakhtin, M. M., 1994b. *Raboty 1920-kh godov* (*Works from the 1920s*), Kiev.

Bakhtin, M. M., 1992a. 'Iz pisem M. M. Bakhtina' ('From the letters of Mikhail Bakhtin'), *Moskva*, 11–12, pp. 175–82.

Bakhtin, M. M., 1992b. 'Pis'ma M. M. Bakhtina' ('The letters of M. M. Bakhtin'), *Literaturnaya ucheba*, 5–6, pp. 153–66.

Bakhtin Centre Analytical Database: Online (available at: http://www.shef.ac.uk/uni/academic/A-C/bakh/bakhtin.html)

Bakhtin Newsletter, 1983: 1; 1986: 2; 1991: 3; 1993: 4; 1996: 5.

Bakhtinskii sbornik 3 (*The Bakhtin Miscellany 3*), ed. V. L. Makhlin, Moscow 1997.

Bakhtinskii sbornik 2: Bakhtin mezhdu Rossiei i Zapadom (*The Bakhtin Miscellany 2: Bakhtin Between Russia and the West*), ed. D. Kuyundzhich *et al.* Moscow, 1991.

Bakhtinskii sbornik 1 (*The Bakhtin Miscellany 1*), ed. D. Kuyundzhich *et al.*, Moscow, 1990.

Barsky, Robert F. and Michael Holquist, eds, 1990. *Social Discourse/Discours social*, III: 1–2 (special issue: 'Bakhtin and otherness').

Bauer, Dale M., 1988. *Feminist Dialogics: A Theory of Failed Community*, Albany and New York.

Bauer, Dale M. and S. Jaret McKinstry, eds, 1991. *Feminism, Bakhtin, and the Dialogic*, Albany and New York.

Bennett, Tony, 1979. *Formalism and Marxism*, London and New York.

Bernard-Donals, Michael F., 1994. *Mikhail Bakhtin: Between Phenomenology and Marxism*, Cambridge.

Berrong, Richard M., 1986. *Rabelais and Bakhtin: Popular Culture in Gargantua and Pantagruel*, Lincoln, Nebraska and London.

Bezmenova, N. A., ed., 1991. *Dialog: Teoreticheskie problemy i metody issledovaniia* (*Dialogue: Theoretical Problems and Methods of Research*), Moscow.

Bibler, V. S., 1991. *Mikhail Mikhailovich Bakhtin, ili poetika kul'tury* (*Mikhail Mikhailovich Bakhtin, or the Poetics of Culture*), Moscow.

Bocharov, S. G., 1993a. 'Ob odnom razgovore i vokrug nego', *Novoe literaturnoe obozrenie*, 3, pp. 70–89 (English translation 1995, 'Around and about one conversation (Conversations with Bakhtin)'), *Russian Studies in Literature*, XXXI: 4, pp. 4–35.

Bocharov, S. G., 1993b. 'Sobytie bytiya' ('The event of being'), *Chelovek*, 4, pp. 137–8; reprinted in extended form 1995, 'Sobytie bytiya: o Mikhaile Mikhailoviche Bakhtine' ('The event of being: on Mikhail Mikhailovich Bakhtin'), *Novyi mir*, 2, pp. 211–21.

Bocharov, S., V. Kozhinov and L. Melikhova, 1994. 'Moral'naya opechatka? Pis'mo v redaktsiyu' ('A moral misprint? Letter to the editor'), *Segodnya*, 82: 4, May, p. 10.

Bonetskaya, N. K., 1993. 'M. M. Bakhtin i rossiiskie kul'turnye traditsii' ('Mikhail Bakhtin and Russian cultural traditions'), *Voprosy filosofii*, 1, pp. 83–93.

Booker, M. Keith and Dubravka Juraga, 1995. *Bakhtin, Stalin, and Modern Russian Fiction: Carnival, Dialogism, and History*, London and Westport, Connecticut.

Booth, Wayne C., 1982. 'Freedom of interpretation: Bakhtin and the challenge of feminist criticism', *Critical Inquiry*, XI: 1, pp. 45–76 (reprinted in Morson 1986, pp. 145–76).

Brandist, Craig, 1995. 'British Bakhtinology: an overview', *Dialog Karnaval Khronotop*, 1, pp. 161–71.

Brandist, Craig and Galin Tihanov, eds, 2000. *Materializing Bakhtin: The Bakhtin Circle and Social Theory*, Basingstoke and New York.

Broitman, S. N., 1990. 'Dve besedy s M. M. Bakhtinym' ('Two conversations with Mikhail Bakhtin'), in Gorbanev et al. 1990, pp. 110–14.

Castellanos, Gabriela, 1995. Laughter, War, and Feminism: Elements of Carnival in Three of Charlotte Brontë's Novels, New York.

Cavanagh, Claire, 1993. 'Pseudorevolution in poetic language: Julia Kristeva and the Russian avant-garde', Slavic Review, LII: 2, pp. 283–97.

Cerquiglini, Bernard, 1986. 'The syntax of discursive authority: the example of feminine discourse', Yale French Studies, 70, pp. 183–98.

Clark, Katerina and Michael Holquist, 1986. 'A continuing dialogue', Slavic and East European Journal, XXX: 1, pp. 96–102.

Clark, Katerina and Michael Holquist, 1984. Mikhail Bakhtin, Cambridge, Mass., and London.

Clifford, James, 1983. 'On ethnographic authority', Representations, I: 2, pp. 118–46.

Coates, Ruth, 1999. Christianity in Bakhtin: God and the Exiled Author, Cambridge.

Crapanzano, Vincent, 1985. Waiting: The Whites of South Africa, London.

Cunliffe, Robert, 1993. 'Charmed snakes and little Oedipuses: the architectonics of carnival and drama in Bakhtin, Artaud, and Brecht', in Shepherd 1993a, pp. 48–69.

Curtis, James, 1986. 'Michael [sic] Bakhtin, Nietzsche and Russian pre-revolutionary thought', in Bernice Glazener Rosenthal, ed., Nietzsche in Russia, Princeton, pp. 331–54.

Danow, David K., 1991. The Thought of Mikhail Bakhtin: From Word to Culture, New York.

Danow, David K., 1986. 'Dialogic perspectives: the East European view (Bakhtin, Mukařovský, Lotman)', Russian Literature, XX: 2, pp. 119–41.

Dentith, Simon, ed., 1995. Bakhtinian Thought: An Introductory Reader, London.

Dialog Karnaval Khronotop (Dialogue Carnival Chronotope), 1992: 1; 1993: 1–3; 1994: 1–4; 1995: 1–4; 1996: 1–4; 1997: 1–4; 1998: 1–; 1999: 1–4.

Dialogism: An International Journal of Bakhtin Studies, 1998: 1; 1999: 2–3; 2000: 4.

Diaz-Diocaretz, Myriam, ed., 1989a. Critical Studies, I: 2 (special issue: 'The Bakhtin Circle today').

Díaz-Diocaretz, Myriam, 1989b. 'Bakhtin, discourse, and feminist theories', in Díaz-Diocaretz 1989a, pp. 121–39.

Díaz-Diocaretz, Myriam, 1989c, 'Sieving the matriheritage of the sociotext', in Elizabeth Meese and Alice Parker, eds, *The Difference Within: Feminism and Cultural Theory*, Amsterdam, pp. 115–47.

Duvakin, V. D., 1996. *Besedy V. D. Duvakina s M. M. Bakhtinym* (*Conversations of Viktor Duvakin with Mikhail Bakhtin*), Moscow.

Eagleton, Terry, 1981. *Walter Benjamin, or Towards a Revolutionary Criticism*, London, pp. 143–56.

Emerson, Caryl, 1997. *The First Hundred Years of Mikhail Bakhtin*, Princeton, New Jersey.

Emerson, Caryl, 1996. 'Stoletnii Bakhtin v angloyazychnom mire glazami perevodchika' ('Bakhtin at 100 in the anglophone world through the eyes of a translator'), *Voprosy literatury*, 3, pp. 68–81.

Emerson, Caryl, 1993. 'Bakhtin and women: a nontopic with immense implications', in Helena Goscilo, ed., *Fruits of Her Plume: Essays on Contemporary Russian Women's Culture*, London and New York, pp. 3–20.

Emerson, Caryl, 1992. 'The shape of Russian cultural criticism in the postcommunist period', *Canadian Slavonic Papers*, xxxiv: 4, pp. 353–72.

Erdinast-Vulcan, Daphna, 1995. 'Bakhtin's homesickness: a late reply to Julia Kristeva', *Textual Practice*, IX: 2, pp. 223–42.

Erdinast-Vulcan, Daphna, 1994. 'Narrative, modernism, and the crisis of authority: a Bakhtinian perspective', *Science in Context*, VII: 1, pp. 143–58.

Eremeev, A. F. *et al.*, eds, 1992. *M. M. Bakhtin: esteticheskoe nasledie i sovremennost'* (*M. M. Bakhtin: Aesthetic Legacy and Contemporaneity*), vol. 2, Saransk.

Eremeev, A. F. *et al.*, eds, 1989. *M. M. Bakhtin: esteticheskoe nasledie i sovremennost'* (*M. M. Bakhtin: Aesthetic Legacy and Contemporaneity*), vol. 1, Saransk.

Estifeeva, V. B., 1995. 'Drevo zhizni. K 100-letiyu so dnya rozhdeniya M. M. Bakhtina. Vospominaniya o Bakhtine' ('The tree of life: to mark the 100th anniversary of Mikhail Bakhtin's birth. Recollections of Bakhtin'), *Strannik*, 1: 37–43; 2: 110–16; 3: 25–32; 4: 71–84; 5: 76–94.

Farmer, Frank, ed., 1998. *Landmark Essays on Bakhtin, Rhetoric, and Writing*, New Jersey.

Farrell, Thomas J., ed., 1995. *Bakhtin and Medieval Voices*, Boca

Raton, Florida.

Fielder, John, 1996. 'The reception of Bakhtin in Australia', in Lee and Thomson 1996, pp. 189–96.

Frow, John, 1986. *Marxism and Literary History*, Oxford.

Gabinskii, G. A. *et al.*, eds, 1994. *Bakhtinskie chteniya. Filosofskie i metodologicheskie problemy gumanitarnogo poznaniia (The Bakhtin Readings: Philosophical and Methodological Problems of Cognition in the Humanities)*, Orel.

Gardiner, Michael, 1992. *The Dialogics of Critique: M. M. Bakhtin and the Theory of Ideology*, London and New York.

Gershkovich, E. V. and S. V. Khatchaturov, eds, 1996. *'Svoe–chuzhoe' v kontekste kul'tury novogo vremeni: Sbornik statei (k 100-letiyu so dnya rozhdeniya M. M. Bakhtina ('One's Own–Another's' in the Context of the Culture of the Modern Era. A Collection of Articles to Mark the 100th Anniversary of Mikhail Bakhtin's Birth)*, Moscow.

Ginsburg, Ruth, 1996. 'Bakhtin criticism in Israel: a short story of a non-reception', in Lee and Thomson 1996, pp. 179–88.

Godzich, Wlad, 1991. 'Correcting Kant: Bakhtin and intercultural interactions', *Boundary 2*, XVIII: 1, pp. 5–17.

Godzich, Wlad, 1985. 'Foreword', in M. M. Bakhtin and P. N. Medvedev, *The Formal Method in Literary Scholarship: A Critical Introduction to Sociological Poetics*, Cambridge, Mass., and London, pp. vii–xiv.

Gogotishvili, L. A. and R. S. Gurevich, eds, 1992. *M. M. Bakhtin kak filosof (Mikhail Bakhtin as a Philosopher)*, Moscow.

Gorbanev, N. A. *et al.*, eds, 1990. *Khronotop: Mezhvuzovskii nauchno-tematicheskii sbornik (Chronotope: An Inter-Institutional Collection)*, Makhachkala.

Grigor'ev, V. P., 1979. *Poetika slova: Na materiale russkoi sovetskoi poezii (The Poetics of the Word, with Reference to Soviet Russian Poetry)*, Moscow, pp. 109–23.

Gushchina, V. A., ed., 1995. *Chteniya: Nevel'skii krug M. M. Bakhtina (26–29 sentiabria 1994 g. Nevel'. Tezisy dokladov (Readings: The Nevel' Circle of Mikhail Bakhtin [26–29 September 1994, Nevel']. Abstracts of Papers)*, Moscow.

Hadjukowski-Ahmed, Maroussia, 1990. 'Bakhtin and feminism: two solitudes', in Thomson 1990, pp. 153–63.

Hale, Dorothy J., 1994. 'Bakhtin in African-American literary theory', *English Literary History*, 61, pp. 445–71; reprinted in Hale 1998, *Social Formalism: The Novel in Theory from Henry James to the Present*, Stanford, California.

Hall, Jonathan, 1995. *Anxious Pleasures: Shakespearean Comedy and the Nation State*, London, Madison and Teaneck.

Haynes, Deborah, 1995. *Bakhtin and the Visual Arts*, Cambridge.

Herndl, Diane Price, 1991. 'The dilemmas of a female dialogic', in Bauer and McKinstry 1991, pp. 7–24.

Herrmann, Anne, 1989. *The Dialogic and Difference: An/Other Women in Virginia Woolf and Christa Wolf*, New York.

Hirschkop, Ken, 1999. *Mikhail Bakhtin: An Aesthetic for Democracy*, Oxford.

Hirschkop, Ken, 1989. 'Critical work on the Bakhtin circle: a bibliographical essay', in Ken Hirschkop and David Shepherd, eds, *Bakhtin and Cultural Theory*, Manchester, pp. 195–212.

Hirschkop, Ken, 1986. 'The domestication of M. M. Bakhtin', *Essays in Poetics*, II: 1, pp. 76–87.

Hitchcock, Peter, ed., 1998. *South Atlantic Quarterly*, XCVII: 3–4 (special issue: 'Bakhtin/"Bakhtin". Studies in the archive and beyond').

Hitchcock, Peter, 1996. 'Events in anglophone Bakhtinian scholarship', in Lee and Thomson 1996, pp. 257–64.

Hohne, Karen and Helen Wussow, eds, 1994. *A Dialogue of Voices: Feminist Literary Theory and Bakhtin*, London and Minneapolis.

Holquist, Michael, 1990. *Dialogism: Bakhtin and His World*, London.

Holquist, Michael, 1985. 'Bakhtin and the Formalists: history as dialogue', in Robert Louis Jackson and Stephen Rudy, eds, *Russian Formalism: A Retrospective Glance*, New Haven, pp. 82–95.

Howard, Jacqueline, 1994. *Reading Gothic Fiction: a Bakhtinian Approach*, Oxford.

Isupov, K. G. et al., eds, 1991. *Problemy bakhtinologii, chast'* 1: *M. M. Bakhtin i filosofskaya kul'tura XX veka* (*Bakhtinology 1: M. M. Bakhtin and the Philosophical Culture of the Twentieth Century*), St Petersburg.

Isupov, K. G. et al., eds, 1995. *Problemy bakhtinologii, chast'* 2: *Bakhtinologiya: Issledovaniya, perevody, publikatsii* (*Bakhtinology 2: Research, Translations, Publications*), St Petersburg.

Ivanov, V. V., 1995. 'Ob avtorstve knig V. N. Voloshinova i P. N. Medvedeva' ('On the authorship of the books by V. N. Voloshinov and P. N. Medvedev'), *Dialog Karnaval Khronotop*, 4, pp. 134–9.

Ivanov, V. V., 1973. 'Znachenie idei M. M. Bakhtina o znake, vyskazyvanii i dialoge dlya sovremennoi semiotiki', *Trudy po znakovym sistemam*, VI, pp. 5–45 (English translation 1973:

'The significance of M. M. Bakhtin's ideas on sign, utterance and dialogue for modern semiotics', *Soviet Studies in Literature*, Spring–Summer, pp. 186–243).

Ivanova, N., 1993. 'Bakhtin's concept of the grotesque and the art of Petrushevskaya and Tolstaya', in Helena Goscilo, ed., *Fruits of Her Plume: Essays on Contemporary Russian Women's Culture*, London and New York, pp. 21–32.

Jaireth, Subhash, 1995. 'Russian and non-Russian readings of Bakhtin: contours of an emerging dialogue', *Southern Review*, 28, pp. 20–40.

Jha, P., 1985. 'Lukács, Bakhtin, and the sociology of the novel', *Diogenes*, 129, pp. 63–90.

Joki, Ilkka, 1993. *Mamet, Bakhtin and the Dramatic: The Demotic as a Variable of Addressivity*, Turku.

Kagan, Yu. M., 1992. 'O starykh bumagakh iz semeinogo arkhiva. (M. M. Bakhtin i M. I. Kagan)' ('Old papers from a family archive: M. M. Bakhtin and M. I. Kagan'), *Dialog Karnaval Khronotop*, 1, pp, 60–88.

Karpunov, G. V., L. S. Konkin and O. E. Osovskii, 1989. *Mikhail Mikhailovich Bakhtin: Bibliograficheskii ukazatel'* (*Mikhail Mikhailovich Bakhtin: A Bibliographical Guide*), Saransk.

Kershner, R. B., 1989. *Joyce, Bakhtin, and Popular Literature: Chronicles of Disorder*, Chapel Hill, North Carolina.

Kinser, Samuel, 1990. *Rabelais's Carnival: Text, Context, Metatext*, Berkeley, California, and Oxford.

Knowles, Ronald, ed., 1998. *Shakespeare and Carnival: After Bakhtin*, Basingstoke, London and New York.

Konkin, S. S., 1996., 'Mikhail Bakhtin v Saranske' ('Mikhail Bakhtin in Saransk'), *Nevel'skii sbornik*, 1, pp. 50–60.

Konkin, S. S., et al., eds, 1992. *M. M. Bakhtin: problemy nauchnogo naslediia*. (*Mikhail Bakhtin: Problems of the Scholarly Legacy*), Saransk.

Kovács, A., 1980. 'On the methodology of the theory of the novel: Bakhtin, Lukács, Pospelov', *Studia Slavica Hungaricae*, 26, pp. 377–93.

Kozhinov, V. V., 1996. 'Bakhtin v zhivom dialoge' ('Bakhtin in living dialogue'), in Duvakin 1996, pp. 272–81.

Kozhinov, V. V., 1995. 'Kniga, vokrug kotoroi ne umolkaiut spory' ('A book around which arguments never fall silent'), *Dialog Karnaval Khronotop*, 4, pp. 140–7.

Kozhinov, V. V., 1992. 'Kak pishut trudy, ili proiskhozhdenie nesozdannogo avantyurnogo romana (Vadim Kozhinov rasskazyvaet o sud'be i lichnosti M. M. Bakhtina)' ('How works are written, or the origins of an unwritten adventure novel: Vadim Kozhinov on the fate and personality of M. M. Bakhtin'), *Dialog Karnaval Khronotop*, 1, pp. 109–22.

Kozhinov, V. V., 1988. 'Tak eto bylo ...' ('That's the way it was ...'), *Don*, 10, pp. 156–9.

Kozhinov, Vadim, 1977. 'The world of M. M. Bakhtin', *Soviet Literature*, 1, pp. 143-4.

Kuyundzhich, D., 1990. 'M. Bakhtin i poststrukturalistskaya situatsiya' ('Bakhtin and the poststructuralist situation'), in Gorbanev *et al.*, 1990, pp. 20–7.

Kuwano, Takashi, 1996. 'Bakhtin in Japan', in Lee and Thomson 1996, pp. 55–66.

LaCapra, Dominick, 1983. 'Bakhtin, Marxism and the carnivalesque', in *Rethinking Intellectual History: Texts, Contexts, and Language*, Ithaca, New York, pp. 291–324.

Lähteenmäki, Mika, 1998. 'Introduction', in Mika Lähteenmäki, ed., *The Relevance of Bakhtin's Ideas in an Interdisciplinary Context*, Jyväskylä.

Lee, Scott and Clive Thomson, eds, 1996. 'Bakhtin around the World' *(The Bakhtin Newsletter, 5)*.

Lodge, David, 1995 [1990]. *After Bakhtin: Essays on Fiction and Criticism*, London.

MacCannell, Juliet, 1985. 'The temporality of textuality: Bakhtin and Derrida', *Modern Language Notes*, C: 5, pp. 968–88.

Makhlin, V. L., 1997 [1995]. *Ya i drugoi (istoki filosofii 'dialoga' XX veka)* (*I and Other: Sources of the Philosophy of 'Dialogue' of the Twentieth Century*), St Petersburg.

Makhlin, V. L., 1996a. 'Listom k litsu: programma M. Bakhtina v arkhitektonike bytiya-sobytiya XX veka', *Voprosy literatury*, 3, pp. 82–8 (English translation: 'Face to face: Bakhtin's programme and the architectonics of being-as-event in the twentieth century', in Adlam *et al*,. 1997b, pp. 45–53).

Makhlin, V. L., 1996b. 'Sistematicheskoe ponyatie (zametki k razvitiiu Nevel'skoi shkoly)' ('Systematic understanding: notes towards the development of the Nevel' school'), in Maksimova 1996a, pp. 75–88.

Makhlin, V. L., 1996c. 'Vremya sbrasyvaet maski' ('Time casts aside masks'), in *Bakhtin pod maskoi. Tom. 5. Maska pyataya (pervaya polumaska). V. N. Voloshinov, P. N. Medvedev, I. I. Kanaev. Stat'i*, Moscow.

Makhlin, V. L., 1995a. 'Tretii Renessans' ('The third Renaissance'), in Isupov *et al.* 1995, pp. 132–54.

Makhlin, V. L., 1995b. 'Za tekstom: koe-chto o zapadnoi bakhtin-istike s postoyannym obrashcheniem k postsovetskoi. (Vmesto obzora)' ('Beyond the text: a few words on Western Bakhtin studies, with constant reference to post-Soviet Bakhtin studies. In place of a survey'), in Yurchenko 1995, pp. 32–54.

Makhlin, V. L., ed., 1994. *M. M. Bakhtin i perspektivy gumanitarnykh nauk: materialy nauchnoi konferentsii (Moskva, RGGU, 1–3 fevralya 1993 goda) (M. M. Bakhtin and the Prospects for the Humanities: Material from an Academic conference [Moscow: RGGU, 1–3 February 1993])*, Vitebsk.

Makhlin, V. L., 1993. 'Bakhtin i Zapad (Opyt obzornoi orientatsii)' ('Bakhtin and the West: an attempted overview'), *Voprosy filosofii*, 1, pp. 94–114; 3, pp. 134–50.

Makhlin, V. L., 1991. '"Dialogizm" M. M. Bakhtina kak problema gumanitarnoi kul'tury XX veka' ('M. M. Bakhtin's "dialogism" as a problem of the culture of the twentieth-century humanities'), in Kuyundzhich *et al.* 1991, pp. 107–29.

Makhlin, V. L., 1988. 'Dialog kak sposob novogo myshleniya: (kul'turologicheskaya kontseptsiya M. M. Bakhtina i sovremennost')' ('Dialogue as a means for new thinking: Mikhail Bakhtin's culturological concept and contemporaneity'), in T. G. Yurchenko, ed., *Chelovek v zerkale kul'tury i obrazovaniya*, Moscow, pp. 82–91.

Makhlin, V. L. and Morson, G. S., 1991. 'Perepiska iz dvukh mirov' ['Correspondence from two worlds'], in Kuyundzhich *et al.* 1991, pp. 31–43.

Maksimovskaya, L. A., 1996. 'Gazeta *Molot* (1918–1920)' ('The newspaper *Molot* (1918–1920)'), *Nevel'skii sbornik* 1, pp. 147–58.

Mandelker, Amy, ed., 1996. *Bakhtin in Contexts: Across the Disciplines*, Evanston, Illinois.

Medvedev, Yu. P., 1995. 'Pis'mo v redaktsiyu zhurnala *Dialog Karnaval Khronotop*' ('A letter to the editors of the journal '*Dialog Karnaval Khronotop*'), *Dialog Karnaval Khronotop*, 4, pp. 148–56.

Medvedev, Yu. P., 1992. 'Nas bylo mnogo na chelne ...' ('There were many of us in the boat ...'), *Dialog Karnaval Khronotop*, 1, pp. 89–108.

Mihailovic, Alexandar, 1997. *Corporeal Words: Mikhail Bakhtin's Theology of Discourse*, Evanston, Illinois.

Morris, Pam, ed., 1994. *The Bakhtin Reader: Selected Readings of*

Bakhtin, Medvedev, Voloshinov, London, New York, Melbourne and Auckland.

Morson, Gary Saul, 1997. 'Professor Morson otvechaet' ('Professor Morson replies'), in *Bakhtinskii sbornik 3*, pp. 383–4.

Morson, Gary Saul, 1991. 'Bakhtin, genres and temporality', *New Literary History*, 22, pp. 1071–92.

Morson, Gary Saul, ed., 1986. *Bakhtin: Essays and Dialogues on His Work*, Chicago and London.

Morson, Gary Saul, 1981. *The Boundaries of Genre: Dostoevsky's 'Diary of a Writer' and the Traditions of Literary Criticism*, Austin, Texas.

Morson, Gary Saul, 1978. 'The heresiarch of meta', *PTL: A Journal for Descriptive Poetics and Theory of Literature*, 3, pp. 407–27.

Morson, Gary Saul and Caryl Emerson, 1990. *Mikhail Bakhtin: Creation of a Prosaics*, Stanford, California.

Morson, Gary Saul and Caryl Emerson, eds, 1989. *Rethinking Bakhtin: Extensions and Challenges*, Evanston, Illinois.

Nikolaev, N. I., 1996. 'Dostoevskii i antichnost' kak tema Pumpyanskogo i Bakhtina (1922–1963)' ('Dostoevsky and antiquity as a theme in Pumpyanskii and Bakhtin (1922–1963)'), *Voprosy literatury*, 3, pp. 115–27.

Nikolaev, N. I., ed., 1992. 'Lektsii i vystupleniya M. M. Bakhtina 1924-1925 gg. v zapisyakh L. V. Pumpyanskogo' ('Lectures and speeches by M. M. Bakhtin in 1924-1925, from notes by L. V. Pumpyanskii'), in L. A. Gogotishvili and P. S. Gurevich, eds, *M. M. Bakhtin kak filosof*, Moscow, 1992, pp. 221-52.

Nikolaev, N. I., 1991, 'Nevel'skaya shkola filosofii (M. Bakhtin, M. Kagan, L. Pumpyanskii) v 1918–1925 gg.: po materialam arkhiva L. Pumpyanskogo' ('The Nevel' school of philosophy (Mikhail Bakhtin, Matvei Kagan, Lev Pumpyanskii) in the years 1919–1925, with reference to materials from Pumpyanskii's archive'), in Isupov *et al.* 1995, pp. 31–43.

O'Connor, Mary, 1990. 'Chronotopes for women under capital: an investigation into the relation of women to objects', in Díaz-Diocaretz 1990, pp. 137–51.

Osovskii, O. E., ed., 1995. *Chelovek v mire slova* (*The Human Being in the World of the Word*), Moscow.

Osovskii, O. E., 1994. 'Retseptsiya idei M. M. Bakhtina v sovremennom literaturovedenii SShA. (Osnovnye etapy)' ('The reception of Mikhail Bakhtin's ideas in contemporary literary theory in the USA: fundamental stages'), in Makhlin 1994, pp. 129–31.

Osovskii, O. E., 1992. 'Bakhtin, Medvedev, Voloshinov: ob odnom iz "proklyatykh voprosov" sovremennogo bakhtinovedeniya' ('Bakhtin, Medvedev, Voloshinov: on one of the "accursed questions" of contemporary Bakhtin studies'), in Aleksandrova and Breikin 1992, pp. 39–54.

Pan'kov, N. A., 1995. 'Mifologema Voloshinova (neskol'ko zamechanii kak by na polyakh arkhivnykh materialov)' ('The mythologeme of Voloshinov: some remarks as if on the margins of archive materials'), Dialog Karnaval Khronotop, 2, pp. 66–9.

Pan'kov, N. A., ed., 1993. "Stenogramma zasedaniya Uchenogo soveta Instituta mirovoi literatury im. A. M. Gor'kogo. Zashchita dissertatsii tov. Bakhtinym na temu "Rable v istorii realizma" 15 noiabria 1946' ('Transcript of a meeting of the Academic Council of the Gorky Institute. Comrade Bakhtin's defence of his dissertation on the theme "Rabelais in the history of realism". 15 November 1946'), Dialog Karnaval Khronotop, 2–3, 1993, pp. 55–103.

Pearce, Lynne, 1994. Reading Dialogics, London.

Pechey, Graham, 1997. 'Bakhtin and the postcolonial condition', in Renfrew 1997, pp. 29–37.

Pechey, Graham, 1994. 'Post-apartheid narratives', in Francis Barker et al., eds, Colonial Discourse/Postcolonial Theory, Manchester, pp. 151–71.

Pechey, Graham, 1990. 'Boundaries versus binaries: Bakhtin in/against the history of ideas', Radical Philosophy, 56, pp. 23–31.

Pechey, Graham, 1987. 'On the borders of Bakhtin: dialogization, decolonization', Oxford Literary Review, 9, pp. 59–84.

Pechey, Graham, 1986. 'Bakhtin, Marxism and post-structuralism', in Francis Barker et al., eds, Literature, Politics and Theory: Papers from the Essex Conference 1976–84, London and New York, pp. 104–25.

Pechey, Graham, 1980. 'Formalism and Marxism' (Review of Bennett 1979), Oxford Literary Review, IV: 2, pp. 72–81.

Perlina, Nina, 1997. (Letter to Gary Saul Morson and Vitalii Makhlin), in Bakhtinskii sbornik 3, pp. 380–2.

Perlina, Nina, 1989. 'Funny things are happening on the way to the Bakhtin forum', Kennan Institute Occasional Papers, Washington, DC.

Perlina, Nina, 1983, 'Bakhtin–Medvedev–Voloshinov: an apple of discourse', The University of Ottawa Quarterly, LIII: 1, pp. 33–50.

Peshkov, I. V., 1996. *M. M. Bakhtin: Ot K filosofii postupka k Ritorike postupka* (*M. M. Bakhtin: From 'Toward a philosophy of the act' to a Rhetoric of the Act*), Moscow.

Pomorska, Krystyna, 1968. 'Foreword', in Mikhail Bakhtin, *Rabelais and His World*, Cambridge, Mass., and London, pp. v–x.

Ponzio, Augusto, 1994. *Man as Sign*, Amsterdam.

Ponzio, Augusto, 1993. *Signs, Dialogue and Ideology*, Amsterdam.

Poole, Brian, 1998. 'Bakhtin and Cassirer: the philosophical origins of Bakhtin's carnival messianism', in Hitchcock 1998, pp. 537–78.

Poole, Brian, 1997. 'Bakhtin's early philosophical anthropology and new archival material', in Ramón Alvarado and Lauro Zavala, eds, *Mijaíl Bajtín: Sexto Encuentro Internacional Mijaíl Bajtín: Cocoyoc, México, Julio 5 al 9, 1993. Sinopsis de ponencias*, Mexico City, unpaginated.

Poole, Brian, 1994. 'Mikhail Bakhtin i teoriya romana vospitaniya' ('Mikhail Bakhtin and the theory of the *Bildungsroman*'), in Makhlin 1994, pp. 62–72.

Presnyakov, O. P., 1978. *A. A. Potebnya i russkoe literaturovedenie kontsa XIX–nachala XX veka* (*A. A. Potebnya and Russian Literary Scholarship in the Late Nineteenth and Early Twentieth Centuries*), Saratov.

Renfrew, Alastair, ed., 1997a. *Exploiting Bakhtin*, Glasgow.

Renfrew, Alastair, 1997b. 'Bakhtin: victim of whose circumstance?', in Renfrew 1997a, pp. v–ix.

Russo, Mary, 1986. 'Female grotesques: carnival and theory', in Teresa de Lauretis, ed., *Feminist Studies/Critical Studies*, Bloomington, Ind., pp. 213–29.

Rutland, Barry, 1990. 'Bakhtinian categories and the discourse of postmodernism', in Thomson 1990, pp. 123–36.

Sadouski, Mary and Clive Thomson, 1983. 'Analytical bibliography of recent criticism in English and French on the Bakhtin Circle', *The University of Ottawa Quarterly*, LIII: 1, pp. 127–31.

San Diego Bakhtin Circle, eds, 2000. *Bucknell Review*, XLIII: 2 (special issue: 'Bakhtin and the nation').

Shaitanov, I., 1996. 'Zhanrovoe slovo u Bakhtina i formalistov', *Voprosy literatury*, 3, pp. 89–114 (English translation: 'The concept of the generic word in Bakhtin and the Russian Formalists', in Adlam *et al.* 1997b, pp. 233–53).

Shaitanov, I. 1994. 'Bakhtin i formalisty v prostranstve istoricheskoi poetiki' ('Bakhtin and the Formalists in the space of historical poetics'), in Makhlin 1994, pp. 16–22.

Shepherd, David, 1996. '"Communicating with other worlds": contrasting views of carnival in recent Russian and Western work on Bakhtin', in Lee and Thomson 1996, pp. 143–60.

Shepherd, David, ed., 1993a. *Critical Studies*, III: 2 and IV: 1–2 (special issue: 'Bakhtin, carnival and other subjects: selected papers from the Fifth International Bakhtin Conference, University of Manchester, July 1991').

Shepherd, David, 1993b. 'Introduction: (mis)representing Bakhtin', in Shepherd 1993a, pp. xiii–xxxii.

Shepherd, David, 1992. *Beyond Metafiction: Self-Consciousness in Soviet Literature*, Oxford.

Shukman, Ann, ed., 1983. 'Editor's introduction', in *Bakhtin School Papers* (*Russian Poetics in Translation*, 10), Oxford, pp. 1–4.

Shukman, Ann, 1978. 'The Moscow–Tartu semiotics school: a bibliography of works and comments in English', *PTL: A Journal for Descriptive Poetics and Theory of Literature*, 3, pp. 593–601.

Smirnov, S. A., 1996. *Opyty po filosofskoi antropologii* (*Chelovek v prostranstve kul'tury*) (*Essays in Philosophical Anthropology: The Human Being in the Space of Culture*), Novosibirsk, pp. 100–14.

Sokoloyansky, Mark G., 1993. 'Mikhail Bakhtin and Grigorij Vinokur: two approaches to scientific poetics', in Ramón Alvarado and Lauro Zavala, eds, *Mijaíl Bajtín: Sexto Encuentro Internacional Mijaíl Bajtín: Cocoyoc, México, Julio 5 al 9, 1993. Sinopsis de ponencias*, Mexico City, unpaginated.

Stallybrass, Peter and Allon White, 1986. *The Politics and Poetics of Transgression*, London and Ithaca, NY.

Stam, Robert, 1989. *Subversive Pleasures: Bakhtin, Cultural Criticism and Film*, Baltimore.

Strada, Vittorio, 1997. Letter to the editor, in *Bakhtinskii sbornik 3*, pp. 373–9.

Thomson, Clive, ed., 1990. *Critical Studies*, II: 1–2 (special issue: 'Mikhail Bakhtin and the epistemology of discourse').

Thomson, Clive and Hans Raj Dua, eds, 1995. *Dialogism and Cultural Criticism*, London, Ontario.

Tihanov, Galin, 1997a. 'Bakhtin, Lukács and German Romanticism: the case of epic and irony', in Adlam *et al.* 1997b, pp. 273–98.

Tihanov, Galin, 1997b. 'Reification and dialogue: aspects of the theory of culture and society in Bakhtin and Lukács', in Miha Javornik *et al.*, eds, *Bakhtin and the Humanities: Proceedings of the International Conference in Ljubljana, October 19–21, 1995/Bahtin in humanisticne vede: Zbornik prispevkov z mednarodnega simpozija v Ljubljani, 19.–21. oktobra 1995*, Ljubljana, pp. 73–93.

Titunik, I. R., 1986. 'The Baxtin problem: concerning Katerina Clark and Michael Holquist's *Mikhail Bakhtin*', *Slavic and East European Journal*, XXX: 1, pp. 91–5.

Titunik, I. R., 1984. 'Bakhtin and/or Voloshinov and/or Medvedev: dialogue and/or doubletalk?', in Lubomir Doložel, I. R. Titunik and B. Stolz, eds, *Language and Literary Theory: In Honor of Ladislav Matejka*, Ann Arbor, Michigan, pp. 535–64.

Todorov, Tzvetan, 1985. 'Humanly plural', *Times Literary Supplement*, 14 June, pp. 675–6.

Todorov, Tzvetan, 1984. *Mikhail Bakhtin: The Dialogical Principle*, London and Minneapolis.

Todorov, Tzvetan, 1977. *The Poetics of Prose*, Oxford.

Turbin, V. N., 1991. '"Ni proizvedenii, ni obrazov Dostoevskogo ... i v pomine net". Pis'mo M.M. Bakhtina ot 19 yanvarya 1963 goda. (Publikatsiya i kommentarii)' ('"There is no sign of Dostoevsky's works or characters ...": a letter from Bakhtin of 19 January 1963. Text and commentary'), in Kuyundzhich *et al.* 1991, pp. 371–3.

Vice, Sue, 1997. *Introducing Bakhtin*, Manchester and New York.

Voronina, N. I. *et al.*, eds, 1995. *M. M. Bakhtin i gumanitarnoe myshlenie na poroge XXI veka: Tezisy III saranskikh mezhdunarodnykh bakhtinskikh chtenii (Mikhail Bakhtin and the Thought of the Humanities on the Threshold of the Twenty-First Century: Abstracts from the Third International Bakhtin Readings in Saransk)*, Saransk.

Vulis, A. Z., 1993. 'U Bakhtina v Maleevke' ('With Bakhtin in Maleevka'), *Dialog Karnaval Khronotop*, 2–3, pp. 190–4.

Walton, William Garrett, Jr, 1981. 'V. N. Voloshinov: a marriage of formalism and Marxism', in Peter V. Zima, ed., *Semiotics and Dialectics: Ideology and the Text*, Amsterdam, pp. 39–102.

Wehrle, Albert J., 1978. 'Introduction: M. M. Bakhtin/P. N. Medvedev', in M. M. Bakhtin and P. N. Medvedev, *The Formal Method in Literary Scholarship: A Critical Introduction to Sociological Poetics*, Cambridge, Mass., and London, pp. ix–xxiii.

Wesling, Donald, 1993. 'Mikhail Bakhtin and the social poetics of dialect', *Papers on Language and Literature*, XXIX: 3, pp. 303–22.

Williams, Raymond, 1986. 'The uses of cultural theory', *New Left Review*, 158, pp. 19–31.

Yudina, M. V., 1993. 'Iz perepiski M. V. Yudinoi i M. M.

Bakhtina' ('From the correspondence between M. V. Yudina and Mikhail Bakhtin'), *Dialog Karnaval Khronotop*, 4, pp. 41–85.

Yurchenko, T. G., ed., 1995. *Bakhtin v zerkale kritiki* (*Bakhtin in the Mirror of Criticism*), Moscow.

Zdol'nikov, V. V., 1993. 'Vopros ostaetsya otkrytym (nemnogo sub"ektivnye zametki o konferentsii "Bakhtin i perspektivy gumanitarnykh nauk", Moskva, RGGU, fevral' 1993 goda)' ('The question remains open: some rather subjective notes on the conference "Bakhtin and the prospects for the humanities", Moscow, RGGU, February 1993'), *Dialog Karnaval Khronotop*, 2–3, pp. 198–201.

Żyłko, Boguslaw, 1996. 'The perception of Bakhtin in Poland', in Lee and Thomson 1996, pp. 39–54.

Index

Note: 'n' after a page reference indicates a note number on that page

MMB = Mikhail Mikhailovich Bakhtin